Open Source
Intelligence Techniques

Resources for Searching and Analyzing Online Information

Fourth Edition

Michael Bazzell

Open Source Intelligence Techniques:
Resources for Searching and Analyzing Online Information
Fourth Edition

Fourth Edition First Published: April 2015

The information in this book is distributed on an "As Is" basis, without warranty. The author has taken great care in preparation of this book, but assumes no responsibility for errors or omissions. No liability is assumed for incidental or consequential damages in connection with or arising out of the use of the information or programs contained herein.

Rather than use a trademark symbol with every occurrence of a trademarked name, this book uses the names only in an editorial fashion and to the benefit of the trademark owner, with no intention of infringement of the trademark.

Library of Congress Cataloging-in-Publication Data
Application submitted

ISBN-13: 978-1508636335

ISBN-10: 15086338

Contents

About the Author

Michael Bazzell

Michael Bazzell spent 18 years as a government computer crime investigator. During the majority of that time, he was assigned to the FBI's Cyber Crimes Task Force where he focused on Open Source Intelligence (OSINT) analysis. As an active investigator for multiple organizations, he has been involved in numerous high-tech criminal investigations including online child solicitation, child abduction, kidnapping, cold-case homicide, terrorist threats, and high level computer intrusions. He has trained thousands of individuals employed by state and federal agencies, as well as the private sector, in the use of his investigative techniques. He has also taught several college courses including Ethical Hacking, Computer Forensics, and Computer Crime Investigation.

The previous editions of "Open Source Intelligence Techniques" and "Hiding from the Internet" have been top sellers in both the United States and Europe. They are used by several government agencies as training manuals for intelligence gathering and securing personal information.

Introduction

Fourth Edition

Keeping a book up to date about ways to access information on the internet is a difficult task. Websites are constantly changing or disappearing, and the techniques for collecting all possible public information from them are affected. While the third edition of this book is still highly applicable, a lot has changed over the past 18 months. Much of this book contains new techniques that were not available previously. The Facebook Graph search options alone have grown considerably. An entire new chapter on Android emulation will provide many new methods of obtaining information.

Fortunately, knowing methods for accessing data on one website often carry over nicely to other websites. This entire fourth edition was accurate as of April 1, 2015. If, or more likely when, you find techniques that no longer work, use the overall lessons from the entire book to push through the changes and locate your content. Once you develop an understanding of the data, you will be ready to adapt with it. As always, I will publish updates to my online blog and free newsletter. I will also post new video tutorials for the members of my online training program. You can access all of this, including my current investigation tools and links, on my website at **IntelTechniques.com**.

Open Source Intelligence (OSINT)

Open Source Intelligence, often referred to as OSINT, can mean many things to many people. Legally, it is defined as any intelligence produced from publicly available information that is collected, exploited, and disseminated in a timely manner to an appropriate audience for the purpose of addressing a specific intelligence requirement. For the CIA, it may mean information obtained from foreign news broadcasts. For an attorney, it may mean data obtained from official government documents that are available to the public. For most people, it is publicly available content obtained from the internet.

What is this book?

Overall, this book includes over 250 sources of free and open data which could identify personal information about anyone. All of the resources are 100% free and open to the public. Each resource is explained, and any creative search techniques involving the resource are detailed. When applicable, actual case examples are provided to demonstrate the possibilities within the methods. The book can be read in any order and referenced when a specific need arises. It is a guidebook of techniques that I have found successful in my investigations.

Locating this free online information is not the final step of OSINT analysis. Appropriate collection methods will be detailed and referenced. Whether the data you obtain is for an investigation, a background check, or identifying problem employees, you must document all of your findings. You cannot rely on the information being available online forever. A website may shut down or the data may be removed. You must preserve anything of interest when you find it. The free software solutions presented here will help you with that.

OSINT search techniques do not apply only to websites. There are many free programs that automate the search and collection of data. These programs, as well as application programming interfaces, will be explained to assist the advanced investigator of open source intelligence.

In summary, this book is to serve as a reference guide to assist you with conducting more accurate and efficient searches of open source intelligence.

What the book is not...

This is not a debate about the ethics or politics of online reconnaissance for personal information. It is not a historical look at OSINT or a discussion of administrative policy. There are better books that tackle these subjects. Further, it is not a how-to guide for criminals to steal your identity. Nothing in this book discusses illegal methods of obtaining information.

Book Audience

When I first considered documenting my OSINT techniques, the plan was to post them on my website in a private area for law enforcement. This documentation quickly turned into over 250 pages of content including screen shots. It had grown too big to place on my site in a manner that was easy to digest. I changed course and began putting together this book as a manual to accompany my multiple-day training sessions. I now hope that a wider investigation community can gain something from these techniques. Intelligence analysts can apply these methods to a large part of their daily work.

I now offer my OSINT training to the private sector, especially global security divisions of large corporations. This book can help these teams locate more concise and appropriate information relative to their companies. These methods have proven successful for employees that monitor any type of threat to their company, from physical violence to counterfeit products.

I encourage the use of these techniques to institutions that are responsible for finding and eliminating "bad apples". This may be the human resources department, applicant processing employees, or "head hunters" looking for the best people. The information about a subject found online can provide more intelligence than any interview or reference check.

Parents and teachers are encouraged to use this book as a guide to locating social media content posted by children. In many households, the children know more about the internet than the adults. The children use this to their advantage and often hide content online. They know that it will not be located by their parents and teachers, and often post inappropriate content. This book can empower the adults and assist with identifying important personal information.

Finally, a large portion of my intended audience is private investigators. They can use this book to find information without possessing a deep understanding of computers or the internet. Explicit descriptions and screen captures will ensure that the techniques can be recreated on any computer.

I realize that people who use these techniques for devious purposes will read this book as well. Colleagues have expressed their concern about this possibility. My decision to document these techniques came down to two thoughts. First, anyone that really wants to use this information in malicious ways will do so without this book. There is nothing in here that could not be duplicated with some serious searching and time. The second thought is that getting this information out to those that will use it appropriately is worth the risk of a few people using it for the wrong reasons.

Please act responsibly with this information.

Chapter One

Search Engines: Google & Bing

The first stop for many researchers will be a popular search engine. The two big players in the United States are Google and Bing. This chapter will go into great detail about the advanced ways to use both. Most of these techniques can apply to any search engine, but the examples will be specific for these two.

Google (google.com)

There are entire books dedicated to Google searching and Google hacking. Most of these focus on penetration testing and securing computer networks. These are full of great information, but are often overkill for the investigator looking for quick personal information. A few simple rules can help locate more accurate data. No book in existence will replace practicing these techniques in a live web browser. When searching, you cannot break anything. Play around and get familiar with the advanced options.

Quotation Marks

Placing a target name inside of quotation marks will make a huge difference in a quick first look for information. In Figure 1.01, I conducted a search for my name without quotes. The result is 47,300 pages that include the words *Michael* and *Bazzell*. These pages do not necessarily have these words right next to each other. The word *Michael* could be next to another person's name, while *Bazzell* could be next to yet another person's name. In one of the results, you can see how this provides inaccurate information. In Figure 1.02 you can see how a result contains a page including a reference to *Michael Santo* and *Barry Bazzell*.

Since technically the words *Michael* and *Bazzell* appear on that page, you are stuck with the result in your list. In order to prevent this, you should always use quotes around the name of your target.

Searching for the term "*Michael Bazzell*", including the quotes, reduces the search results to 4,090.

Each of these pages will contain the words *Michael* and *Bazzell* right next to each other. While Google and other search engines have technology in place to search related names, this is not always perfect, and does not apply to searches with quotes. For example, the search for *Michael Bazzell*, without quotes, located pages that reference *Mike Bazzell* (instead of *Michael*). This same search with quotes did not locate these results. Placing quotes around any search terms tells Google to search exactly what you tell it to. If your target's name is *Michael*, you may want to consider an additional search for *Mike*. If a quoted search returns nothing, or few results, you should remove the quotes and search again.

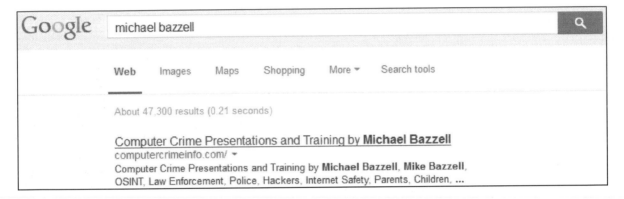

Figure 1.01: A standard Google results page without quotes.

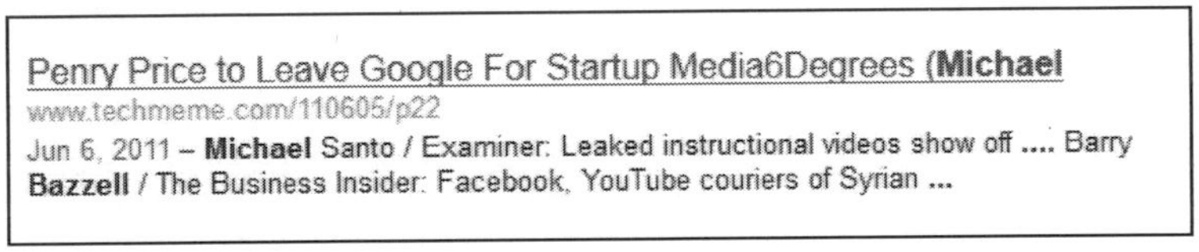

Figure 1.02: Google result displaying unwanted information.

This search technique can be vital when searching email addresses or user names. When searching Michael@inteltechniques.com, I receive 8,070 results. When I search "Michael@inteltechniques.com", I receive the only four results that actually contain that email address.

When your quoted search, such as "*Michael Bazzell,*" returns too many results (Figure 1.03), you should add to your search. When I add the term "*police*" after my name, the results reduce from 4,090 to 1,870. These results all contain pages that have the words *Michael* and *Bazzell* next to each other, and include the word police somewhere on the page. While all of these results may not be about me, the majority will be and can easily be digested.

Adding the occupation, residence city, general interest, or college of the target may help eliminate unrelated results.

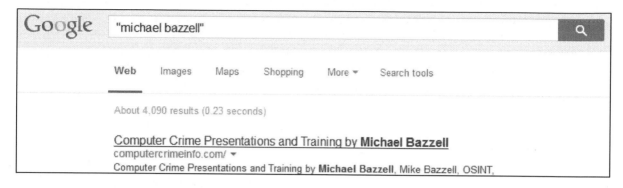

Figure 1.03: A standard Google results page with a quoted search.

Site Operator

Google, and other search engines, allow the use of operators within the search string. An operator is text that is added to the search, which performs a function. My favorite operator is the "site:" function. This operator provides two benefits to the search results. First, it will only provide results of pages located on a specific domain. Second, it will provide all of the results containing the search terms on that domain.

Figure 1.04 displays the results for a search for Kevin Rose. One of these results is a link to the website crunchbase.com. This page is one of several pages on that domain that includes a reference to Kevin Rose. However, this search of Kevin Rose on Google only included one page on that domain. If you want to view every page on a specific domain that includes your target of interest, the site operator is required. Figure 1.05 displays the results of all pages on the domain of crunchbase.com that include a reference to Kevin Rose. This technique can be applied to any domain. This includes social networks, blogs, and any other website that is indexed by search engines.

In another example, Google will allow us to effectively search the site reocities.com. ReoCities is an archive of many of the GeoCities web pages that were removed in 2009. GeoCities was an online portal ran by Yahoo that possessed approximately 38 million user created websites. When Yahoo shut the system down, these pages were no longer available on their servers. Before elimination, a few sites such as ReoCities attempted to collect as much data as possible. With millions of pages, cataloging the data in a searchable format is difficult. A search beginning with "site:reocities.com" will tell Google to only search within the referenced site. A search of "site:reocities.com "leo laporte"" returned 18 websites that have specific information within Reocities about Leo Laporte. Locating this information would have been extremely difficult since a generic search for Leo Laporte produces over 7 million results.

Figure 1.04: A standard Google search response for "Kevin Rose".

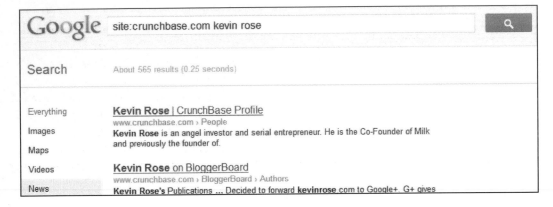

Figure 1.05: A Google result page with a "site" operator.

Another simple way to use this technique is to locate every page that is part of a specific domain. A search query of "site:computercrimeinfo.com" displays all 137 pages that are publicly located on my personal website. This can be a great way to review all of the contents of a target's personal website without attempting to navigate the actual site. It is very easy to miss contents by clicking around within a website. With this technique, you should see all of the pages in a format that is easy to digest. Also, some of the pages on a website that the author may consider "private" may actually be public if he or she ever linked to them from a public page. Once Google has indexed the page, we can view the content using the "site" operator.

Real world application: While conducting private background checks, I consistently use the site operator. I was once supplied a cellular telephone number of an applicant for a very public position. A search on craigslist.org of this number revealed no results. A Google search of "site:craigslist.org and the phone number revealed archived expired posts by the applicant promoting himself as a male prostitute. More methods of Craigslist searching are detailed later in this book. Additionally, using a search such as "site:amazon.com" and the target name can reveal interesting information. A recent background check of an applicant that signed an affidavit declaring no previous drug or alcohol dependencies produced some damaging results. The search provided user submitted reviews that he had left on Amazon in reference to books that he had purchased that assisted him with his continual addiction to controlled substances. Again, this result may have appeared somewhere in the numerous general search results of the target, however the site operator directed me exactly where I needed to look.

Linkto Operator

Another Google operator that can be beneficial to an investigator is the "link" function. This operator specifies a search for any website that contains a link to a specific domain. This operator can also be combined with other search terms to filter search results. Below are examples of a few ways to use this technique.

Providing a search term of "linkto:computercrimeinfo.com" results in several websites that possess a link to my website, computercrimeinfo.com (Figure 1.06). This could be very useful when attempting to identify associates with a target of interest. If the target maintains a blog online, it is common for that target to maintain relationships with other subjects that maintain blogs. Most likely, these associates will have posted a link to the target's website. Websites can provide valuable intelligence about the original target. Unfortunately, the majority of the results from this query are actually references to pages located within this website. In general, I do not want to see these pages in my results, and I only want results on other web pages. In order to accomplish this, we will add an additional operator to our search.

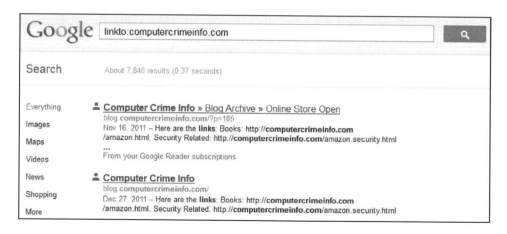

Figure 1.06: A Google result page with a "linkto" operator.

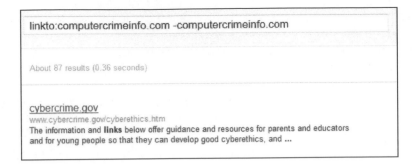

Figure 1.07: A Google result page with "linkto" and "-" operators.

In Figure 1.07, I used the "linkto" operator as well as the "-". This tells Google that I want to find all of the websites that have links to my website; however, I do not want any of the pages on my website to be listed in the results. This is helpful when you are searching a website that has many pages.

Google Search Tools

There is a text bar at the top of every Google search result page. This allows for searching the current search terms within other Google services such as Images, Maps, Shopping, Videos, and others. The last option on this bar is the "Search Tools" link. Clicking this link will present a new row of options directly below. This will give you new filters to help you focus only on the desired results. The filters will vary for each type of Google search. Figure 1.08 displays the standard search tools with the time menu expanded.

Figure 1.08: Google's Search Tools menu.

The "Any time" menu will allow you to choose the time range of visible search results. The default is set to "Any time" which will not filter any results. Selecting "Past hour" will only display results that have been indexed within the hour. The other options for week, month, and year work the same way. The last option is "Custom range". This will present a popup window that will allow you to specify the exact range of dates that you want searched. This can be helpful when you want to analyze online content posted within a known time.

Real World Application: Whenever I am assigned a missing person case, I immediately search the internet. By the time that the case is assigned, many media websites have reported on the incident and social networks are full of sympathetic comments toward the family. In order to avoid this traffic, I set the search tools to only show results up to the date of disappearance. I can now focus on the online content posted about the victim before the disappearance was public. This often leads to more relevant suspect leads.

Google can be very sporadic when it comes to supplying date information within search results. Sometimes you will see the date that a search result was added to the Google index and sometimes you will not. This can be frustrating when you desire this information in order to identify relevant results. There is a fairly unknown technique that will force Google to always show you the date of each search result.

When you choose the "Time" option under the Search Tools menu, you will always see a date next to each result. If you are only searching for recent information, this solves the issue. However, if you are conducting a standard search without a specific date reference, the dates next to each result are missing. To remedy this, you can conduct a specific search that includes any results indexed between January 1, 1 BC and "today". The appropriate way to do this is to add "&tbs=cdr:1,cd_min:1/1/0" at the end of any standard Google search. Figure 1.09 displays the results of a standard search for the terms OSINT Tools. The exact URL of the search was "google.com/?#q=osint+tools". Notice that the result does not include a date next to the item. Figure 1.10 displays the results of this same search with the specific data added at the end. The exact URL of this search was the following address.

"google.com/?#q=osint+tools&tbs=cdr:1,cd_min:1/1/0"

Notice that the result now has the date that the content was indexed by Google. You can also now sort these results by date in order to locate the most recent information. Figure 1.10 displays this menu option.

The search tools menu also offers an "All results" menu that will allow you to choose to see "all results" or "Verbatim". The All Results will conduct a standard Google search. The Verbatim option searches exactly what you typed. One benefit of the Verbatim option is that Google will often present more results than the standard search. It digs a little deeper and gives additional results based on the exact terms you provided.

Figure 1.09: A standard Google search without date information.

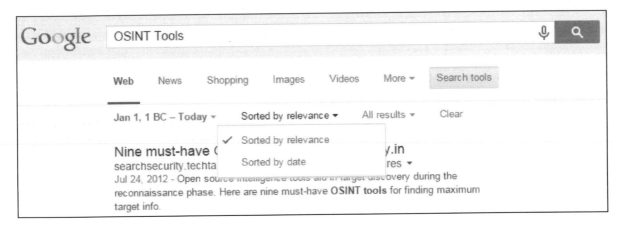

Figure 1.10: A Google search with date information added.

The location option in the search tools will identify the location where Google believes you are located based on your IP address. Google will then try to place priority on that location with your search results. For example, if you are in Chicago, and Google knows this, Google may provide content relative to Chicago in the immediate results. This can either be valuable or a hindrance. If you really are in Chicago, but the person or business that you are investigating is in Dallas, this can harm your investigation. Fortunately, Google allows users to change this location to any zip code desired. Google does not believe that you are in the location that you provide. Instead, it displays the results that would be provided to a person that really was in that location. Figure 1.08 displays my current location as Edwardsville, IL. If you click on this menu, you will see the option to modify this data.

Filetype Operator

Another operator that works with both Google and Bing is the "Filetype" command. In Figure 1.11, the search "Jake Jarvis resume filetype:pdf" in Bing provides results of PDF files that include the word "resume" and the name of the target.

Figure 1.11: A Bing search result with the "filetype" operator.

This search technique often provides resumes created by the target which can include cellular telephone numbers, personal addresses, work history, education information, references, and other personal information that would never be intentionally posted to the internet. The "filetype" operator can identify any file by the file type within any website. This can be combined with the "site" operator to find all files of any type on a single domain (Figure 1.12). By conducting the following searches, I was able to find several documents stored on the website irongeek.com.

site:irongeek.com filetype:pdf
site:irongeek.com filetype:ppt
site:irongeek.com filetype:pptx

These searches provided links to 33 PDF files and 34 PowerPoint files. These files could then be downloaded and archived.

Figure 1.12: A Google results page with the "site" and "filetype" operators.

InURL Operator

We can also specify operators that will focus only on the data within the URL or address of the website. Previously, the operators discussed applied to the content within the web page. My favorite search using this technique is to find File Transfer Protocol (FTP) servers that allow anonymous connections. The following search would identify any FTP servers that possess PDF files that contain the term OSINT within the file.

inurl:ftp -inurl:(http|https) filetype:pdf "osint"

The following will dissect how and why this search worked.

Inurl:ftp – Instructs Google to only display addresses that contain "ftp" in the URL.

-inurl:(http|https) – Instructs Google to ignore any addresses that contain either http or https in the URL. The separator is the pipe symbol (|) located above the backslash key. It tells Google "OR". This would make sure that we excluded any standard web pages.

Filetype:pdf – Instructs Google to only display PDF documents.

"osint" –Instructs google to mandate that the exact term osint is within the content of the results.

Figure 1.13 displays the results of this search. It identified 43 documents. You can see in the address under the first document that the file is a PDF located within an FTP server.

Figure 1.13: A search result identifying files within an FTP server.

Google Alerts (google.com/alerts)

When you have exhausted the search options on search engines looking for a target, you will want to know if new content is posted. Checking Google results every week on the same target to see if anything new is out there will get mundane. Utilizing Google Alerts will put Google to work on locating new information. While logged into any Google service, such as Gmail, create a new Google Alert and specify the search term, delivery options, and email address to send it to.

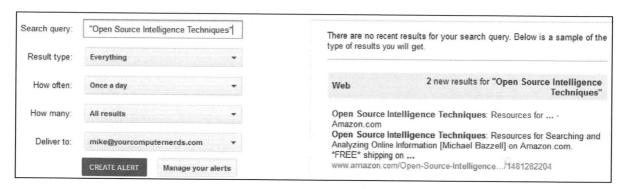

Figure 1.14: A Google Alerts configuration page.

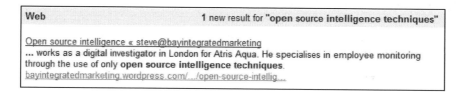

Figure 1.15: A Google Alerts email.

In Figure 1.14, Google will send an email daily as it finds new websites that mention "Open Source Intelligence Techniques" anywhere in the site. Figure 1.15 displays a result received via email. One of my alerts is for my personal website. I now receive an email when another site mentions or links to my website. Parents can use this to be notified if their child is mentioned in a website or blog. Investigators that are continuously seeking information about a target will find this beneficial.

Real world application: A police detective was assigned a runaway case where a 15 year old had decided to leave home and stay with friends at an unknown location. After several extensive internet searches, a Google Alert was set up using the runaway's name and city of residence. Within three days, one of the alerts was for a blog identifying the runaway and where she was currently staying. Within 30 minutes, the unhappy child was back home.

Bing (bing.com)

Google is not the only great search engine. While Google is the overwhelming choice of search engines used today, other sites should not be ignored, especially when having trouble locating any information on a subject. Bing is Microsoft's competition to Google, which provides a great search experience. In 2009, Yahoo search (yahoo.com) began using the Bing search engine to produce search results. This makes a Yahoo search redundant if a Bing search has already been conducted.

The same tactics described above, and in the numerous Google books, can be applied to any search engine. The "site" operator and the use of quotes both work with Bing exactly as they do with Google. Bing also recently introduced time filtered searching that will allow you only show results from the last 24 hours, week, or month. There are a couple of additional operators that are important that only apply to Bing.

Bing offers an option that will list every website that a target website links to. This is different than the "link" operator that Google uses. Google provides any websites that link to the target site. Bing does the opposite, and is the only search engine that offers this service.

In Figure 1.16, I conducted a search on Bing of "LinkFromDomain:computercrimeinfo.com". Note that there are no spaces in the entire search string. This operator creates a result that includes every website that I have a link to on any of the pages within my website.

This can be useful to an investigator. When a target's website is discovered, this site can be large and contain hundreds of pages, blog entries, etc. While clicking through all of these is possible, sometimes links are hidden and cannot be seen by visually looking at the pages. This operator allows Bing to pull links out of the actual code of the website.

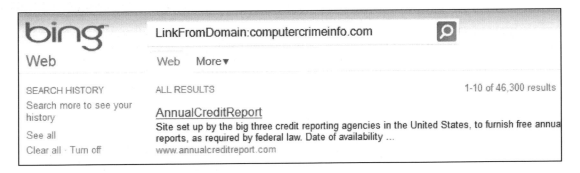

Figure 1.16: A Bing results page with the "LinkFromDomain" operator.

Google Images (images.google.com)

Google Images scours the web for graphical images based on a search term. Google obtains these images based on keywords for the image. These keywords are taken from the filename of the image, the link text pointing to the image, and text adjacent to the image. This is never a complete listing of all images associated with a subject, and will almost always find images completely unrelated to a target. In the case of common names, one should enclose the name in quotes and follow it with the city the subject lives in, place of employment, home town, or personal interests. This will help filter the results to those more likely to be related to the subject.

When results are displayed, clicking the "Search tools" button will present six new filter menus. Figure 1.17 displays these options with the type menu expanded. This menu will allow you to filter results to only include images that are photos, contain a human face, or contain artwork. If your target's last name is "Ford", you may be presented with images of vehicles. Choosing the "Face" option should eliminate most of these results and focus on people. The other menus will allow you to specify color, size, and time range of your results.

Bing Images (bing.com/images)

Similar to Google, Bing offers an excellent image search. Both sites auto load more images as you get toward the end of the current results. This eliminates the need to continue to load an additional page, and leads to faster browsing. Bing also offers the advanced options available on Google, and adds the ability to filter only files with a specified layout such as square or wide. Bing provides a filter for images of people with the options of "Just faces" and "Head & shoulders".

Bing provides suggested filters with every image search. In Figure 1.18, I have conducted a search of "David Prager" on the Bing Images home page. The menu at top includes links to image searches of more specific areas of interest.

Figure 1.17: Google Images search tools.

Figure 1.18: A Bing Images result page with "Related Topics".

Clicking these inks may provide additional photographs of the specific target based on the listed criteria. This intelligence can lead to additional searches of previously unknown affiliations.

Google Cache (google.com)

Occasionally, you will try to access a site and the information you are looking for is no longer there. Maybe something was removed, amended, or maybe the whole page was permanently removed. Google Cache can remedy this. When conducting a Google search, notice the result address directly below the link to the website. You will see a green down arrow that will present a menu when clicked. This menu will include a link titled "Cached". Clicking it will load a version of the page of interest from a previous date. Figure 1.19 displays a search for phonelosers.com which returns a result that includes a cached version of the page. This version was taken four days prior to the current date, and displays information differently than the current version. Figure 1.20 displays the banner of the cached result from Google.

If you have a specific page within a website that you want a cached view of, type the exact website into Google to link to the cached page. For example, if I wanted to see a previous view of the blog for The Phone Show, a podcast about telephone pranks, I could conduct a Google search for the site "thephoneshow.blogspot.com". This will return the main landing page as well as sub-pages that will each have a historical view. If any of these pages were to go offline completely, Google would hold the last obtained version for viewing.

Figure 1.19: A Google search result displaying the "Cached" option.

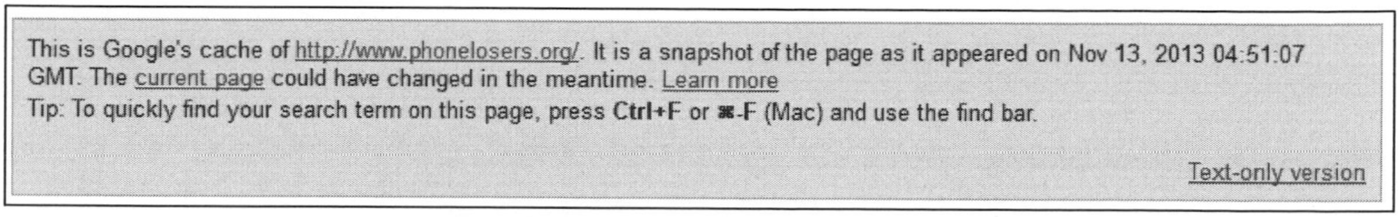

This is Google's cache of http://www.phonelosers.org/. It is a snapshot of the page as it appeared on Nov 13, 2013 04:51:07 GMT. The current page could have changed in the meantime. Learn more
Tip: To quickly find your search term on this page, press Ctrl+F or ⌘-F (Mac) and use the find bar.

Text-only version

Figure 1.20: A banner of a cached page on Google.

Bing Cache (bing.com)

Similar to Google, Bing offers a cached view of many websites. Searching for a domain name, such as phonelosers.com will present many results. The first result should link to the actual website. Directly next to the website name is a small green down arrow. Clicking it will present the option of "Cached page". Clicking this link will display a previous version of the target website as collected by Bing. Figure 1.21 displays the menu option while Figure 1.22 displays information about the collection listed above the cached page.

If your target website has several different cached pages, you may want an automated solution. Recover My Website (recovermywebsite.com) allows you to enter the target website and your email address. It will fetch all of the cached pages and email you the files. This is great for archiving.

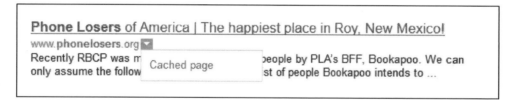

Figure 1.21: A Bing cached page search option.

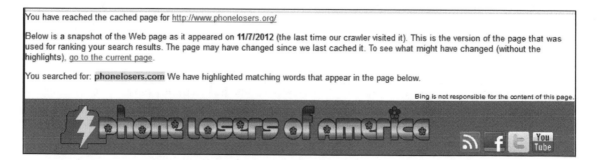

Figure 1.22: A Bing cached page with information banner.

The Wayback Machine (archive.org/web/web.php)

The Wayback Machine will provide a much more extensive list of options in viewing a website historically. Searching for phonelosers.org displayed a total of 915 captures of the site dating from 12/21/1997 through 07/11/2011 (Figure 1.23). Clicking through the links presents quite a display of how the site has changed. Graphics are archived as well, proving that we should always think twice about which photos we post to the internet. Each view of the archived page will allow the user to click through the links as if it were a live page on the original web server. Clicking through the timeline at the top of each page will load the viewed page as it appeared on the date selected.

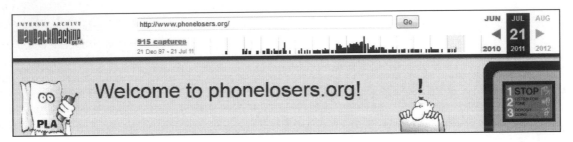

Figure 1.23: A Wayback Machine results page with timeline.

Additional Archive Options

There are two additional options for historic archives of web pages. However, neither of them is very powerful and my successes with these services have been minimal. **Archive Today** (archive.today) will allow you to search a domain and display any captured archives of the home page. They also offer a wildcard service that will search an entire domain for any captured pages. If I wanted to search inteltechniques.com for any archived pages, I would enter the following two queries into the search field.

http://inteltechniques.com/*
*.inteltechniques.com

The first would look for any archived pages within the chosen domain. The second would look for any sub-domains such as mail.inteltechniques.com or ftp.inteltechniques.com. I have rarely received results from the sub-domain search through this service. **Coral** (coralcdn.org) offers a different spin on web archiving. Instead of a collection of historic caches of a website, it retrieves snapshots of any website that might not be obtainable by your connection. I have used this many times in the past when I cannot connect to a website due to overload on the providing server. This could happen when a small website receives an abundance of visits due to instant popularity on a service such as Reddit. If I cannot load the desired page, I will attempt to view it through Coral. To do this, I append the website address with ".nyud.net". If I were attempting to view inteltechniques.com, I would instead navigate to the following exact URL. This will generate a current snapshot of the target page. It is obtained by a series of servers that have the power to retrieve online content that is otherwise restricted due to high demand.

http://inteltechniques.com.nyud.net

Google Translator (translate.google.com)

Many websites exist in non-English languages. As internet enthusiasts, we tend to focus on sites within our home area. There is a wealth of information out there on sites hosted in other countries which are presented in other languages. Google Translator will take text from any site or document and translate the text to a variety of languages (Figure 1.24). Usually, the service will automatically identify the language of the pasted text. Selecting the desired output will provide the translation.

Alternatively, you can translate an entire website in one click which will give a native view of the layout of the site. Instead of copying individual text to the search box, type or paste in the exact URL (address) of the website you want translated (Figure 1.25). Clicking the "Translate" button will load a new page of the site, which will be translated to English (Figure 1.26).

This translation is rarely, if ever, perfect. However, it should give you an idea of the content presented on the page. This will also work on social network sites such as Twitter. In Figure 1.27, a comparison is displayed of a Twitter page in Spanish translated to English through Google Translator.

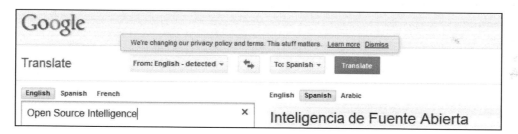

Figure 1.24: A Google Translate page translating individual text.

Figure 1.25: A Google Translate page translating an entire website.

Figure 1.26: A website translated to English through Google Translate.

Figure 1.27: A comparison of a Twitter feed (Left) and English translation (Right).

Bing Translator (bing.com/translator)

A few years after Google introduced free translation services, Bing created their own product. At first glance, it looks like a replica of Google's offering. However, Bing possesses one unique feature that convinced me to use it instead of Google for all of my translations.

The basic Bing translator site allows you to copy and paste foreign text into a search box and it will provide immediate translation. It will be English by default if you are viewing from the United States. Similar to Google, you can also type or paste an entire foreign website to conduct a translation of everything on the target page. However, this is where the similarities stop.

After you translated an entire page and see the results in English, you can control the view and include both the original and translated text. Figure 1.28 displays the search bar with view options on the right. The default view will display the original text as you hover your cursor over any translated text. Figure

1.29 displays the result of hovering over a Spanish comment translated to English. The next option allows you to view the page as it originally appeared and hover over text to see the translation (Figure 1.30). The last two options allow us to view a top and bottom or side by side translation. Figure 1.31 displays a side by side result that allows me to see the original and translated page in a single view.

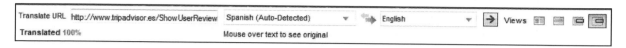

Figure 1.28: The Bing Translator search bar.

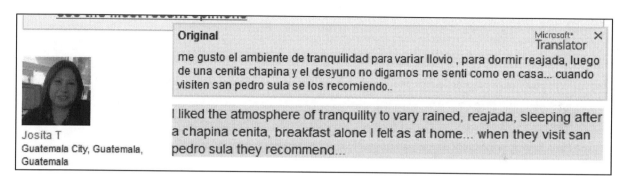

Figure 1.29: A Bing Translator result with the original content.

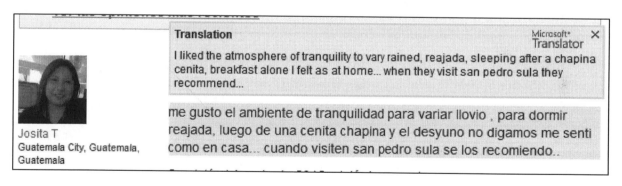

Figure 1.30: A Bing Translator result with translated content.

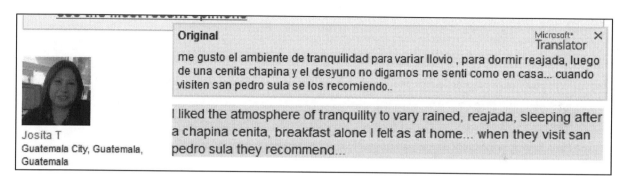

Figure 1.31: A Bing Translator result with side by side content.

Non-English Google Results

Not every piece of information that will be useful to you will be obtained by standard searches within English websites. Your target may either be from another country or have associates and affiliations in another country. While Google and Bing try to pick up on this, the technology is not perfect. Google has a search site and algorithm that change by location. For example, google.fr presents the French search page for Google. While this may produce the same overall results, they are usually in a different order than on google.com. Google maintains a page with links to each international version of its search at google.com/language_tools. This can allow you to search each site for variations, but I have a preferred method.

2Lingual (2lingual.com)

This page will allow you to conduct one search across two country sites on Google. The Google search (2lingual.com/2lingual-google) will display a plain search box and choices of two countries. The results will display in single columns next to each other (Figure 1.32).

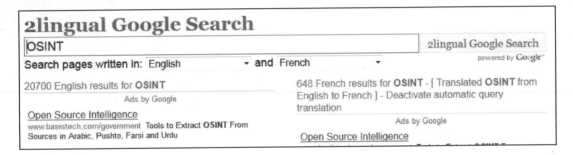

Figure 1.32: The 2lingual Google search page displaying dual search feeds.

Additionally, the foreign results will be automatically translated to English. This feature can be disabled if desired. The first few sponsored results (ads) will be similar, but the official results following should differ.

Groups (groups.google.com / groups.yahoo.com)

Google Groups provides access to both Usenet groups and Non-Usenet Google groups. Usenet groups are similar to mailing lists. The Usenet archive is complete and dates back to 1981. Since many people posted to these groups using their real name or email address, identifying their opinions on controversial topics is effortless. Additionally, searching a real name will often provide previous email addresses that may not be known to the searcher. This provides new intelligence for future searches. While none of this is usually damaging to the submitter, it helps provide an overall view of the target of interest.

Many of the newer groups used are created through Google and conform to practically any interest imaginable. Most users continue to use a real name, screen name, email address, or a combination of all three. Searching these posts is similar to any Google search. I suggest leaving the "all groups" option checked unless you are only looking for a specific Google Group.

While this will search many of the online groups, it will not pick up all of the Yahoo Groups. The content of most Yahoo Groups is public and will allow viewing without membership. Searching by real name or screen name will often produce results.

Google News Archive (news.google.com)

This can be an amazing resource of information about a target. In the past, if someone relocated to a new geographical area, he or she could leave the past behind and start over. Today, that is difficult. Google's News Archive is continually adding content from both online archives and digitized content from their News Archive Partner Program. Sources include newspapers from large cities, small towns, and anything in between. The link referenced above will allow for a detailed search of a target's name with filters including dates, language, and specific publication (Figure 1.33). In order to display this menu, click on the down arrow to the right of the search box. This can quickly identify some history of a target such as previous living locations, family members through obituaries, and associates through events, awards, or organizations.

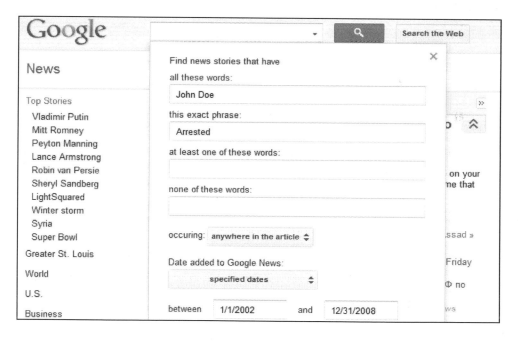

Figure 1.33: A Google News options menu.

Newspaper Archive (newspaperarchive.com)

Google's news search can provide a news article that references your target, but may not include the entire entry as it appeared in an actual newspaper. Google also has an emphasis on digital content and does not archive historic content from all print publications. The website Newspaper Archive provides digital scans of entire newspapers dating back to 1753. The scans are fully searchable by keyword and 2.5 million pages are added every month. This premium service can be purchased for as little as $5.99 per month, but the website states that you can currently view two newspapers per day for free. In the previous edition of this book, you needed to create a free account on the site. This process encouraged you to choose a premium paid account, but the free account was all that was necessary. This method is no longer effective and a new free account only prompts you to purchase a premium subscription.

Beginning in June of 2013, many people began reporting that they were no longer able to create a free account on Newspaper Archive. They were only allowed to create a premium account for a fee. I was able to recreate this problem by requesting a new account. I found that by signing in with a Facebook account as offered on their home page, this bypassed the requirement to create a premium account. Unfortunately, I was still bombarded by requests to create a premium account and it took a lot of effort to finally see the data that I was searching for. I have abandoned this method of access and I currently retrieve content from the service with the following method.

Instead of searching for my target on Newspaper Archive, I search through Google with the site operator discussed earlier. If I were searching for articles about Marcos Pulido, I would conduct the following exact query on Google.

Site:newspaperarchive.com "Marcos Pulido"

This will present the exact search results that would appear on Newspaper Archive; however, we now have the benefit of a direct link to the page that offers the article and content. Clicking any of the links will forward you directly to the page on Newspaper Archive that will display the article of the search result. You are still limited to two free newspaper views per day. I have found that deleting your internet cache, or "cookies", in your web browser will reset this limitation. This will eliminate the need to search in a different browser in order to get two additional searches. Before September of 2013, I could click on the Google Cache results from Newspaper Archive within the Google search and bypass any limitation for page views. This was later blocked. As of this writing, this trick is working again. I encourage you to try this technique whenever any service limits the amount of content you can see.

Regardless of the technique that you use to access a newspaper, the toolbar at the top of each page will allow you to zoom, magnify an area, print, save, and edit. The content is easiest to read by using the "Full Screen" tool to magnify the image. The result is a digital scan of the entire newspaper from the selected publication for the selected date. To document your findings, the entire page can be printed. Additionally, the embedded viewer will allow you to crop a specific portion of the page and save or print the selection. Figure 1.34 displays an excerpt of a newspaper from 1998 about hackers that identified several subjects that were criminally charged. This lesser known article from a Kansas newspaper was found searching for a target's name. Replicating this search on the newspaper's own website produced no results. This type of search will often reveal information about a target that cannot be found by any other technique. While these printed publications are probably archived in storage or at a local library, global immediate access is now possible through the internet. The limitation of two results per day is controlled by the web browser. If you have multiple browsers on your computer, you can increase this limitation. However, if the service provides value, please consider purchasing a premium account.

Figure 1.34: An excerpt from an article on Newspaper Archive.

Google Advanced Search (google.com/advanced_search)

If the search operators discussed in this chapter seem too technical, Google offers an advanced search page that simplifies the process. Navigating to google.com/advanced_search will present the same options in a web page that are possible by typing out the operators. This will help get familiar with the options, but it will be beneficial to understand the operators for later use.

The Advanced Search page will allow you to specify a specific phrase that you are searching for, just like the quotes in a search will allow. The site operator used earlier can be achieved by entering the desired website in the last field on the page (Figure 1.35). The file type option on this page is limited to popular file types, where the "filetype" operator can handle any file extension.

Bing Advanced Search (search.yahoo.com/web/advanced)

Bing does not technically provide an advanced search page similar to Google's. However, since Yahoo uses Bing's search, you can use Yahoo's advanced search page as a replacement. This page will allow you to easily create a search that filters by individual terms, exact phrases, omitted terms, specific domains, file formats, and languages. Figure 1.36 displays a portion of this useful page.

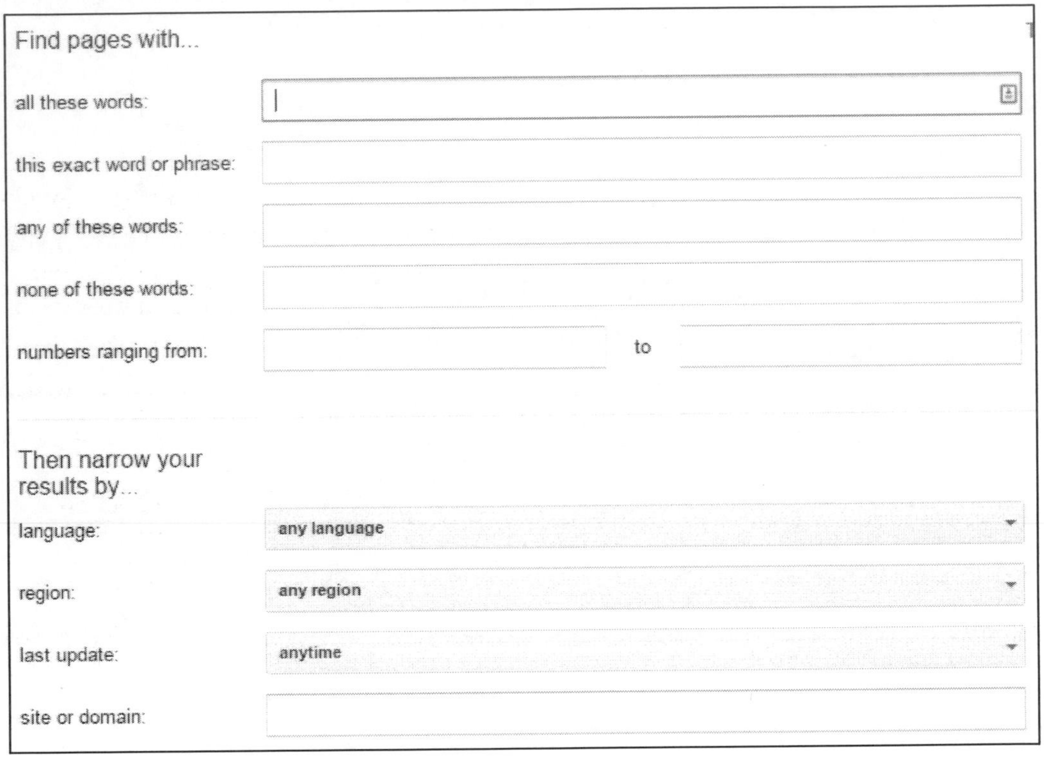

Find pages with...

all these words:

this exact word or phrase:

any of these words:

none of these words:

numbers ranging from: to

Then narrow your results by...

language: any language

region: any region

last update: anytime

site or domain:

Figure 1.35: Google's Advanced Search page with embedded search operators.

Additional Google Engines

Google isolates some search results into specialized smaller search engines. Each of these focuses on a unique type of internet search. The following engines will likely give you results that you will not find during a standard Google or Bing search.

Blogs (google.com/?tbm=blg)

Google removed its blog search in 2014. However, you can currently access this search database by entering "?tbm=blg" after a traditional Google search. This option will only display results from blogs.

This can be very beneficial when you only want user submitted content and not a lot of commercial websites.

Patents (google.com/webhp?tbm=pts)

Goggle probably has the best patent search option on the internet. It allows you to search the entire patent database within any field of a patent. This can be useful for searching names associated with patents or any details within the patent itself. If you need further help, Google offers an advanced patent search at google.com/advanced_patent_search.

Scholar (scholar.google.com)

Google Scholar is a freely accessible web search engine that indexes the full text of scholarly literature across an array of publishing formats. It includes most peer-reviewed online journals of Europe and America's largest scholarly publishers, plus many books and other non-peer reviewed journals. My favorite feature of this utility is the case law and court records search. I have located many court records through this free website that would have cost money to obtain from private services.

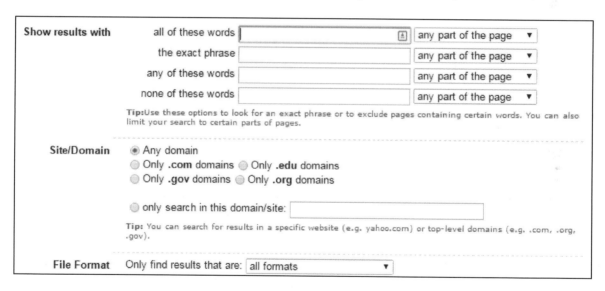

Figure 1.36: A Yahoo advanced search page using Bing's search index.

Google What Do You Love? (wdyl.com)

Another Google search option is the "what do you love?" page that allows a search of any name or topic. The results will be a collection of search hits across all of Google's search services. This will include location data, videos, documents, blogs, books, images and more.

Bing vs. Google (bing-vs-google.com)

This website gives an immediate view of the differences in results from Google and Bing displayed on a single page. If you tend to use only one of these search engines while avoiding the other, changing your home page to this website will remind you to look at the other option. Figure 1.36 displays the side-by-side results for the term "OSINT".

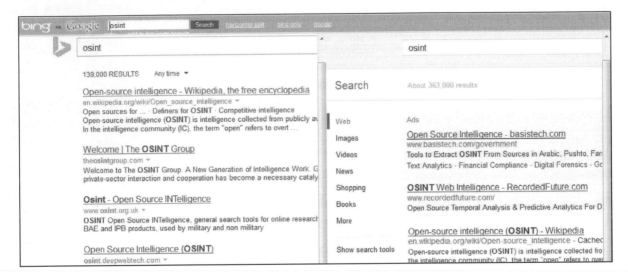

Figure 1.37: Results from a search on Bing vs. Google.

Keyword Tool (keywordtool.io)

Keyword Tool displays autocomplete data from Google, Bing, YouTube, and the App Store. You have likely noticed that Google quickly offers suggestions as you type in your search. This is called autocomplete. Figure 1.38 displays the results when I typed "macb" into Google. It prompted me to choose from the most popular searches when people typed those letters. This information may lead you to new terms to search in reference to your investigation. The advantage of Keyword Tool over Google is that Google only provides the four most popular entries. Keyword Tool provides the ten most popular entries. Additionally, you can choose different countries to isolate popular terms. You can also see results from similar searches that Google does not display. Figure 1.39 displays a partial result for the same search that provides additional information.

Real world application: I have successfully used this technique during the investigation of many businesses. I was once asked by a medium sized business to investigate reports of a faulty product that they had recently recalled. They wanted to see customer complaints. After searching the typical review websites, I conducted a search with Keyword Tool. I discovered that the 9th most popular search involving this specific product name included a term that was a misspelling of the product name. It was different enough in spelling that my searches were missing this content. Knowing this information, I was able to locate more relevant data for the client.

Figure 1.38: A Google autocomplete result.

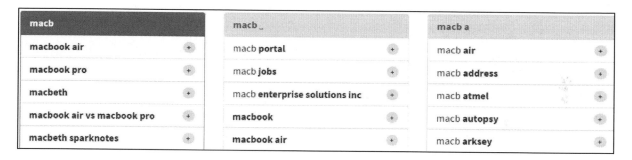

Figure 1.39: A Keyword Tool autocomplete result.

Google Custom Search Engines (google.com/cse)

Now that you are ready to unleash the power of Google, you may want to consider creating your own custom search engines. Google allows you to specify the exact type of searches that you want to conduct, and then create an individual search engine just for your needs. Many specialty websites that claim to search only social network content are simply using a custom engine from Google. For our first example, we will create a basic custom search engine that only searches two specific websites.

After you log into a Google account, navigate to the website listed above. If you have never created an engine, you will be prompted to create your first. Enter the first website that you want to search. In my example, I will search inteltechniques.com. As you enter any website to search, Google will automatically create another field to enter an additional website. The second website that I will search is computercrimeinfo.com. Provide a name for your custom engine and select "Create". You now have a custom search engine.

You can either embed this search engine into a website or view the public URL to access it from within any web browser. Figure 1.40 displays results from my custom engine when I searched the term "osint". Notice that the results are all located within the two websites that I provided.

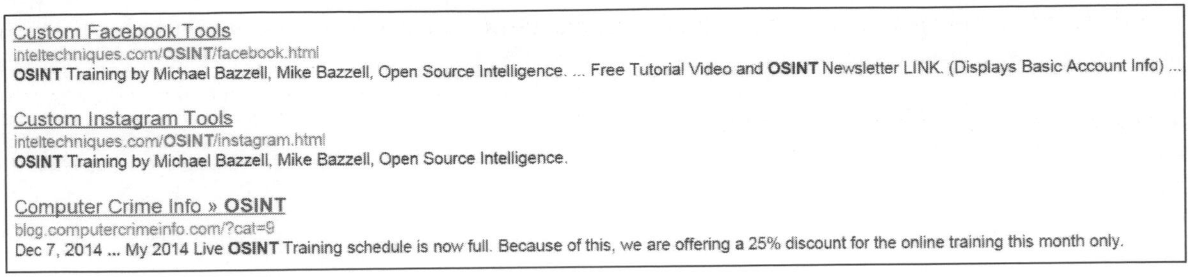
Custom Facebook Tools
inteltechniques.com/**OSINT**/facebook.html
OSINT Training by Michael Bazzell, Mike Bazzell, Open Source Intelligence. ... Free Tutorial Video and **OSINT** Newsletter LINK. (Displays Basic Account Info) ...

Custom Instagram Tools
inteltechniques.com/**OSINT**/instagram.html
OSINT Training by Michael Bazzell, Mike Bazzell, Open Source Intelligence.

Computer Crime Info » **OSINT**
blog.computercrimeinfo.com/?cat=9
Dec 7, 2014 ... My 2014 Live **OSINT** Training schedule is now full. Because of this, we are offering a 25% discount for the online training this month only.

Figure 1.40: The results from a Google Custom Search Engine.

This basic functionality can be quite powerful. It is the method behind my custom Pastebin search engine discussed in Chapter Eight. In that example, I created a custom search engine that scoured 101 specific websites in order to retrieve complete information about specific topics. This is only the first layer of a Google custom search engine.

Google offers an additional element to its custom search engines. This new layer, labeled refinements, allows you to specify multiple actions within one custom search engine. The best way to explain this is to offer two unique examples.

For the first example, I want to create a custom search engine that will allow us to search several social networks. Additionally, we will isolate the results from each network across several tabs at the top of our search results. The first step will be to create a new custom search engine in the same way that we did previously. Instead of specifying the two websites mentioned earlier, we will identify the websites to be searched as the following.

Facebook.com
Twitter.com
Instagram.com
LinkedIn.com
YouTube.com
Plus.Google.com
Tumblr.com

While this is not a complete list of active social networks, it represents the most popular social networks at the time of this writing. At this point, our custom search engine would search only these websites and provide all results integrated into one search result page. We now want to add refinements that will allow us to isolate the results from each social network.

After you have added these websites, navigate to the control panel option in order to view the configuration of this custom search engine. On the left menu, you should see an option called "Search Features". This will present a new option at the top of the page labeled "Refinements". Click the "add" button to add a new refinement for each of the websites in this example. You should create these in the same order that you want them to appear within the search results. For this demonstration, I created the following refinements in order. Figure 1.41 displays this menu with the refinements that match the websites used in this example.

Facebook
Twitter
Google+
Instagram
LinkedIn
YouTube
Tumblr

When each refinement is created, you will have two options of how the search will be refined. The option of "Give priority to the sites with this label" will place emphasis on matching rules, but will also reach outside of the rule if minimal results are present. The second option of "Search only the sites with this label" will force Google to remain within the search request and not disclose other sites. I recommend using the second option for each refinement.

Now that you have the refinements made, you must assign them each to a website. Back on the "Setup" menu option; select each social network website to open the configuration menu. Select the dropdown menu titled "Label" and select the appropriate refinement. Figure 1.42 displays my Tumblr.com site options with the "Tumblr" refinement selected. Repeat this process for each website and save your progress.

Figure 1.41: The refinements menu of a custom Google search engine.

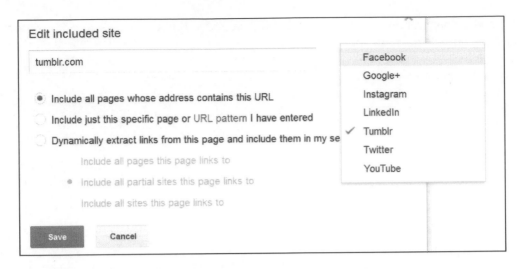

Figure 1.42: The site configuration menu of a custom Google search engine.

You should now have a custom search engine that will not only search several specific social network websites, but it should also allow you to isolate the results for each network. Navigate back to the control panel view and select the Public URL button to see the exact address of your new engine. Go to that address and you should see a very plain search engine.

You can now search any term or terms that you want and receive results for only the social networks that you specified. Additionally, you can choose to view all of the results combined or only the results of a specific network. Figure 1.43 displays the results when I searched the term osint. In this example, I have selected the Twitter refinement in order to only display results from twitter.com.

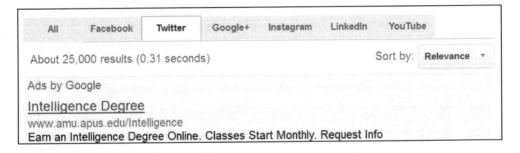

Figure 1.43: A Google custom search engine for social networks.

You can now bookmark this new search engine that you created and visit it whenever you have a target to search. You can take your custom search engines to another level by adding refinements that are not website specific. In the next example, we will make a search engine that will search the entire internet and allow us to filter by file type.

Create a new custom search engine and title it "Documents". Add only "google.com" as the website to be searched. We do not actually want to search google.com, but a website is required to get to the control panel. Save your engine and open the control panel to configure the options. In the "Sites to search" portion, choose the "Search only included sites" option and change it to "Search the entire web but emphasize included sites" option. Delete google.com from the sites to be searched. You now basically have a custom search engine that will search everything. It will essentially do the same thing as Google's home page. You can now add refinements to filter your search results.

Navigate to the search features menu and add a new refinement. Title the new refinement "PDF", leave the default setting of "Give priority to the sites with this label", and enter the following in the "Optional word(s) field.

ext:pdf

This will create a refinement that will allow you to isolate only PDF documents within any search that you conduct. Save this setting and create a new refinement. Title it DOC, leave the default search setting, and place the following in the optional word(s) field.

ext:doc OR ext:docx

This will create a new tab during your search results that will allow you to isolate Microsoft Word documents. By entering both the doc and docx formats, you will be sure to get newer and older documents. The word "OR" tells Google to search either format. Repeat this process for each of the following document types with the following language for each type. Do not enter anything in (parentheses).

XLS (Excel Spreadsheets) – ext:xls OR ext:xlsx OR ext:csv
PPT (PowerPoint Files) – ext:ppt OR ext:pptx
TXT (Text Docs) – ext:txt OR ext:rtf
WPD (Word Perfect Docs) – ext:wpd
ODT (Open Office Docs) – ext:odt OR ext:ods OR ext:odp
ZIP (Compressed Files) – ext:zip OR ext:rar OR ext:7z

Figure 1.44 displays the results of a search for the term osint within this new engine. The PPT tab is selected which reveals 53 PowerPoint presentations that contain the term. There are endless possibilities with this technique. You could make an engine that searched for audio and video files with extensions such as mp3, mp4, mpeg, avi, mkv, etc. You could make an engine that isolated images with extensions such as jpg, jpeg, png, bmp, gif, etc. You could also replicate all of this into a custom engine that only searched a specific website. If you were monitoring threats against your company, you could isolate only these files that appear on one or more of your company's domains.

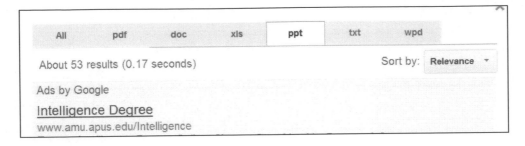

Figure 1.44: A Google custom search engine result for document file types.

As a service to my readers, I have created several custom search engines that are publicly available. You can either connect to them through my website under the OSINT Links section, or navigate to the following addresses.

Social Networks: http://inteltechniques.com/OSINT/social.networks.html
Smaller Networks: http://inteltechniques.com/OSINT/smaller.networks.html
Dating Sites: http://inteltechniques.com/OSINT/dating.networks.html
Pastebins: http://inteltechniques.com/OSINT/pastebins.html
Cloud Documents: http://inteltechniques.com/OSINT/docs.html
Document Formats: http://inteltechniques.com/OSINT/docs.format.html

One negative aspect to custom Google search engines is that they only display the most relevant 100 results. These are presented in ten pages of ten results per page. If you are searching very specific terms, this may not be an issue. However, standard searches can be limiting. The fix for this is an amendment to the URL of the custom search engine. As an example, I will use the social network engine that was created earlier. The public URL of this engine is the following address.

https://www.google.com/cse/publicurl?cx=001580308195336108602:oyrkxatrfyq

Figure 1.45 displays the result of the terms "OSINT Tools" within the Twitter option of this engine. Google announces that 927 results are available. However, you can only view the first 100 within this custom engine. Figure 1.46 displays the bottom of the last page of these results identifying the 100th result. If you copy the search engine ID you can create a new address that will lift this limit to 1000 results. The following URL will expand this specific search engine.

http://www.google.com/custom?cx=001580308195336108602:oyrkxatrfyq&num=100&filter=0

Figure 1.47 displays the results from the earlier search with this new option. While the look and feel is different, the results are the same. However, you can now view ten pages of 100 results each for a total of 1000 results.

Figure 1.45: A custom Google search identifying over 100 results.

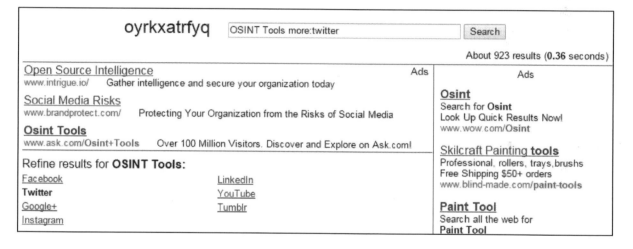

Ethan Bayne on Twitter: "@th3j35t3r looks like a good list of **tools** ...
https://twitter.com/docforensics/status/260678069331845120
Oct 23, 2012 ... BLOG UPDATE: 'Jester's Loadout: **OSINT Tools**', plus a spoiler & unprecedented code release (okay it's old but.
Labeled Twitter

1 2 3 4 5 6 7 8 9 **10**

Figure 1.46: A custom Google search displaying only 100 results.

oyrkxatrfyq   OSINT Tools more:twitter   Search

About 923 results (**0.36 seconds**)

Open Source Intelligence   Ads
www.intrigue.io/   Gather intelligence and secure your organization today

Social Media Risks
www.brandprotect.com/   Protecting Your Organization from the Risks of Social Media

Osint Tools
www.ask.com/Osint+Tools   Over 100 Million Visitors. Discover and Explore on Ask.com!

Refine results for **OSINT Tools:**

Facebook   LinkedIn
Twitter   YouTube
Google+   Tumblr
Instagram

Ads

Osint
Search for **Osint**
Look Up Quick Results Now!
www.wow.com/Osint

Skilcraft Painting **tools**
Professional, rollers, trays, brushs
Free Shipping $50+ orders
www.blind-made.com/**paint-tools**

Paint Tool
Search all the web for
Paint Tool

Figure 1.47: A custom Google search with expanded results.

Chapter Two

Search Engines: Other Alternatives

Google and Bing are great, but they do not do it all. There will always be a need for specialized search engines. These engines usually excel in one particular search method which justifies the lack of search power in other areas. The sites listed in this chapter represent the extreme minority when it comes to search traffic. It is often sites like these that implement the technologies that we later take for granted in more popular engines.

iSEEK (iseek.com)

One site that can be of assistance is iSEEK. This site provides categories of search results based on the information stored about the target. A search for "Glenn McElhose" provides search results similar to Google and Bing; however, there is an additional feature. The left column of the screen includes categories created by the search results (Figure 2.01).

The results include topics, people, places, and organizations related to the target. Clicking these categories will filter the search results to only match the topic, person, place or organization that is selected. Clicking the selection again will un-filter the results. This can be very helpful when the target has a common name. The results can be overwhelming, but the categories may provide a filter that can be applied that will make the results more manageable.

Carrot2 (carrot2.org)

This is another clustering search engine that groups search results into sets of topics. One way that this service stands out from the others is that it offers three different layout formats for viewing and filtering the results. The initial search will produce categories in a left menu similar to the previously mentioned sites. The "Circles" and "Foam Tree" tabs will change these text options into interactive graphics. Figure 2.02 displays the circle graphic identifying categories of topics that relate to the target.

The size of each section correlates to the amount of search results that fit into that topic. In this example, the third largest topic relating to my target is "RAM Analysis". Clicking that piece filters the search results to only include related entries to the right.

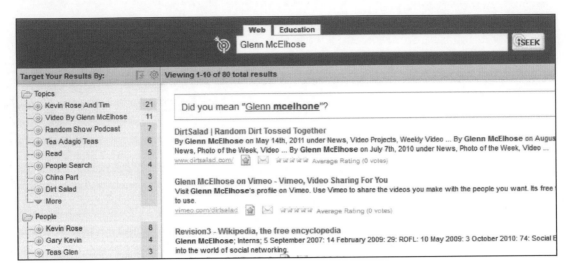

Figure 2.01: An iSeek search results page with categories.

Exalead (exalead.com)

Headquartered in Paris, this search engine has gained a lot of popularity in the United States. The main search engine provides many results on popular searches. I have found that individual targets without a strong internet presence do not get many, if any, results on this site. However, this site excels in two areas.

Exalead works well in finding documents that include the target mentioned within the document. The "filetype" operator used in other engines works the same here. The document search option was also included in FOCA, the metadata scraper that will be discussed later in this book.

Voxalead, an Exalead search engine, searches within audio and video files for specific words. This is thanks to speech to text technologies. Voxalead will search within all of the spoken audio of a file for references to the text searched. The results are presented in a timeline view. Currently, the majority of the results of this new product link to news media and public news video files.

Million Short (millionshort.com)

This website offers one unique function that is not found on any other search engine. You can choose to remove any results that link to the most popular one million websites. This will eliminate popular results and focus on lesser known websites that can get lost in traditional results. You can also select to remove only the top 100,000, 10,000, 1,000, or 100 results.

Million Tall (milliontall.com)

This is the direct opposite of Million Short. This engine only searches the one million most popular websites. Similar to Million Short, you can also filter by the top 100,000, 10,000, 1,000, or 100 websites.

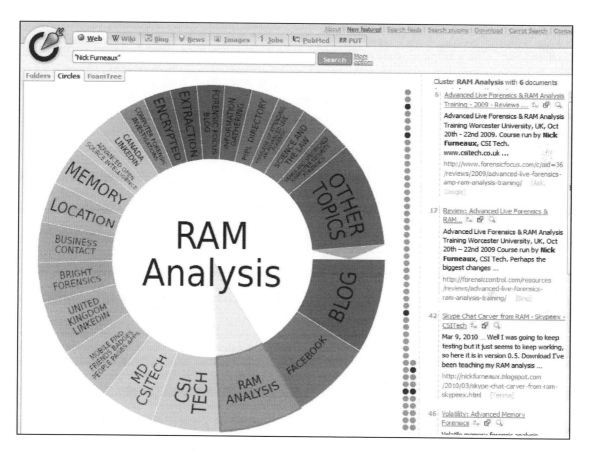

Figure 2.02: A search result on Carrot2 filtered by the "Circles" view.

International Search Engines

U.S. based search engines are not the primary search sites for all countries. Visiting search sites outside of the U.S. can provide results that will not appear on Google or Bing. In Russia, Yandex (yandex.ru) is the chosen search engine. Yandex offers an English version at yandex.com. These results are often similar to Google's, however are usually prioritized differently. In the past, I have found unique intelligence from this site when Google let me down.

In China, most people use Baidu (baidu.com). Baidu does not offer an English version. However, the site is still useable. Striking the "enter" key on the keyboard after typing a search will conduct the search without the ability to understand the Chinese text. New results not visible on Google or Bing may be rare, but an occasional look on these sites is warranted.

Yandex (yandex.com)

In the previous edition of this book, I only made a brief reference to Yandex and quickly moved on. In the past year, I have discovered many advanced features of Yandex which justify an expanded section. Visually, the Yandex home page and search result pages do not possess additional search operators. These options are only available by issuing a direct command within your search. While this can be more cumbersome than a Google search, the results can include much new data. Some of these searches can be overkill for daily use, but those who conduct brand reputation monitoring or extensive background checks may take advantage of the possibilities.

Exact terms: Similar to Google and Bing, quotation marks will search for exact terms. Searching "Michael Bazzell" inside of quotes would search only those terms, and would avoid "Mike" or "Bazel".

Missing word: You can search an exact phrase without knowing every word of the phrase. A search for "Open Source * Techniques" inside of quotation marks will identify any results that include that phrase with any word where the asterisk (*) is located. This identified not only results with the title of this book, but also results for "Open Source Development Techniques" and "Open Source Responsive Techniques". This search can be very useful for identifying a person's middle name. "Michael * Bazzell" produced some interesting results.

Words within the same sentence: The ampersand (&) is used in this query to indicate that you want to search for multiple terms. "Hedgehog & Flamingo", without the quotation marks, would identify any websites that contained both of those words within one sentence. If you want the results to only include sentences that have the two words near each other, you can search "Hedgehog /2 Flamingo". This will identify websites that have a sentence that includes the words Hedgehog and Flamingo within two words of each other.

Words within the same website: Similar to the previous method, this search identifies the searched terms within an entire website. "Hedgehog && Flamingo" would identify pages that have both of those words within the same page, but not necessarily the same sentence. You can also control the search to only include results that have those two words within a set amount of sentences from each other. A search of "Hedgehog ?? /3 Flamingo", without the quotation marks would identify websites that have those two words within three sentences of each other.

Include a specific word: In Google and Bing, you would place quotation marks around a word to identify pages that contain that word in them. In Yandex, this is gained with a plus sign (+). Michael +Bazzell would mandate that the page has the word Bazzell, but not Michael.

Search any word: In Google and Bing, you can use "OR" within a search to obtain results on any of the terms searched. In Yandex, this is achieved with the pipe symbol (|). This is found above the backslash (\) on your keyboard. A search of "+Bazzell Michael|Mike|M ", without quotation marks, would return results for Michael Bazzell, Mike Bazzell, and M Bazzell.

Exclude a word: Google and Bing allow you to use a hyphen (-) to exclude a word in a search. Yandex does not technically support this, but it seems to work fine. The official Yandex operator is the tilde (~). A typical search would look like "Michael Bazzell ~ Mike", without the quotation marks. This would identify websites that contained Michael Bazzell, but not Mike Bazzell. I prefer to stick with the hyphen (-) until it no longer works.

Multiple identical words: This is a technique that I have needed several times in the past before I learned of Yandex's options. You may want to search for websites that contain a specific word more than once. An example might be if you are searching for someone that has two identical words in his or her full name. "Carina Abad Abad" would fit in this scenario. You could use quotation marks to identify the majority of the results, but you would filter out anything that was not exact such as Abad,Abad, Abad-Abad, or AbadAbad. This is where the exclamation point (!) comes in. A search of "!Carina !Abad !Abad", without quotation marks, would identify any results that included those three words regardless of spacing or punctuation.

Date specific searches: While Google provides a menu to filter your searches by date, Yandex makes you work harder for it. You must specify the date range within the search. The following queries should explain the options.

date:20111201..20111231 OSINT – Websites mentioning OSINT between December 1-31, 2011
date:2011* OSINT – Websites mentioning OSINT in the year 2011
date:201112* OSINT – Websites mentioning OSINT in December of 2011
date:>20111201 OSINT – Websites mentioning OSINT after December 1, 2011

Standard operators: Most of the operators explained earlier for Google and Bing should also work in Yandex. The commands for Site, Domain, Inurl, and Intitle should work the same way. Yandex maintains a list of operators at help.yandex.com/search/how-to-search/search-operators.xml. All Yandex operators work together and multiple operators can be used to form very specific searches. Figure 2.03 displays the results for a search of any websites from 2013 with the phrase Michael Bazzell and the word OSINT while excluding any websites with the word Mike.

Figure 2.03: A specific Yandex search with operators.

Search Engine Colossus (searchenginecolossus.com)

This website is an index of practically every search engine in every country. The main page offers a list of countries alphabetically. Each of these links connects to a list of active search engines in that country. I stay away from this service when searching American based subjects. However, if my target has strong ties to a specific country, I always research the engines that are used in that area through this website.

Duck Duck Go (duckduckgo.com)

This search engine with a clean interface offers two unique services. It has gained a lot of popularity because it does not track anything from users. Engines such as Google record and maintain all of your search history and sites visited. This can be a concern to privacy advocates and those with sensitive investigations. Additionally, it uses information from crowd sourced websites such as Wikipedia and Wolfram Alpha to augment traditional results and improve relevance. You will receive fewer results here than at more popular search engines, but the accuracy of the results will improve.

Global File Search (globalfilesearch.com)

Most File Transfer Protocol (FTP) servers have been indexed by Google. While I prefer the technique explained in the previous chapter, and referenced again in a moment, there are other options. Overall use of FTP to transfer files is minimal compared to a decade ago, but the servers still exist. Global File Search provides one of the only web based engines for searching files on these public servers. In Figure 2.04, a specific search identified PDF documents in reference to a hospital available for public download. At the time of this writing, the site claims to have indexed 243 terabytes of files in public FTP servers. Anyone searching for intelligence on any business should take a look at this site.

File Mare (filemare.com)

Although it has indexed a smaller amount of data than the others, File Mare should be visited to locate possible FTP content. Much of the data on this website is no longer available. However, knowing the IP address of a previous FTP server with desired content could be valuable to your investigation.

Napalm FTP (searchftps.org)

This FTP search engine often provides content that is very recent. After each result, it displays the date that the data was last confirmed at the disclosed location. This can help locate relevant information that is still present on a server.

Manual FTP Search

I still prefer the manual method of searching Google for FTP information. As mentioned earlier, Google and Bing index most publicly available data on FTP servers. A custom search string will be required in order to filter unwanted information. If I were looking for any files including the term "confidential" in the title, I would conduct the following search on Google and Bing.

inurl:ftp -inurl:(http|https) "confidential"

The result will include only files from ftp servers (inurl:ftp), will exclude any web pages (-inurl: (http|https)), and mandate that the term "confidential" is present ("). I have located many sensitive documents from target companies with this query. The above search yielded 1,200,000 FTP results.

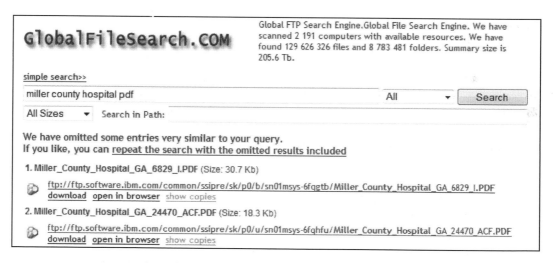

Figure 2.04: PDF files found on a FTP server found with Global File Search.

Nerdy Data (search.nerdydata.com)

Google, Bing, and other search engines search the content of websites. They focus on the data that is visually present within a web page. Nerdy Data searches the programming code of a website. This code is often not visible to the end user and exists within the HTML code, JavaScript, and CSS files that most users are not familiar with. This code can be extremely valuable to research in some scenarios. Viewing the source code of a website can be done by right-clicking on the background of a page and selecting "View Source". The following two examples should explain a small portion of the possibilities with this service.

In Chapter Twelve, you will learn about free services that try to identify additional websites that may be associated with your target website. The backbone of these services relies on the indexing of programming data of websites. Nerdy Data may be the most pure way of searching for this data. If you were to look at the source code of one of my websites, yourcomputernerds.com, you would see at the bottom that I use a service called Google Analytics. This service identifies the number of visitors to a website and the general area where they are located. The following is the actual code.

```
<script type="text/javascript">
try {
var pageTracker = _gat._getTracker("UA-8231004-3");
pageTracker._trackPageview();
} catch(err) {}</script>
```

The important data here is the "UA-82310004-3". That is my unique number for Google Analytics. Any website that I use the service with will need to have that number within the source code of the page. If you search that number on Nerdy Data, you will get interesting results. Figure 2.05 displays the partial results of this search. Nerdy Data identified three websites that are using that number including computercrimeinfo.com and two additional sites that I maintain for a law firm. You can often find valuable information within the source code of your target's website.

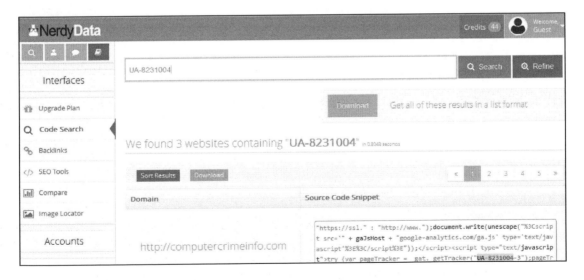

Figure 2.05: A search result on Nerdy Data.

Many web designers and programmers steal code from other websites. In the past, this would be very difficult to identify without already knowing the suspect website. With Nerdy Data, you can perform a search of the code of concern and identify websites that possess the data within their own source code. In 2013, I located a custom search website at the YGN Ethical Hacker Group that inspired me to create my own similar search service. I was curious if there were any other search websites that possessed this basic code that might give me more ideas. I looked at the source code of the website and located a small piece of code that appeared fairly unique to that service. I conducted a search on Nerdy Data for the following code.

<li>http://yehg.net/q?[keyword]&c=[category] (q?yehg.net&c=Recon)</li>

This code was within the JavaScript programming of the search website. The search results identified 13 websites that also possessed the same code. Two of these results were hosted on the creator's website, and offered no additional information. Three of the results linked to pages that were no longer available. Three of the results linked to pages that were only discussing the code within the target website and how to improve the functionality. However, four of the results identified similar search services that were also using the programming code searched. This revealed new search services that were related to the website that I was interested in. This same technique could be used to identify websites that are stealing proprietary code, locate pages that were created to attempt to fool a victim into using a cloned site, or validate the popularity of a specific programming function being used on hacking websites globally.

You may have noticed other search possibilities within Nerdy Data. These options will be explained in other more appropriate areas of this book.

Qwant (qwant.com)

Qwant attempts to combine the results of several types of search engines into one page. It was launched in 2013 after two years of research. It has an easily digestible interface that displays results in columns titled Web, News, Knowledge, Social, and Shopping. There is a Google "feel" to it and the layout can be changed to your own preferences. A default search of my own name provided the expected results similar to Google and Bing. Clicking on the "People" tab at the top introduced new results not found on the other engines. The results included recent posts from Twitter, Facebook, LinkedIn, and MySpace from and about people with my name.

Talk Walker Alerts (talkwalker.com/en/alerts)

The previous chapter explained Google's alert option. While this is the current standard for email alerts on search terms, there are other options. Some people choose not to use Google because of privacy concerns. Some just want alternatives to obtain complete results. Talk Walker Alerts has a feel very similar to Google Alerts. The main difference is that it does not require a Google account.

Custom Search Tool (inteltechniques.com/OSINT/user.html)

At this point, you may be overwhelmed with the abundance of search options. I can relate to that, and I do not take advantage of every option during every investigation. During my initial search of a target, I like to rely on the basics. I first search Google, Bing, Yandex, and the smaller Google search engines. In order to assist with this initial search, I created a custom tool that will allow you to quickly get to the basics. Figure 2.06 displays the current state of this online website.

The main set of search options will allow you to individually search directly through Google, Bing, Yahoo, Yandex, Exalead, Google Newsgroups, Google Blogs, FTP Servers, Google Scholar, Google Patents, Google News, Baidu, Duck Duck Go, Blekko, and Qwant. Each search that you conduct will open within a new tab within your browser. This tool is based on simple JavaScript and your queries are never seen nor stored on my server. The search all takes place on your computer.

The last search option will allow you to provide any search term that will be searched across all of the services listed. Each service will populate the results within a new tab in your internet browser. Please note that this works best within Firefox. Specifically, Google Chrome occasionally prohibits this type of behavior and will only load one tab at a time. You can also use any of the search operators discussed previously within this tool.

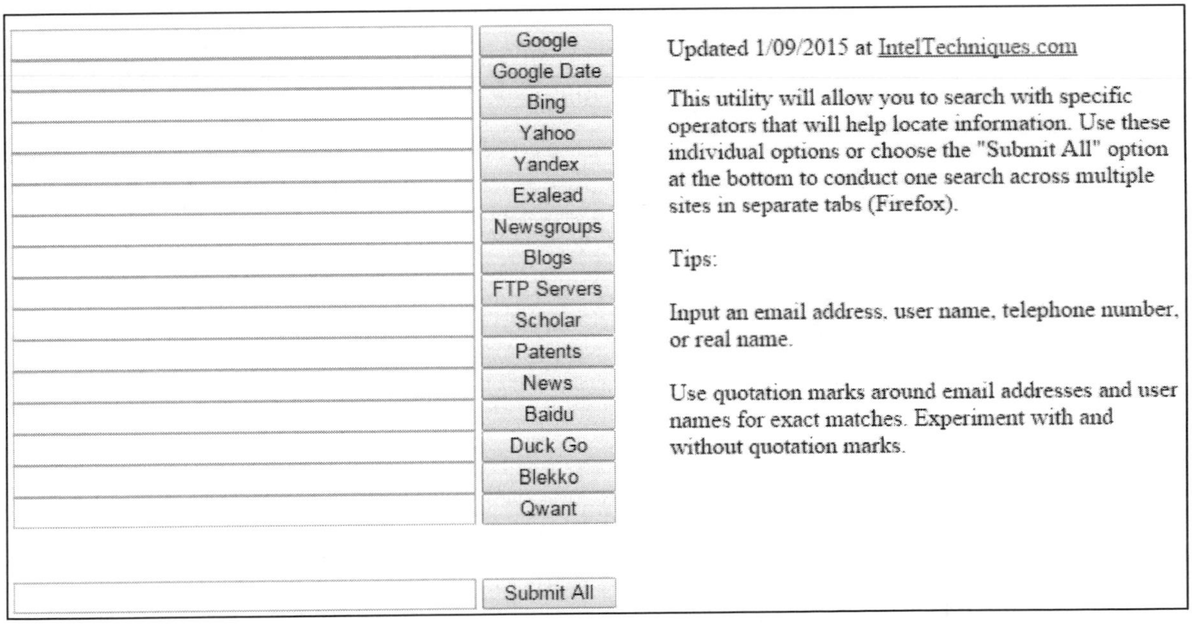

Figure 2.06: A custom search tool from IntelTechniques.com.

Chapter Three

Social Networks

There are hundreds of social networks that act as storage for details of a person's life. Information that was once held privately within a small group of friends or family is now broadcasted to the world via public websites. Searching these websites has always been a high priority for intelligence gathering. This chapter should identify some new techniques that can be applied on any target.

Facebook (facebook.com)

Facebook users tend to keep their information a little more secure than users of other social networking sites. By default, a new Facebook user must specify the privacy settings to their account during the creation of their profile. This is mostly thanks to privacy advocates that continuously protest Facebook's privacy policies. Many of these user settings simply do not promote privacy and leave the user's information exposed for anyone to see. This section will explain numerous ways to obtain user information that is not visible on the public profile.

Facebook's search options are severely limited without being logged into an account. In fact, I do not recommend trying any searches on Facebook without an account. Creating an account is free and can be completed using fictitious information. Once logged in, a simple search field will be present at the top of any Facebook page. Typing in the target's real name should lead to some results. Unlike Twitter, Facebook users usually use their real name when creating a profile. This profile is also usually linked to a graduating high school class as well as college alumni. Once a user's profile is located, the default view is the "timeline" tab. This will include basic information such as gender, location, family members, friends, relationship status, interests, education, and work background. This page will also commonly have a photo of the user and any recent posts on their page. With over a billion active users, it will be likely that you will locate several user profiles under the same name as your target. There are a few things that you can do to find the right target.

If your target's name is Tom Johnson, you have your work cut out for you. This does not mean that you will never find his Facebook page, but you will need to take additional steps to get to your target. When searching the name, several possibilities will appear in a drop down menu. This is obviously not the complete list of Tom Johnsons that are present on Facebook. At the bottom of this list is an option to see all of the profiles with your target name. After scrolling down through this list, you can select "See more results" to continue loading profiles with your target's name. You can look through these and hope to identify your target based on the photo, location, or additional information displayed in this view.

In 2013, Facebook introduced the Graph search, which eliminated some of the search filters visible on the people search pages. These filters were still available throughout 2014, but you needed to enter specific words into the search form to use them. This was often achieved by common phrases such as "people named Tom Johnson who live in Chicago, Illinois". If your wording was perfect, you would receive accurate results. In February of 2015, Facebook removed the ability to conduct detailed searches for user profiles within the search field. Prior to this time, you could enter the following queries directly into a Facebook page and receive matching results.

People named "John Smith"
People who work at Microsoft
People who work in Chicago
People who live in Chicago
People who like OSINT
People who attended Arlington High School
People born in 1980
People who visited Peru
People who speak Russian

Facebook now requires a specific address (URL) in order to search this type of information. It is not as user friendly as their previous option, but we can recreate each query. The following section will identify the types of information you can search and the necessary detailed structure of each address. At the end, I will present my custom online Facebook search tool that will simplify the entire process.

Name

Facebook still offers native name searching within any page. However, I have received better results by using a custom address. The following page would identify any profiles with my name. Note the "%20" in the URL represents a space. Most browsers will automatically convert a space to this format.

https://www.facebook.com/search/str/Michael%20Bazzell/users-named

Employment

Facebook can help you find current and past employees of a business. This can be beneficial if you are investigating a shady company and would like to contact employees that can assist with your investigation. I have also used this to gather intelligence from employees that were committing illegal acts while at their workplace. Knowing a suspect's friends that they work with can be valuable during an interview. Knowing the names of people that work with your suspect, but are not necessarily friends with the suspect, can be more valuable. I might focus on these people as potential witnesses since they probably do not have as much loyalty to the suspect as one of the target's friends. If I wanted to locate all Facebook profiles of Microsoft employees, the following address would provide the results.

https://www.facebook.com/search/str/Microsoft/pages-named/employees/present

Changing "present" to "past" within this address will identify profiles of people that are likely no longer employed by the target company. You can also combine search options into one URL. You need to place each search structure into a single address and add "intersect" at the end. If you wanted to search for all previous Microsoft employees named "Mike Smith", the following address would produce results.

https://www.facebook.com/search/str/Mike%20Smith/users-named/str/Microsoft/pages-named/employees/past/intersect

Location

Searching profiles by location can be extremely beneficial when you do not know the name of your target. If you know the city where your target lives, you can use this as a filter. The address of a search to identify every user that currently lives in Denver is as follows.

https://www.facebook.com/search/str/denver/pages-named/residents/present

This will reveal an enormous amount of profiles. You can filter them by adding more search criteria. The following URL would display only users that live in Denver and are chefs.

https://www.facebook.com/search/str/Denver/pages-named/residents/present/str/chef/pages-named/employees/present/intersect

If you know that your target's name is Sarah, and she lives in Denver, and she is a chef, the following URL will identify the one person on Facebook that matches this search.

https://www.facebook.com/search/str/Denver/pages-named/residents/present/str/chef/pages-named/employees/present/str/Sarah/users-named/intersect

Likes

Facebook will allow you to filter results by a topic of interest. When people click the "like" button on a Facebook page, their profiles can be searched by this data. The URL to view every Facebook user that likes Budweiser would be as follows.

https://www.facebook.com/search/str/budweiser/pages-named/likers

I was recently asked to look into an incident at a community college where vulgar graffiti was found next to a spray painted logo of a specific local musical group. I searched for people that liked this band on Facebook and attended the target high school. This produced a list of four subjects that attended the school and were fans of the band. All four subjects were questioned and one of them confessed to being present at the scene and identified the culprit. If I were searching for Harvard students that like the band Thrice, the following address would produce the results.

https://www.facebook.com/search/str/Harvard/pages-named/students/str/Thrice/pages-named/likers/intersect

Education

Facebook will also allow you to search for students of a specific school without knowing names. This can help create a list of potential witnesses to an event and will allow you to analyze friendships. The following search would identify current and past students of Harvard University:

https://www.facebook.com/search/str/harvard/pages-named/students

Age

I have found age range searching beneficial when my target is using a false name on Facebook or an alias that I do not know. This has also been used to identify sex offenders that provide real information, but change their name on Facebook to avoid detection. Choosing the age range and city of residence of your target may provide any Facebook pages that fit the criteria. You may receive several results that do not apply to your subject, but finding your target within these pages can be very gratifying. The following URL would identify people named Brad O'Neal between the ages of 37 and 40.

https://www.facebook.com/search/str/Brad%20O'Neal/users-named/str/37/40/users-age-2/intersect

If you know the exact year of birth of your target, you can also search by this data. If you know that your target's name is Tim Smith, and that he was born in 1980, the following address would display the appropriate results. This filtered numerous people with a common name to only seven profiles.

https://www.facebook.com/search/str/Tim%20Smith/users-named/str/1980/date/users-born/intersect

Visited

Facebook allows users to "check in" to places that they visit. Searching this data can help identify people that were present at a specific location or event. The address to search every user that visited Wrigley Field is the following. You could easily add additional filters to identify a target.

https://www.facebook.com/search/str/wrigley%20field/pages-named/visitors

Language

Many people identify the languages that they speak within their Facebook profile. You can search this content with a query similar to the previous. The URL to identify every user that speaks Japanese and lives in Denver would be the following.

https://www.facebook.com/search/str/Japanese/pages-named/speakers/str/Denver/pages-named/residents/present/intersect

Gender

When you do not know your target's name you will likely use the previous techniques to filter the profiles. Filtering further by gender can often remove half of the possibilities. In the past, you could type something similar to "women that work at Microsoft" directly into the search field. Today, that no longer works. However, you can add "/males" or "/females" near the end of every previous address to filter by gender. The following address would display every Facebook profile of female Microsoft employees that live in Seattle. The final section of custom Facebook search tool, which is explained next, allows you to easily specify the gender of users during your searches.

https://www.facebook.com/search/str/seattle/pages-named/residents/present/str/microsoft/pages-named/employees/present/females/intersect

Custom Facebook Search Tool (inteltechniques.com/osint/facebook.html)

This free online tool will create detailed queries within Facebook without the need to memorize the exact search addresses required. Figure 3.01 displays the profile search portion of the Facebook search tool. It occupies the entire right half of this search page. It identifies the type of search within each search box. As an example, typing "Microsoft" in the third search option would immediately display any profiles that previously announced employment at Microsoft. The lower options allow you to combine searches. Entering "OSINT" and "Microsoft" in the "People who like… and worked at…" option would display profiles of former Microsoft employees that clicked "Like" on the OSINT Facebook page. Overall, this tool is not doing anything that you could not do on your own using the methods mentioned previously. Its purpose is to make searching easier.

The Multiple Variables option near the bottom will allow you to select multiple filters and launch the appropriate search. In Figure 3.01, the data entered would search for any Facebook profiles of people named John Smith that currently work at Microsoft and live in Chicago. You can choose as many or few of the following options to generate your own custom search. Clicking "AND" after each input will present an additional search field.

Name
Current Employer or Title
Previous Employer or Title
Current Home Location
Previous Home Location
Language Spoken
School Affiliation
Places Visited
Pages Liked
Year Born

Once you have located the profile of your target, it should be fairly easy to navigate. If the information is public, you can click to see the friends, photos, posts, and basic information about the subject. If the profile is private, you may be limited to what you can see on this screen.

Clicking the "Friends" link in the profile will load a list of the friends in the center column. This can be beneficial to identify associates of the subject. While some people will only list others that they have some type of relationship with, many people will list hundreds of friends that they may or may not actually know. Fortunately, Facebook gives us a search bar that we can use to filter this list. Typing a name or partial name will immediately filter the list. This works on first name or last.

When you locate a comment on a profile, never assume that the comment was not manipulated. Facebook allows a user to change the text posted at any time. Fortunately, the word "Edited" will appear under a comment if any changes have been made. Clicking this link will load a new popup window that will display any edits to the comment and the date and time of each edit. Figure 3.02 displays an edited wall post on the left and the edit history on the right.

The "Photos" option will display any public photos that the target has in his or her profile. The default view will list a photo identifying each album. The total number of photos in the album will be listed below the album name. Clicking on either the photo or the album name will open that album in icon view. If the user has uploaded any videos, clicking the "Photos" dropdown menu and selecting "Videos" will display the videos. I will demonstrate a better way of doing this in a moment.

If the user's page has been marked as private, the information will be limited. This will usually still include a photo and general wall information such as friends that have recently been added. It is possible to hide all information, but that is very rare.

People named....		GO
People who work at....		GO
People who worked at....		GO
People who like....		GO
People who live in....		GO
People who lived in....		GO
School attended....		GO
People who visited....		GO

People who live in....	and like....	GO
People who live in....	birth year....	GO
People who live in....	and work at....	GO
People who live in....	and worked at....	GO

People named....	who live in....		GO
People named....	who like....		GO
People named....	birth year....		GO
People named....	between age....	and....	GO
People named....	who work at....		GO
People named....	who worked at....		GO

People who like....	birth year....	GO
People who like....	and work at....	GO
People who like....	and worked at....	GO

Posts about....	GO

Multiple Variables:

Name ▼	John Smith	AND
Current Employer/Title ▼	Microsoft	AND
Current Location ▼	Chicago	AND

Search

Gender Search:

○ Males ○ Females

who live in....	and like....	GO

○ Males ○ Females

who live in....	with birth year....	GO

○ Males ○ Females

who live in....	and work at....	GO

○ Males ○ Females

who live in....	and worked at....	GO

Figure 3.01: A custom Facebook search tool on IntelTechniques.com.

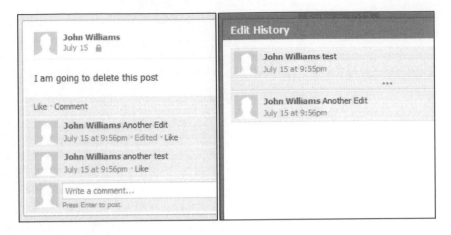

Figure 3.02: An example of an edited comment on Facebook.

All of the Facebook information up to this point applies to the new Timeline view. All profiles have converted over to this more modern view. This will include a large photo at the top of the page and a continuous timeline of data as you scroll down. This will start with the most recent uploads and work backward in time. The Friends, Photos, Map, and Subscribers options can all be found under the main photo in the timeline view.

Search by Email Address

Facebook has another useful search feature. You can enter an email address and it will identify any profile that was created using that email address. In the past, you could provide this address in the main search field on any Facebook page. This technique no longer works. Instead, we must submit the search as an address, or URL. The following website address will identify any Facebook profiles that were registered to tom.smith@gmail.com.

https://www.facebook.com/search/results.php?q=tom.smith@gmail.com

This will link to the profile and provide the basic information associated with the account. This is also beneficial when trying to locate someone that may have a nickname instead of a real name on their profile. Additionally, it may provide alias profiles that were created by someone who did not use an alias email address. Figure 3.03 displays a Facebook URL result from searching the email address lorangb@gmail.com.

Search by Telephone Number

Prior to November of 2012, a telephone number could be typed into the Facebook search form and the results would identify any profiles created with that number. Since Facebook usually requires a cellular telephone number to complete the signup process, this type of search yielded very successful results. Facebook has a great database of cellular telephone numbers and associated users. Unfortunately, this feature was eliminated by Facebook after a security researcher made the vulnerability public. This feature reappeared for several months in 2014 but was later removed. Fortunately, there is a way around this obstacle.

A Facebook account and Yahoo email account will be required for this technique. Through a web browser, log into an alias Facebook account in one tab and log into an alias email account on Yahoo Mail in another tab. If you do not have a Yahoo email account, the creation process is easy at mail.yahoo.com. On the "Contacts" page of your Yahoo account, select "Add a New Contact". This will present a form that will allow you to enter a target telephone number. The "Name" fields can contain any data, and I usually use numbers beginning at 001. Figure 3.04 displays this minimal contact information. Save this entry and go to your Facebook page. Click on the "Find Friends" button next to your name in the upper right portion of the page. This will present several options for importing friends into Facebook. Choose the Yahoo option and provide your Yahoo email address. You will need to confirm that you want to give Facebook access to your Yahoo contacts by clicking "I agree" on the popup window. Facebook will then identify any user profiles that are associated with the target number. Facebook will encourage you to add these friends, but do not choose that option. If you do, your target will be sent a friend request from your account.

This should be a reminder about how important it is to only log into profiles that do not contain any personal information. While the target should never know that you were searching their information, an anonymous profile ensures that your identity is not compromised in case a mistake is made during the search techniques.

In the search demonstrated here, a target number of 314-555-1212 was used since that number will never be assigned to any personal telephone account. The results identified three people that are providing this telephone number as their own to Facebook. Figure 3.05 displays the Facebook accounts that are associated with this number.

This technique usually identifies the current users of cellular telephone numbers regardless of how the cellular number was registered. This is often successful in identifying owners of cash telephones that could not be identified through traditional resources.

There is one easier way of searching by telephone number on Facebook, and I am surprised that it still works. There is a Facebook website that allows you to reset your password if you have forgotten it. This page can be located at the following address.

https://www.facebook.com/login/identify?ctx=recover

This will present a single search field that will accept an email address, a telephone number, a user name, or a real name. If you enter any of this information about your target, you should receive a result identifying the profile. Figure 3.06 displays a result from an email search. Notice that the information provided now identifies other partial email addresses and the last two digits of a telephone number attached to the account. This would have also worked by searching his cellular telephone number. Do not click "Continue" on this screen, as it will send a password reset request to that individual. This would not lock him out of the account or gain you access, but it will raise suspicion.

Figure 3.03: A search result from an email address on Facebook.

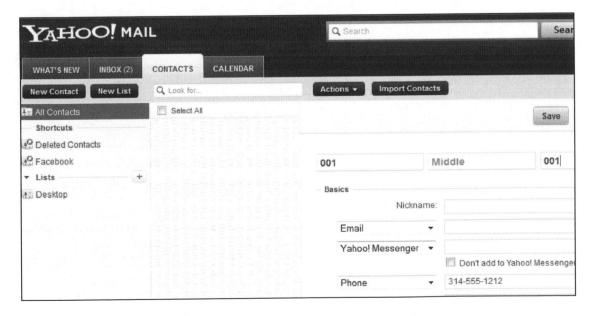

Figure 3.04: A Yahoo Mail contact entry.

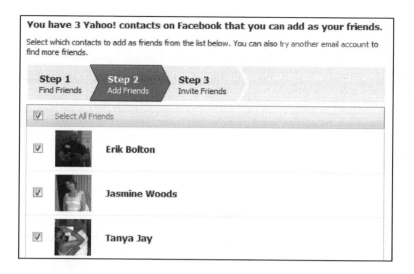

Figure 3.05: A Facebook result from a telephone number search.

Figure 3.06: A Facebook password reset search.

Identify User's Email Address

Yahoo can provide additional information that traditional searches cannot. Yahoo can extract the email address of some Facebook users based on the address associated with the Facebook account. This method will only work if you are friends on Facebook with the target profile. Often a simple friend request to the target will result in an accepted connection.

While logged into your Yahoo email account, click on the "Contacts" tab and then the "Import Contacts" button. This will present four options, and you should choose the first option titled

"Facebook". You will be asked to confirm that you want Yahoo to access your Facebook contacts. Yahoo will then identify your Facebook friends and extract their information into your Yahoo contacts. This will often include the user's full name and any email addresses associated with the target.

Search Posts

In the first edition, I recommended third party websites to search Facebook post content. Some of these sites still exist, but most have either shut down or stopped functioning. In order to present a more permanent solution, I have identified a new way to do this through Facebook.

While logged into a Facebook account, one should be able to natively search within the content of public posts. However, at the time of this writing, the basic search option was not functioning. A search of the term "OSINT" in the Facebook search field only identifies Facebook groups that contain the term within the group name. A search of "posts about "OSINT"" also produces zero results. Figure 3.07 displays this result including the URL created by Facebook. The reasons that this search does not work are unknown. However, we do know that Facebook does support this type of search.

Instead of searching from the search field, you should conduct your query through the URL. You can successfully perform the previous failed search by entering the following address directly into your browser. Figure 3.08 displays the result. Notice that the search field is identical in each example, but only the direct URL retrieved results.

https://www.facebook.com/search/str/OSINT/stories-keyword

Real world application: A large company with thousands of employees wanted to see if any employees were online discussing sensitive information about a stealth product. Several searches on specific employee profiles returned no results. A search on Facebook of the name of the secret project identified two employees leaking inappropriate information.

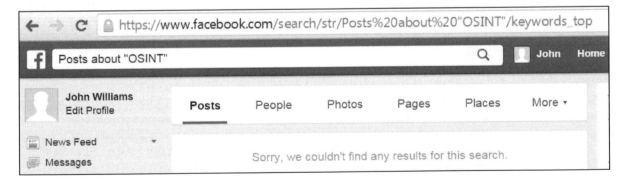

Figure 3.07: A failed topic query from the Facebook search field.

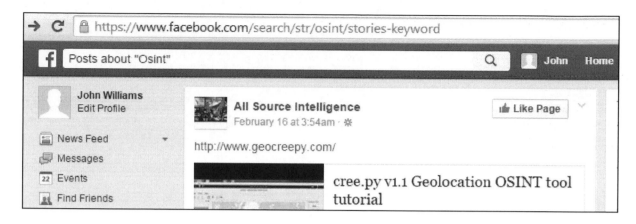

Figure 3.08: A successful topic search from the URL.

Additional Personal Information

At this point, you should be able to locate a target's profile, analyze the publicly available content, and search by topic. That is just the tip of the iceberg. Facebook collects a lot of additional information from everyone's activity on the social network. Every time someone "Likes" something or is tagged in a photo, Facebook stores that information. Until recently, this was sometimes difficult to locate, if not impossible. You will not always find it on the target's profile page, but the new Facebook Graph search allows us to dig into this information.

The official way to search this data on Facebook has flaws. You can type in what you are looking for and Facebook will give you results based on your friends and people close to your network. As an example, when I conduct a search for photos liked by Tom Merritt, I am given no results. If I had typed "Photos liked by" and then the name of one of my friends, it would have worked fine. Since our target is not likely to be on our friends list, we must get creative in order to obtain this information.

In order to conduct the following detailed searches, you must know the user number of your target. This number is a unique identifier that will allow us to search otherwise hidden information from Facebook. The easiest way to identify the user number of any Facebook user is through the Graph API. While you are on a user's main profile, look at the address (URL) of the page. It should look something like Figure 3.09.

The address of the page is https://www.facebook.com/bart.lorang. This identifies "bart.lorang" as the user name of the user. In order to obtain the user number, replace "www" in the address with "graph". Figure 3.10 displays the results when this is conducted on the same target.

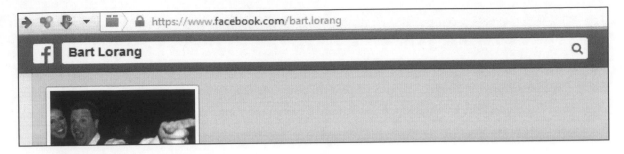

Figure 3.09: A web address (URL) of a Facebook Profile.

```
id: "651620441",
name: "Bart Lorang",
first_name: "Bart",
last_name: "Lorang",
link: http://www.facebook.com/bart.lorang,
username: "bart.lorang",
gender: "male",
locale: "en_US"
```

Figure 3.10: A web address (URL) of a Facebook Graph profile.

The first number that you see in this result is the target's user number on Facebook. This data will allow us to obtain many more details about the account. If we want to see any photos on Facebook that this subject has "liked", we can type the following address into a web browser.

https://www.facebook.com/search/651620441/photos-liked

This basic structure contains the website (facebook.com), the action (search), the user number (651620441), and the requested information (photos-liked). Figure 3.11 displays the partial results of this address.

Notice the "Refine this search" option in the upper right. Hovering over this expands the options which will allow us to filter the results by the people in the photo, location, time, and the person that posted the photo. This allows me to display only recent photos or focus only on a specific location. Since these are photos that were "liked" by the target, the results will include photos on other people's pages that would have been difficult to locate otherwise.

Figure 3.11: A web address (URL) of a "liked photo" page of a Facebook user.

If we had asked Facebook for this information with only the name of the target, we would have been denied. If your target has a common name, this would not work. The method described here works because we know the target's user number. There are many other options with this search. We can navigate to the following addresses to see more information about our target (user number 651620441). Explanations of each address will be explained after the list.

https://www.facebook.com/search/651620441/places-visited
https://www.facebook.com/search/651620441/places-liked
https://www.facebook.com/search/651620441/pages-liked
https://www.facebook.com/search/651620441/photos-by
https://www.facebook.com/search/651620441/photos-liked
https://www.facebook.com/search/651620441/photos-of
https://www.facebook.com/search/651620441/photos-commented
https://www.facebook.com/search/651620441/videos
https://www.facebook.com/search/651620441/videos-by
https://www.facebook.com/search/651620441/videos-of
https://www.facebook.com/search/651620441/videos-liked
https://www.facebook.com/search/651620441/videos-commented
https://www.facebook.com/search/651620441/apps-used
https://www.facebook.com/search/651620441/friends
https://www.facebook.com/search/651620441/events
https://www.facebook.com/search/651620441/events-joined
https://www.facebook.com/search/651620441/stories-by
https://www.facebook.com/search/651620441/stories-commented
https://www.facebook.com/search/651620441/stories-tagged
https://www.facebook.com/search/651620441/groups
https://www.facebook.com/search/651620441/relatives

The "places-visited" option will display locations that the target has physically visited and allowed Facebook to collect the location information. This is often completed through a smart phone, sometimes unintentionally. This can be used to disprove alibis or verify trips.

The "places-liked" option will display any physical locations that the target has clicked "like". This will often identify vacation spots, favorite bars, and special restaurants. This can be priceless information for an investigator or skip-tracer.

The "pages-liked" option will display any Facebook pages that the target clicked "like". This will often display interests of the target such as a favorite sports team, musical group, or television show. These results will include a button labeled "liked by". Clicking this will identify everyone on Facebook that liked that item. This can quickly identify the people that visit a hole-in-the-wall bar that you are investigating.

The "photos-by" option will display Facebook photos that were uploaded by the user. These will likely already be visible on the target's photos page. However, this search could potentially reveal additional images.

The "photos-liked" option was explained on the previous page. This can be beneficial if your target has a private profile. If the photos of interest are on someone else's profile that is not private, you will be able to see all of them.

The "photos-of" option will display any photos that the target has been tagged in. This search has already proved very effective in many investigations. This will immediately locate additional photos of your target that may not be visible on the target's profile. This is helpful when the photos are private on one person's page, but not others.

The "photos-commented" option will display any photos on profiles where the target left a comment on the photo. This can be important because the target may not have "liked" the photo or been tagged in it. The option may produce redundant results, but it should always be checked.

The "videos" option will display videos visible on the target's profile. These may or may not be directly connected to the target. They could also be videos linked to the original source with no personal ties to the subject.

The "videos-by" option will display videos that were actually uploaded by the target. These will be much more personal to the subject and will usually include more relevant content.

The "videos-of" option is similar to the "photos-of" filter. This will display videos that supposedly contain images of the target within the video itself. It could be compared to "tagging" someone inside a video.

The "videos-liked" option will display any videos that the target clicked "like". This can also be used to establish personal interests of the target and are often of interest to parents.

The "videos-commented" option will display any videos on profiles where the target left a comment on the video. Again, this can be important because the target may not have "liked" the video or been tagged in it. The option may produce redundant results, but it should always be checked.

The "apps-used" option will display the apps installed through Facebook. These are usually games that can be played with other people. Many of these specify the environment that they work with such as "IOS". This would indicate that the target is using an iPhone or iPad instead of an Android device.

The "friends" option should display a list of all of the target's friends on Facebook. This will be the same list visible on the main profile page. If you receive no results, the target likely has the friend's list set to "private".

The "events" option will display any Facebook events that your target was invited to attend. These often include parties, company events, concerts, and other social gatherings. This will usually display events that are not listed on the target's profile.

The "events-joined" option will only display the Facebook events that the target acknowledged attendance. This could be in the form of a "R.S.V.P." or confirmation by the target that he or she is currently at the event. I have used this resource to question an alibi of a suspect.

The "stories-by" option will display any public posts by the target. This can often identify posts that are not currently visible on the target's profile.

The "stories-commented" option will display any public posts by any users if the target entered a comment. This is useful in identifying communication from a target with a private profile. The standard privacy options do not prevent a search of your comment history on public posts.

The "stories-tagged" option will display any posts that were tagged by the target. This tagging is usually performed because of an interest in the post.

The "groups" option will display any groups that the target is a member of. This is beneficial in identifying stronger interests of the target. In my experience, a target must only have faint interest to "like" something. However, the interest is usually strong if a group related to the topic is joined.

The "relatives" option will display a list of people that the target has identified as a relative. Often, this will display relatives even if the target has the friend's list set to "private".

Friends' Information

Occasionally, you may find that your target's Facebook profile possesses minimal information. The techniques mentioned previously may not locate any valuable information if your target does not provide any content to his or her profile. Therefore, knowing the overall interests of someone's friends on Facebook may assist with your analysis of the target. The following direct addresses focus only on the friends of an individual. The results will display items in order from the most commonalities between friends to the least. Explanations of each URL will follow the list. Similar to the previous example, a user number is already included in the address (678216059). You should replace this with the user number of your target.

https://www.facebook.com/search/678216059/friends/places-visited
https://www.facebook.com/search/678216059/friends/places-liked
https://www.facebook.com/search/678216059/friends/pages-liked
https://www.facebook.com/search/678216059/friends/photos-by
https://www.facebook.com/search/678216059/friends/photos-liked
https://www.facebook.com/search/678216059/friends/photos-of
https://www.facebook.com/search/678216059/friends/photos-commented
https://www.facebook.com/search/678216059/friends/videos
https://www.facebook.com/search/678216059/friends/videos-by
https://www.facebook.com/search/678216059/friends/videos-of
https://www.facebook.com/search/678216059/friends/videos-liked
https://www.facebook.com/search/678216059/friends/videos-commented
https://www.facebook.com/search/678216059/friends/apps-used
https://www.facebook.com/search/678216059/friends/friends
https://www.facebook.com/search/678216059/friends/events
https://www.facebook.com/search/678216059/friends/events-joined
https://www.facebook.com/search/678216059/friends/stories-by
https://www.facebook.com/search/678216059/friends/stories-commented
https://www.facebook.com/search/678216059/friends/stories-tagged
https://www.facebook.com/search/678216059/friends/groups
https://www.facebook.com/search/678216059/friends/relatives

The "friends/places-visited" option will display the common places that your target's friends visit. This may identify local hangouts and favorite bars.

The "friends/places-liked" option will display the common places that your target's friends like on Facebook. This can also identify locations of interest to the investigator.

The "friends/pages-liked" option will display the common pages that your target's friends like on Facebook. This will usually identify products and items of interest instead of places. I have used this to determine if my target's friends were mostly interested in drugs or other criminal activity.

The "friends/photos-by" option will display the photos uploaded by your target's friends. This can quickly identify interests and recent locations visited by the subjects. Occasionally, you may locate untagged photos of your target in this collection.

The "friends/photos-liked" option will display the photos "liked" by your target's friends. This can provide an indication of interests by both the target and the friends.

The "friends/photos-of" option will display the tagged photos of your target's friends. This will quickly display images which may identify recent locations visited by the friends.

The "friends/photos-commented" option will display the photos on Facebook that your target's friends placed a comment on. This often includes communication otherwise difficult to find.

The "friends/videos" option will display the videos on your target's friends' pages.

The "friends/videos-by" option will display the videos uploaded by your target's friends.

The "friends/videos-of" option will display the videos containing your target's friends. This may include video taken at events where your target was present.

The "friends/videos-liked" option will display the videos "liked" by your target's friends. This can provide an indication of interests by both the target and the friends.

The "friends/videos-commented" option will display the videos on Facebook that your target's friends placed a comment on. This often includes communication otherwise difficult to find.

The "friends/apps-used" option will display the apps that your target's friends use on Facebook.

The "friends/friends" option will display the friends of your target's friends on Facebook.

The "friends/events" option will display the common events that your target's friends were invited to on Facebook. This may identify upcoming large local gatherings. I have successfully used this information to conduct surveillance for a wanted fugitive.

The "friends/events-joined" option will display the common events that your target's friends attended.

The "friends/stories-by" option will display the Facebook posts that your target's friends posted.

The "friends/stories-commented" option will display the common Facebook posts that contain comments from your target's friends. This can often display valuable communication that would otherwise be very difficult to locate.

The "friends/stories-tagged" option will display the common Facebook posts that your target's friends tagged as interesting.

The "friends/groups" option will display the Facebook groups that contain the most members of your target's friends. This is another valuable source for locating possible interests of your target.

The "friends/relatives" option will display the relatives of your target's Facebook friends. I once found value in this when trying to locate people that may cooperate with an investigation. During a homicide investigation, many of the people involved refuse to talk to the police. However, reaching out to relatives often provides more support.

Common Results

The previous options will easily allow you to view sensitive information about an individual target. Repeating these queries on additional individuals may allow you to recognize common patterns. This may identify relationships between individuals that are not obvious through their profiles. Knowing that two people both joined a local event, liked a rare page, commented on a specific photo, or joined a small group can generate a new lead in an investigation. Much of this information would not be visible on an individual's profile. Instead of manually analyzing multiple profiles for common information, consider a specific URL address that will only display combined results.

Facebook supports this type of analysis within the standard search field. Entering "Pages liked by Mark Zuckerberg and Chris Hughes" will display numerous profiles and pages that both subjects "liked". The flaw with this type of search is that it is not unique per Facebook profile. There are dozens of profiles for people named Chris Hughes. This native search does not know which Chris Hughes you have an interest in. Therefore, I never recommend this type of written query. Instead, the following URL will display only pages liked by both Mark Zuckerberg (Facebook user number 4) and Chris Hughes (Facebook user number 5).

https://www.facebook.com/search/4/pages-liked/5/pages-liked/intersect

This specific structure is important for the query to function. The URL begins with the same terms that you learned in the previous section (facebook.com/search/user number/pages-liked). It is followed by a second search for an additional user (user number 2/pages-liked). The final term of "intersect" instructs Facebook to only list results that apply to both users listed. You could continue to add users to this search. The following URL will display the five Facebook pages liked by Mark Zuckerberg (Facebook user number 4), Chris Hughes (Facebook user number 5), and Arie Hasit (Facebook user number 7).

https://www.facebook.com/search/4/pages-liked/5/pages-liked/7/pages-liked/intersect

This method could be applied to all of the techniques that were explained earlier in reference to an individual. The following URL queries would identify common elements between Mark Zuckerberg and Arie Hasit. It should be noted that I am using these examples because of the single digit user numbers. Your user number searches will likely be much longer and appear similar to "17893008278".

https://www.facebook.com/search/4/places-visited/7/places-visited/intersect
https://www.facebook.com/search/4/places-liked/7/places-liked/intersect
https://www.facebook.com/search/4/pages-liked/7/pages-liked/intersect
https://www.facebook.com/search/4/photos-liked/7/photos-liked/intersect
https://www.facebook.com/search/4/photos-of/7/photos-of/intersect
https://www.facebook.com/search/4/photos-commented/7/photos-commented/intersect
https://www.facebook.com/search/4/videos/7/videos/intersect
https://www.facebook.com/search/4/videos-of/7/videos-of/intersect
https://www.facebook.com/search/4/videos-liked/7/videos-liked/intersect
https://www.facebook.com/search/4/videos-commented/7/videos-commented/intersect
https://www.facebook.com/search/4/apps-used/7/apps-used/intersect
https://www.facebook.com/search/4/events/7/events/intersect
https://www.facebook.com/search/4/events-joined/7/events-joined/intersect
https://www.facebook.com/search/4/stories-commented/7/stories-commented/intersect
https://www.facebook.com/search/4/stories-tagged/7/stories-tagged/intersect
https://www.facebook.com/search/4/groups/7/groups/intersect
https://www.facebook.com/search/4/relatives/7/relatives/intersect
https://www.facebook.com/search/4/friends/pages-liked/7/friends/pages-liked/intersect

Real world application: I have found myself in interview rooms with suspects that claim to not know the co-suspects being investigated. Locating rare and specific Facebook interests or photos in common with both suspects always gave me an edge in the interview. The suspects would have a hard time explaining the coincidence. In one case, two suspects that swore they did not know each other had both referenced going to a party together within the comment area of a long forgotten photo on Facebook.

Common Friends

Facebook will often display all of the friends of a target. However, it does not natively display a set of friends that two users have in common. We can accomplish this with a URL trick. First, consider scenarios of when this might be useful.

A law enforcement officer that has two suspects in custody for a homicide is getting little cooperation from the duo. Identifying only the people that are friends with both of them may provide an opportunity to interview someone that has direct knowledge of the incident.

A teacher or counselor that is trying to resolve ongoing issues between two students is having a hard time getting them to talk about the situation. Casually talking to a couple of people that are friends with both of the subjects may lead to better details about the real problems.

Finally, an investigator is looking for evidence of a cheating spouse. Looking at the photos on the Facebook pages of friends of both the cheating spouse and the new boyfriend or girlfriend may provide the final piece of the investigation.

The structure of the address that will conduct this search is as follows.

https://www.facebook.com/USER NAME ONE/friends?and=USER NAME TWO

If we wanted to display only the friends of both Bart Lorang (bart.lorang) and Mark Shaker (mark.shaker.39), the following address would be appropriate.

https://www.facebook.com/bart.lorang/friends?and=mark.shaker.39

This exact search identified 16 people of interest. Figure 3.12 displays the partial result including the exact address that was submitted. This link could be saved as a bookmark and you can check it often to identify anyone new that has been added to this circle of friends. Comparing a new search to a previous screen capture of this data may also identify anyone that has been removed from this group. An individual no longer accepted by his former friends may make a great candidate for an interview if this group was involved in an incident you are investigating.

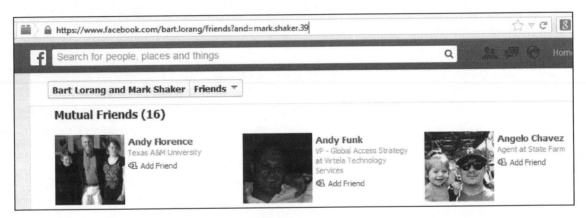

Figure 3.12: A Facebook URL result identifying friends in common with two people.

You can use a similar technique to discover the length of time that two users have been friends on Facebook and immediately see commonalities of both users. The URL structure is as follows.

https://www.facebook.com/USER NAME 1?and=USER NAME 2

If you wanted to see information of the two users that were mentioned earlier (Mark Zuckerberg and Chris Hughes), you would enter the following URL.

https://www.facebook.com/zuck?and=ChrisHughes

Note that these searches use the Facebook user names and not user numbers. Figure 3.13 displays the result of this search. It identifies their Facebook friendship start date of November 2006, and displays that they both work at Facebook and studied at Harvard. This technique can quickly inform an investigator of the main areas in common between two Facebook users.

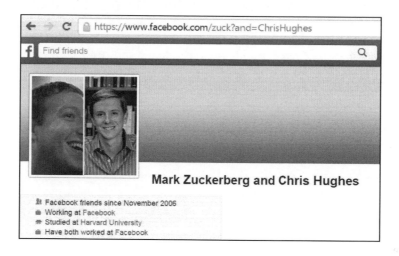

Figure 3.13: A Facebook search result identifying commonalities between two users.

Custom Search Tool (inteltechniques.com/osint/facebook.html)

You may now be wondering how you are going to implement all of these searches in an easy format. I had the same thought and developed my own web tools to handle this task. Navigate to the above website in order to access an all-in-one option.

This is the same page that was referenced earlier while explaining advanced profile search options. The entire left side of this page will allow you to conduct all of the Facebook Graph searches that were mentioned in this section. The current state of this tool is visible in Figure 3.14.

The first group of searches will display the individual "liked", "tagged", "event", and "by" information that we previously discussed. The next option will conduct all of the searches at one time into separate tabs in your browser. Make sure you are logged in to a Facebook account for this to function. I also recommend using the Firefox browser which will be discussed in Chapter Fifteen. Chrome tends to block the script required to make this work.

The next group will conduct the friends in common search that was previously explained. It will work best with user names instead of Facebook user numbers. The final group will replicate the most popular commonality searches that were discussed previously.

Finally, the last option (not visible in Figure 3.14) will perform an entire Graph search from Facebook on a target. The details of this search will be explained in Chapter Fourteen.

Private Friends

Many Facebook users have chosen to make their list of Facebook friends private. When this occurs, you will not see any friends listed through either the native profile view or the "Displays Friends" option in the custom search tool page. Facebook puts a lot of effort into hiding the information when this security option is selected. However, there is a fairly sneaky method of identifying these details. The following instructions should identify the entire list of friends on any protected profile.

✓ Create a new Facebook account. This must be an account that has never been used before. Do not provide any personal details.

✓ Click the "Find Friends" tab within your account. Confirm that Facebook has no friend recommendations.

✓ Search for your target's profile. Click the "Add Friend" button. Immediately hover over this button and choose "Cancel Friend Request".

✓ Click the "Find Friends" tab again. You should now be presented a list of your target's friends.

There are concerns while using this technique. Most importantly, your target may be notified of the friend request. If you are using a new (and generic) account, your target will not know your identity. Most Facebook users get random unknown friend requests weekly. Additionally, you will have no way of knowing the accuracy of this technique. In my tests, the lists have been practically identical.

Changed User Name

If you have an ongoing investigation, you should make note of your target's Facebook user ID number. If he or she changes the real name or user name of the Facebook profile, this user ID will always connect to the live account. A previous Graph example displayed a Facebook user number of 651620441. You can now always navigate to the following address to view this profile.

facebook.com/651620441

If this user changes his user name to bart.lorang.2 or his real name to John Doe, the above address will still find the profile. A standard search would not. This will always be the easiest way to follow the activity of a target. If you are going to create a bookmark of this subject's page, make sure it is using the number instead of the name. It is very popular with young people and online criminals to change this information often. It introduces confusion for the authorities that are monitoring. Meanwhile, any friends of the target do not experience any connection issues and any changes carry over to them.

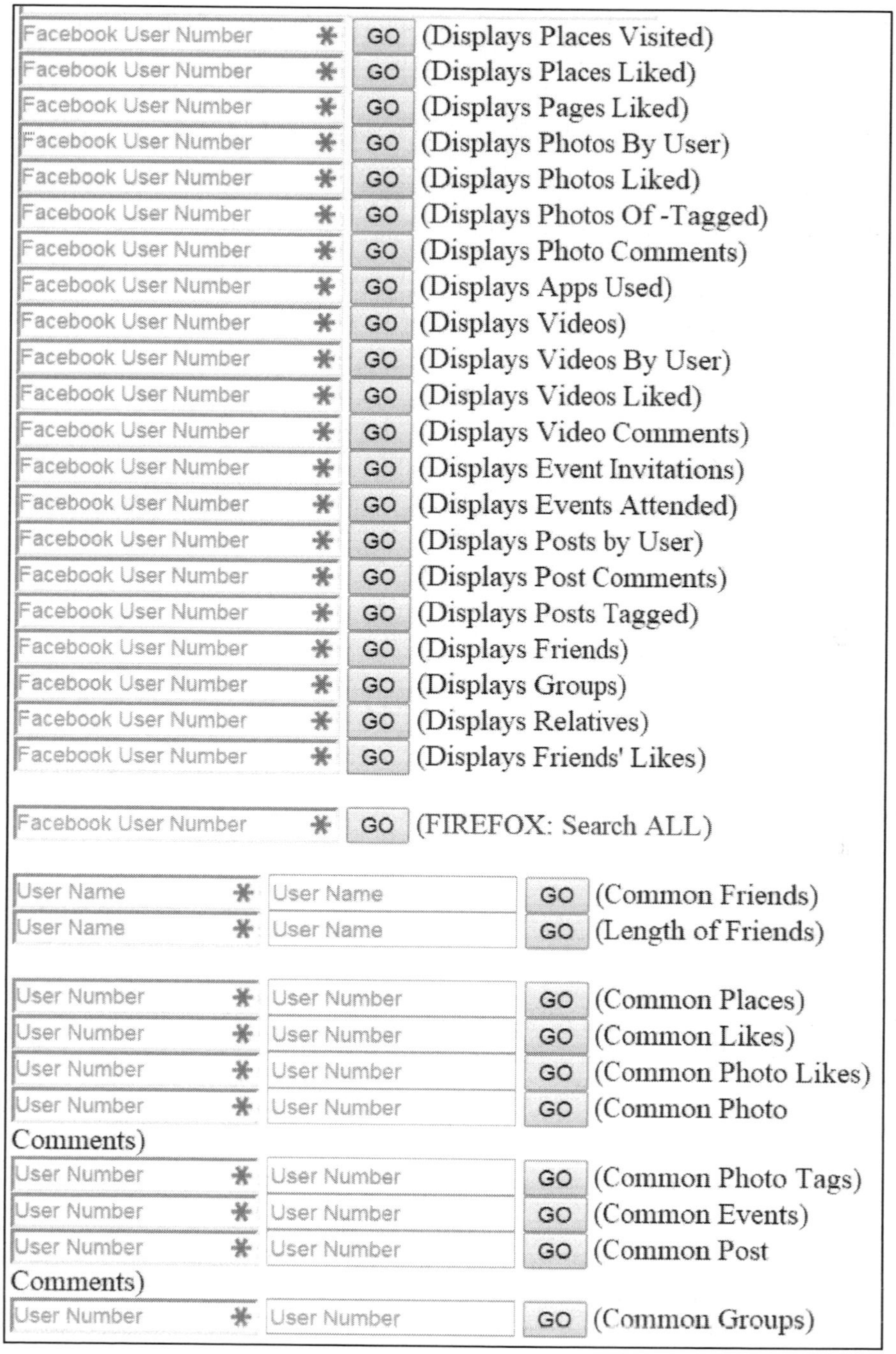

Facebook User Number	✱	GO	(Displays Places Visited)
Facebook User Number	✱	GO	(Displays Places Liked)
Facebook User Number	✱	GO	(Displays Pages Liked)
Facebook User Number	✱	GO	(Displays Photos By User)
Facebook User Number	✱	GO	(Displays Photos Liked)
Facebook User Number	✱	GO	(Displays Photos Of -Tagged)
Facebook User Number	✱	GO	(Displays Photo Comments)
Facebook User Number	✱	GO	(Displays Apps Used)
Facebook User Number	✱	GO	(Displays Videos)
Facebook User Number	✱	GO	(Displays Videos By User)
Facebook User Number	✱	GO	(Displays Videos Liked)
Facebook User Number	✱	GO	(Displays Video Comments)
Facebook User Number	✱	GO	(Displays Event Invitations)
Facebook User Number	✱	GO	(Displays Events Attended)
Facebook User Number	✱	GO	(Displays Posts by User)
Facebook User Number	✱	GO	(Displays Post Comments)
Facebook User Number	✱	GO	(Displays Posts Tagged)
Facebook User Number	✱	GO	(Displays Friends)
Facebook User Number	✱	GO	(Displays Groups)
Facebook User Number	✱	GO	(Displays Relatives)
Facebook User Number	✱	GO	(Displays Friends' Likes)

| Facebook User Number | ✱ | GO | (FIREFOX: Search ALL) |

| User Name | ✱ | User Name | GO | (Common Friends) |
| User Name | ✱ | User Name | GO | (Length of Friends) |

User Number	✱	User Number	GO	(Common Places)
User Number	✱	User Number	GO	(Common Likes)
User Number	✱	User Number	GO	(Common Photo Likes)
User Number	✱	User Number	GO	(Common Photo Comments)
User Number	✱	User Number	GO	(Common Photo Tags)
User Number	✱	User Number	GO	(Common Events)
User Number	✱	User Number	GO	(Common Post Comments)
User Number	✱	User Number	GO	(Common Groups)

Figure 3.14: A website of custom Facebook search tools on IntelTechniques.com.

Embedded Photos

As with any other online evidence, you should download and archive any Facebook photos of interest of your target. After you locate a photo using any of the methods explained in this chapter, click on it to expand the image inside Facebook's default image viewer. Facebook compresses all photos that are uploaded, and this view is smaller than the original uncompressed version. The best way to manually save the photo will vary based on the web browser that you are using. Overall, right-clicking and selecting "Save image as" will work.

Tracking Photos

The first two editions of this book discussed a website that would track a photo hosted on Facebook. If you encountered an image that had been posted to a non-Facebook site, but the original link was obviously from a Facebook server, you could use this service to identify the Facebook profile connected with the image. This could also be used to search links to Facebook photos that were sent via text message or chat room. This service, as well as others like it, stopped functioning in 2013. However, we can still perform this type of search manually. The following scenario should explain the process.

Imagine that you have located a photo that was posted to an online forum or blog. It could have also been sent as a text message. The link to the actual image is the following address. Figure 3.15 displays the live photo.

https://fbcdn-sphotos-c-a.akamaihd.net/hphotos-ak-xpa1/t31.0-8/1614393_10101869091776891_1149281347468701704_o.jpg

Figure 3.15: A Facebook photo discovered from a direct address (URL).

The domain "fbcdn.net" indicates that this image is stored on a Facebook server, and that it is connected to a Facebook profile. However, we do not know the associated profile. There are three groups of numbers listed in this link, and each is separated with an underscore (_). We are interested in the second number (10101869091776891). We should construct a new address based on the following structure.

https://www.facebook.com/photo.php?fbid=NUMBER

If we enter that second number at the end of this address, it will connect us to the original photo page that possesses the image of interest. This will identify the person that possesses this picture on their profile, any tagged information, the date it was added, and any comments on the photo. The actual address for this example is the following.

https://www.facebook.com/photo.php?fbid=10101869091776891

Figure 3.16 displays the result. We now know that Mark Zuckerberg originally posted this photo on his Facebook page. We can analyze the page to determine the date it was posted and any communication in reference to the image. If the photo that you connect to is private, you will receive a "This page is not available" error.

Figure 3.16: A Facebook page identified by reverse image number searching.

Facebook continuously makes both minor and major changes to their search functions. Some of these instructions may not work one day and work fine the next. Hopefully, this section has given you new ideas on ways to completely analyze your next target on Facebook.

Facebook Friends Extraction

I was recently presented a Facebook scenario without any obvious solution. Assume that you find the Facebook profile of your target, and there is a large list of "Friends". You want to document this list, and a screenshot is not good enough. You want to capture the hyperlinks to each account and have a data set that can be manipulated or imported elsewhere. There are several outdated online tools that claim to "scrape" this data, but none of them work. Earlier this year, Facebook changed their TOS and have now blocked any type of scraping of Friend data. Further, the Facebook API no longer allows the display of this data either. There is a solution, and it will involve minimal geek work.

First, identify the page of your target. For this example, I will use the following public profile:

https://www.facebook.com/darya.pino/friends

She has several friends, so I will hold down the Space Bar on my keyboard to load the entire page. I will now highlight her entire friends list and use ctrl-c or right-click>copy to copy the data. I find it best to click directly above the left side of the first friend and hold until the lower right area of the last friend. The friends list should highlight. Now, open Microsoft Excel. Click on the "B" in column B to highlight the entire column. Paste the content with either ctrl-v or right-click>paste. This will appear disorganized, but the data is there. The images will be on top of the user data, which will not work for a final report. Figure 3.17 (left) displays the result.

Use F5 to launch the "Go To" menu and select "Special" in the lower left. Select "Objects" and click OK. This will select all of those images. Hit the delete key to remove them. You will now see only the text data (with hyperlinks). Now click on the "A" in column A and paste the friend content again with either ctrl-v or right-click>paste. Right-click any cell in this column and choose "Clear Contents". This will remove any text, but keep the images.

Place your mouse in between columns A and B and re-size column A to be a bit larger than one of the images. Do the same with Column B to fit in all of the text. Use the "Find and Replace" feature to find every instance of "Add Friend" and replace it with nothing. This will remove those unnecessary entries. In the "Home" menu, choose "Format" and then "Auto Fit Row Height". This will eliminate unnecessary spacing. Select Column B and Left Justify the text. Your final result will be a clean spreadsheet with all of the images, names, and active links from your target's Facebook page. Figure 3.17 (right) displays my final result. This is not the cleanest way of doing things, but it will work.

Figure 3.17: An import of Facebook friends into Excel.

Twitter (twitter.com)

Twitter is a social network and micro blogging service that limits each post to 140 characters. In 2014, Twitter reported that there were 500 million Twitter posts, or "tweets", posted every day. Basically, users create a profile and post tweets announcing their thoughts on a topic, current location, plans for the evening, or maybe a link to something that they feel is important. A user can "follow" other users and constantly see what others are posting. Likewise, a user's "followers" can constantly see what that user is up to. The premise is simply sharing small details of your life for all of your friends to see, as well as the rest of the world. Most users utilize the service through a cellular phone, which can capture the user's location and broadcast the information if the location feature is enabled. Obtaining information from Twitter can be conducted through various procedures.

Twitter Search (twitter.com/search)

This is the official site's search interface. The results can be overwhelming and unrelated to your interest. This is only appropriate when looking for recent news, gossip, and trends on Twitter.

Twitter Advanced Search (twitter.com/search-advanced)

This page will allow for the search of specific people, keywords, and locations. The problem here is that the search of a topic is often limited to the previous seven to ten days. Individual profiles should display tweets as far back as you are willing to scroll though. This can be a good place to search for recent data, but archives of a topic will not be displayed.

In the Figure 3.18, submitting this query would receive results for any posts by "JohnDoe92" that included the words "Bomb" and "Threat" sent from the zip code "77089". This precise search can provide the exact results desired. Unfortunately, this can also limit the information received. Including a location can be beneficial in some situations. If you did not know the user name of a post, a location may help you find your target. When you already know the user name, I do not recommend using the location feature. If the user had the GPS turned off, or if the data was inaccurate, you would miss out on good information. Any time you use the location feature, regardless of any other filters; you will only receive results from users that have their location enabled. Many users, especially those with evil plans, turn this feature off. This example would have been more appropriate by excluding either the user name or the location.

This Twitter search does not take advantage of quotes to identify exact word placement. Instead, conduct the search in the "This exact phrase" box to get precise results. Typing any words in the "None of these words" box will filter out any posts that include the chosen word or words. The "Hashtags" option will locate specific posts that mention a topic as defined by a Twitter hashtag. This is a single word followed by a pound sign (#) that identifies a topic of interest. This allows users to follow certain topics without knowing user names of the user submitting the messages.

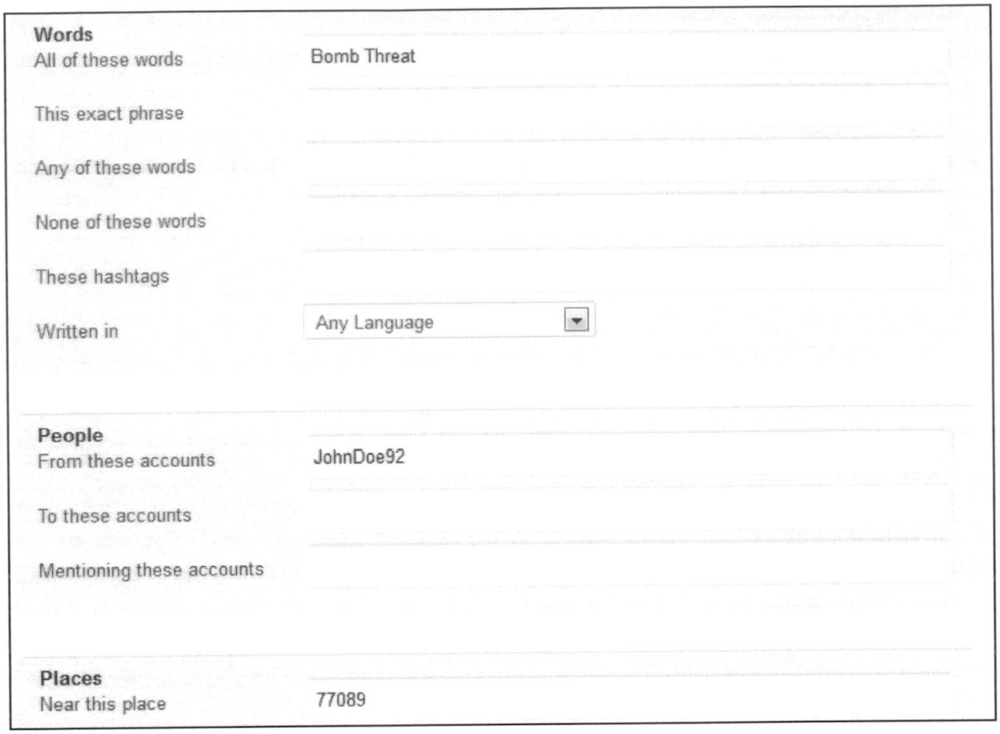

Figure 3.18: The Advanced Twitter Search page.

The "People" section allows you to search for tweets from a specific user. This can also be accomplished by typing the user name into the address bar followed by the Twitter domain. An example for the previous user would be www.twitter.com/JohnDoe92. This will display the user's profile including recent tweets.

The "To these accounts" field allows you to enter a specific Twitter user name. The results will only include tweets that were sent to the attention of the user. This can help identify associates of the target and information intended for the target to read.

The "Places" field allows for the input of a zip code and selection of distance. The default 15 miles setting would produce tweets posted from within 15 miles of the perimeter of the zip code supplied. If using this option, I recommend choosing the 1 kilometer option, as it is the most constrictive radius that can be searched. In a moment, I will explain a more effective search technique for location.

The results of any of these searches can provide surprisingly personal information about a target. Much of the content may be useless banter. This data can be used for many types of investigations. Law enforcement may use this data to verify or disprove an alibi of a suspect. When a suspect states in an interview that he was in Chicago the entire weekend, but his Twitter feed displays his tweet about a restaurant in St. Louis, he has some explaining to do. Private investigators may use this content as documentation of an affair or negative character. Occasionally, a citizen will contact the authorities when evidence of illegal activity is found within a person's tweets. The possibilities are endless.

Real world application: On several occasions, Police Officers have used this service to locate runaway children. Additionally, teenagers tend to brag about their activities on sites like Twitter, including vandalism, theft, and violence. While these posts do not prove a crime was committed, it provides a great lead and jury appeal at a trial.

Twitter Person Search (twitter.com/#!/who_to_follow)

Locating your target's Twitter profile may not be easy. Unlike Facebook and Google+, most Twitter users do not use their real name as their profile name. You need a place to search by real name. I recommend Twitter's "Who to follow" search page. Loading this page presents a single search option under the Twitter bar that can handle any real name.

In Figure 3.19, I am presented with numerous people with the name of "Sarah Lane". Scrolling down the list I can look through the photo icons and brief descriptions to identify my target. Clicking on the user name will open the user's Twitter profile with more information.

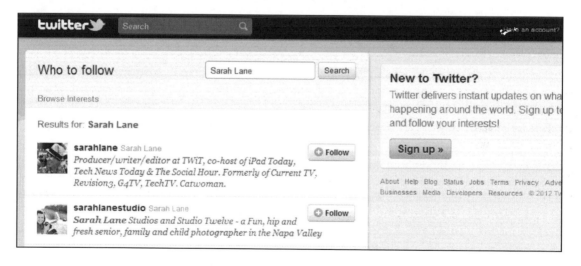

Figure 3.19: Results from Twitter's "Who to follow" option.

Followerwonk Bios (followerwonk.com/bio)

Twitter's Who To Follow option can be great when you know the exact name that a target used when creating an account. If you are unsure of the real name, or if the target has a very common name, Followerwonk can help you identify the profile that you are looking for. This service allows you to search Twitter profiles for any keyword that may help you locate a profile of interest. You can choose the default "Profiles" search or the focused "Twitter Bios Only" option. The "More Options" under the main search box will display numerous fields including Location, Name, and Follower details.

A search of "John Smith" reveals 21,156 Twitter profiles. However, a search of "John Smith" from "New York City" reveals only 81 profiles. Filtering out profiles that have not posted at least 100 Tweets reveals only 31 profiles. This is a manageable number of profiles that can be viewed to identify the target.

Twitter Directory (twitter.com/i/directory/profiles)

If you still cannot locate your target's profile, you may need to resort to the Twitter Directory. This awkward and difficult monstrosity tries to allow you to browse through the millions of Twitter profiles alphabetically. First, choose the first letter of the first name of your target. This will present a range of options. When I chose the letter "M", I was presented with the following name ranges.

m — Maggie San Tzu
Maggie San. — Manish Chandna
Manish Chandna — marcopt
marcoptique — mariabrea
MariaBreezyThorpe — marisol
marisol — Martin en Jo Holman

Martin Radio — matiasardito
matias arias — maxime lattreche
Maxime Latulipe — Megz
Megz — MerleTherrien
MERLETM — Michael Walz
Michael Walz — Mike

Mike — mirella ringler
mirella rios — Mohamed Zarouf
mohamed zaroug-Morgan Huff
Morgan Huff- muhammad naser
Muhammad Naser — mzzzzzme

I would now need to select the range that my target would be listed in, and that selection would open a new window with hundreds of name range options such as "Mike Hall – Mike Hirsch". You will need to keep using this drill-down method until you reach a list of actual profiles that meet your criteria. I do not enjoy this method, but sometimes it is all that you have. I once found my target this way after he used a misspelled version of his real name.

Twitter API View

June 11, 2013 was a sad day for me. For years, I had been using the Twitter Application Programming Interface (API) to access otherwise hidden information inside user's accounts. However, Twitter closed the original API on this date and eliminated all of the techniques that went with it. Fortunately, much of the information that I received from the original API is now available from newer methods.

Search by Location

If you are investigating an incident that occurred at a specific location and you have no known people involved, Twitter will allow you to search by GPS location alone. The Twitter Advanced search allowed us to search by zip code, but that can be too broad. The following specific search on any Twitter page will display Tweets known to have been posted from within one kilometer of the GPS coordinates of 43.430242,-89.736459.

geocode:43.430242,-89.736459,1km

There are no spaces in this search. This will be a list without any map view. They will be in order chronologically with the most recent at top. The "1km" indicates a search radius of one kilometer. This can be changed to 5, 10, or 25 reliably. Any other numbers tend to provide inaccurate results. You can also change "km" to "mi" to switch to miles instead of kilometers. If you wanted to view this search from the address bar of the browser, the following page would load the same results.

https://twitter.com/search?q=geocode:43.430242,-89.736459,1km

You can add search parameters to either of these searches if the results are overwhelming. The following search would only display Tweets posted at the listed GPS coordinates that also mention the term "fight".

geocode:43.430242,-89.736459,1km fight

Notice that the only space in the above search is between "km" and "fight". The results of a similar search can be seen in Figure 3.20. This was a search for any Tweets posted from Lambert Airport in St. Louis. The first two results validate that the location is correct.

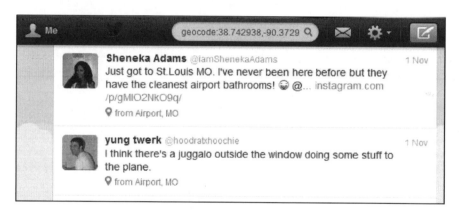

Figure 3.20: A location only search through Twitter.

Mandatory and Optional Search Terms

You may have a scenario that requires a specific search of both mandatory and optional terms. Twitter does not provide a published solution for this. However, it does support this type of search. Assume that you are investigating threats against your target named Michael Parker. You believe that people may be tweeting about him with reference to violence. Searching his name alone produces too many results. Since you only want posts that include violent terms, the following search on any Twitter page may be appropriate.

"Michael Parker" kill OR stab OR fight OR beat OR punch OR death OR die

The name within quotes forces Twitter to only give you results on those exact terms. That is your mandatory portion. The words kill, stab, fight, beat, punch, death, and die are all optional because the term "OR" is between each. This term must be uppercase, and will only require one of the optional words be present within the search results.

Specific Date Search

If you are searching vague terms, you may want to filter by date. This option is now available on the advanced search page, but I believe it is important to understand how Twitter performs this task. Assume that you are investigating a bomb threat that occurred several weeks or months ago. A search on Twitter of the terms "bomb threat" will likely apply only to recent posts. Instead, consider a date specific search. The following query on any Twitter page would provide any posts that mention "bomb Threat" between January 1, 2015 and January 5, 2015.

since:2015-01-01 until:2015-01-05 "bomb threat"

First Tweet (discover.twitter.com/first-tweet)

In 2014, Twitter released a feature that allows you to view any user's first Tweet. This was designed to be fun and see how people started their Twitter accounts. I am more interested in the date and time associated with this information. Figure 3.21 displays a person's first Tweet. Notice the date and time below the content. This helps identify the length of time a person has been using a specific Twitter account.

Figure 3.21: A first Tweet on Twitter.

First Tweet – Keyword (http://ctrlq.org/first)

If you are ever following a trending hashtag or unique keyword, you may want to know the user that first posted the topic. This is not available natively within Twitter, but you can use this website to perform the search. Figure 3.22 displays the result for the first time a person used the hashtag of OSINT (#OSINT). It displays the message and the date of October 27, 2008.

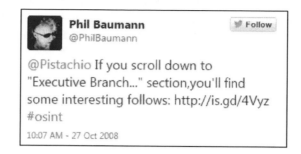

Figure 3.22: The first post to mention #OSINT as identified by ctrlq.org.

First Follower (socialrank.com/firstfollower)

It may be beneficial to know the first follower of your target on Twitter. This will likely be the person that introduced the target to Twitter and can often identify a former associate. If you want only this one piece of information, First Follower will give you the result. However, I recommend taking this idea to further extremes with Tweet Tunnel.

Tweet Tunnel (tweettunnel.info)

This website will identify all of a person's Twitter followers in the order that they started following the target. When you enter the target Twitter user name under the "FIRST FR" option in the main menu, you will see the followers beginning with the first follower. Figure 3.23 displays this result for the same user name from the First Tweet example previously. This partial view identifies the first three people and last three people that followed the target. This can often identify friends from when the target started the account or recent connections that may be more relevant.

Figure 3.23: The first three and last three followers of a target from Tweet Tunnel.

Deleted, Suspended, and Missing Tweets

Twitter users may delete their own accounts if there is suspicion that an investigation is under way. If this happens, searching on Twitter will not display any of the posts. Further, a person may only delete individual Twitter posts that are incriminating, but leave non-interesting posts on the profile to prevent raising suspicion associated with deleting an entire account. Some users may find their accounts suspended for violating Twitter's terms of service. In any of these scenarios, it is still possible to retrieve the missing posts using various techniques.

Google Cache (google.com)

If I encounter a Twitter user that has recently deleted some or all of their messages, I conduct a cache search of their profile. There are various ways to do this, and I will demonstrate the most common. In this example, I conducted a search on Twitter for "just deleted all my tweets". This provided many users that recently posted that they had just deleted all of their content. This helped me identify a good target for this type of demonstration. The first user I located was "AimeeLakic". Figure 3.24 displays his live profile. Notice that he only had one Tweet and that it referenced deleting his content.

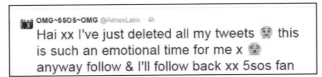

Figure 3.24: A user that recently deleted all Tweets.

I then went to Google and conducted a search for Twitter AimeeLakic. The first search result was a link to the user's live Twitter page. Instead of clicking on the link, I chose the Google Cache view of his profile by clicking the small green "down arrow" next to the URL and selecting "Cached View". Figure 3.25 displays a portion of this result. Notice that this view identifies six Tweets. You can now see deleted messages from this account.

Figure 3.25: A user's deleted Tweets.

This may be enough for your investigation. Occasionally, I need to identify content that was deleted weeks or months before my investigation. The previous technique will likely not provide much assistance because the Google Cache is probably a recent copy of their live page. The cache will also be missing the Tweets you want to see. For this example, I chose another user that had deleted all of their Tweets on the day of this writing. Twitter user MLGReilly possessed only one Tweet titled "Just deleted all my tweets". Figure 3.26 displays this post from 15 hours prior. I navigated to Google and conducted the following exact search.

site:twitter.com/MLGReilly

This instructs Google to search only the website twitter.com/MLGReilly. Since Twitter creates an individual page for every Tweet, and each of these pages start with twitter.com and then the person's user name, we should receive a large list of results. These results will include many individual messages that have been deleted from Twitter. Figure 3.27 displays the result from my search. Notice that Google located 349 unique pages in reference to this target user name. Figure 3.28 displays the result received when opening the second link which is connected to an individual message. This notification reveals that this specific message has been removed from Twitter.

Instead of clicking the live link, you should click the small green "down arrow" next to the URL and select "Cached View". Figure 3.29 displays the result which contains the deleted Tweet including the date and time it was posted. You may notice that the message in this Tweet does not match the description within the Google search result. This is because the individual message was part of a larger conversation on Twitter. The graphical cached view does not display the entire conversation and clicking any links within the cached result will send you back to a live page. Instead, choose the "Text-only version" link in the upper right of the cached page. This will present a text view of the cached Twitter message page. Figure 3.30 displays a portion of the text result which identifies the entire conversation.

Figure 3.26: A Twitter post announcing Tweet deletion.

Figure 3.27: A Google search result identifying specific Tweets by a user.

Sorry, that page doesn't exist!

You can **search Twitter** using the search box below or **return to the homepage.**

Figure 3.28: A Twitter notification that a post has been removed.

Figure 3.29: A recovered Tweet from Google cache.

1. homegirl **megansuxatlife** Dec 27

   Obs is picking my capture card up like this but the aver media driver thingy is picking it up perfectly so??

2. Reilly **MLGReilly** Dec 27

   megansuxatlife delete and re add it as a source

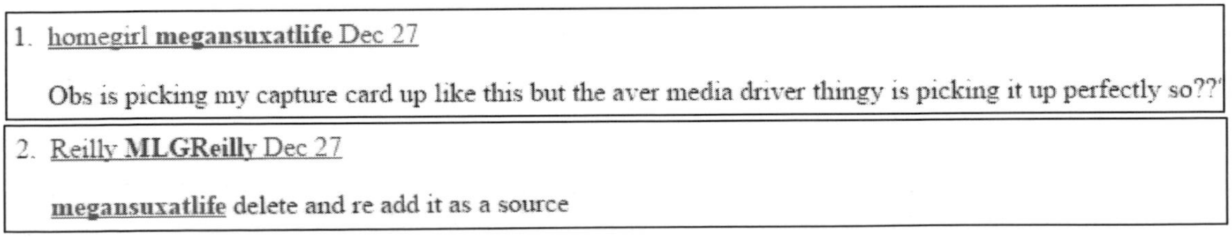

Figure 3.30: A Text view of a deleted Tweet from Google Cache.

Topsy (topsy.com)

Topsy is commonly used to monitor social traffic by topic and is explained later in this book. Another hidden use is to recreate a person's Twitter account that is no longer available through the official website. For this technique, it is not advised to search your target's Twitter name within the search field on the main Topsy website. This will identify any Twitter post that includes this text, which will include re-tweets and posts that mention the searched term. This can produce false positives. Instead, edit the address of the website, also called the URL, and include the Twitter name. For example, if you navigate to the following address, you should see a professional wrestler's page that has minimal Tweets.

http://twitter.com/ryback22

I use this as an example because this subject commonly deletes all of his posts. If you take that user name, ryback22, and add it to the Topsy address, you should receive the previous Twitter posts that were created with that account. The proper format is as follows:

http://topsy.com/twitter/ryback22

Note that in the above address "/twitter/" is included. This is mandatory for this technique. The above link identifies 6 pages of posts that were created on this subject's Twitter account before they were deleted. These can now be viewed and documented. Figure 3.31 displays the last page of the result, which identifies Tweets from two years prior.

This method can immediately produce results that were otherwise unavailable. Analyzing the content is easy when an account was completely deleted or has been suspended. The results will not be as obvious if an account exists and has messages still available on Twitter. If someone has deleted individual messages but left the rest of the account visible, you will need to recreate the previous steps and analyze both the live data from Twitter and the archived data on Topsy. You will need to manually compare the results and look for any messages present on Topsy that are not present on Twitter. After Twitter changed their API in 2013, Topsy's success rate with this technique has become sporadic. If your target has deleted their Tweets or disabled the account, you should find all of their posts on Topsy within a week after the activity. Tweets that were deleted months and years prior are not always available as seen in this example. My personal success rate is still over 50% with this technique.

Undetweetable (undetweetable.com)

Undetweetable was a website that collected deleted Twitter posts. It has been shut down by Twitter and they no longer collect new content. However, you can search the database of previously collected Tweets for free. Your results will vary. I have had many successes and failures using this service.

Figure 3.31: A Topsy search result of deleted Tweets.

Custom Twitter Tools

I find myself using many of these manual Twitter techniques daily. In order to prevent repetitive typing of the same addresses and searches, I created a custom web page with an all-in-one solution. Navigate to the following website to access this resource.

http://inteltechniques.com/osint/twitter.html

This page includes embedded JavaScript that will structure and execute web addresses based on your provided information. Figure 3.32 displays the current state of this tool. Any utilities that do not look familiar will be described in the remaining pages of this book. This tool will replicate many of the Twitter searches that you have read about here.

Location Information by User

Most people post to Twitter through their smart phones. This allows users to take advantage of location aware apps such as Foursquare, which they can use to "check-in" to places and let their friends know their location. While privacy-aware individuals have disabled the location feature of their accounts, many users enjoy broadcasting their location at all times. Identifying a user's location during a Twitter post is possible through various methods. Please note that the following methods will only work if your target has not disabled the geo-locate settings within Twitter.

GeoSocial Footprint (geosocialfootprint.com)

My current favorite tool for identifying recent location information from a specific Twitter profile is GeoSocial Footprint. This service will only search for location data within the most recent 200 posts. It is a great resource for identifying the current or recent location of a target. Using this website is fairly straight forward and does not require a Twitter account.

On the main page, enter the target Twitter user name and click "Retrieve Tweets". This will produce a map with markers identifying the most recent locations of that target. You can click on each marker to see the content of the message, but not the date and time. This overall view provides a quick glimpse into the general location of the target. Figure 3.33 displays a typical map with a view of a post.

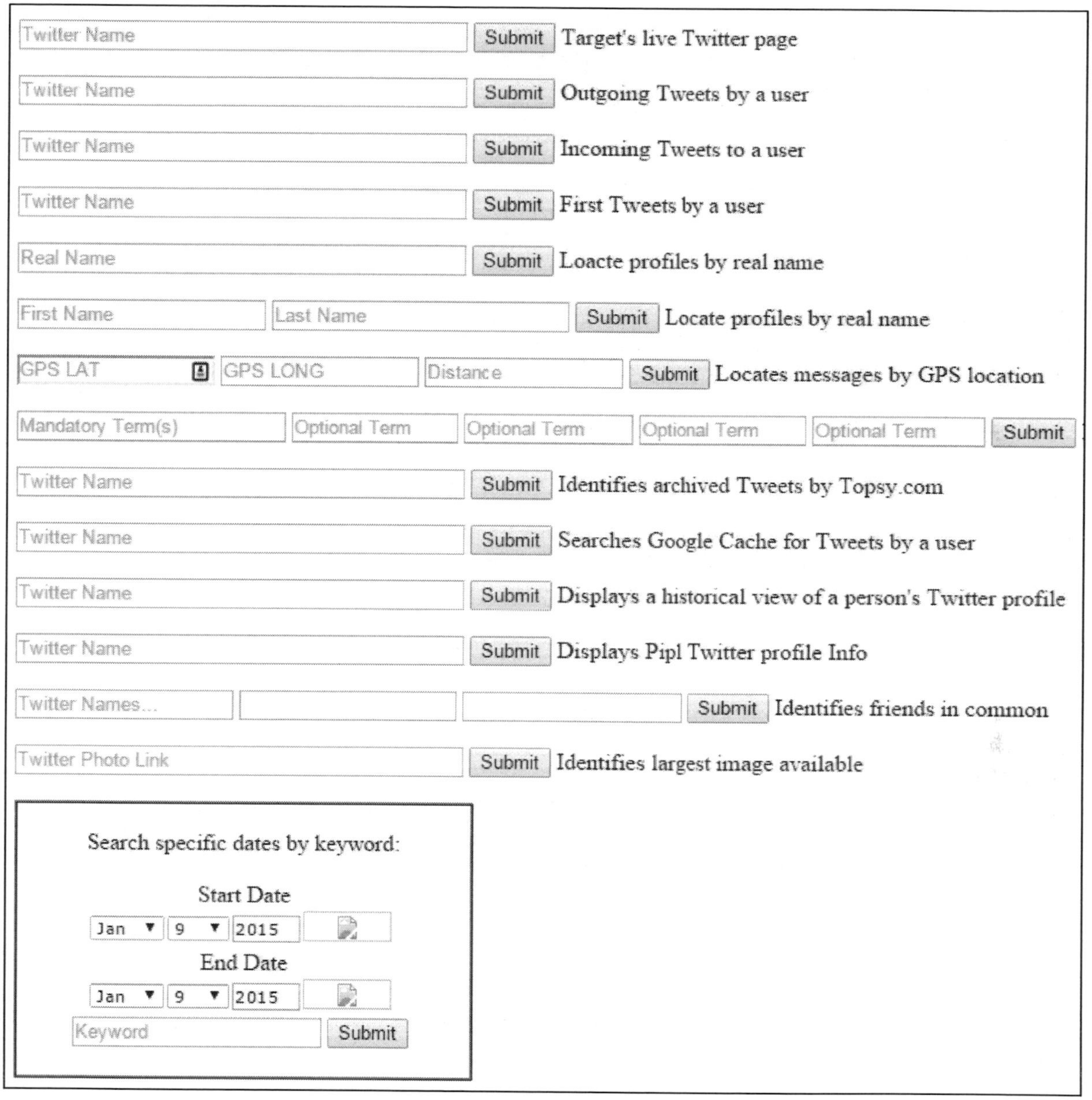

Twitter Name	Submit	Target's live Twitter page
Twitter Name	Submit	Outgoing Tweets by a user
Twitter Name	Submit	Incoming Tweets to a user
Twitter Name	Submit	First Tweets by a user
Real Name	Submit	Loacte profiles by real name
First Name	Last Name	Submit	Locate profiles by real name
GPS LAT	GPS LONG	Distance	Submit	Locates messages by GPS location
Mandatory Term(s)	Optional Term	Optional Term	Optional Term	Optional Term	Submit
Twitter Name	Submit	Identifies archived Tweets by Topsy.com
Twitter Name	Submit	Searches Google Cache for Tweets by a user
Twitter Name	Submit	Displays a historical view of a person's Twitter profile
Twitter Name	Submit	Displays Pipl Twitter profile Info
Twitter Names...			Submit	Identifies friends in common
Twitter Photo Link	Submit	Identifies largest image available

Search specific dates by keyword:

Start Date

Jan ▼ 9 ▼ 2015

End Date

Jan ▼ 9 ▼ 2015

Keyword   Submit

Figure 3.32: A custom Twitter Tools page from inteltechniques.com.

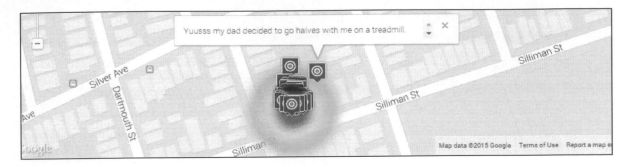

Figure 3.33: A map view from GeoSocialFootprint.

In order to view more detailed information about these posts, click on the "Download Tweets" button. This will generate a plain text file with no file extension titled "Download". Open this file within a text viewer such as Notepad to display the content. The text below is the actual content received during the previous search. The message contents were redacted for space and privacy. Note that you can now view the actual GPS coordinates and the date and time of each message. This could also be imported into a spreadsheet or database.

Sat Jan 10 09:22:46 +0000 2015,37.7296498,-122.4118834,Having our second unit be able to
Sat Jan 10 09:21:30 +0000 2015,37.7296699,-122.4118867,These Warrior games have been amazing.
Sat Jan 10 09:20:45 +0000 2015,37.7296699,-122.4118867,"@ItsFoodPorn: The whole point of dating
Sat Jan 10 09:18:08 +0000 2015,37.7296397,-122.4117785,You'd almost swear Imma thoughtful person

Tweetpaths (tweetpaths.com)

You will need to sign in to Tweetpaths using your Twitter account information in order to conduct any searches. The results will be limited to the most recent 75 Tweets. However, you can use advanced options to expand this restriction. Similar to GeoSocial Footprint, input your target's Twitter name and the resulting map will focus on the geographical area of where the target was located while posting. Figure 3.34 displays the result of a search. The popup window identifies detailed information about a selected message.

If you want to search a specific range of dates, click the "Show advanced options" link directly below the search field. This will expand the menu and allow you to enter a start date and end date. This can allow you to expand your search beyond the 75 Tweet limit. If your target is an active user, you may want to search one week at a time and document the results.

A great feature of Tweetpaths is that you can identify several users on the same map. Figure 3.35 displays a map with Google's satellite view enabled. Three Twitter users were searched and the results identify each with a different color of marker. This can be beneficial by showing three or more targets that were present at the same location during an incident. A user name is required to see any activity with this service. Several new websites have surfaced that will allow us to view recent Tweets from a specified area without knowledge of any user names involved.

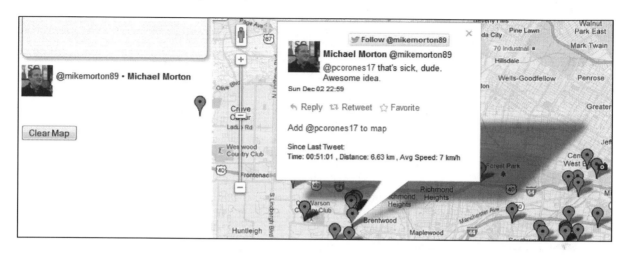

Figure 3.34: A Tweetpaths search result.

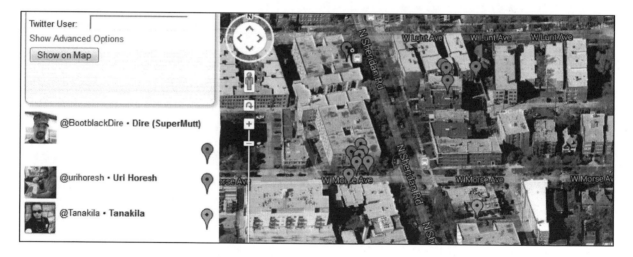

Figure 3.35: A Tweetpaths search result with satellite view and multiple accounts.

Information by Physical Location

A manual Twitter search method for identifying posts by location was explained earlier. This technique is best for recent or live information. You may have a need for historical details from previous posts from a specific location. There are several third party websites that can assist.

EchoSec (app.echosec.net)

One of the best location based search websites for Twitter is a service called EchoSec. This Canadian website will display Twitter, Instagram, Panoramio, Foursquare, and Flickr data on one screen. While these additional networks will be explained later, this one-stop-shop is a great resource for this combined data. The main page will present a satellite view Google map focused on the San Francisco area. You can click the interactive map to navigate to a different area or type in an address in the search field in the lower right. Once you have your area of interest visible on the map, click on the "Select Area" button and draw a box around the perimeter that you want to search. The map will populate with posts from the area and the markers will identify the social network. Below, you will see the content of your results. This will identify messages and photos from within the searched area. Figure 3.36 display a search of a baseball stadium.

Figure 3.37 displays the message results that appear below the map. The selection identifies the numerous posts from the inside of the stadium on the field. One advantage of this website is that it identifies the device or service that was responsible for delivering the Tweet. In Figure 3.37, you can see that the messages were posted to Twitter via Foursquare, Instagram, and 360 Panorama. This will often identify posts made by either Android or iPhone devices. This minor piece of information can help build the overall picture of your investigation.

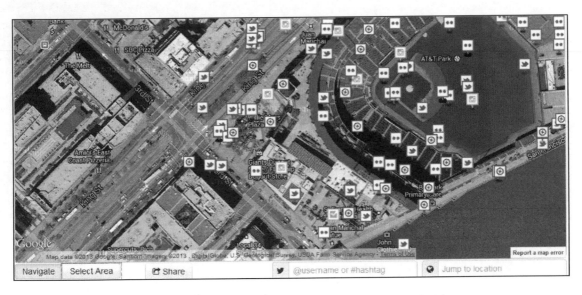

Figure 3.36: Mapped results from a perimeter search on EchoSec.

Figure 3.37: Message results from a perimeter search on EchoSec.

MapD: MIT (http://mapd.csail.mit.edu/tweetmap/)

MapD is a massive database platform being developed through collaboration between MIT and Harvard. Currently, each college has their own interface into this data, which usually supplies Twitter posts from the last twenty days of activity. The Harvard website states that it will eventually provide real-time streaming data on top of the billions of historic posts. Each interface provides new ways of searching information. Figure 3.38 displays the entire screen of a search result, which will be referenced during this section.

This website can search by topic, user name, or location. It can also combine all three options to conduct a detailed search. The first search field, titled "What", can accept any keywords and identify location enabled Tweets that meet the criteria. The second field, "Who", can only accept a Twitter user name and will not function with a real name. The third search field, titled "Where", can accept GPS coordinates, a zip code, or a street address. This data will zoom the map to a more detailed level. Figure 3.38 displays a neighborhood in Kansas City and the small dots indicate Tweets posted from the identified locations. The column on the left displays the Twitter message content that is represented in the map view. Finally, the graph at the bottom right identifies message volume in the chosen area. Clicking the right arrow button at the bottom will "play" the map and highlight the Tweets in the chronological order of post.

The view in Figure 3.38 is not the default configuration. When you first load this website, a dark map is displayed without satellite view. This can be changed by clicking on the blue plus sign in the upper right area. Clicking on each visible dot will display the details of the message. This will include exact date and time, the message content, and user that posted the Tweet. The area in the lower left (not visible in Figure 3.38) is a word cloud that identifies words that appear in messages more commonly than others.

MapD: Harvard (http://worldmap.harvard.edu/tweetmap)

Harvard's version of this data interface is more basic with fewer options. This may not sound like a desirable trait. However, the clean interface makes room for a feature that may not work properly on MIT's contribution. The compressed view in Figure 3.39 displays a small box around a group of Tweets posted from a parking lot on the map. This square is executed when clicking on any portion of a visible map. Any Twitter posts existing within the square will be presented in a popup window that will identify the Tweets and all available details about them. The box at the bottom will allow you to filter the results by date of key word. The view from a monitor with decent resolution will provide a better spacious view.

Overall, both of these services are displaying identical data. You should experiment with both until you gain your own personal preference. I believe that the MIT option is the more advanced and preferred route to go. In order to view live streaming data, we will need to use another service.

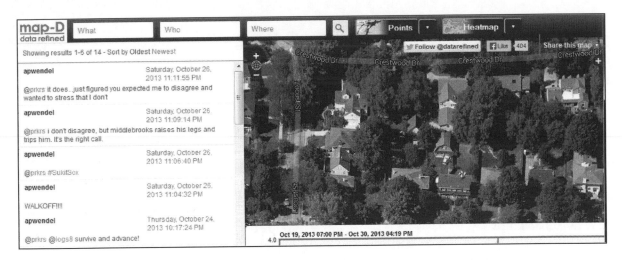

Figure 3.38: A MapD search result on a MIT page.

One Million Tweet Map (onemilliontweetmap.com)

This service only displays the most recent one million tweets on an international map. They do not have access to every Tweet available, often referred to as the "fire hose", but they offer new Tweets every second. I would never rely on this map for complete data about a location. However, monitoring a large event can provide live intelligence in an easily viewed format. I recommend using a mouse scroll wheel to zoom into your location of interest. Once you are at a level that you can see single Tweets, you can click any of them to see the content. The page will automatically refresh as new information is posted.

Figure 3.39: A MapD search result on a Harvard page.

Now Tweets (nowtweets.com)

Now Tweets is similar to the previous Tweet mapping websites. The difference is that it only displays current Tweets. You will not see any historical posts. As Tweets are posted from the location that you are searching, the website will update with the new content. This service is in "Beta" stage right now and is far from complete.

Search by Email Address

Technically, Twitter does not allow the search of a Twitter user by providing an email address. If you attempt this type of search on Twitter, you will receive no results, even if a profile exists for a user with that email address. To bypass this limitation, you can use a feature offered by online email providers that will communicate with Twitter.

This technique will require a Twitter account and Yahoo email account. Through a web browser, connect to an alias Twitter account in one tab and connect to an alias email account on Yahoo Mail in another tab. If you do not have a Yahoo email account, the creation process is easy at mail.yahoo.com. On the "Contacts" page of your Yahoo account, select "Add a New Contact". This will present a form that will allow you to enter the email address of the target. The "Name" fields can contain any data, and I usually use numbers beginning at 001. Save this entry and go to your Twitter page. Click on the "Discover" tab at the top and then "Find Friends" in the left menu. This will present several options for importing friends into Twitter. Choose the Yahoo option and provide your Yahoo email address. You will need to confirm that you want to give Twitter access to your Yahoo contacts by clicking "I agree" on the popup window. Twitter will then identify any user profiles that are associated with the target email address. Twitter will encourage you to add these friends, but do not choose that option. If you do, your target will be sent a notification from your account. Figure 3.40 displays the result when importing a contact with a target's email address.

Figure 3.40: A Twitter email address import search result.

Embedded Photos

It is very common for users to include digital photos within their Tweets. There are multiple ways to do this. Regardless of the method, it is always important to save a copy of any photos of interest to your investigation. This section will explain the ideal process to obtaining the largest possible photos.

The most likely way that a person will add photos to their Twitter posts is through Instagram. This popular service will be explained in more detail later. The priority for now is to download the digital photos with the best quality available. Figure 3.41 displays a Twitter post that has a link to an Instagram photo. This link opens a new tab that will load the photo within the Instagram page. This photo will not have any options to download or save the data. If you right-click on it, you will not be given an option to save-as or download the image as you would on standard websites. Instead, we must manually archive this file.

Figure 3.41: A Twitter post with Instagram link.

The process for archiving an embedded photo in Instagram will vary based on your browser. The easiest is with Firefox. Right-click on the image of interest and select "View background image". This will present the actual jpeg image, which can be saved by right-clicking again and choosing "Save image as".

If you are using Internet Explorer, you can right-click on the image and select "View source". This will open a new window with a text only display of the code to this web page. On the left will be a column of numbers, which refers to the line number of each line of programming code. In the area of the line 38, you should see an address (URL) of a photo file. This is the actual location of this full sized image. Copy and paste this information into a web browser to load the image. You can right-click it at this point to save it easily. Figure 3.42 displays this source code that identifies the location of the image.

```
36    <meta property="og:site_name" content="Instagram" />
37    <meta property="og:title" content="" />
38    <meta property="og:image" content="http://distilleryimage2.ak.instagram.com/380ebffa42eb11e3ad1322000ab5bf34_8.jpg" />
39    <meta property="og:determiner" content="a" />
40    <meta property="fb:app_id" content="124024574287414" />
41    <meta property="og:url" content="http://instagram.com/p/gK7xDuQRKq/" />
```

Figure 3.42: The source code of an Instagram page identifying embedded photos.

If you are using Chrome, you will see a "Save as" option when you right-click the image. Unfortunately, this is the option to save the entire page and will not always include the original photo. As with Internet Explorer, right-click on the photo and select "View page source". This will open a new window with the source code that will identify the entire address of the jpeg file. Copy and paste this address into any browser and you can easily save the file.

Mac users that have Safari as their default browser can use the same source view method; however the line numbers will not be visible. You will still see the address of the jpeg file, which can be downloaded in the same manner.

If the person used Twitter's native photo sharing ability, you will see a small version of the actual photo or a link within the stream of data in a person's feed. Click on this photo and it will open in a popup window as a larger view. You can now right-click on the photo and save the file. However, this will not be the largest size available through Twitter. Instead, right-click the photo and select "open image in new tab". This will launch a new tab that should only contain the actual image. The address of the image will likely end in a file extension such as jpg. At the very end of the URL for this image, add ":orig" without the quotes. It should open a new version of the photo. This version will likely appear larger and have a higher resolution.

As an example, I located an image at the following address from Twitter. I then added ":orig" at the end and received a much more detailed photo. The second link demonstrates this structure.

https://pbs.twimg.com/media/BstXzBYCAAECMmL.jpg
https://pbs.twimg.com/media/BstXzBYCAAECMmL.jpg:orig

There are several third party options that allow you to extract these types of photos. I do not like to rely on them because their services do not always work properly. I prefer to archive the Twitter information from the actual source. More documentation and archiving options will be explained later.

All My Tweets (allmytweets.net)

This website provides a clean display of all of a user's Twitter posts on one screen. It will start with the most recent post and list previous posts on one line each. This view will display up to 3200 messages on one scrollable screen. This provides two analysis methods for digesting large amounts of data. Holding CTRL and F on the keyboard will present a search box. Any search terms can be entered to navigate directly to associated messages. The page can also be printed for archiving or distribution to assisting analysts. Figure 3.43 displays the format of the results. This is my preferred way of reading through the Tweets of an active user. This also prevents you from constantly loading more Tweets at the end of every page throughout a profile.

Figure 3.43: A search result on All My Tweets.

Conweets (conweets.com)

All My Tweets can be a great resource for location posts published by your target. However, it will only show you one side of the conversation. You would need to perform the same action on ever user associated with the target. Conweets may eliminate this problem. This website allows you to enter two Twitter users and it will identify the conversations between them. It will display them in order from most recent to the oldest. Each section will identify the person that started the conversation and the date. The appearance is similar to a back-and-forth text message session. You will only receive publicly visible Tweets.

Sleeping Time (sleepingtime.org)

This site allows for a search of an exact Twitter profile name, and provides the average time period that this user sleeps. The historical tweets are analyzed according to the times of posts. Data is then presented that suggests when the user is usually sleeping due to lack of posting during a specific time period. A query of Kevin Mitnick revealed that he is likely to be sleeping between 12am and 7am according to his tweets. Although the idea was probably executed as a fun site, it can be quite useful.

Real world application: Police often want the element of surprise on their side when contacting suspects. Whether this is to execute a search warrant or simply contact a subject when he or she is most likely to be home, knowing the habits of the individual can be beneficial. Locating a possible sleep pattern of the individual will decrease the chances of showing up at an empty house, only to discover that the subject works a strange night shift somewhere. Sleeping Time may have alerted an investigator that the average sleep time is 2pm to 10pm, creating an opportunity to catch the subject at home. This also works for process servers, private investigators, bill collectors, and even salesmen.

Tweet Deck (tweetdeck.com)

Tweet Deck is owned by Twitter, and it can take advantage of the Twitter "Firehose". This huge stream of data contains every public post available on Twitter. Many Twitter services do not have access to this stream, and the results are limited.

Tweet Deck requires you to create and log into an account to use the service. This user account is not the same as a Twitter account. The "Create Account" button on the website will walk you through the process. Alias information is acceptable and preferred. The round plus symbol in the upper left area will add a new column to your view. There are several options presented, but the most common will be "Search" and "Tweets". The "Search" option will create a column that will allow you to search for any keywords on Twitter. The following is a list search examples and how they may benefit the investigator:

"Victim Name": A homicide investigator can monitor people mentioning a homicide victim
"School Name": A school can monitor anyone mentioning the school for suspicious activity
"Subject Name": An investigator can monitor a missing person's name for relevant information
"Event": Officials can monitor anyone discussing a special event such as a festival or concert
"Child Name": Teachers can monitor mentions of a student's name to identify problems

The "Tweets" option will allow you to enter a Twitter user name and monitor all incoming and outgoing public messages associated with the user. If several subjects of an investigation are identified as Twitter users, each of the profiles can be loaded in a separate column and monitored. Occasionally, this will result in two of the profiles communicating with each other while being monitored. Figure 3.44 displays one instance of Tweet Deck with a combination of search types.

You can also use the Geo search mentioned earlier within Tweet Deck. A column that searches "geocode:43.430242,-89.736459,1km" will display a live feed of Tweets posted within the specified range. A more precise search of "geocode:43.430242,-89.736459,1km fight" would add the keyword to filter the results.

The columns of Tweet Deck are consistently sized. If more columns are created than can fit in the display, the "Columns" option with left and right arrows will provide navigation. This allows for numerous search columns regardless of screen resolution. This is an advantage of Tweet Deck over the other services discussed.

Figure 3.44: A Tweet Deck search screen.

Hootsuite Feed (hootsuite.com)

While Tweet Deck is my preferred viewer of live Twitter information, it does not display well for large audiences. If I am broadcasting my screen to a digital projector for a room full of people to see, the text is usually too small to accurately view from a distance. Hootsuite offers a solution to this predicament. If you wanted to display a live feed of anyone mentioning "OSINT" on Twitter, you can navigate to the following website in your web browser, after connecting to a Twitter account.

https://hootsuite.com/feed/OSINT+Search

You can replace "OSINT" in the above address with any term or terms of interest. The result will be a live stream with a very large font that could be viewed from a long distance away. Figure 3.45 displays the results on my monitor, which is at 1920x1080 resolution. I purposely left the task bar in the screen shot to demonstrate the size of the text. This view can be beneficial for situations where Twitter streams are monitored by a group of people in an operations center.

Twiangulate (twiangulate.com)

This is one of two websites that I recommend to quickly identify any mutual friends or mutual followers listed on two Twitter profiles. Figure 3.46 displays the result of mutual friends on two specific accounts. Out of 521 people that are friends with one of the subjects, only 15 are friends with both. This can quickly identify key targets associated within an inner circle of subjects. All 15 subjects were listed within the results including full name, photo, bio, and location.

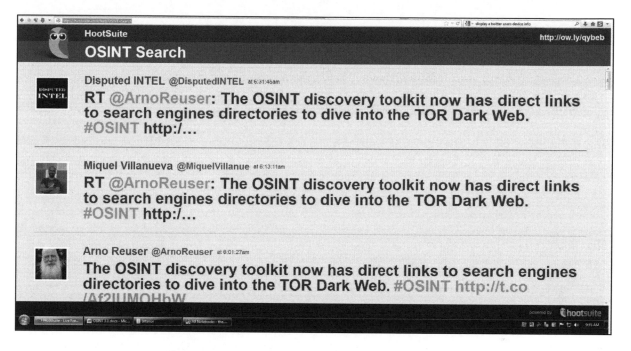

Figure 3.45: A Hootsuite live feed with large text.

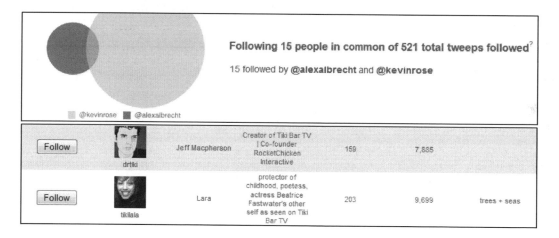

Figure 3.46: A Twiangulate report of mutual friends.

Followerwonk (followerwonk.com)

The second website that I use for group Twitter analysis is Followerwonk. This service offers more options that Twiangulate and will let you compare up to three users. The second tab at the top of the page, titled "Compare Users", will allow you a more thorough search. Figure 3.47 displays the analysis of three subjects. You can see that the first and second subject do not have any people in common that they follow on Twitter. This can indicate that they may not know each other in real life, or that they simply have different tastes in the people that they find interesting. However, the first and third subjects have 79 people in common that they follow on Twitter. This is a strong indication that they know each other in real life and have friends in common. Clicking on the link next to this result will display the identities of these people as seen in Figure 3.48.

This default search on Followerwonk is a good start. A more valuable search is to analyze the people that follow these users. The previous example identified people that our targets followed. This will often include celebrities, businesses, and profiles that probably have no impact on your investigation. However, the people that follow your targets are more likely to be real people that may have involvement in your investigation. Figure 3.49 displays the results of the same targets when the search criteria was changed to "Compare their followers" in the dropdown menu next to the search button. We now see that the first and second subject still have no one in common. The first and third subject has 200 people that follow both of their Twitter feeds. You can click the result link to identify these 200 people.

Followerwonk possesses other search capabilities for user analysis. The first tab at the top of the screen will search any term or terms to identify any Twitter bios that contain those words. This may identify profiles that were missed during the search on twitter.com for messages. The third tab, titled "Analyze Followers", allows you to enter a single Twitter handle and either analyze the people the user follows or the people that follow that user. The second option usually provides more relevant results.

The information provided during this search will display numerous pie charts and graphs about the user. The most useful is the map that identifies the approximate location of the people connected to the person's Twitter account. Figure 3.50 displays a map for one of the users searched previously. This provides a quick indication of the regions of interest to the target. Figure 3.51 displays a detail level of an area near Denver. Each small dot identifies an individual Twitter account of a person that follows the target and lives or works in the general area. This location data is very vague and does not usually correctly correlate with the address on the map. This should only be used to identify the general area, such as the town or city, of the people that are friends with the target on Twitter. In the past, I have used this data to focus only on people in the same area as my homicide victim. I temporarily eliminated people that lived in other states and countries. This helped me prioritize on subjects that could be contacted quickly and interviewed.

Fake Followers

There are a surprising number of Twitter accounts that are completely fake. These are bought and sold daily by shady people that want to make their profiles appear more popular than they really are. I have seen a lot of target profiles that have been padded with these fake followers. There are two websites that will assist in distinguishing the authentic profiles from the fraudulent. Both options will require you to be logged in to a Twitter account.

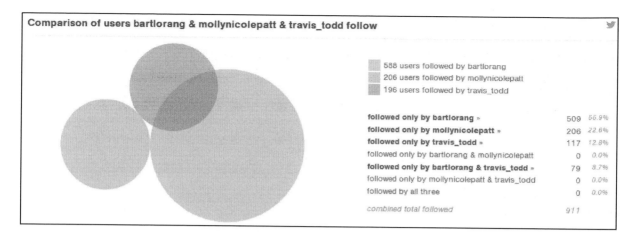

Figure 3.47: A Followerwonk user comparison.

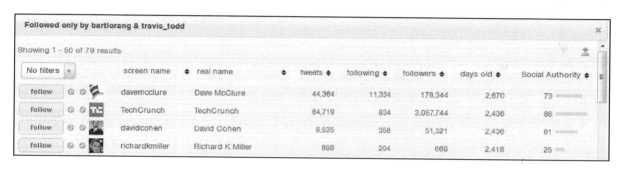

Figure 3.48: A Followerwonk list of users.

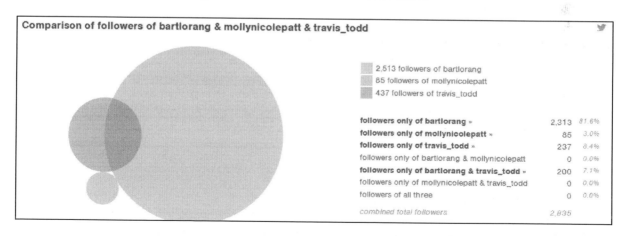

Figure 3.49: A Followerwonk user comparison.

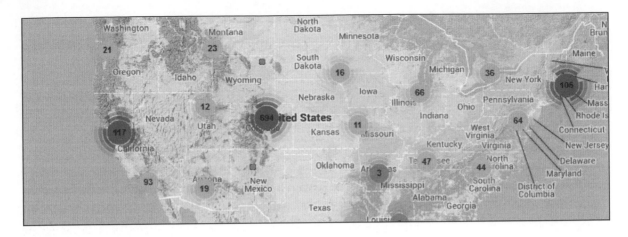

Figure 3.50: A Followerwonk map of users connected to a target.

Figure 3.51: A detailed view of a Followerwonk map of connected users.

Social Bakers (socialbakers.com/twitter/fakefollowercheck)

This service allows you to enter any Twitter handle in the search field. The result will identify the suspicious or empty accounts, inactive accounts, and profiles that appear legitimate. Figure 3.52 displays the results for our target. The eleven accounts that were listed as suspicious are identified on the results page.

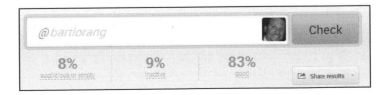

Figure 3.52: A result on Social Bakers to identify fake followers.

Status People (fakers.statuspeople.com)

This service has a strength and a weakness when compared to Social Bakers. The strength is that it gives you additional information such as the languages spoken by the followers, the people that have not posted a Tweet in the past 100 days, and the users that follow less than 250 people. The weakness is that this is a paid service and it limits the free visibility. You are allowed to search only two Twitter handles during your free trial and you can see only two of the fake profiles identified. The website is poorly designed, and I would be skeptical of providing a credit card to the service.

Backtweets (backtweets.com)

Backtweets provides one unique service. It identifies any Twitter posts that included a link to a specified website. This tool works even if the post used a URL shortening service such as bit.ly. Figure 3.53 identifies two Twitter posts that linked to my website. This can be used to locate subjects that are promoting illegal websites, followers of protest movements, or to identify the popularity of a website.

Figure 3.53: A Backtweets report of website links.

Miscellaneous Twitter Sites

Every week, a new site arrives that takes advantage of the public data that Twitter shares with the world. These sites offer unique ways of searching for information that Twitter does not allow on their main page. This partial list is a good start to finding information relevant to your target.

Trendsmap (trendsmap.com)

Monitoring trends on Twitter can provide intelligence on a global scale. The keywords that are currently being posted more than any other terms in a specific area could be of interest. This can identify issues about to surface that may need attention. This type of analysis is common during large events such as protests and celebrations. Several websites offer this service, but I choose Trendsmap. You can search either topics or a location. Searching a location will provide the top keywords being posted as well as a heat map to identify peak usage.

Mention Map (mentionmapp.com)

This service displays a visualization of a user's Twitter connections and topics. It identifies connections to other users based on Twitter traffic. The wider the connecting lines are specifies a stronger connection. Figure 3.54 displays Robert Scoble's connections to TechCrunch, Michael Arrington and others. This can provide a quick look at strong associations without analyzing an official Twitter feed.

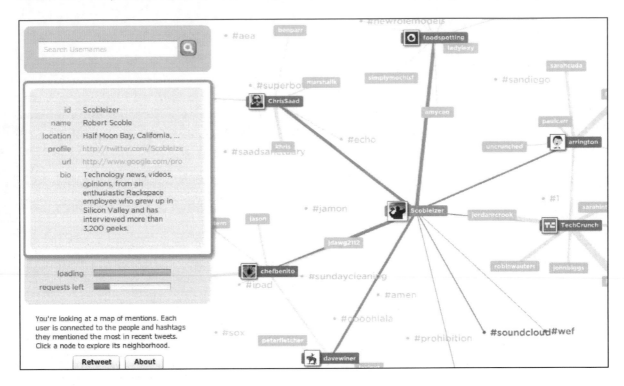

Figure 3.54: A user name mapped out on Mention Mapp.

Tweet Alarm (tweetalarm.com)

This service is similar to Google Alerts. However, it only monitors Twitter. You can enter any terms that you like and it will notify you via email if a post matches your query. In my experience, this has only been useful when I had very unique terms to monitor.

Twitonomy (twitonomy.com)

One Twitter analytics website that stands out from the rest is Twitonomy. This is the most complete analytics service that I have found for a single Twitter handle. A typical user search would fill four pages of screenshots. A search of the user "bartlorang" immediately revealed the following details.

He has posted 6,848 Tweets
He is following 588 people
He has 2,513 followers
He joined Twitter on May 13, 2007
He lives in Boulder, CO
He averages 5 Tweets per day
He has mentioned 2,317 other Twitter users
He replies to 32% of posts to him
He has re-tweeted 1,109 posts (15%)

The remaining sections of this page identify current posts, followers, people following, favorites, and lists. The main analytics portion identifies the average number of posts by day of the week and by hour of the day. It also displays the platforms that the user Tweets from. Figure 3.55 displays this portion. This data discloses that the target has an iPhone and iPad, and that the majority of his Twitter time is spent on the smart phone. This also identifies his preferred web browser (Safari), check-in utility (Foursquare), photo sharing service (Instagram), and video sharing service (Vine). Other information includes his Tweets that are most "favorited" and "retweeted", the users that he replies to most often, and the users that he mentions more than others. If you have a Twitter name of interest, I highly recommend searching it through Twitonomy.

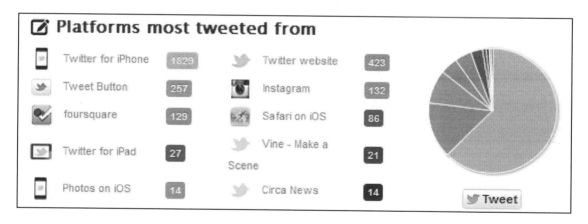

Figure 3.55: A portion of a Twitonomy search result identifying user platforms.

Tweet Topic Explorer (tweettopicexplorer.neoformix.com)

This free Twitter post analysis tool provides a unique service that I have not seen in the numerous competitors. It displays a word cloud view identifying the terms mentioned most often on your target's account. It then allows you to select any term of interest and immediately identifies Tweets containing the selected word. It has helped me quickly identify the main topics of a user's posts. I can then easily isolate the messages that are important to my investigation.

Other Twitter Analyzers

There are dozens of sites that will analyze a person's tweets and provide a summary report. Explaining each of them here would be too redundant. Below is a list of sites that you should experiment with until you find one that you like. An example is shown in Figure 3.56.

Gwittr (gwittr.com)
FollerMe (foller.me)
Twtrland (twtrland.com
Tagwalk (tagwalk.com)
Twitalyzer (twitalyzer.com)
TheArchivist (archivist.visitmix.com)
TweetReach (tweetreach.com)
SocialSearcher (socialsearching.info/#twitter)

Real world application: Parents can benefit from these Twitter searches. Locating a child's profile can provide great detail about portions of the child's life that is not shared with the parent. On one occasion, I was presenting to a group of concerned parents about the dangers of the internet. Afterward, a parent located her child's profile and discovered an abundance of tweets that referenced depression and suicidal thoughts. The parent had no idea that her child was having such thoughts. Professional assistance with the situation was sought. The parent could also identify a specific location that the child was visiting every day after school that was previously unknown to the parents.

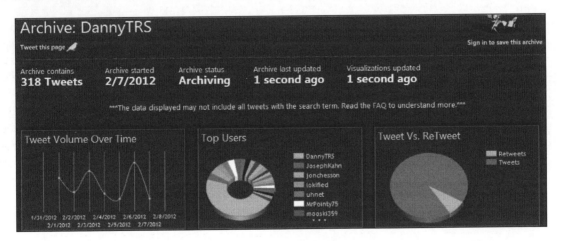

Figure 3.56: An example of a summary result of a Twitter name on The Archivist.

MySpace (myspace.com)

The previous editions of this book possessed a large area devoted to MySpace. It discussed ways to view hidden videos, photos, and comments from a target's profile. In 2013, MySpace redesigned the entire website and all of the original techniques were disabled. We could still search for information, but the methods were much more traditional. The majority of user profiles were marked as private and no content was viewable. In 2015, a new option surfaced that would again allow the display of private video files.

Any MySpace page will have a search option at the bottom of the screen. This is in the form of a small magnifying glass icon. Clicking this will open a new blank page with a cursor flashing. You can type in a real name or user name and will be presented many profile options that match your search. Clicking a result will open that user's profile for analysis. Overall, I rarely see any recent items of interest on MySpace. It is mostly music related now and contains very little communication. However, the entire archive of user's personal videos can be viewed regardless of privacy settings.

In order to see these videos, you must first know either the MySpace user name of your target, the title of the video, or specific terms within the video. I will demonstrate all three in this section. First, assume that your target is MySpace user "butchcassidy8504". Figure 3.57 displays his profile which is set to "restricted". If I want to know if he has videos within his profile, I would conduct the following search on Google.

site:sitemaps.myspace.com ext:xml "www.myspace.com/butchcassidy8504"

The first portion instructs Google to only search the "sitemaps" subdomain of MySpace. This is where MySpace stores thousands of files that contain the locations of all of their videos. The next section instructs Google to only display results that have the xml file extension. The final portion instructs Google to only display results that contain the target user name directly after the MySpace domain. This will eliminate any undesired results that are not directly connected to the target user name. In the example above, 60 results were returned that contain direct links to videos from this user. Because these pages are dynamic, the selected result may not actually contain videos by your target. In these situations, use the Google cache of the MySpace page, or view the necessary video address within the brief description. Figure 3.58 displays the first Google result from this search. Within the description of this result, you can see the address of this "private" video as the following.

https://www.myspace.com/butchcassidy8504/video/big-legs-does-batting-practice/42166588

If you type this URL directly into your browser, MySpace will redirect you to their main page and you will not see the target video. However, you can see within the URL that the video ID number is 42166588. If you add this video ID number to another specific URL, you can watch the entire video. The proper structure of the actual address, using this video ID number as an example, is the following.

https://myspace.com/swfplayer?type=video&id=42166588

Replacing 42166588 in this example with any video ID number that you find should play the video regardless of the profile privacy setting. You can use this same type of Google search to identify videos with specific titles or keywords. The following two examples may give you an idea of how to ask for specific video results. Both of these present interesting results of "private" videos.

site:sitemaps.myspace.com ext:xml "fight" "bus" "seattle"

site:sitemaps.myspace.com ext:xml "21 shots of vodka! in 47 seconds"

Overall, it appears that all MySpace videos are public. If your target has a restricted profile, it does not mean that you cannot view his or her videos. Many readers may question my reasons for mentioning MySpace at all. It is true that most members have abandoned their profiles for the larger and more popular networks. However, very few people deleted their profiles. If you have a target that has been an internet user for several years, you will likely locate a MySpace page for that person. The videos that you find on their private profile were likely long forgotten by the user. This can be very valuable during background investigations. The other relevant area that I still search is the photos that can be accessed by clicking a user's "Photostream" link on the left menu. These images can be useful when conducting reverse photo searches as described in Chapter Nine.

Figure 3.57: A restricted MySpace profile.

Getting - MySpace
sitemaps.myspace.com/VideoSitemap/type1/sitemap_3853.xml
... ny https://myspace.com/swfplayer?type=video&id=42166585 289 https://**www.**
myspace.com/butchcassidy8504/video/big-legs-does-batting-practice/42166588 ...

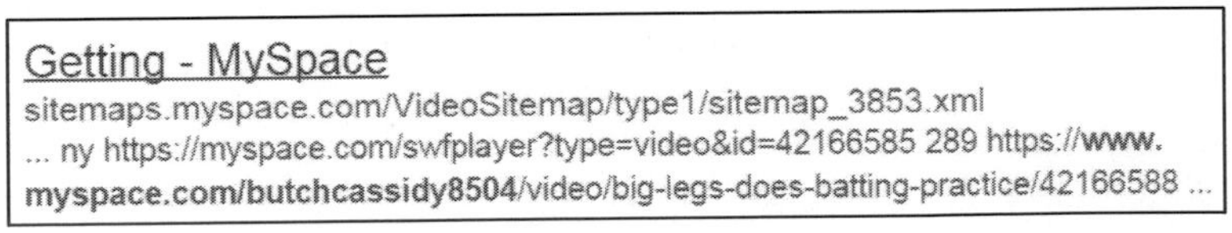

Figure 3.58: A Google search result identifying video ID numbers from restricted MySpace profiles.

Google+ (plus.google.com)

Google's social network is fairly straight forward. All Google+ pages have a search bar at the top ready for a real name to search. While Google has allowed the use of screen names in rare circumstances, a real name is required by the service. After locating the profile of your target, you can click through the options for Posts, About, Photos and Videos. These pages will display information about the target that was supplied by the user. The left column will display a photo posted by the user and an abbreviated list of people involved in "circles" with the user. These circles are Google's way of identifying relationships between users. The right column will identify additional profiles on other networks of the user as well as links uploaded by the user.

For many people, navigating to plus.google.com will present a request from Google to join the social network. This can be difficult to bypass. A solution to avoiding this trap is to conduct a search on Google for the word "plus" followed by any target name. The following example would search for Google+ profiles of Kevin Rose:

plus Kevin Rose

The first result will be a link to a Google+ profile page. Even if it is not the target that you are looking for, you will now have unlimited access to the profile search bar. Figure 3.59 displays a result with the search option at the top of the page.

Figure 3.59: A Google+ profile.

LinkedIn (linkedin.com)

When it comes to business related social networking sites, LinkedIn is the most popular. It currently has more than 330 million subscribers internationally. The site encourages searchers to create a free profile before accessing any data. This is not required and searching a name is easy. There are some protected areas that are not visible without registering for the free account. As with any social network, I recommend creating a basic account with minimal details. The bottom section of the main page offers a search using a real name. These searches will often lead to multiple results that identify several subjects with the same name. The upper right portion of this results page will offer only some basic refinement to the search to filter by country. In order to filter more results, you must sign in to the service.

After logging in to your account, a people search field will be present on the upper right portion of every page. You can type in a real name, business name, or industry to begin locating your target. Knowing the real name will be most beneficial. The results page will include the target's employer, location, industry, and a photo. After identifying the appropriate target, clicking the name will open that user's profile. If searching a common name, the filters on the left portion of the screen will help limit the options. If you would like to filter this information during your search, you can use the advanced search link directly to the right of the general search field. This will allow you to structure the exact search that you want. Figure 3.60 displays a search results page including links to individual profiles.

The profiles on LinkedIn often contain an abundance of information. Since this network is used primarily for business networking, an accelerated level of trust is usually present. Many of the people on this network use it to make business connections. Several of the profiles will contain full contact information including cellular telephone numbers. This site should be one of the first stops when conducting a background check on a target. The target profile often contains previous employment information, alumni information, and work associates.

Aside from searching names and businesses, you can search any keywords that may appear within someone's profile. Since many people include their phone numbers in their profile, this can be an easy way to identify the user of a specific cellular telephone number. Figure 3.61 displays a search of a telephone number and a single matched result. Visiting this profile identifies further information as well as confirmation of the target number (Figure 3.62).

Figure 3.60: A LinkedIn search result.

Figure 3.61: A LinkedIn telephone search result.

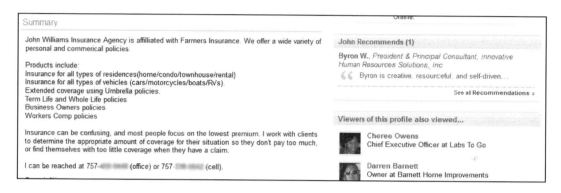

Figure 3.62: A LinkedIn profile containing a telephone number.

Searching by Company

If you are searching for employees of a specific company, searching the company name often provides numerous profiles. Clicking on any of these profiles presents a very limited view, such as the redacted example in Figure 3.63. The name of the employee is not available, but the photo and job description is visible. You are now required to upgrade to a full premium account in order to get further information. Instead, copy the entire job description under the "LinkedIn Member" title, including the business name. In this example, it is "Facebook Client Team, The Client Council". Use this in a custom Google search as displayed in Figure 3.64. The results listed should be the same results as those on LinkedIn. However, these results will have the employee's names. Clicking these links will present the entire public LinkedIn profile for that user (Figure 3.65). An alternative to this approach is to conduct a reverse image search on Google of this photo. This method will be explained in detail in a later chapter.

Figure 3.63: A LinkedIn profile located by a business search.

Figure 3.64: A Google search to locate employee's name of a targeted business.

Figure 3.65: A LinkedIn profile identifying an employee name from a Google search.

Searching by Country

While LinkedIn is an American company, it is a global social network. If you know that your target is in a specific country, you can filter your search accordingly. This can be done manually by navigating to a foreign subdirectory such as uk.linkedin.com (UK), ca.linkedin.com (Canada), or br.linkedin.com (Brazil). This tedious method of searching can be replaced with a custom Google search engine. Navigate to inteltechniques.com/osint/linkedin.country.html. You will see a single search field. Conduct your query and you will be presented with a new window that will filter your search results on LinkedIn by country. Figure 3.66 displays a sample search with the Canadian results selected.

Figure 3.66: A custom Google search engine to filter LinkedIn results by country.

PDF Profile View

Some LinkedIn profiles will mask some details if you are not connected through the network to the person. When this happens, select the down arrow next to the blue "Connect" button and select "Export to PDF". This will open a document that should have the full content in resume format.

Tumblr (tumblr.com)

Tumblr was purchased by Yahoo in 2013. It is half social network and half blog service. It is gaining a lot of popularity with many active users. At the time of this writing, there were 223 million blogs and 103 billion posts. These posts can include text, photos, videos, and links to other networks. The search method and layout is no longer user-friendly. The search feature will only identify blogs that were specifically tagged by the creator with your search terms. I suggest using the Google custom search engine described in Chapter One.

Access to private profiles

There have been "hacks" in the past that would allow a type of "back door entry" into a profile that is marked as private. By the time these methods become known, the vulnerability is usually corrected by the social network host. Websites or applications that publicly claim to be able to access this secured data are most often scams or attempts to steal your own passwords. In my experience, it is best to avoid these traps and focus on finding all available public information.

Chapter Four

Online Maps

Google Maps (maps.google.com)

The presence of online satellite images is not news any more. Most of you have already "Googled" your own address and viewed your home from the sky. This view can get surprisingly detailed when using the zoom feature. Alleys, sheds, and extended driveways that are hidden from the street are now visible thanks to this free service. Many tactical units will examine this data before executing a search warrant at a residence. Aerial maps are helpful for viewing the location of exiting doors, escape routes, stairs, and various obstructions. The rapidly growing availability of the Street View option now gives us more data.

If the Street View option is available, Google has been in the area and captured a photo of the location from the street. Clicking this will open a 360 degree view from the street. This view can be zoomed in by double-clicking and panned left and right by dragging the mouse while holding a left click. Double-clicking an area of the street will refresh the window to the view from that location.

In 2014, Google made several changes to their online maps service. They introduced a new feature with Street View that made the default view full screen. This eliminates the Google search bar, side menu, browser menus, and any other items from blocking a larger view. Additionally, Google streamlined the entire Maps experience to make everything easier to use. Unfortunately, they also eliminated many of the features that were available to researchers and investigators. Fortunately, you can re-enable these missing features with an easy fix.

While viewing any map, satellite image, or street view, click on the small question mark in the lower right portion of the map. This will load a menu that will allow you to select "Return to classic Google Maps". This option will present the exact view and options that were available before the most recent changes. Figure 4.02 displays this option. The following techniques will only work while in this classic view.

In the original Google Satellite or Map view, there are more search options than the current design. Clicking the down arrow in the box directly below the "Satellite" or "Map" option will generate a drop-down list. Clicking the down arrow again will show the entire list of options. Some of these options are helpful for a traveler, but not necessarily great for intelligence collection.

The "Photos" option will display user submitted photos that have been geo-tagged to a location. These are often taken by amateur photographers to document a landmark. The "Webcams" option will identify public webcams that can be viewed live. These are often provided by television stations, local government, and tourism agencies.

Figure 4.01: A Google Maps address result with a Street View option.

Figure 4.02: A Google Maps "Return to classic Google Maps" option.

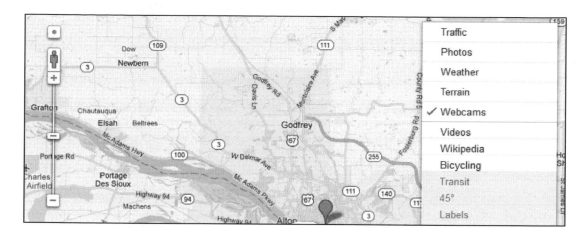

Figure 4.03: The extended options menu in classic Google Maps.

Original Google Maps Labs

If you want to be a true power user of Google Maps, visit the Maps Labs options and enable some advanced features. This area can be accessed by clicking on the tiny "Maps Labs" link in the lower left portion of any Google Maps page. This will present several new options for your mapping experience. I will outline the tools that I have found beneficial to online research. Each tool will have an option to "enable" or "disable" to the right of the option. I recommend only enabling those that you think will be helpful.

Distance Measurement Tool: This has been a valuable asset for law enforcement investigators. Google natively allows you to measure the distance between two locations, but it measures according to the route taken. It does not provide a true measurement of point A to point B. This tool corrects that. Once enabled, you will now see a small ruler in the lower left of the map view. Clicking this ruler will show the measurement options and allow you to click on any point of the map. A second click on a different location will draw a straight line and display the result in either metric or English units. Figure 4.04 displays a typical result that identifies the distance between two houses.

Show Me Here!: This feature adds an option to the context menu that lets you zoom directly to the maximum zoom level at the point under the cursor. You can now right-click any area at any time, choose the "Show me here" option, and the map will zoom into the closest view of that location. This prevents you from zooming in one level at a time looking for the closest option.

Drag 'n Zoom: With this feature enabled, you can now draw a box of any size around an area, and Google will zoom to the level that fits that area into your window. You must first click on the square icon of a magnifying glass directly below the zoom out option on the upper left of any map.

LatLng Tooltip: If you prefer to know the GPS coordinates of a location instead of the address, this feature will add instant availability of this data. You can now press the "Shift" button on your keyboard at any time, and a small notification will appear to identify the coordinates of wherever your mouse is hovering. If you continue to hold this key, it will change the coordinates as you move the mouse. Figure 4.05 displays a typical result.

LatLng Marker: This feature adds an option to the context menu that lets you drop a mini marker showing the GPS coordinates of the position that the cursor was pointing at when the context menu was evoked. Figure 4.06 displays the new option on the right-click menu next to the result of a marker placed with this option.

Smart Zoom: If you have ever zoomed into a satellite view of a location to be informed that imagery did not exist at that level, you may wonder why you were allowed to zoom in that far at all. This feature disables the possibility to go too far. It will stop you at the closest satellite view available for the area you are searching.

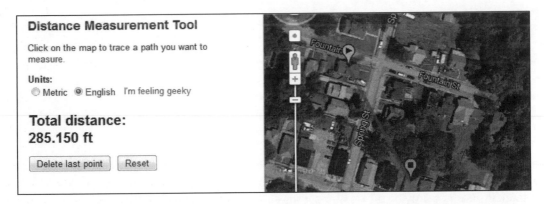

Figure 4.04: The Google Maps Distance Measurement Tool in use.

Figure 4.05: The Google Maps LatLng Tooltip in use.

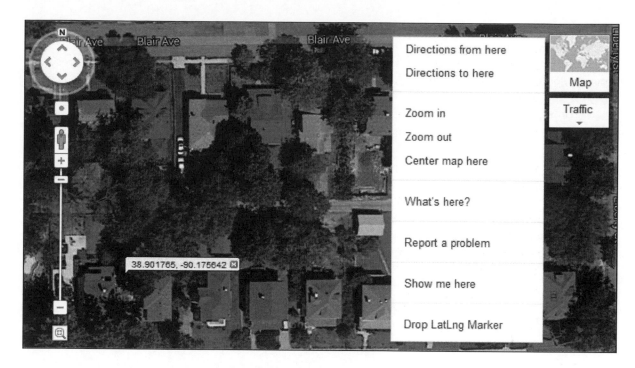

Figure 4.06: The Google Maps LatLng Marker in use.

When you are ready to return to the standard current Google Maps service, simply click on the Google logo in the upper left corner of any Google Maps page. It will return you to a live default version. Google continuously makes changes to this product. A thorough OSINT researcher will use both versions in order to never miss a feature. The current default Google Maps layout will allow you to measure distance without reverting to the classic view. Simply right-click on any area and choose "Measure distance". A small dot will appear and you can select the end point. You can then drag and drop the start and end points as necessary.

Real world application: In 2009, Phillip Garrido was arrested for the kidnapping of Jaycee Lee Dugard in 1991. Several reports stated that the local police were called on numerous occasions to investigate the happenings at his residence, but took no action. A quick look at Google Maps would have shown a backyard full of blue tarps acting as several temporary shelters. Checking out the Street View option would show a subject, which appeared to be Garrido, leaving the residence in a grey van, following the Google Maps vehicle around several blocks. While this doesn't prove anything, or even supply any *vital* evidence, it could have made for some decent intelligence. At the time of this writing, these images were still available on Google Maps. These findings originally appeared on BoingBoing, and are archived at boingboing.net/2009/08/31/did-google-street-vi.html.

Bing Maps (bing.com/maps)

Similar to Google Maps, Bing offers a map view, satellite view, and street view. Bing does offer something that is not available in Google. Bing possesses a "Bird's Eye View" which displays four distinct angled views of a location. This can display signs, advertisements, pedestrians, and other objects with clear visibility. While Google is rolling out their own 45 degree satellite view, the areas covered are minimal at the time of this writing.

In my experience, the satellite imagery provided by Bing is often superior in quality compared to Google Maps. A side by side comparison can be seen in a few pages with the Dual Maps website. In Figure 4.07, a building is displayed with the "Bird's Eye" view enabled. By default, this view will always be of the south side of a location, looking north. The curved arrows in the upper right corner allow you to navigate to three additional views which display the west, north, and east sides of the location. This example displays the north and south views of the same building.

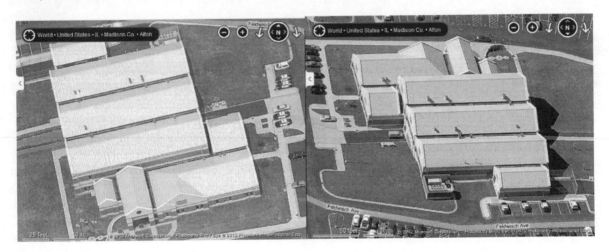

Figure 4.07: Two directional views of a location on Bing Maps.

Dual Maps (data.mashedworld.com/dualmaps/map.htm)

This website provides a satellite view of a location on both Google Maps and Bing Maps simultaneously. The Google view on the left will also contain a search field in the lower left corner. Searching an address in this field will center both maps on the same address. This will provide a comparison of the satellite images stored on each service. This can quickly identify the service that has the better imagery. Figure 4.08 displays one location as seen by Google and Bing.

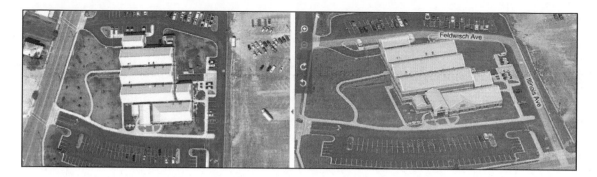

Figure 4.08: A Dual Maps view of a single location.

Custom Maps Tool (inteltechniques.com/OSINT/maps.html)

If the Dual Maps option does not satisfy your craving for multiple satellite views of a single location, my online custom map tool may be what you need. This web page allows you to enter a single set of GPS coordinates and it will display the satellite imagery from multiple providers. It currently fetches images from Google Satellite, Bing Satellite, Bing Bird's Eye, Google Street View, Bing Street View, Mapquest Satellite View, and Google Earth Interactive View. The figures on the following pages display the multiple results from various providers when searching Wrigley Field in Chicago.

GPS Identification

Previously, you read how GPS coordinates could be used to find Twitter posts from that specific area. There are several ways to determine the GPS coordinates of a physical address. One of the easiest is to use Google Maps. Search any address on the main site. Right-click on the marker that identifies the address searched and click on "What's here?". In the search box that you used to search the address, the address will change from the physical address to the GPS coordinates of the address.

Alternatively, you can use GPS Visualizer (gpsvisualizer.com/geocode). This site will allow you to type in any address and will provide the GPS coordinates for the address. By default, this site uses the same Google resource as the example above.

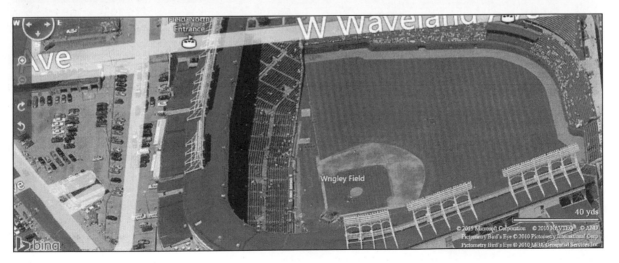

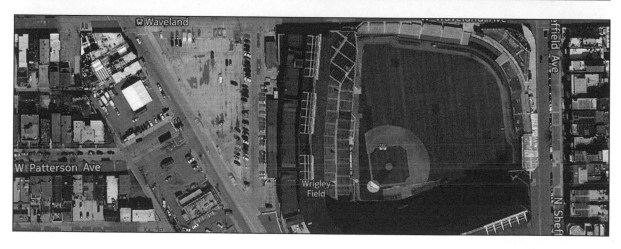

Nokia Maps (here.com)

Another option for an alternative satellite view of a location is Nokia Maps. The areas that display a detailed view are limited, but worth investigating. If you are searching for imagery of a large city, the 3D view displays great detail of the buildings and structures. This imagery is independent of Google and Bing data.

Flash Earth (flashearth.com)

This multiple satellite imagery website presents views from NASA, Bing, Nokia, ArcGIS, and Mapquest. Occasionally, the ArcGIS data is more recent than Google or Bing. The smooth interface will easily provide a comparison of the available images for any location.

Historic Imagery

Researching different satellite views of a single location can have many benefits. These views are all of the current content stored within each service. However, these mapping services continuously update their offerings and usually present the most recent option. You may want to view the previous content that was available before an image was updated. Chapter Fifteen will explain software options for retrieving older images. Additionally, some web based services also offer alternative views.

Google Street View (maps.google.com)

In late 2014, Google began offering the ability to view all stored street view images for any single location. This option is available within the standard street view layout within the search area of the upper left corner. Click on the small clock in order to launch a popup window. This new view will allow you to move a slider bar which will present different views. The month and year of image capture will also appear for documentation. Figure 4.09 displays this method which presents an additional view of a parking lot. This can often reveal additional vehicles or missing structures associated with an investigation.

Historic Aerials (historicaerials.com)

If you need satellite imagery from several years prior, you can visit Historic Aerials. The quality will often be poor, especially as you view imagery from previous decades. After you enter an address, you will be presented all available options on the left side of the page. Figure 4.10 displays several results of the same location over a twenty year period. These views will be unique from all of the previously mentioned services.

Figure 4.09: A Google Maps historical street view.

Figure 4.10: Multiple views of a location through Historic Aerials.

Real world application: Combining several satellite views can provide much information about a target's residence. Before the execution of a search warrant, it is beneficial for police to collect as much map information as possible. This will give updated views of a drawn map, satellite imagery directly above the house, four angled views from the sky, and a complete view of the house and neighboring houses from the street, including vehicles. This can be used to identify potential threats such as physical barriers and fencing, escape routes, and video surveillance systems in place.

Satellite Imagery Update Notification (followyourworld.appspot.com)

It is safe to assume that Google will continue to generate new satellite views of earth as time passes. If you have a specific location of interest, you may want to be notified the moment that a new image is available for view. This Google service does exactly that. After you log into your Google account, you are allowed to select a specific location by address, GPS, or landmark. Google will now email you each time the satellite imagery for this location is updated. This could be useful for monitoring the remote location of a current investigation.

Street View Hyperlapse (http://hyperlapse.tllabs.io)

This new service combines software from four sources and creates the ability to make "videos" from Google's Street View data. Basically, it collects the Street View images from any chosen location and combines them into a playable format. It has the appearance of streaming video, but it is only displaying the views in order. The website lacks many functions and many have complained that the speed of the images is too fast. I have found the following to be the best practice for this service.

Navigate to the website and you will be presented with a random demonstration of the capabilities of the product. Click "Cancel" while the demo is loading and you will be presented with a search field. You can provide an address, GPS coordinates or landmark name. You will see a Google Maps view of the desired location. You can then move both points A and B to any start and end point of the project that you want created. The crosshairs can be moved to identify the direction that you want the street view to be presented. Short distances on a straight road work best.

I have used this to recreate the street view of a suspect residence prior to a search warrant. It provides many additional angles of a building from several points. Pressing the space bar during the interactive display will pause on a single frame. This allows for additional analysis of each view.

Panoramio (panoramio.com)

Panoramio is more of a photo site than a mapping site, but the mapping of the photos is the focus. This service allows users to upload digital photographs that have been geo-tagged to identify the location where they were taken. The images are then searched according to the location instead keywords. Searching locations that are not tourist attractions often reveal personal images that can provide intelligence about the area. The default view displays popular images that are available in Google Earth software. Selecting the option to "Also show photos not selected for Google Earth" will add to the displayed images. The single search field in the upper right portion will allow search by city and state, zip code, or entire address.

Mapify (mapify.us)

Mapify states that it answers the question of "What is happening near a location?". This interactive map presents markers that identify upcoming events being broadcasted by the social networks Facebook, Eventbrite, Meetup and Upcoming. It extracts the data from the content provider and assigns the location based on the announcement address. This can identify upcoming protests, gatherings, flash mobs, and parties.

Scribble Maps (scribblemaps.com)

The default view of mapping services such as Google and Bing may be enough for your situation. Occasionally, you may want to modify or customize a map for your needs. Law enforcement may want to create a map to be used in a court case, a private investigator may want to customize a map to present to a client, or a security director may want to use this service to document the inappropriate Tweets that were found during the previous instructions. Scribble Maps offers one of the easiest ways to create your own map and add any type of visual aids to the final product.

The default view of your new map at Scribble Maps will display the entire world and a menu of basic options. I close this menu by clicking the small "x" in the upper right corner. You can then manually zoom into an area of interest or type in an address in the location bar at the top of the map. This will present you with a manageable area of the map. The lower right corner will allow you to switch from a traditional map view to a satellite or hybrid view.

The menu at the top of the map will allow you to add shapes, lines, text, and images to your map. Practicing on this map can never be replaced with any instruction printed here. Mastering the basics of this application will make occasional use of it easy. Figure 4.11 displays a quick sample map that shows a title, a line, a marker, and graphics. The menu can be seen in the upper left portion. When finished, the "Menu" button will present many options to print, save, or export your map. Some advanced features require you to register for a free account.

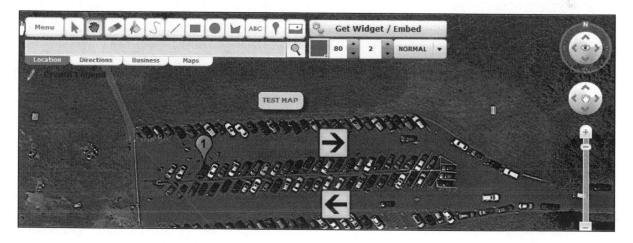

Figure 4.11: A basic custom map created with Scribble Maps.

Chapter Five

People Search Engines

Just as Google and Bing specialize in searching content on the internet, people search engines specialize only in finding content about a particular person. Many of these sites utilize search engines such as Google and Bing to help compile the data, and then present a summary style interface that is easy to consume. The sites listed here each have their own strengths and weaknesses. Standard searches are free on all of them; however, each site generates revenue in some form. Usually, this is by displaying advertisements that often appear to be a report function within the site. I do not recommend purchasing any of the premium paid services until all free options have been exhausted.

That's Them (thatsthem.com)

In late 2014, a new website quietly entered the crowded scene of people search services. On the surface, it was just another service that aggregated publicly available information. However, a closer examination revealed That's Them to contain information that is not available anywhere else for free. This service has many options, and most will be discussed in this book. For the purposes of this chapter, I will focus on the "Name and Address" search option in the top menu of the website. Entering a full name with city and state is preferred. However, a first and last name without location will also display results.

That's Them does not offer a premium service. Everything is included for free. The service requests that you consider a donation in order to prevent fees in the future. A search of "Leo Laporte" in California provided the result in Figure 5.01. It clearly displays the person's age range, month of birth, cell phone number, landline number, full address, religion, and financial details. I searched my own name to test the accuracy of the results. My profile correctly identified similar information as well as the exact VIN number of my current vehicle. This type of data is impressive without any fees. Note that the options to purchase additional information are advertisements from third party companies.

Figure 5.01: A That's Them search result on a name.

Pipl (pipl.com)

This site claims to be "the most comprehensive people search on the web". Putting a first and last name along with a city and state associated with the target will generate a new page full of information. If you are not sure of the location of your target, just enter a first and last name. The first group of data you will see is the "Suggested searches" which identify subjects matching your search along with location information for each. If any appear to reside in a general area that is near your target's last known location, you should investigate the link. The next group will have icons of images from various social networks. Each of these will link to the original image location, which will be a part of a user's social network profile.

The "Profiles" section will present links to social network profiles that belong to users with the name that you searched. Common networks include Twitter, Facebook, Meetup, MySpace, and YouTube. The next section will include web page hits on your target name. These are usually fairly accurate to the target name supplied. These tend to place a stronger emphasis on personal websites and blogs than general pages that a standard search engine might provide.

Ultimately, with Pipl, you want to identify your actual target through a Pipl profile. To do this, you need to filter through the results you receive. In Figure 5.02, I conducted a search for a name without a location. The "Suggested Results" provided the location information for a target. This result links to a Pipl profile with a lot of information about the target.

The left column of this page provides suggested filters for location and age. This will help filter the results in the case of a common name. Once you locate the Pipl profile for your target, it will display all available social network associations that Pipl has on the target. This will include more photo icons that link to the host profile. Many of the links on this page will be "Sponsored" links that will direct you to an advertiser's website. Fortunately, Pipl marks all of these links with the word "Sponsored". I stay away from these traps. Often the link will provide enough visual information that clicking for further data is unnecessary. Sometimes an entire telephone number, age, or family member's name is visible without visiting the sponsored site. The "School & Classmates" section, a sponsored link, will always identify the school attended, years attended, and location of the school in the text of the link without actually clicking on the link.

The "Professional & Businesses" section will usually be limited to LinkedIn profiles. This social network was explained in the previous chapter. The rest of the page will vary depending on how much information is available about your target. Pipl will never present all data that is out there about your target. It is simply a worthwhile stop to begin identifying related content. The information obtained here can be valuable for future searches. Pipl also allows searching through their API, which will be explained later in this book.

In mid-2013, I noticed that Pipl began replacing some valid and useful links with advertisements and sponsored links that provide no valuable information about the target. This has been the trend with most free people search websites including those that follow. Be cautious not to fall into any advertisement traps that try to trick you into purchasing the content.

Figure 5.02: A Pipl search result from a real name.

PeepDB (peepdb.com)

This website provides a unique search interface. The main page offers a search field that does nothing more than a standard Google search. You should avoid it and look below to find the real search options. There will be 50 links representing each state in America. Select the state of your target and a new page with all 26 letters of the alphabet will appear. Select the first letter of your target's last name and another page will load. Select the first two letters of your target's last name and then finally the first three letters of your target's last name. This will finally present you with a list of everyone in that state that meets the criteria that you just selected. Either scroll through to find your subject or use the search option in the lower left portion of the page.

If your target has a common name, you may have several possibilities to go through. Clicking each person's link will open a new page with redacted information. Figure 5.03 displays a typical result. Clicking the "Get the uncensored listing" link will ask you to complete a Captcha to prove you are human and will then display the entire listing without any redactions.

Figure 5.03: A censored result on PeepDB.

KGB People (kgbpeople.com)

Another free people search engine is KGB People. This site tends to provide better international results for those outside of the United States. The results will appear in one of four tabs. The first tab, Social Networks, will search the popular sites such as Twitter, Facebook, and MySpace. To see the results, you must expand each section by either clicking the title or the "+" icon on the right of each title. These results will most likely have already been identified through Pipl or 123 People. The second tab, Search Engines, consists of Bing search results and sponsored advertisement pages. This will rarely be helpful. The third tab, Photo and Video, will link to Flickr and YouTube content. Again, this is a repeat of what the other searches have already provided. The fourth tab is where we see something new. A "Related persons" section will display subjects that may be related to the target. Each of these results will link to the KGB People profile of that person. Browsing the profile may validate the relationship to the target. The next section, Facts, contains brief statements about the target obtained from websites, blogs and social networks mentioning the target. These can provide instant details about the target that would otherwise involve analysis of several sites to obtain.

Zaba Search (zabasearch.com)

This site appears to have several search options at first glance. Unfortunately, all but one will forward to an Intelius site, which will require a fee. Though there is one very specific free option on this page. Providing any real name and state of residence will provide a results page with full name, date of birth, address and phone number. In my experience, this often includes unlisted telephone numbers and addresses. Clicking on practically anything else on this results page will take you to a sponsored link. When I use this resource, I only rely on the information obtained on the first result page.

Intelius (intelius.com)

Intelius is a premium service that provides reports about people for a fee. Most of the information is from public sources, but some of it appears to come from private databases. Searching for any information on the main website will always link you to a menu of pricing options. The information will never be displayed for free. However, the page that lists the report options does possess some interesting information. Figure 5.04 displays a typical result. This free preview identifies an exact age, possible aliases, cities lived in, previous employers, universities attended, and relatives. If the subject is married, this will usually identify the spouse. In most situations, it will identify the maiden name of the person's wife. Anything that you do not see on this main screen, you must pay for. I never recommend purchasing any of this data. Users are usually disappointed with the results.

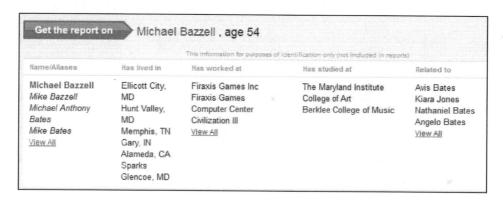

Figure 5.04: An Intelius page that provides some free content.

Radaris (radaris.com)

This service has many similarities to Intelius. However, the data set is unique. The business model is to entice you into purchasing an entire profile. I only use the service for the limited free content available in the preview. After searching a name, select the most appropriate target and choose "Full Profile" in the lower right of the result. This will open the full view of any free information. This will often include the target's middle name, age, current address, previous address, landline telephone number, and links to social networks. The Background Check options will forward you to a third party premium access website that I do not recommend.

Spokeo (spokeo.com)

Spokeo is probably the most well-known of all of the people search engines. There are two very distinct versions of this service, free and premium. The premium service will provide a large amount of accurate data, but at a cost of approximately $15 for three months. The free version provides an interface that is easy to navigate. The results from a target name search will be presented after choosing a state and city. Only the states and cities where the target name has a presence will be shown. The final choice will present partial addresses to help identify the actual target of interest. Choosing this target will display a profile with various information. Within this data will be several attempts to encourage you to purchase a premium account. Basically, anything that you do not see within this profile will cost you money. Any links from the profile will present a membership plan with pricing. There is a lot of data to still obtain for free.

The free version will identify an age range of the target, but not an exact year or birth date. Usually, the last known address and phone number are partially excluded to prevent you from seeing the full information. Though knowing a street name, which is usually visible, can be great start. The "Family Tree" section will include first names and approximate age ranges of immediate family members. I have found any further information from these free profiles to be completely inaccurate and not reliable.

Reverse Genie People (reversegenie.com/people.php)

In early 2015, Reverse Genie added a people search to their existing email and phone search service. While it is not the strongest person search option available, it occasionally offers data the others do not. The majority of the results will simply link to a Facebook profile. Viewing the "full report" will lead you to a premium service requesting payment. I plan to monitor this service and watch for new free features.

Lullar (com.lullar.com)

Lullar will search by email address, user name, or real name. The search excels with an email address or screen name, but I do not recommend the real name option for reliable results. Lullar takes a different approach with the search results. When conducting the search, the results page appears almost immediately. This is because Lullar is not actually conducting any real analysis of user profiles. The results displayed are only the links that would open the page of the target's profile based on the address, or URL, of that profile. For example, if I search for the user name JohnDoe911, Lullar does not check any sites to see if this user has a profile. Instead, it generates the appropriate links that would function for that user name. In the case of Twitter, it creates a link to twitter.com/#!/search/JohnDoe911. This link will be presented whether there is a profile at this address or not. On the down side, you will often be presented with links that do not function. On a positive note, you may get links that do function and are so new that other engines have not indexed them yet.

I often use this service in two scenarios. When I have a partial or questionable user name, I will search it through Lullar and see what the profiles look like. This can tell me right away if I am researching the wrong target name. The other scenario is when I encounter an email address or user name that may have alternatives or aliases. If my target has a user name of TheJohnDoe2, I am curious if the user also possesses TheJohnDoe3, TheJohnDoe4, or maybe TheJohnDoe. Many times, users will need secondary user names and will choose names very similar to their primary names. Lullar will show me what content appears on these profiles without regard to the real name of the user of the accounts. This may lead to unwanted profiles, but has been very successful at locating previously unknown profiles of a target. Lullar inserts ads on their page, as seen in Figure 5.05, however these are usually obvious and easy to avoid.

Figure 5.05: A Lullar results page with assumed links for content.

Yasni (yasni.com)

On the surface, Yasni appears to be another standard people search engine. Much of the content received will be duplicate data, but there are a few areas that Yasni works differently. The home page will give three search options (Figure 5.06). For most OSINT purposes, the last option is the desired search. It will accept a real name or user name and forward you to a results page. Real name search will present a large number of links associated with your target's name. As with other engines, many of these results will be about a person other than your target. The first box on the results page will include a "lives/works in" option that will identify the cities of the users identified with the search. Clicking on a location that looks appropriate for your target will load a new results page that will provide all search results about your specific target. These links could all be found using search engines and operators, but this will take the hassle out of that technique. Though to obtain complete results on a target, you should still visit a standard search engine. This Yasni page will identify news articles, websites and social networks related to your target.

By default, the search is conducted internationally. Yasni is a German site and searching outside of the United States is one of the strengths of the service. The search bar includes an option to filter the results by specific countries, but the United States is not listed as an option. If you have a target that lives in another country, Yasni is a great tool.

Figure 5.06: The Yasni main search options.

Zoom Info (zoominfo.com)

Zoom Info specializes in providing work and career information about a target. The results of a search are presented in a user profile which focuses on employment history, membership and affiliations, and education. It appears to extract data from several online sources to compile enough information to determine a subject's current and previous employers. These profiles are generated automatically by scraping personal websites and blogs. In my profile, the majority of the content appears to have been obtained from my personal website, a news website, a law blog, and my employer's website. While not everything is accurate, the profile creates a fairly complete view of my employment history.

In the case of a common name with hundreds of results, the search menu on the left of the page will help filter through the profiles (Figure 5.07). Supplying the target's job title, company name, or location should present more manageable options. These filters should only be applied one at a time to avoid filtering out wanted information. Zoom Info can be a valuable resource when conducting background checks. Many applicants will omit from an application any previous employers that would provide a negative review of the applicant. This site can identify employers that should be contacted. Highlighting any business name in the employment history menu will present a popup window containing business information including contact information, revenue, amount of employees, and links to the company's social network sites.

Clicking on the "Companies" tab will allow manual searches for business information. This includes websites without a physical presence. These profiles will include links to related companies which also identifies subsidiaries and acquisitions. This can be a good technique for an investigator researching assets of businesses. Similar to most search sites, some of the advanced data will require a paid account.

Figure 5.07: A Zoom Info report with name and location filters.

Custom People Search Tools (inteltechniques.com/osint/person.html)

The abundance of free person search tools can get overwhelming. They each have strengths and weaknesses, and none of them are consistent on accurate results. In years past, I would manually visit each site and enter my target information. This would usually result in small, yet valuable, pieces of information from each service. Today, I use a custom search tool that I created to search all possible sites simultaneously. This free tool will not locate any information that you could not find manually. Instead, it attempts to save you time by automating the process. Figure 5.08 displays the current state of this website.

You can either enter the first and last name of your target within the search fields of each service, or enter this information only once at the final set of search fields. This latter option will launch several new tabs and conduct your search across each service. Note that the Chrome browser tends to block this type of activity. I recommend Firefox. The tool currently searches Pipl, That's Them, Spokeo, Reverse Genie, KGB People, Yasni, Radaris, Zaba Search, Intelius, PeekYou, WebMii, LinkedIn, and Twitter.

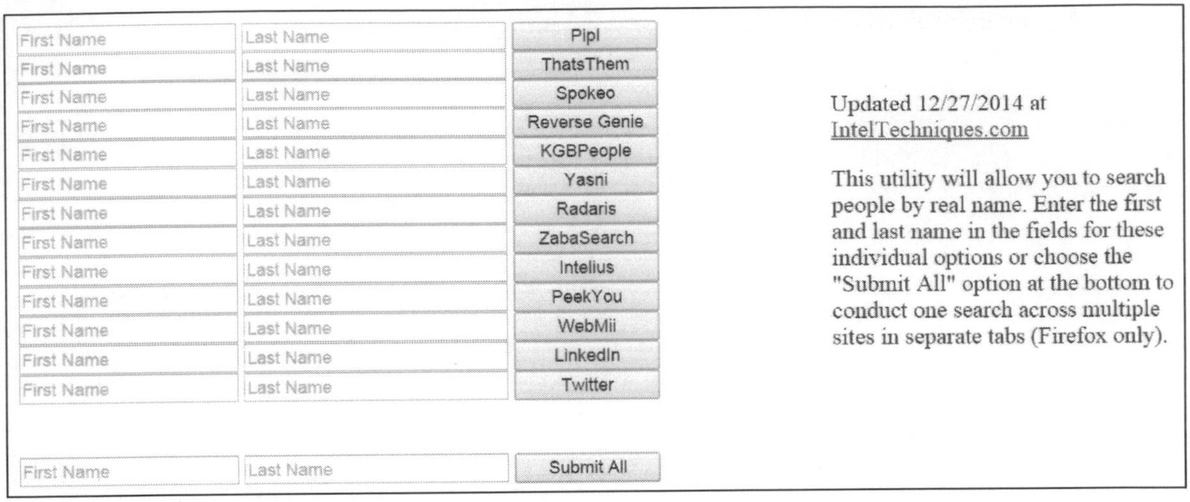

First Name	Last Name	Pipl
First Name	Last Name	ThatsThem
First Name	Last Name	Spokeo
First Name	Last Name	Reverse Genie
First Name	Last Name	KGBPeople
First Name	Last Name	Yasni
First Name	Last Name	Radaris
First Name	Last Name	ZabaSearch
First Name	Last Name	Intelius
First Name	Last Name	PeekYou
First Name	Last Name	WebMii
First Name	Last Name	LinkedIn
First Name	Last Name	Twitter
First Name	Last Name	Submit All

Updated 12/27/2014 at IntelTechniques.com

This utility will allow you to search people by real name. Enter the first and last name in the fields for these individual options or choose the "Submit All" option at the bottom to conduct one search across multiple sites in separate tabs (Firefox only).

Figure 5.08: The custom people search tool available at IntelTechniques.com.

Putting It All Together

At first glance, the results obtained from free people search engines may appear redundant. There are definitely areas that repeat the same information. However, this can be beneficial for verification and building confidence in the results. Occasionally, what appears to be redundant might present further details. This can include a third report of an identical address that now includes an apartment number. In order to display the ways that each service can present unique details about your target, I conducted a query and documented all of the results. I chose the target of Rocco Castoro. He is the reporter that accidently leaked the location of John McAfee during an interview by posting an iPhone photo with GPS included. I began my search with only his first and last name. The following details were identified which include the services that reported the information.

Full Name: Rocco Carl Castoro (Pipl, Intelius)
Age: 33 (Pipl, Intelius, Radaris)
DOB: 01/23/1982 (Yasni, WebMii)
Current Address: XXXXX Beadel St, Apt 1f, Brooklyn, NY (PeekYou, Spokeo)
Current Address: 11211 XXXXXX St, Brooklyn, NY (Yasni, Intelius)
Telephone Numbers: 352-362-7905, 352-335-5305 (Pipl, Radaris)
Previous Address: 3640 Beneva Oaks Blvd, Sarasota, FL (Radaris, Pipl)
Previous Telephone: 941-922-3117 (Pipl, That's Them)
Mother: Karen Castoro-56 (Intelius, Pipl)
Father: John Castoro-57 (Intelius, Pipl)
Email Addresses: rocco.castoro@asaprent.com, rocco.castoro@vice.com (Yasni)
High School: Cardinal Mooney High School, Sarasota, FL, 1996-2000 (Yasni)

College: University of Florida (LinkedIn)
Employer: Vice Media (Intelius, Yasni)
Facebook Profile: rcastoro (Yasni)
Twitter Profile: rocco_castoro (PeekYou)
YouTube Channel: UCn8zNIfYAQNdrFRrr8oibKw (KGB People)
Languages Spoken: Italian (That's Them)
Religion: Catholic (That's Them)

This summary was achieved in less than five minutes. Imagine what you could find if you took the time to continue analyzing social media links. The results above were all obtained from public data. These people search engines can assist greatly by aggregating this information.

How Many Of Me (howmanyofme.com)

This minimalistic site provides a simple interface to find out how many people exist that have a specific name. In my case, there are 16 people in the United States with my name. This is obtained from census data and can help determine how effective a targeted search will be. For example, if your target has a very unique name, you may still get numerous results to links of social network sites. In order to determine the likelihood that all of these profiles apply to the target, How Many Of Me can tell you whether your target is the only person that has that name. This site provides no intelligence about someone with a common name.

Classmates (classmates.com)

Classmates is a very underrated resource for the internet searcher. Unfortunately, you must create a free account to take advantage of the worthy information inside the site. This free account can contain fictitious information and it is necessary to complete a profile on the site to access the premium features. After you are logged in, you can search by first and last name. If you know the school that was attended, the results will be much more accurate. This should provide the school attended as well as the years the target attended the school. My new interest in this site is due to the availability of scanned yearbooks. The collection is far from complete, but there are a surprising number of complete yearbooks available to browse. This includes small towns and large cities. In Figure 5.09, the classmates embedded viewer displays a page from the 1946 Alton High School yearbook. Analyzing this content can be very time consuming, as the yearbook must be manually browsed one page at a time. The information obtained should be unique from any internet search previously conducted.

Mocavo (mocavo.com)

If Classmates does not have the yearbook that you are looking for, Mocavo is the next stop. This collection of yearbooks grows daily, and the scan quality is superb. Searching on the website can be difficult though. Every search will be halted while you are presented a popup that encourages you to purchase a premium account, though this is not mandatory. On the bottom left portion of this window is a link that will allow you to create a free basic account. After creation, you will need to supply your new credentials every time you want to search the site. If you want to avoid this requirement, and only want to browse the yearbooks, this can be avoided by supplying a direct address. If you enter the following address into your browser, you will be forwarded to the yearbook portion of the website that will allow you to filter and browse a specific publication:

http://www.mocavo.com/yearbooks

Avoid the first search field, as this will only present the requirement to create an account. Instead, scroll further down to the area for browsing yearbooks. You can either use the small search field on the right or choose categories to identify a specific location. Figure 5.10 displays an example of a search that would identify any yearbooks with a keyword of "Woodrow" in the Chicago, Illinois area. The first link visible in this example opens the yearbook from the 1936 Woodrow Wilson Junior College. Searching within the search field will bring back the mandatory account requirement, but clicking the link to the yearbook will allow you to browse the entire publication without membership. Registering for the free account will disable most of the annoyances and allow searching from any field.

Figure 5.09: A scanned yearbook embedded into Classmates' site.

Region	State/Province	City		Search	
United State ▼	IL ▼	Chicago ▼	Filter	woodrow	🔍

Title	Collection
Woodrow Wilson Junior College (1936), Chicago, IL	Yearbooks

Figure 5.10: A Mocavo yearbook collection filter.

Indeed (indeed.com)

Resume searching was mentioned earlier in Chapter One. Those methods will identify many documents, especially if the word "resume" is inside the file or file name. Indeed has a powerful collection of resume data. Because the term "resume" is not present in any of the content pages, you will likely not obtain this data during your standard searches. Entering your target name on Indeed under the "Find Resumes" option may present new results. Contact information is usually redacted. However, detailed work experience, education, and location are commonly present.

Ripoff Report (ripoffreport.com)

If your target conducts any type of business with the public, he or she will likely upset someone at some point. If your target regularly provides bad service or intentionally commits fraud within the business, there are likely many upset victims. Ripoff Report is user-submitted collection of complaints about businesses and individuals. I have had numerous investigations of shady people that were benefitted from the information provided by previously unknown victims.

Email Searching

Searching by a person's real name can be frustrating. If you target has a common name, it is easy to get lost in the results. Even a fairly unique name like mine produces almost 20 people's addresses, profiles, and telephone numbers. If your target is named John Smith, you have a problem. This is why I always prefer to search by email address when available. If you have your target's email address or specific user name, you will achieve much better results at a faster pace. There may be thousands of John Wilson's, but there would be only one john.wilson.77089@yahoo.com. Searching this address within quotation marks on the major search engines and Facebook may provide new intelligence. If you receive absolutely no results in your searches, you may want to validate the email address.

Mail Tester (mailtester.com)

When searching for a target by email address, you may find yourself receiving absolutely no results. If this happens, you need to consider whether the email address that you are searching is valid. It is possible that the address was copied incorrectly or is missing a character. There are several websites online that claim to be able to verify the validity of an email address. Most of these do not work with many of the free web based email providers. One service that stands out from this crowd is Mail Tester. The sole purpose of the service is to identify if an email address is active and currently being used. After entering an email address, you will be presented with the results page that will identify if the address is valid or invalid. An invalid notification means that the email address you are researching simply does not exist. Figure 5.11 displays a result on an email address that is valid and can receive emails.

Verify Email (verify-email.org)

If Mail Tester is not functioning, or giving you inaccurate results, you may want to try Verify Email. This is a similar service that tries to identify if an email address is valid. The results should be identical to Mail Tester. This service could be used to verify Mail Tester's response to a query.

Peep Mail (samy.pl/peepmail)

Peep Mail takes the technique used in the previous two examples to confirm valid email addresses and attempts to discover new addresses. It asks for two pieces of information. The full name is the real name of your target. The domain field should be the internet domain of the business where your target is employed. If your target's name is Jarrett Ford, and he works at the Alton, Illinois police department, the following would be the appropriate search information.

Full Name: Ford Jarrett
Domain: altonpolice.com

Placing the last name first usually offers better results. If you do not know the domain of the business, this domain can usually be found with an internet search. The first search result of "Alton, Illinois police department" on Google identifies "altonpolice.com" as the domain. A Peep Mail search with this information identifies the subject's email address as ford@altonpolice.com. You can now conduct new searches on this email address to identify associated content and social networks.

Since the creation of Peep Mail, several additional services have replicated this process. Each has their own look and rules of function. Of the free services, I have had success with the following.

Find Any Email (findanyemail.net)
Voila Norbert (voilanorbert.com)

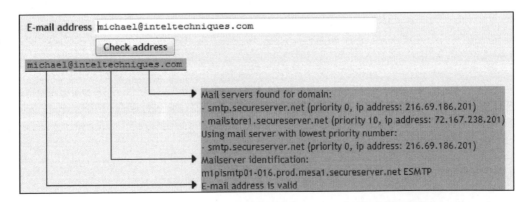

Figure 5.11: A Mail Tester results page for a valid email address.

Email Assumptions

You may not know your target's email address. You may know about one address, but not others. Either way, it can be productive to make assumptions of possible email addresses and use the verifiers to see if they exist. For example, if your target's name is Jay Stewart and he has an email address of jayspice2003@yahoo.com, I will conduct additional searches for the addresses of jayspice2003 @gmail.com, jayspice2003@hotmail.com, and jayspice2003@live.com. These would only be a start. If I had no email address at all for him, but I knew that he worked at the Illinois Medical District Commission, I may start searching for the following email addresses.

jstewart@medicaldistrict.org
jay.stewart@medicaldistrict.org
j.stewart@medicaldistrict.org
stewartj@medicaldistrict.org

These are merely assumptions of potential addresses. Most, if not all, of them do not exist and will provide nothing for me. However, if I do identify an existing address, I now have a new piece of the puzzle to search. Creating a list of possible addresses can be time consuming. I have an online spreadsheet that should make this easier. The following shortened link will open a Google document that will assist with our task.

http://goo.gl/V2xRgP

Figure 5.14 displays a completed search using the same information mentioned earlier. You should provide the first, middle, and last name, if known. The "domain" should be the web domain used by the business where the individual is employed. If your target works at Microsoft, it would be microsoft.com. If she works at Caterpillar, it would be cat.com. As soon as you complete this information, the spreadsheet will generate 48 potential email addresses that are ready for search or validation. This could be completed manually as discussed in the previous chapters, or with the help of applications as discussed in Chapter Fifteen. Searching all of these addresses may seem like a lot of work, and it is. However, if it is the only hurdle in taking your investigation to the next level, it is worth every minute.

At the beginning of this section, I mentioned guessing at personal email accounts such as Gmail and Yahoo. If you already know your target's user name, such as a Twitter handle, you should create a list of potential email addresses. I have also created a Google spreadsheet for this purpose. This document is located at the following shortened address.

http://goo.gl/s5AXRS

Figure 5.12 displays this document with the example data used earlier. The first entry cell is for the user name of your target. This will generate a list of potential email addresses using these providers.

Hotmail	Me	GMX
Gmail	Mail	Facebook
Yahoo	Outlook	Zoho
Live	AOL	Lavabit
Hushmail	AIM	iCloud.com

The final link below the results is a custom Google search that will conduct a query based on these potential email addresses. The search will also place each address in quotation marks for exact identification. Figure 5.13 displays a result when I searched for the user name of "lorangb". The 38 results identified "lorangb@gmail.com" as an active email address.

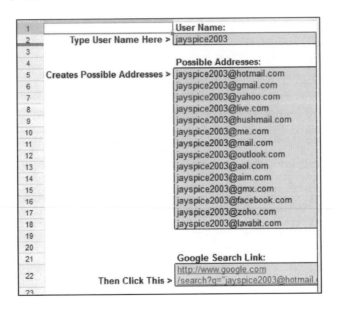

Figure 5.12: A Google Document that provides potential personal email addresses.

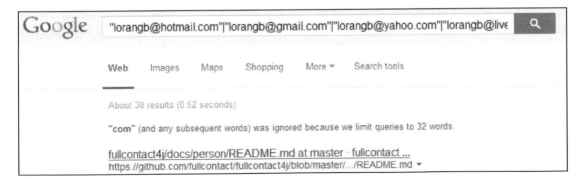

Figure 5.13: A custom Google search result from the online email generator.

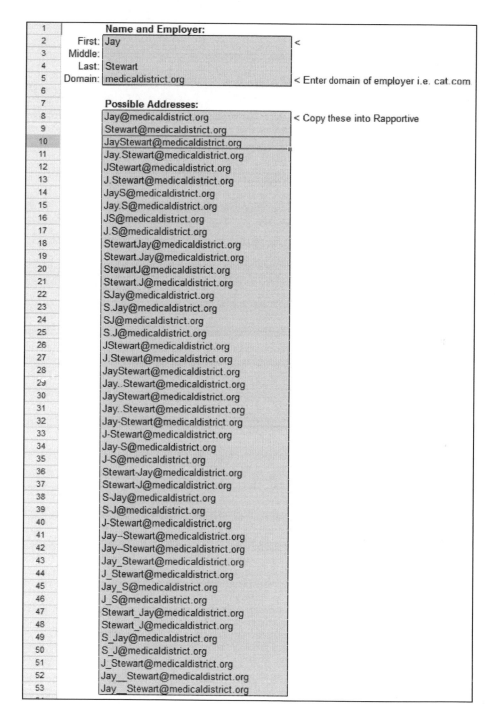

Figure 5.14: A list of potential email addresses generated with a Google document.

jay@medicaldistrict.org
spice@medicaldistrict.org
stewart@medicaldistrict.org
jaystewart@medicaldistrict.org
spicestewart@medicaldistrict.org
jay.stewart@medicaldistrict.org
spice.stewart@medicaldistrict.org
jstewart@medicaldistrict.org
sstewart@medicaldistrict.org
j.stewart@medicaldistrict.org
s.stewart@medicaldistrict.org
jays@medicaldistrict.org
spices@medicaldistrict.org
jay.s@medicaldistrict.org
spice.s@medicaldistrict.org
js@medicaldistrict.org
ss@medicaldistrict.org
j.s@medicaldistrict.org
s.s@medicaldistrict.org
stewartjay@medicaldistrict.org
stewartspice@medicaldistrict.org
stewart.jay@medicaldistrict.org
stewart.spice@medicaldistrict.org
stewartj@medicaldistrict.org
stewarts@medicaldistrict.org
stewart.j@medicaldistrict.org
stewart.s@medicaldistrict.org
sjay@medicaldistrict.org
sspice@medicaldistrict.org
s.jay@medicaldistrict.org
s.spice@medicaldistrict.org
sj@medicaldistrict.org
ss@medicaldistrict.org
s.j@medicaldistrict.org

s.s@medicaldistrict.org
jay-stewart@medicaldistrict.org
spice-stewart@medicaldistrict.org
j-stewart@medicaldistrict.org
s-stewart@medicaldistrict.org
jay-s@medicaldistrict.org
spice-s@medicaldistrict.org
j-s@medicaldistrict.org
s-s@medicaldistrict.org
stewart-jay@medicaldistrict.org
stewart-spice@medicaldistrict.org
stewart-j@medicaldistrict.org
stewart-s@medicaldistrict.org
s-jay@medicaldistrict.org
s-spice@medicaldistrict.org
s-j@medicaldistrict.org
s-s@medicaldistrict.org
jay_stewart@medicaldistrict.org
spice_stewart@medicaldistrict.org
j_stewart@medicaldistrict.org
s_stewart@medicaldistrict.org
jay_s@medicaldistrict.org
spice_s@medicaldistrict.org
j_s@medicaldistrict.org
s_s@medicaldistrict.org
stewart_jay@medicaldistrict.org
stewart_spice@medicaldistrict.org
stewart_j@medicaldistrict.org
stewart_s@medicaldistrict.org
s_jay@medicaldistrict.org
s_spice@medicaldistrict.org
s_j@medicaldistrict.org
s_s@medicaldistrict.org

Above is a list of 67 email addresses created from information provided to an email permutator website. These include combinations of first and last name, as well as an additional nickname or maiden name. The automated service will generate this list. However, the above examples may give you ideas for an individual search. This technique, combined with the Rapportive application discussed in Chapter Fifteen or bulk validation, often identifies the actual target email address.

Email Permutator (inteltechniques.com/OSINT/email.html)

Both of these documents were created after being inspired by the Email Permutator project by Rob Ousbey at distilled.net. Several similar attempts have been made to improve on the original design. One effort that showed promise was the Email Permutator+. However, modern browsers now block that website as malicious. I decided to create my own tool that would provide enhanced features valuable to my own investigations. The advantage with this version is that you can enter a nickname and multiple domains for your search. This is then used to create several additional potential addresses. The nickname field could also be used for a maiden name in case an email address was not converted after a recent marriage. A search of only the information referenced earlier with an added nickname of "Spice" resulted in 67 potential email addresses which are listed on page 146.

This tool offers two phases of a potential email address search. By default, it will automatically check the custom email domain provided as well as eleven additional popular domains. The included domains for the default "Global" setting are Hotmail, Gmail, Yahoo, Live, Hushmail, Me, Mail, Outlook, AOL, iCloud, and GMX. Figure 5.15 (left) displays the current state of the first phase of tool including the details used previously. The result was 420 potential email addresses as seen in Figure 5.15 (right). Notice that these results include potential addresses for multiple domains.

The second phase of the tool is directly below the first search box. It allows you to copy the entire list of generated potential email addresses and paste them into the search box. The tool will generate direct search links for each email address through Google, Bing, and Facebook. Each link can now be clicked to open a new tab to search for the chosen email address. The Google and Bing columns will each launch a quoted search of the exact email address while the Facebook links will display any profile created with the chosen address. Figure 5.16 displays a small portion of the results. This method can still be time consuming, but it is not as tedious as manual entry. The Russia, Germany, and Asia options will change the included domains to those most popular in each region.

This technique will work with any domain name. You can remove any domains desired in order to prevent those results. Knowing the domain of the target's employer is a great scenario. Identifying a person's email address will often lead to their social networks, blogs, and other online accounts.

Bulk Validation (e-mailvalidator.com)

When using the previous technique to create potential email addresses, you will need a way to distinguish valid accounts from invalid. This can be done individually with the mail validation methods described earlier or in bulk with the website listed above. The bulk search will identify any valid email addresses that were created with the Permutator tool. This saves time compared to a manual search. You must create a free account and will be limited to 100 free searches. That will suffice for this technique. Creating new accounts only requires a valid email address and ownership is not verified.

Figure 5.15: An email assumption search tool (left) and results (right).

Google Links	Bing Links	Facebook Links
jay@medicaldistrict.org	jay@medicaldistrict.org	jay@medicaldistrict.org
spice@medicaldistrict.org	spice@medicaldistrict.org	spice@medicaldistrict.org
stewart@medicaldistrict.org	stewart@medicaldistrict.org	stewart@medicaldistrict.org
jaystewart@medicaldistrict.org	jaystewart@medicaldistrict.org	jaystewart@medicaldistrict.org

Figure 5.16: Hyperlink results from an email assumption search.

Email Format (email-format.com)

If the previous email assumption techniques were unproductive or overkill for your needs, you may want to consider Email Format. This website searches a provided domain name and attempts to identify the email structure of employee addresses. When searching medicaldistrict.org, it provided several confirmed email accounts under that domain and made the assumption that employee emails are formatted as first initial then last name. Our target would have an email address of jstewart@medicaldistrict.org according to the rules.

Toofr (toofr.com)

A more sophisticated way of conducting this same technique is through Toofr. This premium service will allow you five free searches per month for free with a registered account. They also have an API option which will be explained in Chapter Fourteen. A test search of "Jay Stewart" that works at Microsoft produced the results visible in Figure 5.17.

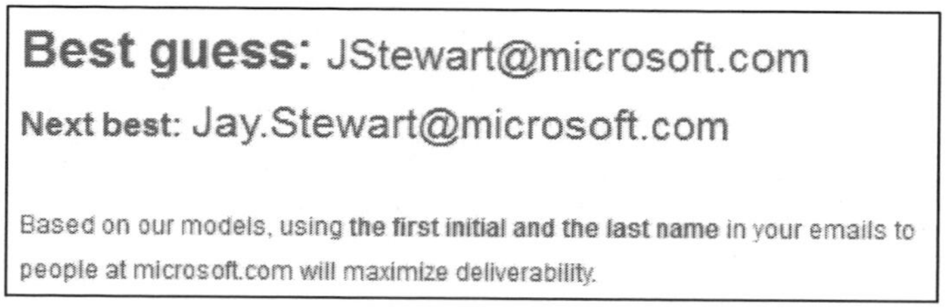

Best guess: JStewart@microsoft.com

Next best: Jay.Stewart@microsoft.com

Based on our models, using **the first initial and the last name** in your emails to people at microsoft.com will maximize deliverability.

Figure 5.17: A Toofr search result.

This information is based on the number of validated email addresses for the specified business. These results are constantly analyzed and assumptions are made from the name information provided within the searches. This response data is often very accurate.

Emails 4 Corporations (sites.google.com/site/emails4corporations)

This is a free email format identification service similar to Toofr. It only searches approximately 1,000 companies with known email formats. It does not appear to have been updated since 2013.

Email Sherlock (emailsherlock.com)

This website is one of many all-in-one email search engines. As with all of them, results will vary drastically. Additionally, any email account that you search through this tool will receive a message announcing that the email address was searched. This notification will also include the city and state of your IP address. If this might jeopardize your investigation, and I think in most cases it would, do not use this tool. A successful search might identify the social networks, websites, and personal details of the user of an email address. I believe the most valuable part of this service is the free access to Full Contact's data. This paid service is explained in Chapter Fourteen. I know of no other free website that allows unlimited access to this premium data. A search for "lorangb@gmail.com" confirmed the address as valid and located the following social network information.

Fullname: Bart Lorang
Gender: Male
Location: Denver, Colorado
Linkedin: https://www.linkedin.com/in/bartlorang
Facebook: https://www.facebook.com/bart.lorang
Klout: http://www.klout.com/user/lorangb
Googleprofile: http://profiles.google.com/114426306375480734745
Lastfm: http://www.last.fm/user/ILuchinni
Aboutme: http://about.me/lorangb
Flickr: http://www.flickr.com/people/39267654@N00/
Youtube: http://www.youtube.com/user/lorangb

Picasa: http://picasaweb.google.com/lorangb
Foursquare: https://www.foursquare.com/user/10245647
MySpace: http://www.myspace.com/137200880
Quora: http://www.quora.com/Bart-Lorang
Googleplus: https://plus.google.com/114426306375480734745
Gravatar: http://gravatar.com/blorang
Twitter: http://twitter.com/bartlorang

That's them Email/User Name (thatsthem.com)

Unfortunately, the valuable person search technology behind That's Them did not carry over to their email and user name search options. The majority of the email addresses and user names I have searched through this service returned no results. However, on occasion I received detailed results such as full name, address, phone number, and vehicle information. Although this is rare, I believe that That's Them should be on your list of email and user name search resources.

Reverse Genie Email (reversegenie.com/email.php)

Reverse Genie offers several reverse search options. The strongest are the phone and email search. It will search an email address through several application programming interfaces (API's) for positive results based on the email address. This will include social networks, such as Facebook and Twitter, which were created with the target email address. A search on one of my real email addresses identified an alias Flickr page that I carelessly associated with a real email account. Entering the email lorangb@gmail.com resulted in direct links to his accounts on Me, Facebook, Flickr, Foursquare, Google+, Google Profile, Gravatar, Klout, LastFM, LinkedIn, MySpace, Picasa, Quora, Twitter, and YouTube. This would have taken hours to discover through traditional methods.

Pipl (pipl.com)

Pipl was explained earlier as an effective real name search engine. Their email search option is just as robust. Enter any email address and you will be presented a dossier style of report of all available information. Figure 5.18 displays a result of the email address "lorangb@gmail.com". Much of this data has already been received from other sources. However, the user name portion often includes unseen details. The associated subjects or often non-relatives that do not appear in other search results. If you want a more detailed report, consider the Application Programming Interface (API) version of Pipl that is explained in Chapter Fourteen.

Figure 5.18: A Pipl email search result.

User Name Search Engines

Once you have identified a user name for an online service, this information may lead to much more data. Internet savvy people often use the same user name across many sites. For example, the user "amandag62002" on MySpace may be the same "amandag62002" on Twitter and an unknown number of other sites.

When you identify an email address, you may now have the user name of the target. If a subject uses mpulido007@gmail.com as en email address, there is a good chance that he or she may use mpulido007 as a screen name on a number of sites. If the target has been an internet user for several years, this Gmail account was probably not the first email address used by the target. Searches for mpulido007@yahoo.com, mpulido007@hotmail.com, and mpulido007@aol.com may discover new information.

Manual searching of this new user name information is a good start. Keeping up with the hundreds of social websites available is impossible. Visiting the following services will allow you to search user names across several websites, and will report links to profiles that you may have missed.

Knowem (knowem.com)

Knowem is one of the most comprehensive search websites for user names. The main page provides a single search field which will immediately check for the presence of the supplied user name on the most popular social network sites. In Figure 5.18, a search for the user name "mikeb5" provides information about the availability of that user name on the top 25 networks. If the network name is slightly transparent and the word "available" is stricken, that means that there is a subject with a profile on that website using the supplied user name. When the website is not transparent and the word "available" is orange and underlined, there is not a user profile on that site with the supplied user name. For an online researcher, these "unavailable" indications suggest a visit to the site to locate that user's profile. The results in Figure 5.18 indicate that the target user name is being used on MySpace and Twitter, but not Flickr or Tumblr.

The link in the lower left corner of Figure 5.19 will open a new page that will search over 500 social networks for the presence of the supplied user name. These searches are completed by category, and the "blogging" category is searched automatically. Scrolling down this page will present 14 additional categories with a button next to each category title stating "check this category". This search can take some time. In a scenario involving a unique user name, the search is well worth the time.

Name Chk (namechk.com)

Name Chk provides a similar service. It does not search as many sites as Knowem, however it provides a feature that is a great convenience for the researcher. Entering a unique user name in the search field at the top of the page will immediately identify the presence of that name within 159 popular social networks. A green background and the word "available" indicates that the user name is not in use on that site while a red background and the word "taken" indicates that a user account exists on the site. Figure 5.20 displays a partial view of the results of this type of search. The advantage with this site is that clicking on any of the "taken" results will forward directly to the profile with the supplied user name on that specific website. This eliminates the need to manually navigate to the specified social network and search for the target user name.

Check User Names (checkusernames.com)

This site combines the search engine of Knowem and the features of Name Chk. It searches approximately one third of the sites on Knowem, but it links directly to the target's profile when one is identified. Figure 5.21 shows the similarity between this site and the others. Ultimately, you will need to determine which of these sites works best for your preferences.

Name Checkr (namecheckr.com)

This service appeared in late 2014 and conducts the same type of search as the previous competitors. The only slight advantage here is that the search is conducted faster than other sites. Additionally, you have a live hyperlink that will navigate to any identified accounts with the target user name.

User Search (usersearch.org)

This service stands out a bit from the others in that it only provides actual profile results. It searches the supplied user name for a presence on 45 of the most popular websites (basic option) or 115 total websites (advanced option) and returns a list of identified profiles matching the target. This service is the slowest of all of the options. However, this could be an indication of account verification for more accurate results. I have found their email address search occasionally valuable. However, their telephone search option has yet to return an accurate result.

NameVine (namevine.com)

This user search service provides a unique feature missing in the rest. It allows you to begin typing any partial user name and it will immediately identify registered accounts within the top ten social networks. This could be beneficial when you are not sure of the exact name that your target is using. If your target has a Twitter user name of "Bazzell", the previous services will easily identify additional accounts that also possess this name. If you think that your target may be adding a number at the end of the user name, it could take some time to search all of the possibilities. With NameVine, you can quickly change the number at the end of the user name and get immediate results. It will search Twitter, Facebook, Pinterest, YouTube, Instagram, Tumblr, Wordpress, Blogger, and Github. It will also check for any ".com" domains that match. Figure 5.22 displays the results of my search of Bazzell2 as a user name. This identifies potential accounts belonging to the target on Twitter and YouTube. The benefit of this service is the speed of multiple searches.

Pipl (pipl.com)

Pipl has been discussed a great site for searching a person's real name and email address. This site performs equally as well at locating people by a user name. Inserting a user name in the same field that a person search would be conducted will display results of subjects using this user name on social networks. It will also attempt to determine vital information about the user including age, location, employer, and interests. Finally, it will display small images that are associated with the user's social network accounts.

An important part of searching by user name is the attempted searches of unknown user names. In all of the examples above, the user name "mikeb5" was used. If you know that your target is using this name, you may want to take a quick look at the user names of "mikeb", "mikeb1", "mikeb2", etc. While these profiles may not belong to your target, you could discover new profiles that would otherwise have been missed.

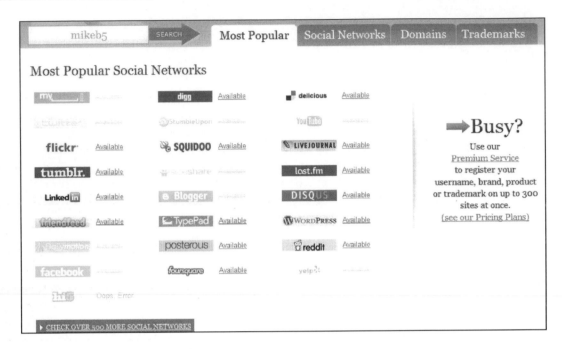

Figure 5.19: A Knowem search result identifying target profiles.

Figure 5.20: A Name Chk search result identifying target profiles.

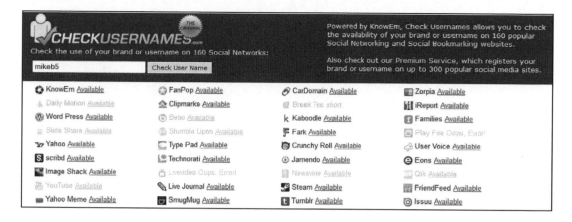

Figure 5.21: A Check User Names search result identifying target profiles.

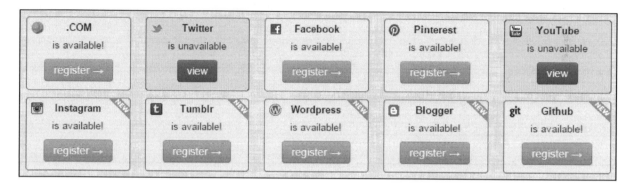

Figure 5.22: A search result of a user name on NameVine.

University Homepages

These automated searches for user names can be very productive. However, they will not locate accounts within all online communities. One large untapped resource is the massive presence of university personal web pages and user names. Almost every university issues each student a university email address. These usually follow a standard naming convention such as the following.

lastname.firstname@university.edu

If you can identify the convention that the school uses and know the full name of the target, you can determine the email address of the student. This address can be searched for any websites and social networks that may have been missed. Further, the first part of that address is usually the user name that would have been issued to the student for a homepage. The target may have never used this email address online and a search result may appear empty. That does not mean that there is not data available. The chance that the target created some type of homepage while attending the university is high. Finding the content is easy.

Hopefully, the searches explained earlier have helped in identifying a university that the target attended. A search for the university's website will reveal the domain name that the university uses. For example, Southern Illinois University at Edwardsville's website is siue.edu. We can now take that information and conduct a specific search for any personal pages on their domain. The search should look like:

site:siue.edu laura

I picked the name of Laura at random just to identify any student or employee personal website on the SIUE domain. One of the results was a link to a personal website belonging to "Laura Swanson". The link was:

www.siue.edu/~lswanso/

This indicates that the naming convention for personal websites is a tilde (~) followed by the first initial and then the first six letters of the last name. If the target of interest was "Scott Golike", the personal website would probably be at:

www.siue.edu/~sgolike/

We can also assume the possibility of his school issued email account to be sgolike@siue.edu. A few searches using previously discussed techniques should confirm if this address belongs to the target. A search using the email to Facebook profile technique may identify an abandon profile.

We can now navigate to this personal school page and see if there is any content. If there is, we can collect the data and conduct an analysis for intelligence and further research leads. If there is no page at this address, it does not mean that there has never been data there. This only indicates that there is no current content on this website. When students graduate, universities will usually remove all of the personal content from the servers. As discussed in Chapter One, this is never an excuse to stop looking. You can now take the URL of a target and conduct a search on The Wayback Machine (wayback.archive.org).

As an example, I can navigate to the first personal link above for "Laura Swanson". Figure 5.23 displays a portion of the live page at www.siue.edu/~lswanso/. If this page did not exist and the site contained no content, you could check on The Wayback Machine. Figure 5.24 shows the search results for this personal page and identifies numerous archives dating back to 1997 for this site. Checking all of these options presents the many different versions of the site including one from 2005 (Figure 5.25) and the first capture from 1997 (Figure 5.26). This presents new data that would not have been uncovered with conventional searches. When a personal website is located, earlier versions should be archived.

Real world application: While assisting another agency, a suspect had been developed in a priority investigation. After all online search attempts revealed nothing of value in locating the subject, a deleted student personal page was located using this method. It contained a list of friends, roommates, family members, and interests that were not previously known. This information helped locate the individual within hours.

It should be noted that some institutions will not follow a standard naming convention for all students and faculty. Additionally, there will be occasions when two or more students will have a name similar enough to create the same user name. Usually, there is a plan in place to thwart these duplications. Sometimes it is as simple as adding the number "2" after the user name.

Universities are not the only places that create personal web pages based on a member name. Several internet service providers allow each subscriber a personal space online as part of the provider's main website. Comcast provides 25MB of storage in a folder with the title of the subscriber's user name. For example, if the email address of the customer was laurenanddan@comcast.net, the user name for the service would be laurenanddan. The URL to view the personal web page would be:

home.comcast.net/laurenanddan

The following is a sample list of personal web page addresses from additional internet providers, using "laurenanddan" as a user name example. You should also search for internet providers in the target's area and attempt to find deleted pages on The Wayback Machine.

360.yahoo.com/laurenanddan
laurenanddan.webs.com
laurenanddan.weebly.com
webpages.charter.net/laurenanddan
sites.google.com/laurenanddan
about.me/laurenanddan

angelfire.com/laurenanddan
geocities.com/laurenanddan
reocities.com/laurenanddan
laurenanddan.tripod.com
home.earthlink.net/~laurenanddan
home.comcast.net/~laurenanddan

Peek You (peekyou.com)

The previous edition of this book listed Peek You in the following "Additional Sites" section. Lately, this service has introduced new search options and better accuracy. The standard landing page encourages a search of a person's first and last name. A filter by country option exists which may eliminate unwanted results. This often identifies a target's Twitter page, Facebook profile, and related accounts. This basic data is only the beginning of the service's offerings.

The "Username" search option performs a query similar to Knowem that will identify social networks that possess a user account with the specified user name. On occasion, this has located new internet profiles that other services missed. The "Work" search option attempts to locate people by their employer.

Figure 5.23: A current personal page on a university website.

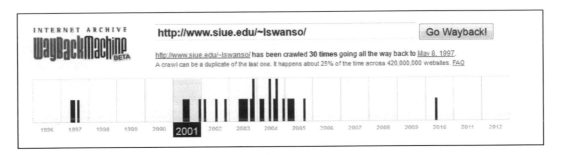

Figure 5.24: A Wayback Machine timeline of available versions of a website.

Figure 5.25: A previous version of the website.

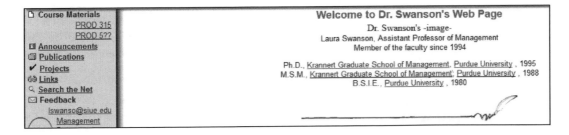

Figure 5.26: A previous version of the website.

This produces surprisingly accurate results. I recently conducted a search of a local small newspaper. This service identified 17 current and past employees with links to each person's Peek You profile. A typical profile included current position at the company, links to social networks and blogs, and possible interests. Premium search results will also be displayed that only connect to paid content options. I try to avoid those.

The "School" search option will allow you to enter any school name to identify current and past attendees. This was once useful when trying to locate a woman with an unknown married name. Searching the small high school that she attended quickly located her current profile with the new name. The "Phone" option was the least successful of all searches. I was unable to locate information on either private cellular numbers or public landline accounts.

Overall, this free service has become a staple in my search options. If your target has a decent internet presence, you are likely to find some type of content about them through this website. Some of the information is older data that has since been updated on the target's profile. This can be beneficial when you are seeking content that has been recently changed.

Additional Sites

Discussing every people search engine is impossible since some sites tend to shut down as quickly as new sites pop up. It is also common that larger sites will acquire smaller sites and forward searches to the larger site. After you visit a handful of these, you will start to see duplicate information that may get frustrating. If you make it through all of the sites detailed in this chapter and still crave more information, the following can be searched:

YoName (yoname.com)
InfoSpace (infospace.com)
Whozat (whozat.com)
WebMii (webmii.com)
CVGadget (cvgadget.com)

Chapter Six

Social Network Traffic

We now know that locating someone's social network profile can reveal quite a lot about them. Just knowing a target name can make use of the people search engines that will identify places to seek more information. Unfortunately, sometimes the investigator does not know the target's name. A common scenario is an investigation about some type of event. This could be a specific violent crime, a bomb threat on a campus, or inappropriate chatter about a particular business. All of these scenarios require search engines that monitor social network traffic. There is an abundance of these types of services. Some will work better on reactive investigations after an incident while others show their strength during proactive investigations while monitoring conversations. Many of the sites in this chapter will find the same results as each other. They are all presented for you to practice with and identify which services are most appropriate for your needs. Two of the strongest methods of searching social network traffic have already been discussed in the Facebook and Twitter sections of Chapter Three.

Custom Search Engines

Chapter One discussed the creation of custom search engines on Google. Two of the final products created were the Social Networks Search Engine and the Smaller Networks Search Engine. Both of these offer a quick and thorough search of both popular and lesser known social networks. They can often identify communication involving your target. I have found these to be the best initial search for general content about a specific topic, user name, real name, or event. Both of these engines can be found on the Intel Techniques website under Resources > Custom Search Tools. Additionally, they can be accessed at the below URL's.

Social Networks: http://inteltechniques.com/OSINT/social.networks.html
Smaller Networks: http://inteltechniques.com/OSINT/smaller.networks.html

The Social Networks engine searches all content indexed by Google on Facebook ,Twitter, Google+, Instagram, LinkedIn, YouTube, and Tumblr. Each service has isolated results within the respective tabs at the top of the engine. The Smaller Networks engine scours MySpace, Orkut archives, TheHoodUp, BlackPlanet, MiGente, and AsianAve.

Social Searcher (social-searcher.com)

I had previously discouraged users from attempting searches on the first version of Social Searcher. Since then, I have begun to rely on their free service to digest data located on the main social networks. You can provide any keywords, user names, or terms and receive the most recent results from Facebook, Twitter, Google+, and the overall web. It allows email alerts to be created for notification of new content matching your query. One of the unique features of this website is the free ability to export search results into CSV format. The following portion was exported during a search for the term "OSINT". This obtained the Twitter user name, date & time, and entire message among other information. Having this in a spreadsheet format can be incredibly beneficial.

http://twitter.com/borderpol	Sun Feb 01 22:43:51	Experts raise alarm as plague kills dozens in Madagascar http://t.co/gyetAXF6zd
http://twitter.com/dzhray	Sun Feb 01 22:11:48	RT @Robert4787: @dzhray I hope so. Robert at OSINT NEWS: http://t.co/WHZ5
http://twitter.com/3XPlo1T2	Sun Feb 01 21:50:25	although on our last one we used #SET after #OSINT and got access in 7 secs....
http://twitter.com/nipunjaswal	Sun Feb 01 21:39:01	British army creates team of Facebook warriors	http://t.co/6WZng
http://twitter.com/josealegria	Sun Feb 01 21:37:45	HP Security Research OSINT (OpenSource Intelligenc... http://t.co/F3pmB

Convoflow (convoflow.com)

Convoflow aggregates social network traffic from several sources. It separates the results by each source and includes data from Twitter, FriendFeed, YouTube, MetaCafé, Blog Catalog, and Flickr. The traffic appears to be indexed within one minute. The links provided forward straight to the actual social network source, and advertisements are minimal.

Ice Rocket (icerocket.com)

Ice Rocket provides a clean interface and quick results. Instead of merging all social network traffic together in one result, it isolates each source for separate view. The default view will search blogs. The five tabs above the search field on every page will provide results for Blogs, Twitter, Facebook, Images, and Big Buzz. Clicking on any of these tabs will conduct a search of the previous search term without reentering the words. When searching blogs, the menu on the left will allow you to specify search results from today, the past week, the past month, or any time. The final option will allow you to define a specific range of dates to limit the search results. The Twitter search will identify tweets from the past 24 hours beginning with the most recent traffic. The compressed view of these tweets presents a photo icon, user name, message, links, and hash tags all in a single horizontal line. The Facebook search results are identical to the Twitter results. The images search seems to focus mostly on Flickr photos. This type of search should also be conducted on other image search sites. The Big Buzz feature presents a combination of all of these searches on a single page. This can be convenient if you have developed specific keywords that return few results. By default, the ability to automatically refresh the content on this page is disabled. To enable this live stream, choose a time interval in the upper right corner of the screen.

Topsy (topsy.com)

Topsy offers a few options that the other social network traffic search sites do not. A search of any term or terms will present a default view of several results sorted by relevance. This means that results from a few minutes ago could be combined with the results from several days ago. Clicking the "latest results" option in the left menu will present only recent posts about the supplied search. By default, this will only include Twitter posts. Filter options include the ability to filter content from the past hour, day, seven days, or month. A unique feature on Topsy is the ability to create an email alert for your search terms. On any search result page, there is a link to "create email alert" directly above the first search result. Clicking this link will force you to sign into either a Twitter or Facebook account in order to proceed with the alerts. This is in place to prevent abuse by automated systems. The account used for verification does not require any personal information. After verification, you will be allowed to insert an email address when clicking this link which will then email you any time a new result appears in reference to your desired search terms. I highly recommend conducting a very detailed search if you choose this option. Otherwise, you will receive daily emails full of unwanted search results. Personally, I do not use this technique.

Social Mention (socialmention.com)

Social Mention searches the same traffic as most of the other social search sites. This is one of the few sites that offer real-time statistics within the search results that can be beneficial to a researcher. These new sources of information include a sentiment reading, a passion reading, an average time frame per comment, and the top keywords present for the search conducted. This data will notify the researcher if the overall results for the search are negative, positive, or neutral. Further, the identification of the most used keywords may provide further intelligence about additional terms that should be searched. Figure 6.01 displays this combined view of data.

Who's Talkin (whostalkin.com)

This is yet another site that searches for social traffic on the web. In contrast to the other sites mentioned in this chapter, Who's Talkin searches a few lesser known sites that are often ignored. These include Bebo, Friendster, and Reddit. The interface is not always user friendly. It can be difficult to specify search results by category instead of a single website. If your searches with the other sites appear overwhelming with results from Twitter and Facebook, this site can help filter out the popular results. Figure 6.02 displays a filtered result of WordPress blogs that contain specific search terms.

Figure 6.01: A search result from Social Mention.

Figure 6.02: Search results on Who's Talking filtered by Wordpress Blogs.

Delicious (delicious.com)

Delicious is a social bookmarking web service for storing, sharing, and discovering internet bookmarks. It is owned by Yahoo and has several million users. The benefit of this site for OSINT investigations is twofold. A standard topic search will identify subjects with an interest in your investigation while a user search will display websites of interest to that person. Both searches have roadblocks, but we can get around those with two techniques.

The keyword search will identify subjects that have bookmarked a page about the topic of your investigation. This can provide potential targets and information about other interests of any subjects identified. Delicious recently removed the search option from the home page which would display this information, but we can achieve the same result through either a sub-domain or Google.

If you want to perform a standard search through all Delicious content, navigate to the following exact website.

https://previous.delicious.com/

This will take you to the previous design of Delicious which contains a search bar at the top of every page. Here you can search any topic of interest to your investigation. The search works well with single and multiple terms, but does not work well with website addresses. For that we will use Google.

Assume that you are investigating an incident that involved a fight on a bus. A related video was uploaded to YouTube and you located the video at http://www.youtube.com/watch?v=lQJFv9SMSMQ. After watching the video and gathering information about the uploader, you want to know other people in your area that also found and watched the video. This may identify actual witnesses that saved the bookmark to show to others. You could search for the presence of that video on Delicious through the following Google search.

site:delicious.com "lQJFv9SMSMQ"

You should also attempt a standard search on previous.delicious.com for "lQJFv9SMSMQ" to identify possible connections. A search for the video mentioned here identified 16 people that had this same video in their bookmarks. Figure 6.03 displays one of the results that identify a user name of b8akaratn and a comment about the video. Clicking the user name will open a page of all of that individual's bookmarks in chronological order beginning with the most recent. Figure 6.04 displays this user's profile which identifies a real name of Kara Owens, a join date of 03/08/2008, and a last access date of 10/11/2013. You can also see that the user has bookmarked 426 links. Navigating through these can give a very detailed view of the subject's interests, hobbies, and activities.

If the user possesses hundreds or thousands of links, navigating through all of them can be burdensome. The new Delicious site does not offer an official way of searching through an individual's links, but we can accomplish this with a URL trick. Assume that we want to find any bookmarks from our example user that mentions the word "vegan". We can type the following address directly into any web browser and receive the result visible in Figure 6.05.

https://delicious.com/b8akaratn/vegan

This technique allows us to quickly find any content of interest. If I have a target of interest with many links, I will conduct a detailed search for any bookmarks that include "map", "maps", "directions", or "route". This often identifies saved direction information from an online mapping service. Often, this includes the subject's residence as the starting point. Think for a moment of the interesting bookmarks in your browser. What would they tell about you if they were public?

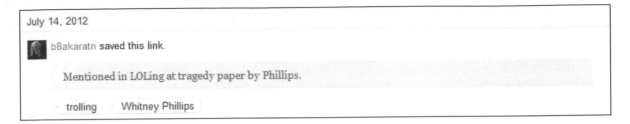

Figure 6.03: A Delicious search result by keyword.

Figure 6.04: A Delicious search result by user name.

Figure 6.05: A Delicious search result by keyword and user name.

If you already know the user name of your target, such as their Twitter handle, you can enter this directly into a web address to see if a page exists. If your target's user name on other services is "bbrenner", you could load the following URL into your browser.

delicious.com/bbrenner

You may find that more subjects do not use Delicious than those that do. However, a positive hit can provide great information about a target's interests, skills, future plans, friends, education, and employment. Even if a user has moved on to newer technology, the old bookmarks can tell a powerful story.

Stumble Upon (stumbleupon.com)

A more modern and very popular alternative to Delicious is Stumble Upon. It is not necessarily a bookmarking service, but it is a way for people to share their favorite links with their friends. Searching directly within the service is difficult, if not impossible. A search for the same video mentioned previously through Google with the "site" operator identified one post on Stumble Upon. Figure 6.06 displays the search terms and redacted result. Clicking this link opens the video within the Stumble Upon environment. The default view will not tell you anything about the person that shared the video. However, if you click on the small exclamation point in the upper right corner of the video, it will load the user information. The link mentioned here was posted by a user name of iyannaw08. This information can now be searched to learn more about this subject.

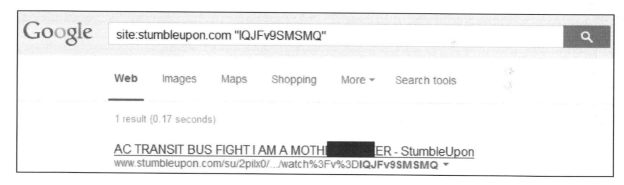

Figure 6.06: A Google search for Stumble Upon content.

Chapter Seven

Online Communities

Online communities are very similar to social networks. While social networks cater to a broad audience with many interests, these communities usually relate to a specific service or lifestyle. Many online communities do not get indexed by search engines. Therefore, the presence of a target's participation will not always be found through Google or Bing. Any time that a target's interests or hobbies are located through the previous search techniques, you should also seek the online communities that cater to that topic. This can often identify information that is very personal and private to the target. Many people post to these communities without any regard to privacy. Some communities require registration to see the content, which is usually free. Occasionally, a cached version of the pages on the site is available without registering. This chapter will provide methods of infiltrating these communities to maximize the intelligence obtained.

Craigslist (craigslist.org)

Craigslist is one big online classified ad for every area of the world. The site can ease the pain of finding an apartment, provide numerous options for buying a vehicle locally, or assist in locating just about any item or service that you can imagine that is within driving distance of your home. It is also a landing spot for stolen goods, illegal services, and illicit affairs. While Craigslist offers a search option, the results are limited to active posts only. You can also only search within one category at a time. You can browse through the posts individually, but this will be overwhelming.

Government and private investigators have found much success in locating stolen goods within this site. To start, you must find the Craigslist site for your area. Often, simply visiting craigslist.org will direct you to the landing page for your geographical area. If this does not happen, navigate through your country, then your state, then your metropolitan area to see listings around you. If the theft occurred recently, a live search in the "for sale" section may produce results. I do not recommend searching from the main page, as there are no advanced options. Instead, click on any section title. For example, clicking on the "for sale" section will take us to that area. The top of the page will have a search field that will search all of the categories in this section. Additionally, we can filter by price range, posts that contain images, or terms that only appear in the title of the post.

In Figures 7.01 through 7.04, you can see the difference in the search results. The first was a search for "laptop" anywhere in the post, which returned 1346 posts for the St. Louis area. The second search was the same term, but only for results that contained the term in the title of the post. This resulted in 736 posts in the St. Louis area. The third search was for "laptop Edwardsville", within the entire post, which returned 28 posts containing the term laptop in the Edwardsville, Illinois area. Finally, adding the "pic" option to the same search provides links to the 20 posts that include photos of the items. Figure 7.05 displays one of the results found from this search. If this had been a stolen item, the investigator could use this photo to confirm any details provided by the victim.

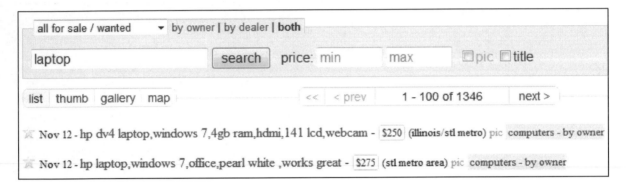

Figure 7.01: A Craigslist search by search term.

Figure 7.02: A Craigslist search by search term within the title only.

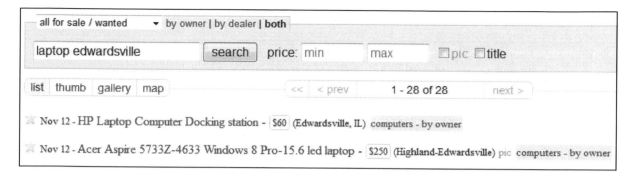

Figure 7.03: A Craigslist search by search term including location.

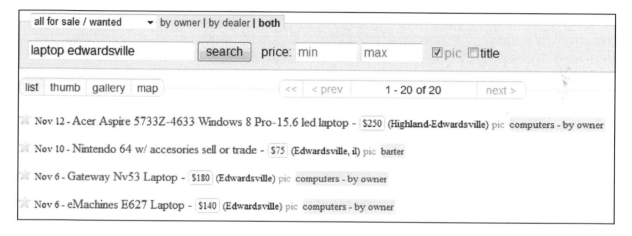

Figure 7.04: A Craigslist results page from search term, location, and images.

Craigslist recently added new features that allow you to view results by list view, gallery view, or map view. Figure 7.06 displays the same laptop results by image gallery while Figure 7.07 displays the results on a map. These locations will only refer to the city of the item, and not exact GPS location. The gallery view can be used as a "photo lineup" to identify a stolen item. The map view can be beneficial when only looking for items within surrounding areas.

Four new options on the upper right of every result page allow you to sort the items by newest listings (default), relevance, lowest price, and highest price. This option is visible in Figure 7.06. Most pages with items for sale will also allow you to filter the results so that only items being sold by individuals are listed. This would eliminate businesses and dealers. The default is to show both and I recommend leaving that unless you are overwhelmed by the number of results. This option can be seen in Figures 7.01 through 7.04.

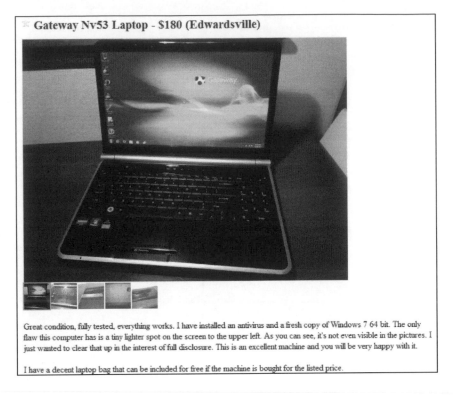

Gateway Nv53 Laptop - $180 (Edwardsville)

Great condition, fully tested, everything works. I have installed an antivirus and a fresh copy of Windows 7 64 bit. The only flaw this computer has is a tiny lighter spot on the screen to the upper left. As you can see, it's not even visible in the pictures. I just wanted to clear that up in the interest of full disclosure. This is an excellent machine and you will be very happy with it.

I have a decent laptop bag that can be included for free if the machine is bought for the listed price.

Figure 7.05: A Craigslist post with images.

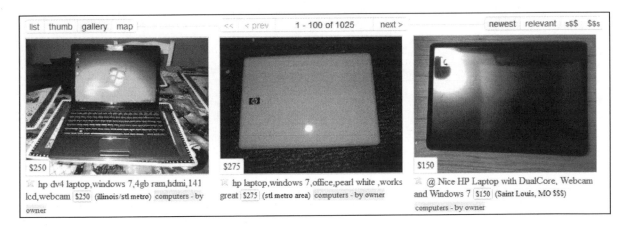

Figure 7.06: A partial gallery view of items on Craigslist.

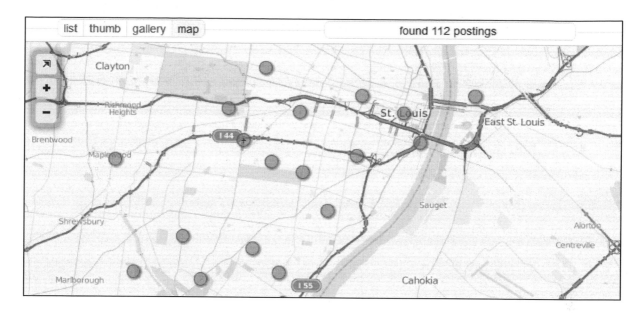

Figure 7.07: A map view of laptops for sale on Craigslist.

If a thief sells the item on Craigslist, he or she will usually delete the post after the transaction is complete. If the post is deleted, it will not be listed in the results of a search on Craigslist. This is where Google and Bing come in.

Both Google and Bing collect information from Craigslist posts to include in their search results. This collection can never be complete, but a large archive of posts is available for searching. Searching Google or Bing with "site:craigslist.org" (without quotes) will search through archived posts on Craigslist that are both active and removed. Similar to the previous example, you can search "site:craigslist.org laptop Edwardsville" without the quotes. Figure 7.08 displays this search, which produced 798 results that match these criteria on Google. These include the current posts that were available with the live search on craigslist.org as well as posts that have been recently deleted from Craigslist. If you wanted to focus only on a specific regional area of Craigslist, changing the search to "site:stlouis.craigslist.org laptop Edwardsville" would filter results. This example would only show listings from the St. Louis section of Craigslist. You can use any region in your custom searches.

The results that are still current will link to the actual post and display all content of the post. If a search result links to a post that has been deleted from Craigslist, a standard "page not found" error will be returned. You can still get additional information from this deleted post by looking through the text supplied on this search page. The brief description will often disclose an email address or telephone number. Some listings may have a cached view, but lately this has been rare.

Figure 7.08: A Google search result page of Craigslist posts with specific terms.

In a scenario where thousands of search results are presented by Google or Bing, you can add search terms to filter to a more manageable amount of posts. Adding the make or model number of the product may quickly identify the stolen property.

You can also search by terms other than the product of interest. Many people that use Craigslist do not want to communicate through email sent from the website. Most users will include a telephone number in the post as a preferred method of communication. The overwhelming majority of these telephone numbers belong to the cellular telephone of the user submitting the post. This can be a huge piece of intelligence for an investigator attempting to identify a person associated with a telephone number. It is common that a criminal will purchase a cellular telephone with cash and add minutes to it as needed. This makes it difficult for someone to identify the criminal from the phone number. Ironically, the same criminal will post the telephone number as well as a name on a public internet site for the world to see. Sometimes, a person will post both a cellular and a landline telephone number on the same post. This allows an investigator to associate these two numbers, and a quick internet search should identify the owner of the landline telephone number.

In Figure 7.09, a search is conducted on the official Craigslist site for a cellular telephone number of interest. This search produces 177 results of items currently listed for sale by the owner of the cellular telephone. None of these posts identify the target by name. Each post, however, lists an additional telephone number where the person can be contacted (Figure 7.10). Searching the secondary landline telephone number on whitepages.com reveals the name and address of the owner of this landline telephone (Figure 7.11). This does not prove that the same subject owns the original cellular telephone number of interest, but it does indicate some type of association.

Another way to search Craigslist posts is to identify screen names within the post. Craigslist discourages inserting a screen name or email address within a post, however, most people have figured out how to bypass this limitation. Instead of someone typing their email address within their posts, they will insert spaces between the first portion of the email address (user name) and the second portion of the email address (domain name). For example, instead of the user typing their email address as JohnDoe911@gmail.com, he or she may identify the account as "JohnDoe911 at gmail com". This would be enough to prevent Craigslist's servers from identifying the text as an email address and prohibiting the post. Fortunately for the investigator, this information is indexed by

Craigslist and other search engines to be retrieved. In Figure 7.12, a search is conducted on Craigslist for a specific user name believed to be associated with a target. The single search result opens a Craigslist post that includes the target's first name, full email address, and telephone number (Figure 7.13).

---

for sale / wanted

search for: 314 ▓▓▓▓   in: all for sale / wanted ▾   ○ title only ● entire post [Search]

price: min max   ☐ has image

sort by **most recent** best match low price high price

Found: 177 Displaying: 1 - 100
[1 | 2]

Feb 10 - (2) 5 ft Trailer Ramps - $30 (ferguson) auto parts - by owner pic

Feb 10 - Good Easton Pitch Back - $35 (north county) sporting goods pic

---

Figure 7.09: A Craigslist search by telephone number.

---

(2) 5 ft Trailer Ramps - $30 (ferguson)

uncategorized

prohibited

spam/overpost

best of craigslist

Date: 2012-02-10, 11:47AM CST
Reply to: see below [Errors when replying to ads?]

I have (2) 5 ft trailer ramps. There are minor scratches and markings on them from use. There are also minor surface rust in some spots. One is gray and the other is gold. They are in good condition. I delete postings when sold, if interested call Tony @314 ▓▓▓▓ or 314 ▓▓▓▓. Please no text messages, I don't reply to them because I don't know how to use it.

Figure 7.10: A Craigslist result by telephone number including secondary landline number.

---

2 Results for 314-▓▓▓▓

See in map»

You?
Claim &
edit »
   Anthony ▓ ▓▓▓▓
(Age 45-49)

▓▓▓▓ ▓▓
Saint Louis, MO

Associated people:
Corey Drewes
+ more...
See full listing»

Figure 7.11: A White Pages search result for the landline telephone number.

You can search any keyword in either the official Craigslist site or on Bing using the "site" operator. In my experience, Bing offers more results of archived Craigslist posts than Google. But, if you do not have success with Bing, Google should be searched as well. Many private investigators find the "personals" section of interest. The "Casual encounters" area is well known for extra-marital affairs. If you want to only search all live Craigslist posts, regardless of which geographical area it exists, you can use sites such as totalcraigsearch.com, adhuntr.com, and searchalljunk.com.

Real world application: Many thieves will turn to the internet to unload stolen items. While EBay requires banking information or a credit card to use their services, most thieves prefer Craigslist's offer of anonymity. My local police department successfully located a valuable stolen brass instrument this way and set up a sting to arrest the thief. Often, the thief will be willing to bring the item to you in order to get some quick cash.

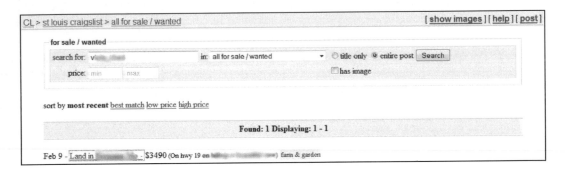

Figure 7.12: A Craigslist search by user name.

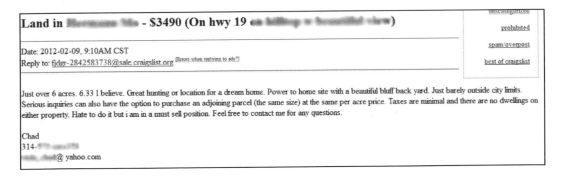

Figure 7.13: A Craigslist post associating a user name with a name and telephone number.

NotiCraig (noticraig.com)

NotiCraig.com is a free tool for automated Craigslist searches. Instead of spending your time searching Craigslist, NotiCraig will send you a notification as soon as the item of interest becomes available. There is no signup required and it is a free service. To use the website, you provide any applicable details such as the item you are looking for, the geographical area of interest, and an email address to receive the results. Law enforcement can use this tool to monitor stolen goods, collectors can use it to avoid missing desired items, and companies can use it to monitor fraudulent merchandise.

EBay (EBay.com)

EBay is an online auction site. Since the site requires a user's financial information or valid credit card to post items for sale, many thieves have moved to Craigslist to unload stolen goods. EBay offers an advanced search that will allow filters that limit to auctions from a specific location, or specified distance from the location. On any search page, there is an "Advanced" button that will display new options. Of these options, there is a category titled "show results". The last option in this category is titled "items near me". Here, you can select a zip code and filter results to a minimum of 10 miles from the zip code selected. This will now allow you to search for any item and the results will all be from sellers near a specific zip code. This location option, as seen in Figure 7.14, will remain active as you search for different keywords. These searches will only search current auctions that have not expired. In order to search past auctions, select the "Completed listings" option under the category of "Search including".

Flippity (flippity.com)

An alternative to the location feature on the official EBay site is Flippity. This site performs the same function as mentioned previously, but with less work on the user's part. The results of your search will appear on a map with the ability to minimize and expand the radius as desired. This is a quick way to monitor any type of items being sold in a specific community.

GoofBay (goofbay.com)

Not everyone uses spellcheck. Some people, especially criminals, will rush to list an item to sell without ensuring that the spelling and grammar are correct. You could conduct numerous searches using various misspelled words, or you can use GoofBay. This site will take your correctly spelled keyword search and attempt the same search with the most commonly misspelled variations of the search terms. Once this helped me identify a thief selling a "saxaphone". Another alternative to this service is Fat Fingers (fatfingers.com)

Figure 7.14: An EBay search page using the optional location-based search.

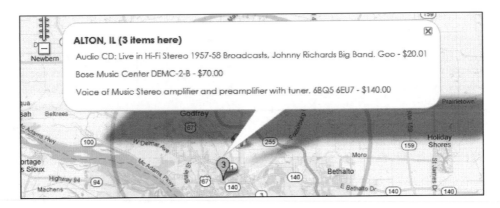

Figure 7.15: A Flippity search result.

Search Tempest (serchtempest.com)

If you find yourself searching multiple geographical areas of Craigslist and EBay, you may desire an automated solution. Search Tempest will allow you to specify the location and perimeter for your search. It will fetch items from Craigslist, EBay, and Amazon. You can specify keywords in order to narrow your search to a specific area. One feature that some users overlook is the option to display expired posts. The feature is titled "Hide Expired Posts" under the preferences menu in the upper right portion of every page. By default, this option is selected in order to hide any posts that have been removed by the author. I recommend disabling this option in order to display these expired posts that would not be seen on a live Craigslist search.

To demonstrate this feature, I searched for "Jailbroken Apple TV 2" on the St. Louis Craigslist page on February 1, 2015. It returned the two available items as seen in Figure 7.16. I repeated this same search on Google with the exact search of site:stlouis.craigslist.org "jailbroken apple TV 2". This returned five results with the oldest dated December 26, 2014. Google will usually only reveal posts from the past 60 days. I then conducted the same search on Search Tempest and received six results with the oldest also dated December 26, 2014. However, when I changed the Search Tempest setting of "Hide Expired Posts" to "No", I received an additional two results with the oldest dated November 20, 2014. Figure 7.17 displays the two expired posts. When clicking this link, I was presented a Craigslist error page notifying me that the post had been deleted.

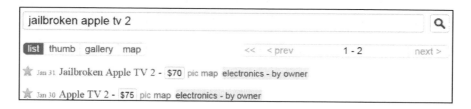

Figure 7.16: A live Craigslist search showing only current items.

Figure 7.17: A Search Tempest result displaying deleted posts.

Real world application: While investigating numerous vehicle burglaries, police detectives knew that the thieves were targeting high dollar stereo equipment. Without the exact details of model numbers, vague searches for stereo equipment were overwhelming. Utilizing the advanced search option on EBay, the detectives could specify a search of car stereos being sold in their zip code. Instantly, they were presented with a pattern of one individual user that seemed to be selling used car stereos with exposed wiring on a weekly basis. After verification that the stolen items matched those in the reports, a subpoena to EBay provided a verified name, banking information, billing address, and complete history of all transactions since the account was created. The detectives obtained a search warrant to the suspect's residence as well as for his arrest.

Dating Websites

When investigating cheating spouses, background information, personal character, or applicant details, dating sites can lead to interesting evidence. The presence of a dating profile does not mean anything by itself. Millions of people successfully use these services to find mates. When a target's profile is located, it will usually lead to personal information that cannot be found anywhere else.

Match (match.com)

As the most popular of the online dating sites, the chances of locating a target's profile will be highest here. In order to properly search and view complete profiles, you will need an account. Account creation is simple and free. False information can be used to create the account. You will not be able to make contact with other users with this free trial, but you can browse without limitation. Most profiles are not attached to an actual full name. If you know the target's screen name on other websites and social networks, it may be worthwhile to search for this user on Match. Limiting the searches to an exact zip code of the target may work as long as accurate information was used in the profile. Knowing the interests of a target may help identify the profile as well. Otherwise, limiting to an age range and general location will present you with many profiles that can be browsed by photo to identify the target. Other popular dating sites include Plenty of Fish (plentyoffish.com), eHarmony (eharmony.com), and OK Cupid (okcupid.com).

In my experience, if a user has a profile on one dating website, he or she most likely has others. These can usually be located with a user name search on each website. Another successful technique is to conduct a reverse image search on any photos of the target within the profile. This method will be explained in Chapter Nine.

Real world application: In 2013, I was teaching an OSINT course in Canada. During a break, one of the attendees asked for assistance with a sexual assault case that involved the dating website Plenty Of Fish. The unknown suspect would meet women through the online service and rape them. All of the information on his profile was fake, and the photos were of poor quality and unhelpful. Together, we conducted a Google search that had worked in the past for this type of situation. We copied and pasted each sentence that he had written in his bio for the profile. Eventually, we found one that was very unique and grammatically worded poorly. A quoted Google search of this sentence provided only one result. It was the real profile of the suspect, under his real name, that contained the same sentence describing himself. The high quality photos on this legitimate page were used to verify that he was the suspect. An arrest was made within 24 hours.

Ashley Madison (ashleymadison.com)

The motto of the site is "Life is short, have an affair". The premise of the site is a place for married individuals to meet and have a fling with other married individuals. Registration is free and allows unlimited browsing. Contacting someone through the site will cost money. As with other dating websites, many users will use the same screen name here as they would on their other public profiles. The advanced search options will allow you to search by a screen name. If this information is not available, standard filters such as location, age, and race will help you filter out unwanted results. This site is the first stop for a private investigator hired by an attorney representing a divorce client.

Additional Dating Sites

There are many other online dating websites that all function similarly. A website devoted to identifying the top 100 dating websites can be found at 100bestdatingsites.org. The most popular include Match, eHarmony, Adult Friend Finder, Christian Mingle, and Plenty of Fish. I also maintain a custom search engine that searches any user name or keyword at the following URL.

http://inteltechniques.com/OSINT/dating.networks.html

True Dater (truedater.com)

This is a portal for the review of online dating relationships. As you may suspect, most of these are negative. It is a place for someone to vent about a jerk they met online, a liar that tried to take advantage of them, or a subject that turned out to be married. Searches here are done by the user name provided on the dating site, so identifying the target's user name needs to be completed first.

Meetup (meetup.com)

Meetup is not necessarily a dating website. It consists of users, groups, and events. Each user creates a profile that includes the person's interests, photos, and user name. A group is created by one or more users and is focused on a general interest in a specific location. An example would be the "Houston Dog Park Lovers", which is a Houston based group of dog owners that meet at dog parks. Each group will post events that the members can attend. The majority of the events posted on Meetup is visible to the public and can be attended by anyone. Some groups choose to mark the location of the event as private and you must be a member to see the location. Membership is free and personal information is not required.

You can search Meetup by interest or location on practically any page. Once you locate a group page, you can browse the members of the group. This group page will also identify any future and past events sponsored by the group. These past events will identify the users that attended the event as well as feedback about the event. This site no longer offers the option to search by user name. In order to do this, you will need to use a search engine such as Google or Bing. In Figure 7.18, a Google search using the "site" operator reveals 466 results on Meetup for "John Morrison". These results could be filtered by adding interests or a location that would likely relate to the target. The user profile, as seen in Figure 7.19, will often include links to social networks and messages from associates on the website. Additionally, these profiles will identify any future Meetup events that the user plans on attending. Because of this, the site has been used in the past by civil process servers, detectives, and the news media to locate people that had been avoiding them.

Figure 7.18: A Google search result for a user on Meetup.

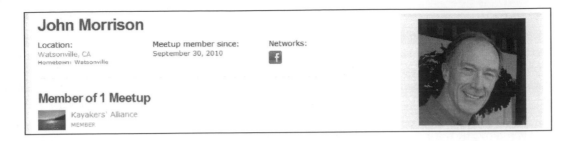

Figure 7.19: A user profile on Meetup.

Forums and Message Boards

Online forums provide a unique place for discussion about any topic. If you can think of the subject, an entire site full of people is probably hosting a discussion about the topic. These are usually referred to as user forums. Sometimes, these sites are excluded from being indexed by search engines. This can make locating them difficult. A new wave of forum search sites fills this void. Each of the following sites will search the forum communities, message boards, discussion threads, and other general interest groups that post messages back and forth.

Oh My God I Love It (omgili.com)

OMGILI is my first choice for online forum searching. The content on here is not limited only to third party forum sites. OMGILI also has its own forum for commenting about other websites and forums. Searching a user name is the most helpful here. A topic search may work, but you may need to search for something precise. Note that the default search is now limited to only one day. You can change this within the search area and select "any time".

Board Reader (boardreader.com)

Board Reader offers an advanced search which allows you to choose keywords, language, data range, and specific domain. If you have trouble filtering results on other forum search sites, this can be useful.

Real world application: Police were investigating a violent incident where someone was injured during an attack. The unknown suspect, a person the victim met on an online gaming forum, was not immediately identified. After receiving cooperation from the victim, these forum search sites were used to locate other gaming sites that the suspect used. In one of these sites, he openly bragged about his participation in the felony. Two subpoenas later, detectives were able to contact and arrest the "anonymous" suspect.

Craigslist Forums (craigslist.org)

One individual online forum that deserves mentioning is the Craigslist forum. This forum is categorized by topic instead of location, but location filtering is supported. These forums are not indexed by most search engines, so a manual search is the only way to see the content. Figure 7.20 displays the Craigslist Forums home page with some conversation topics. In order to search these areas, you must create a free user account. As usual, you can use fictitious information in your profile. After logging in, you can search by keyword on this main page, but not by screen name. This option will identify posts matching the search terms within any of the topics. Figure 7.21 shows a search by telephone number to identify posts mentioning the number.

The "Handle" option will search by user name but can only be seen by clicking on any topic. In Figure 7.22, I entered the "Yoga" room which displays the additional "Handle" search option. This will identify the posts of an individual user. I have found this "handle" option useful to an investigator. As a general rule, most people will use the same user name across several sites. Craigslist is no exception. If you have identified a user name of a target, a search on the Craigslist forums is worth a look. Although you will not get a result every time you search, the commentary is usually colorful when you do.

When you locate a user name of a target on the Craigslist forums, searching that user name will provide an abundance of information within the user's profile page. Figure 7.23 displays a forum user and identifies a forwarding email address, date joined, photograph, and up to 50 posts made during the past 31 days. These can provide great intelligence on the target.

adoption ℝ 130	dance 1	gift ideas 13	outdoors ℝ+ 95	self-employment ℝ 47
alt energy ℝ 9	death & dying ℝ+ 106	haiku hotel ℝ+ 89	over 50 club ℝ 109	shopping forum 5
alt housing 4	design & decor 8	health & healing ℝ 270	p.o.c. forum ℝ+ 144	spirituality ℝ 221
antiques 9	dieting ℝ+ 55	history forum ℝ 95	parenting ℝ 7264	sports ℝ 298
apple / mac ℝ+ 88	disabilities ℝ+ 6	housing ℝ+ 366	pĕrsonal forum ℝ 2	std info 5
arts forum ℝ+ 310	disaster relief ℝ	insomnia 1	pet & animal ℝ+ 2142	supernatural ℝ+ 135
astronomy 14	divorce ℝ+ 200	job market ℝ+ 226	philosophy ℝ+ 185	tax forum ℝ 75

Figure 7.20: A portion of the Craigslist Forums home page.

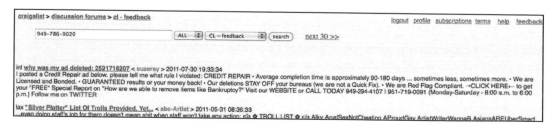

Figure 7.21: A Craigslist Forums search result for a telephone number.

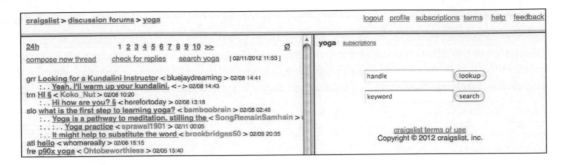

Figure 7.22: A Craigslist Forum discussion room with search options.

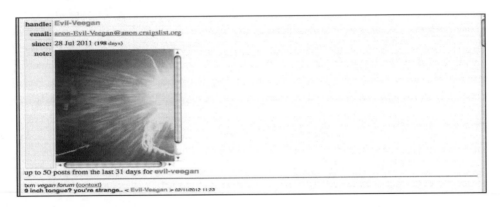

Figure 7.23: A Craigslist Forum handle search identifying a user profile.

Online Newspaper Comments

Practically every newspaper now has some sort of online presence. Most digital editions allow readers to leave comments about individual articles. These comments can usually be seen at the bottom of each web page. While the value that these comments add to the newsworthiness of each piece of news is debatable, the content can be important to an investigation. In years past, most newspapers hosted their own digital comment delivery system within their website. This often resulted in a large headache while trying to maintain order, prevent feuds between readers, and delete direct threats. Today, most news websites use third party services to host these comments. The most popular are Facebook and Disqus. When Facebook is utilized, most people use their real names and behave better than when using only a user name on Disqus. Any complaints about the comment activity can be referred to Facebook since they technically store the content. Searching Facebook comments can be conducted through the technique explained in Chapter Three.

In order to search for content within the Disqus comment system, you can conduct a custom Google search. First, it is important to understand how the Disqus system is recognized by Google. Figure 7.24

displays a typical comment area of a website. There is an option to log into a Disqus account and you can "upvote" or "downvote" each comment to show your approval. The words visible on this page that were provided by Disqus are important for the search. The word "comments" will be visible on every Disqus provided environment and there will also be a link to disqus.com. Therefore, the following search on Google should provide any websites that have the Disqus comment delivery system and also have a reference to OSINT.

"osint" "disqus" "comments"

This may produce some non-Disqus results that happen to possess all three words, but those should be rare. This will also identify many pages that do not contain any comments whatsoever. In order to only receive results that actually have some comments, alter your Google search to the following.

"osint" "disqus" "1..999 comments"

This instructs Google to only display results that contain the keywords "OSINT" and "Disqus" and also contain the exact phrase of any number between 1 and 999 followed immediately by the term "comments". This would provide the example in Figure 7.24 that contains "5 Comments" as a result. The "1..999" portion is the Google range operator that will display any number within the specified range.

Figure 7.24: A typical Discus comment environment.

Ethnicity Specific Communities

There are several social websites that focus on one specific race. While these communities do not prohibit members of another race from joining, the great majority of the members are of a single race. Black Planet (blackplanet.com) has a large African-American presence, MiGente (migente.com) has a large Latino-American presence, and Asian Avenue (asianave.com) has a large Asian-American membership. Each of these has extensive search capabilities. The easiest option is to provide a user name which may identify a target's profile.

The Hood Up (thehoodup.com)

This interesting website has a subtitle of "Where American Hoods Connect!". The index page has categories for open discussion, the East Coast, the West Coast, the Midwest, and "Down South". The premise of the site is a place for "gangsters" and "hoods" to communicate with each other in an uncensored environment. A quick look into the Midwest group displayed numerous conversations about criminal activity, gangs, and violence. Each page has a search option for any keyword. A search of "Chicago Gaylords" resulted in 799 posts discussing everything from the history of the gang to debates about current and future plans. Any of this would be great intelligence for the gang units of the Chicago Police Department.

Online Prostitution

Craigslist was once used by many prostitutes nationwide as an avenue to meeting "Johns". Likewise, many people used the site to locate a prostitute. In 2009, Illinois Attorney General Lisa Madigan convinced Craigslist to remove the "Erotic Services" section that hosted these posts announcing illegal activity. Today, it is difficult to find a post offering prostitution on Craigslist. Unfortunately, this does not mean that the prostitutes and their clients simply stopped the illegal behavior. Instead, they found new resources. There are many sites online that aid in prostitution and human trafficking. A few of the big players are listed here.

Backpage (backpage.com)

When Craigslist turned off the "Erotic Services" section, the traffic immediately went to Backpage. After selecting your location on this site, you will be presented with a main page of categories including the "Adult" area. This will include subsections of Escorts, Body Rubs, Stripper & Strip Clubs, Dom & Fetish, Trans-Sexuals, Male Escorts, and Adult Jobs. It should be no surprise that the posts inside of these sections include blatant ads for prostitution. Almost all of them include photos, many of them nude, and prices for various services. Cellular telephone numbers are common, but are usually spelled out in text. Instead of typing an area code of "314", the user may type "three one four". Because of this, an investigator must get creative with the searches. A search field is at the top of every page and allows for any keyword search. Several cases of juvenile prostitution have started with a visit to Backpage.

Real world application: Officials in Bridgeport Connecticut made several arrests of a prostitution ring that included 14 year old girls after an investigation into Backpage. Such stories are common nationwide. A quick look into any major city will display several prostitutes waiting for their next client.

National Blacklist (nationalblacklist.com)

Three interesting new blacklist services for prostitutes arrived in 2013. The first, and most popular, is National Blacklist. This website is self-described as "Serving the escort community" as a deadbeat registry. Most of the user submitted posts appear to be escorts warning other women about people that do not show up, refuse to pay for sexual services, or harass the prostitutes in any way. The forums are categorized by city, and Chicago currently has over 5,000 posts. Figure 7.25 displays a menu of messages announcing potential covert police officers, liars, abusers, and a client that canceled an appointment. The website does not offer a search option. I recommend browsing by city or using the Google "site" operator to find anything specific.

10/18/13	Chicago	Benny	He a known liar, fake broke black
10/15/13	Chicago	Robber!	When you not being outright robbed
10/15/13	Chicago	Police	Police
10/14/13	Chicago	Cop ?	i suspect he's a cop. Asks way to m
10/11/13	Chicago	Bad Trick!	After he parked his car behind mine
10/09/13	Chicago	cluelss caller or a cop	Asking stuff about sex and what's o
10/09/13	Chicago	abuser	woman beater!!!
10/08/13	Chicago	Tyron Talbort	Client cancels last minute then whe

Figure 7.25: A National Blacklist user forum.

Backpage Blacklist (backpageblacklist.com)

This service offers an avenue for prostitutes to report no-shows and file "incident reports" after an unwanted encounter. The website allows you to search by cellular telephone number or keyword within a report. Anyone can post anything to these services without validation, so you must always question how accurate the information is. I once found the cell number of a background check target on one of these sites. During an interview, he confessed to the activity.

City Vibe (cityvibe.com)

This site offers a search for "escorts" after choosing a geographical location. This will present a page full of posts from local women offering various services for money. Many include a nude photograph, details of the service provided, breakdown of the fees, and whether they will travel to a location (outcall) or demand a client come to them (incall). Several also offer a personal website link with even further information. It is also common for the user to include a cellular telephone number to be used for contact. The search function on this site is fairly weak. Searching a user's name will usually present results, but searching a full telephone number often returns no results. To correct this, only search the last four digits of a telephone number to get a result. Many times, doing this will discover many women using the same contact number, which often actually connects to a pimp. Law enforcement agencies take advantage of this site to set up prostitution stings.

Escort Review Websites

These types of services may be difficult for some readers to understand. I was also surprised when I first found them. This is where prostitution clients communicate with each other and leave reviews of their experiences with the prostitutes. These "Johns" document the slightest details of the experience including price, cleanliness, and accuracy of the photograph in the ad. Further, this is the first location that will announce an undercover operation by the police. This is important for law enforcement, as this could create an officer safety issue. It is also how the police can determine when a new name or photo should be used in future covert ads. Another purpose for this data is to create documentation of the reviews of an arrested prostitute. This can prove valuable in court for the prosecution of offenses. There are several of these services, and every metropolitan area will have a preferred website by the customers. A Google search of "Escort reviews Anaheim" will get you to the popular options. Of course, replace Anaheim with your city of interest. The following techniques can be useful when you identify the service relevant to your investigation.

Rate That Provider (ratethatprovider.com)

Rate That Provider, and many others, requires an account to access the forums. This can be covertly created, or you can often use a search engine to get around the limitation. A search on Google of "site:ratethatprovider.com chicago", without the quotes, identifies 32,500 results of forum posts. Figure 7.26 displays this search with active links that connect to the posts created. Usually, this link will forward you to a login page. Credentials must be provided before you can see the content. Accessing the Google Cache of each link will likely bypass this demand and display the content information without membership. Practically every post on this forum can be accessed with this method.

Figure 7.26: A result page on Google for a prostitution rating site.

The Erotic Review (theeroticreview.com)

If you do not know of any individual services that prostitution clients are using in your area, The Erotic Review is a safe bet. Practically every metropolitan area has a presence here. Much of this site will not be available unless you join as a premium member. However, there should be plenty of visible free content for basic investigations. Figure 7.27 displays a partial post by TRH2323, a client of "Jayda Noir". The rest of the post was unsuitable for this book.

> saw jaydas post on rs2k. I really go for hot ebony girls so when I saw her pics I could not resist. emailed her in the morning and got a prompt reply. set up an appointment for later that afternoon. I am from central Illinois so a trip to Chicago can be an adventure. I ran late be she was very understanding. when I finally arrived at her incall I was about 45 minutes late. exchanged some pleasant chit chat. she brewed me a cup of coffee then laid on the bed looking extremely sexy in a tight purplish dress. then the fun began.

Figure 7.27: A review of a prostitute on The Erotic Review.

Escort Ads (escortads.xxx)

This adult website sponsored by pornography ads allows you to enter the cellular telephone number of a suspected sex provider. The results will include all of the profiles that have been associated with the number. It will also combine these results and display a convenient summary of the cities where ads were posted, ages used in the ads, and every photo posted. It will even remove the duplicate photos.

Real world application: While participating in an FBI Operation, I focused on locating juvenile prostitutes and women forced into the sex industry by pimps. One easy way to determine if a sex worker was traveling extensively was to search her number through the Escort Ads website. If it returned numerous cities with postings, that was a strong indication that she was a full time sex worker and was likely not traveling alone. Every contact that we made with traveling prostitutes resulted in the identification of the pimps that transported them to the stings.

Exposing Johns (exposingjohns.com)

This service is somewhat of a flipside of prostitution review sites. Instead, Exposing Johns identifies the sex buyers that are attempting to solicit sex through Backpage. These reports are crowd sourced and submitted by strangers, so the data will not always be accurate. Many people will post fake ads as a prostitute and expose all of the men that try to buy sex through the ad. The cellular number of the "John" will then be searched on Facebook and connected to a true identity if possible. The service offers a search function to help you quickly look for the owner of a cell phone number.

Amazon (amazon.com)

Amazon is the largest online retailer. Users flock to the site to make purchases of anything imaginable. After the receipt of the items ordered, Amazon generates an email requesting the user to rate the items. This review can only be created if the user is logged in to an account. This review is now associated with the user in the user profile. An overwhelming number of users create these product reviews and provide their real information on the profile for their Amazon account. While Amazon does not have an area to search for this information by user name, you can do it with a search engine. Figure 7.28 displays a search on Amazon for a specific user which returns zero results. A search on Google (Figure 7.29) links to an Amazon profile and several item reviews. The first link (Figure 7.30) displays the user profile including photo, location, and the user's review of products purchased.

This technique of using Google or Bing to search for profiles on websites that do not allow such a search can be applied practically everywhere. Many sites discourage the searching of profiles, but a search on Google such as "site:targetwebsite.com John Doe" would provide links to content matching the criteria. The difficulty arises in locating all of the sites where a person may have a profile. By now, you can search the major communities, but it is difficult to keep up with all of the lesser known networks. This is where the user name search engines mentioned earlier assist.

Amazon does offer a native Wish List search option. If you navigate to amazon.com/gp/registry/search, you can type any name or email address to search for that target's wish list, baby registry, or wedding registry. I have found this type of information useful during criminal interrogations. While these details do not insinuate any criminal activity, telling a suspect that I know this information can be interesting. I once had a suspect convinced that I had no evidence against him in reference to a child pornography investigation. When I "slipped" and told him I knew the books that he wanted for Christmas two years prior, a look of fear replaced his arrogant attitude. He began questioning his lack of confidence in my investigation.

Figure 7.28: An Amazon user search without results.

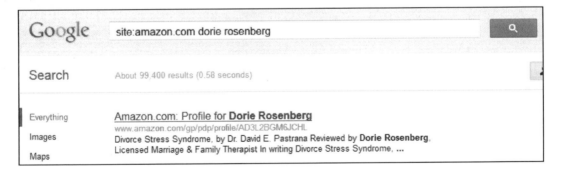

Figure 7.29: A Google search for an Amazon user name.

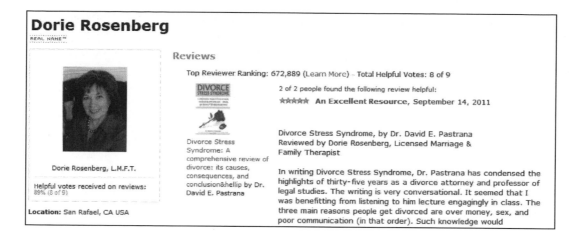

Figure 7.30: An Amazon user profile with review information.

Pinterest (pinterest.com)

Pinterest is an online "pinboard" where users can share photos, links, and content located anywhere on the internet. It is a way to re-broadcast items of interest to a user. People that follow that user on Pinterest can keep updated on things that the user is searching and reading. The search feature on the main website is useful for keyword searches only. It will search for any term and identify posts that include those words within the description. A search of my last name displayed several photos of people. Clicking each of these links will present the full page view of the photo and any associated comments. This page will also identify the full name of the person that uploaded the content and the original online source. Clicking on the full name of the user will open the user profile which should include all "pinned" content. Unfortunately, you cannot search a person's full name or user name on Pinterest and receive a link to their profile page. To do this, you must use Google. The following search on Google will identify the user name and a link to the profile page of "Helen Cargile".

Site:pinterest.com "Helen Cargile"

Figure 7.31 displays the result of this search. The link identifies the user's screen name as "cornhuskdolls". If you knew the user name but did not know the person's real name, you could change the search to the following.

Site:pinterest.com "cornhuskdolls"

You would receive a similar result as seen in Figure 7.31 and would now know the full name of that user.

Figure 7.31: Identifying a user profile on Pinterest.

Reddit (reddit.com)

Reddit is a social news and entertainment website where the registered users submit content in the form of either a link or text. Other users then vote the submission up or down, which is used to rank the post and determine its position on the website's pages. The submissions are then discussed on the "comments" page of every entry. There are categories, referred to as sub-Reddits, which cover practically any topic you can imagine. As of May 2013, there were over 5,000 sub-Reddits. Three of these categories can aid researchers with many types of investigations.

Reddit Bureau of Investigation (reddit.com/r/rbi)

This active community helps other Reddit users solve crimes and other problems. Internet gurus will help find deadbeat parents, computer specialists will aid in tracking stolen devices, and private investigators will assist with investigation techniques.

Real world application: I have used this sub-reddit several times in the past three years. The most successful cases involved hit and run traffic crashes. In 2013, I assisted a northern Illinois police department with the investigation of a fatal car crash. The offender fled the area and an elderly woman died. Three small pieces of the offending vehicle were left at the scene. After posting this information to local media outlets, I submitted it to RBI. Within minutes, several vehicle body shop employees were tracking down the parts and eventually tied them to a specific year and model of a 10 year old vehicle. This information led to the arrest of the subject.

Figure 7.32 displays a post from 2013. A victim of a hit and run traffic crash posted a blurry photo of the suspect vehicle and asked for assistance. Within hours, a Reddit user identified the license plate through digital correction techniques.

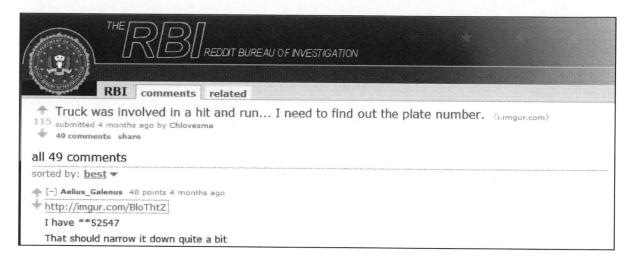

Figure 7.32: A post on Reddit's RBI forum.

Pic Requests (reddit.com/r/picrequests)

A constant frustration in my work is blurry, out of focus, or grainy digital images. Commonly, I will receive surveillance photos that are too dark or light to identify anything of value in the image. Occasionally, I will find images on social networks that could be beneficial if they were just a touch clearer. Pic Requests saves the day. This sub-Reddit consists of digital photo experts that can perform Photoshop magic on practically any image. Many Reddit users will request old photos colorized, torn photos digitally repaired, or unwanted subjects removed from an image. I have uploaded several surveillance images to this group with a request for assistance. The users have been incredibly helpful by identifying digits in blurred license plates and turning dark surveillance footage into useful evidence.

What Is This Thing? (reddit.com/r/whatisthisthing)

I am consistently amazed at the results from this sub-Reddit. What Is This Thing is a place that you can post a digital photo of practically anything, and someone will know exactly what it is while providing detailed and sited additional information. Many users post images of old antiques and intricate items hoping to identify something valuable in their collection. I use it to identify tattoo meanings, graffiti, suspicious items mailed to politicians, vehicle parts, and just about anything else that is presented to me during my investigations.

Real world application: In 2012, I was asked to assist with a death investigation of a "Jane Doe". I submitted a sanitized version of a tattoo on her back that appeared to be Chinese symbols. Within five minutes, a Reddit user identified the symbols, their meaning, and references to the region of China that would probably be related to my investigation. A reverse image search of his examples led to information about a human trafficking ring that the victim was associated with.

At the time of this writing, a user was requesting information about the tattoo visible in Figure 7.33. Reddit user "hihrince" identified the tattoo as a reference to Dihydroxyphenylacetaldehyde, user "xgloryfades" provided an explanation of the chemical compound, and user "WTF-BOOM" provided a link to over 50 online photos of people with the same tattoo. This all occurred over a period of one hour.

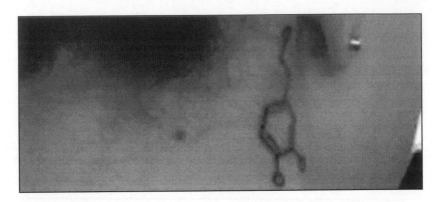

Figure 7.33: An unknown tattoo submitted to Reddit.

If you plan to use these techniques on Reddit, please consider a few things. You should create a free account now and hold on to it. Creating a new account and asking for help minutes later can be viewed as rude. I like to use accounts that appear to have been established a long time ago. If you are visible as an active member of Reddit with a history of comments, this might encourage other active members to assist you. You should never be demanding in your requests. Remember, these people are volunteering to help you. Many of them possess a skill set that cannot be found elsewhere.

I also never upload any content that is not already publicly available. If digital images were released to the press, I have no problem releasing them to Reddit. If my target image is already on a public social network, I see no reason it cannot be linked to through Reddit.

Reddit Search

While the search option on Reddit is not perfect, it is the best option for identifying posts of interest. The search area in the upper right of every page will allow you to query any terms. The results will be from all pages, including thousands of sub-Reddits. If you want a more detailed search, you can use Google or Bing. The following query would identify any posts that included the word "surveillance" within the sub-Reddit "RBI".

site:reddit.com/r/rbi "surveillance"

You can modify this search to look for any word of interest within any other category. You could also eliminate the category option and search the entire website. The search on Reddit will not search for posts from a specific user. If you know the user name of your target, you can enter it within the address (URL). The example below would present the Reddit page of the user "jforrler".

http://www.reddit.com/user/jforrler

This page will display every post and comment by that subject. It is important to note that users can delete their posts. If you suspect that this has occurred recently, you can search for this user on Google and check the "Cached" copy of the profile. This has produced many results for me in the past.

Compromised Accounts

Email addresses are compromised regularly. Hacker groups such as Lulzsec and Anonymous often publicly post databases of email addresses and corresponding passwords on websites such as Pastebin. These types of websites are detailed in Chapter Eight. Manually searching for evidence of compromised accounts can get complicated and results are rarely complete. Several newer services aid with this type of investigation.

Should I Change My Password (shouldichangemypassword.com)

Should I Change My Password has been created to help the average person identify if his or her email accounts have been compromised and need to have the passwords changed. This site uses a number of databases that have been released by hackers to the public. No passwords are stored in their database, and a result appears immediately after a search. This result identifies the amount of references to the email address online and the date it was compromised.

Hack Notifier (hacknotifier.com)

Hack Notifier is the only one of these services that will attempt to link the searcher to information about the compromised account. A link is included in the positive match result that will forward to an online source that explains the security breach. This will often be the news report that first published the details of the hacked accounts. If an email address is suspected of being compromised, all three of these services should be searched.

In 2014, several new services began offering their own compromised email notification websites. Many of these "hacked" databases are identical, but some may possess newer data than others. Those that I have successfully used previously include Breach Alarm (breachalarm.com) and Have I Been Pwned (haveibeenpwned.com).

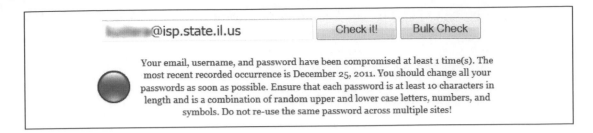

Figure 7.34: A compromised email account on shouldichangemypassword.com.

Broadcastify (broadcastify.com)

Broadcastify is much more than an online community. It is an online portal for scanner enthusiasts. It contains the most comprehensive database of radio frequencies that can be monitored on personal radios and scanners. The forums are very active with conversations about emergency radio traffic, hardware reviews, amateur radio, and frequency monitoring software. This can all be interesting content to search, but will rarely provide valuable intelligence. The real interest for OSINT analysts is the live and archived audio.

The live audio feeds are free and do not require an account to access them. You will be presented a map that you can navigate to the state and county of interest. This will present all of the live audio feeds of public scanner frequencies that can be monitored over the internet. Figure 7.35 (left) displays a web player monitoring the live audio of Chicago Police radio traffic. In the background is a partial list of other Chicago area emergency frequencies that can be monitored.

These live audio feeds are provided by individual listeners within the area of the frequency coverage. A user leaves a personal scanner on the frequency and broadcasts the audio through a computer with internet access. You will find audio feeds in all parts of the country. This includes large cities, small towns, and rural counties. This can provide immediate information about live events anywhere. You no longer need to be in a specific location to receive radio traffic from that area. For historical content, information can be obtained from the archives.

Most live audio feeds have an option within the player window of "Feed Archives". This will take you to a menu that will provide several dates to choose from, a time frame of a chosen date, and an embedded player that will play the radio feed from the time specified. Figure 7.35 (right) displays an active channel. Additionally, you can choose the "save as" feature to download a copy of the communication as a MP3 file for archiving. This will provide the emergency services radio traffic during an event of interest. The archive function requires a user account.

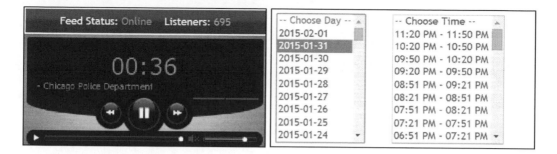

Figure 7.35: A live audio stream (left) and an archived audio stream (right) on Broadcastify.

Web SDR (websdr.org)

The previous technique connected you to shared radio scanners set to a specific frequency. There is another community that allows you to control the target frequency. A Web SDR is a Software-Defined Radio receiver connected to the internet. It allows many listeners to listen and tune it simultaneously. SDR technology makes it possible that all listeners tune independently, and thus listen to different signals. This is in contrast to the many classical receivers that are already available via the internet. This page will direct you to over 100 online receivers waiting for your connection. The list will identify the location, frequency range, and antenna in use. The world map at the bottom of the page will help you quickly locate receivers in your targeted area.

Figure 7.36 displays a receiver available at the University of California Berkeley. It is tuned to 144391.60 KHz and is monitoring a digital communication over an analog signal. This tone can be converted to the text that it is sending to another device. I have used this in the past to monitor marine, citizen band, and ham signals in geographical areas of an active investigation.

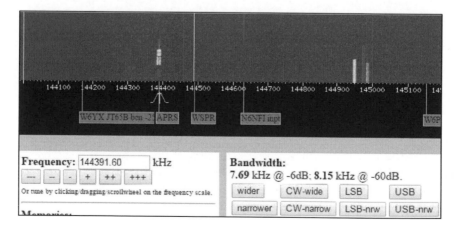

Figure 7.36: A WebSDR live audio feed from a controllable analog receiver.

Chapter Eight

Documents

The open source intelligence discussed up to this point has focused on websites that include valuable information about a target. A category of intelligence that is often missed during OSINT research is documents. This type of data usually falls into one of three classes. The first is documents that include information about the target within the contents of the file. These can include online PDF files that the target may not know exist. The second class is documents that were actually created by the target. These files can make their way into public view unintentionally. Finally, the third class includes the metadata stored within a document that can include vital information about the true source of the document. The following techniques explain manual searching and retrieving of documents. Later in this book, automated software solutions will be detailed.

Google Searching (google.com)

A very basic way of locating documents that are publicly available on a specific website or related to a specific topic is to use Google. The "filetype" search operator explained in Chapter One can be used for this task. An example of a search query for all Microsoft Word documents stored on the domain of cryptome.org would be:

site:cryptome.org filetype:doc   or   site:cryptome.org filetype:docx

As seen in Figure 8.01, this search on Google provided 95 documents. If you wanted to locate all documents that reference a specific topic, you can use the filetype operator without a specific website listed. An example of a search query for all Excel spreadsheets that contain a list of members of the Harrodsburg First Program would be:

filetype:xls"Harrodsburg First"

Figure 8.02 displays this search with 27 results for Excel documents. The first result is a spreadsheet that contains the member names, affiliated businesses, addresses, phone numbers, and websites (Figure 8.03). If you wanted to search for a specific person's name within any spreadsheets, you would type the following query.

filetype:xls TARGET NAME

Using this technique with one of the people listed within this document also provided a link to the same document (Figure 8.04).

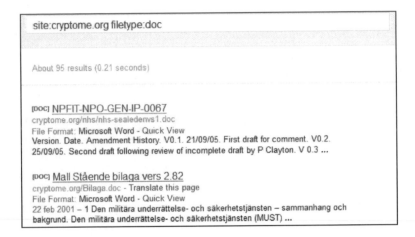

Figure 8.01: A Google search result of Word documents.

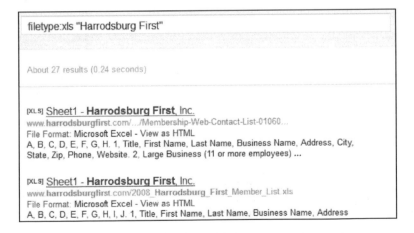

Figure 8.02: A Google search result of Excel documents.

	Title	First Name	Last Name	Business Name	Address	City, State, Zip	Phone	Website
1	Title	First Name	Last Name	Business Name	Address	City, State, Zip	Phone	Website
2	Large Business (11 or more employees)							
3	Mr.	Dixon	Dedman	Beaumont Inn	638 Beaumont Inn Dr.	Harrodsburg, Ky 40433	859-734-3381	www.beaumontinn.com
4				Community Trust Bank	570 Chestnut St	Harrodsburg, Ky 40433	859-73404354	
5	Mr.	Allen	White	Farmers National Bank	776 S. College St	Harrodsburg, Ky 40433	859-734-9953	www.fnbky.com

Figure 8.03: An Excel spreadsheet located containing personal information.

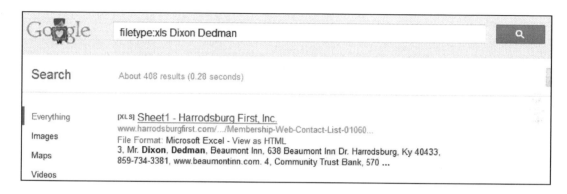

Figure 8.04: A document search by name with identical result.

The following table includes the most common document file types and the associated file extensions. Both Google and Bing are capable of searching any file type regardless of the file association.

Microsoft Word	DOC, DOCX
Microsoft Excel	XLS, XLSX, CSV
Microsoft Powerpoint	PPT, PPTX
Adobe Acrobat	PDF
Text File	TXT, RTF
Open Office	ODT, ODS, ODG, ODP
Word Perfect	WPD

If you wanted to search all of these file types at once, the following string in Google or Bing would find most documents on the topic of OSINT. You could change that term to anything else of interest.

OSINT filetype:pdf OR filetype:doc OR filetype:xls OR filetype:xlsx OR filetype:docx OR filetype:ppt OR filetype:pptx OR filetype:wpd OR filetype:txt

This query basically tells the search engine to look for any reference to the term OSINT inside of a PDF file, Microsoft Word file, et cetera, and display all of the results. The Google Custom Search Engine described in Chapter One is a great resource for this exact type of search. However, I highly recommend having an understanding of the manual search process. It will give you much more control than any automated solution.

The first three editions of this book contained several third party document search services. Most of them either disappeared or now rely solely on a Google custom engine. Therefore, I no longer recommend any of them. They simply cannot compete with a properly structured document search on Google or Bing.

Scribd (scribd.com)

The idea of storing user created documents on the internet is gaining a lot of popularity. Keeping these files "in the cloud" eliminates the need for personal storage on a device such as a CD or flash drive. In addition, storing files on the internet allows the author to access and edit them from any computer with an internet connection. A common use of these document-hosting sites is to store them only during the editing phase. Once the document is finished and no longer needed, the user may forget to remove it from public view. Scribd is one of the most popular document storage websites. It allows users to embed the stored documents into their own websites if desired. Searching the site is relatively easy.

A search field is at the top of every page on the site. Searching for your target name should produce any public documents stored through this service that includes the target name on any page of the document. Most of these documents are intentionally stored on the site and any groundbreaking evidence of criminal activity will not be included. Instead, the primary use of the site for OSINT investigations is the large number of documents related to businesses. Entering any large corporation name should display several pages of viewable documents related to the company. Often, these include documents that the company's security personnel would not authorize to be online. Searching for "FOUO", an acronym for "for official use only", produced hundreds of results. While none of these appeared to be officially classified, they were not intended to be posted to a public website. If you are presented with an unmanageable amount of results, the filter options appear directly above the first document result. These will allow you to search by language, size, file type, and date uploaded. Figure 8.05 displays the previously mentioned search and a small selection of the results.

Identifying the user that uploaded a document is as easy as locating the document. On the upper-right side of any page containing a document, there is an area that will identify the subject that uploaded the file. This also acts as a link to this user's profile on the website. The profile will display any information that the user supplied as well as a feed of recent activity of that user on the site. This can help identify other documents uploaded by a specific user. Figure 8.06 shows the first page of a document with the user name of the person responsible for the upload to the right of the document.

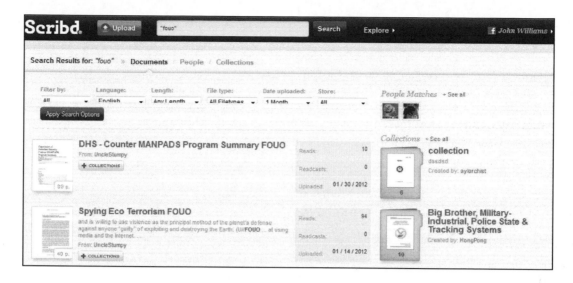

Figure 8.05: Sensitive document results found on Scribd.

Doc Stoc (docstoc.com)

Doc Stoc is self-described as "Documents and resources for small businesses and professionals". The majority of the users on this website use it for legitimate purposes. Just like other websites, there are users that take advantage of these free services with unintended usages. This is a popular site for users to store "leaked" documents. These often include internal memos and policy guides from large corporations that were never meant to be released to the public. Conducting a few creative searches revealed several hundred private documents created by large financial institutions. Security personnel from these types of businesses should continually check sites like Doc Stoc and Scribd for proprietary information. If any are found, an official letter from the legal department of the company should result in a quick removal.

Figure 8.06: A partial view of a document and the user name of the provider.

Presentation Repositories

With unprecedented online storage space at all of our fingertips, many people choose to store PowerPoint and other types of presentations in the cloud. Several free services have appeared to fill this demand. Of those, the following have the majority of publicly available documents.

Slide Share (slideshare.net)
ISSUU (issuu.com)
Prezi (prezi.com)

Slide Share and ISSUU allow native searching within their websites. However, Prezi does not have this option. For all three, I recommend a custom Google search with the site operator. If I want to locate presentations including the term OSINT from Slide Share, I would use the following query.

site:slideshare.net "OSINT"

Google Docs (docs.google.com)

Many Google Mail (Gmail) users take advantage of Google's free service for document storage called Google Docs. When a document is created, it is private by default and not visible to the public. However, when people want to share documents with friends or coworkers, the sharing properties must be changed. While it is possible to privately share files with individual Google users, many people find it easier to make the documents public. Most of these users probably assume that the files will not be seen by anyone other than the intended recipients. After all, who would go out searching for other people's documents? We will.

The Google Docs and Google Drive websites do not offer the option to search these public files, but you can do this using Google search. Now that the Google Docs allows search engines to index most of the public files, you should be able to find them with some specific search methods. The following search examples will explain a few of the options that would be conducted on google.com. The exact search is listed with the expected result. These should be used as a starting point for the many possibilities of document searching.

site:docs.google.com "resume" - 22,700 online resumes
site:docs.google.com "resume" "Williams" – 2,491 resumes with the name Williams
site:docs.google.com "Corey Trager" - 1 document (resume) belonging to the target
site:docs.google.com 865-274-2074 - 1 document containing the target number

Google categorizes the documents that are created by the user. The examples below identify searches that would display documents by type.

site:docs.google.com/presentation/d – 865,6000 PowerPoint presentations
site:docs.google.com/drawings/d – 68,600 Google flowchart drawings
site:docs.google.com/file/d – 6,945,000 images, videos, PDF files, and documents
site:docs.google.com/folder/d – 94,000 collections of files inside folders
site:docs.google.com/open – 1,400,000 external documents, folders and files

In 2013, Google began placing some user generated documents on the "drive.google.com" domain. Therefore, any search that you conduct with the method described previously should be repeated with "drive" in place of "docs". The previous search for the telephone number would be the following.

site:drive.google.com 865-274-2074

The target could be added to the previous examples to filter results. Figure 8.07 displays a search result from a Google query of site:docs.google.com/drawings/d "kim williams"

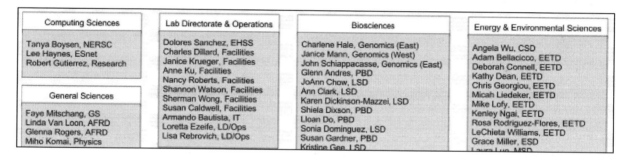

Figure 8.07: A Google Docs search result file.

Microsoft OneDrive (onedrive.live.com)

Similar to Google Drive, Microsoft's OneDrive offers that ability to store and share documents. The service is not as popular as Google Drive. However, there are thousands of publicly visible documents waiting to be found. The shared files are stored on the onedrive.live.com domain. A query for resumes would be as follows. This search could be conducted on Google or Bing. The result on Google was 3,550 resume files with personal information.

site:onedrive.live.com "resume"

Dropbox (dropbox.com)

The same technique used for Google Docs will also work with public Dropbox documents. There will be fewer results, but searching is still worthwhile. The following search revealed five digital scans of tax documents containing sensitive information:

site:dl.dropbox.com "taxpayer"

Note that "dl." is included before the domain instead of after. This is a unique requirement for Dropbox. Lately, I am seeing fewer results from this technique.

Amazon Web Services (aws.amazon.com)

Amazon Web Services is a large collection of servers that supply storage and internet application hosting in "the cloud". Instead of purchasing expensive hardware, many companies and individuals rent space on these servers. There are numerous documents available for download from these servers when searched appropriately. The following structure will identify documents indexed on google.com:

site:s3.amazonaws.com

The following search examples will explain a few of the options. The exact search is listed with the expected result. These should be used as a starting point for the many possibilities of document searching.

site:s3.amazonaws.com ext:xls "password" – 27,000 Excel spreadsheets
site:s3.amazonaws.com (504) 390-6582 – 1 PDF file with target number
site:s3.amazonaws.com "lionheart201" – 1 PDF file with user name reference

Custom Search Engine (http://inteltechniques.com/osint/docs.html)

If these operators seem overwhelming, I have created a Google Custom Search Engine that will apply many of the methods discussed here. This website will present a simple search field ready for any keyword desired. The results will include content obtained from Google Drive, SlideShare, AmazonAWS, DropBox, ISSUU, Scribd, DocStoc, and Prezi. Figure 8.08 displays the result of searching the term OSINT within SlideShare.

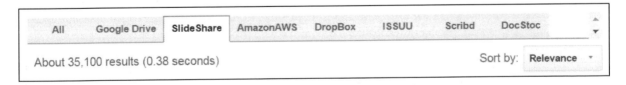

Figure 8.08: A search result page from a custom documents search engine.

WikiLeaks (search.wikileaks.org)

Some websites are created for the sole purpose of leaking sensitive and classified documents to the public. Wikileaks is such a site. When an Army soldier named Bradley Manning was arrested in 2010 for uploading classified government information to the site, Wikileaks became a household name. People then began to flock to the site to catch a glimpse of these controversial documents and videos. The official Wikileaks site finally provides a working search option. It will allow you to enter any search terms and will provide results of any leaked documents that contain these terms. Both the government and the private sector should be familiar with this site and the information that is identified with their agency.

Cryptome (cryptome.org)

Another site that strives to release sensitive and classified information to the public is Cryptome. Most of the information is related to freedom of speech, cryptography, spying, and surveillance. Much of the content could be considered conspiracy theories, but several official documents get released daily. Cryptome does not provide a search for their site and there are no third party providers that cater to this service. Therefore, we must rely on Google to find the documents. A structured query such as the following should function well.

site:cryptome.org "NAME OR TOPIC"

This technique using the search terms of "bradley manning" linked to 77 documents surrounding his investigation.

FOCA Online (informatica64.com/foca)

When an original document is found online, it is obviously important to analyze the visible content of the file. This includes the file name, written text, and an original location of the document. Digging deeper will expose more information. There is data embedded inside the document that cannot be seen by simply looking at the content of the file. This data is called metadata and can be very valuable to any type of investigation. This data can often include the computer name the document was created on, the user name of the computer or the network, the software version used, and information about the network that the computer is connected to. The best way to view all this information is to use a software solution which will be discussed later in book. It is also possible to view this "hidden" information online through a web browser.

The FOCA Online site will allow you to upload documents for analysis. To do this, click the "browse" button on the page. This will enable a file explorer that will allow you to select the document that you want analyzed. Figure 8.09 displays the results of an outdated America Online law enforcement manual uploaded in PDF format. The result identifies a created and modified date, the original title, three applications used to create the document, and a user name. A further search of this user name through the previously discussed techniques produced a wealth of information about the author of the document.

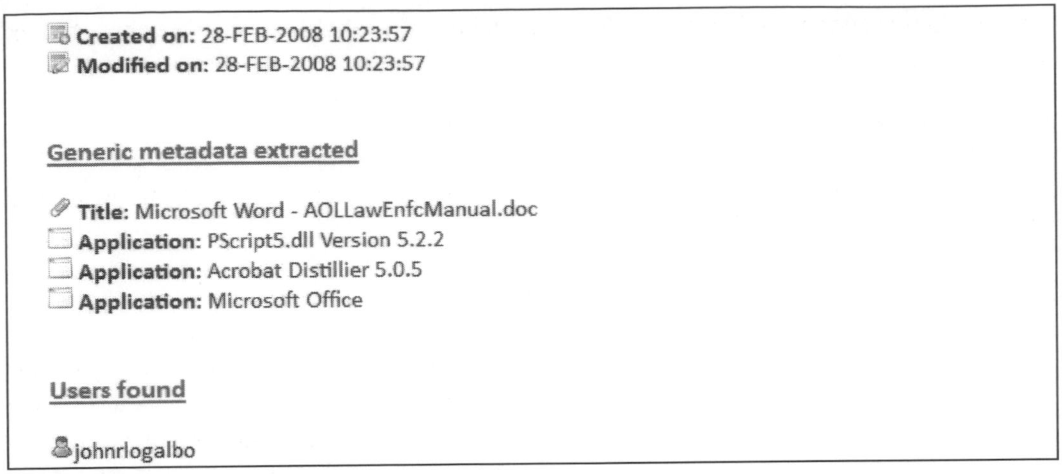

Figure 8.09: A FOCA document metadata result.

Real world application: Dennis Lynn Rader, also known as the BTK killer, sent a floppy disk to the Wichita Police Department containing a Microsoft Word document in reference to his killings. The police examined the metadata of this document and determined that it was made by a subject named "Dennis". Links to a Lutheran church was also located within this data. Conducting OSINT searches on these two pieces of information help identify the suspect and make an arrest.

Free OCR (free-ocr.com)

You may occasionally locate a PDF file that has not been indexed for the text content. These types of PDF files will not allow you to copy and paste any of the text. This could be due to poor scanning techniques or purposely to prohibit outside use of the content. You may desire to capture this text for a summary report. These files can be uploaded to Free OCR and converted to text documents. OCR is an acronym for optical character recognition. Basically, a computer "reads" the document and determines what the text is inside the content. The result is a new document with copy and paste capability.

Rental Vehicle Records

The details of rental vehicles are not technically documents, but the data seemed to fit this category the best. The following options have been controversially received during training and may not be appropriate for everyone. I present these methods to you as theories, and you should evaluate if the techniques are suitable for your research.

Several vehicle rental companies offer an option to access your receipts online. This is probably designed for customers that leave a vehicle at the business after hours and later need a receipt. While the processes to retrieve these documents are designed to only obtain your own records, it is very easy to view the records of other people.

Enterprise (enterprise.com)

At the bottom of every Enterprise web page is an option to "Print your receipt". Clicking this will present a form that must be completed before display of any details. Enterprise will need the target's country, driver's license number, and last name. Providing this information will display the user's entire rental history for the past six months. Testing with my own data provided two years' worth of results. Each document will link to the entire receipt from that rental. These receipts include the start date and time, end date and time, vehicle make and model, location picked up, total mileage, lease name, and form of payment. This information could be very beneficial to any drug case or private investigation. Figure 8.10 displays the search requirements and Figure 8.11 displays a detailed receipt.

Hertz (hertz.com)

Similar to Enterprise, Hertz has a link at the bottom of every page titled "Find a receipt". You can search by driver's license number or credit card number and will need a matching last name. The receipt will be very similar to the example in the Enterprise demonstration.

Alamo (Alamo.com)

Alamo also titles their receipt retrieval link "Find a Receipt" and it is located in the lower right portion of every page. The process is identical to the previous two examples. The only difference is that you must choose a date range. I usually select a start date of one year prior to the current date and the end date of the current date.

E-Z Rental (e-zrentacar.com/ez_rental_receipt.asp)

This company does not have an easily located search option. The link above will connect you to a request form that must be completed and submitted. You must include the driver's license number and zip code of the target. You must also include a valid email address where the receipt can be sent via email. I have not personally used this option in the past.

Thrifty (thrifty.com)

Thrifty requires you to log into your account in order to view receipts. This requires a password and is definitely outside the scope of OSINT. However, some have reported success by requesting a forgotten member number on the page located at www.thrifty.com/bluechip/forgotid.aspx. The site requires only the last name, date of birth, and DL number of the target.

Country in which Vehicle was Rented:	Select a Country ▾	**Note:** To protect your identity, your drivers license number will only appear online at time of entry.
Driver's License Number:		
	(Tip: 1-20 Alphanumeric Characters)	Special Characters
Last Name:		
	(e.g. Smith)	

Figure 8.10: The Enterprise rental receipt request form.

Enterprise Location: 7135 Gilespie St
Las Vegas, NV 89119-4267
US
Tel.: 7958842

Driver: MICHAEL BAZZELL

Start Date:	End Date:	Make/Model	Start Miles	End Miles	Miles Driven
May 13, 2011 @ 8:10 am	May 16, 2011 @ 3:34 pm	CALIBER SXT	24,232	24,432	200
Total Miles					**200**

Charge Description	Quantity		Per	Rate	Total
Rate	4		Day	16.56	66.24
COLLISION DAMAGE WAIVER FULL	4		Day	7.50	30.00
DISCOUNT					(19.87)
					Subtotal: USD 76.37

Taxes and Surcharges

CONCESSION RECOVERY FEE 10 PCT	8.42
CONSOLIDATED FACILITY CHG 3.75/DAY	15.00
CLARK COUNTY TAX 2 PCT	1.53
VEHICLE LICENSE FEE 1.95/DAY	7.80
NV GOV SURCHG	9.98
SALES TAX	3.76
	Subtotal: USD 122.86

Total Charges:	**USD 122.86**

Payment Information

CREDIT CARD MC	122.86

Figure 8.11: A receipt visible from Enterprise's website.

There are probably other options for the remaining vehicle rental companies. Google or Bing may find what you are seeking. Most of these options will involve knowledge of the target's driver's license number. While this may appear to be available only to law enforcement, visit Chapter Thirteen for an open source solution.

Paste Sites

Paste Sites are not technically documents. They are websites that allow users to upload text for public viewing. These were originally designed for software programmers that needed a place to store large amounts of text. A link would be created to the text and the user could share the link with other programmers to review the code. This is still a common practice, but other users have found ways to abuse this technology. Many hacking groups will use this area of the internet to store compromised account information, user passwords, credit card numbers, and other sensitive content. There are dozens of sites that cater to this need, and very few of them have a search feature.

Pastebin (pastebin.com)

Pastebin is the most popular paste site in the United States. This site has created over 13 million pages of content in the last few years. Hacker groups often use this site to release illegally obtained data to the public. A recent release included the home addresses and personal information of many police officers near Ferguson, Missouri. This is one of the sites that will allow for a search from within the site. This function performs a search through Google in the same way we could with the "site" operator. Typing in a target name, email address, or business name may reveal private information not intended for the public. For law enforcement, typing in the last four digits of a stolen credit card number may identify the user name of the thief. If successful, the target is most likely outside of the country. Regardless, this is a valuable piece to the case and an impressive explanation to the victim. Unfortunately, most of the users leave a default user name of "Guest".

Pastebin Alerts (andrewmohawk.com/pasteLert)

This free service will allow you to set up an alert for any search terms that appear on Pastebin. Similar to the Google Alerts service mentioned in Chapter One, this service continually monitors any keywords. If a new entry appears on the site that meets your criteria, you will receive an email notification. This can be beneficial to a business trying to monitor any fraudulent activity related to various services or products. Additionally, an individual could monitor a real name or partial credit card number for any personal content that shows up.

There are over 100 online paste sites and more are added monthly. Searching all of them can be overwhelming. A custom search website that queries all known paste sites is located at the following address. At the time of this writing, it searched over 100 websites commonly used to host criminal information. A complete list of sites can be found on the website.

http://inteltechniques.com/OSINT/pastebins.html

Chapter Nine

Photographs

Thanks to increased broadband speeds and cameras on every data cellular phone, digital photograph uploads are extremely common among social network users. These images can create a whole new element to the art of open source intelligence analysis. This chapter will identify various photo sharing websites as well as specific search techniques. Twitter photos alone require unique searches in order to be located properly. Later, photo metadata will be explained that can uncover a new level of information including the location where the picture was taken, the make, model and serial number of the camera, original un-cropped views of the photos, and even a collection of other photos online taken with the same camera. After reading this information, you may question if your online photos should stay online.

Twitter Images

For the first several years of Twitter's existence, it did not host any photos on its servers. If a user wanted to attach a photo to his or her post, a third party photo host was required. These have always been free and plentiful. Often, a shortened link was added to the message, which forwarded to the location of the photo. Twitter can now host photos used in Twitter posts, but third party hosts are still widely used. The majority of the images will be hosted on Instagram, which is explained in Chapter Three and detailed further in upcoming pages. If you have already identified your target's Twitter page, you will probably already have the links you need to see the photos uploaded with his or her posts.

Many Twitter messages have embedded images directly within the post. Twitter now allows you to search keywords for photo results. After you conduct any search within the native Twitter search field, your results will include a filter menu to the left. Figure 9.01 displays this menu with the "Photos" option selected. The results will only include images that have a reference to the searched keyword within the message or hashtag. You can also filter this search for people, videos, or news.

Figure 9.01: A Twitter search filtered by photos.

Chapter Three already explained the process of obtaining copies of the images in the highest resolution possible. If you do not have an identified target yet, you will need a search engine to find the images. Standard Google and Bing searches will not always suffice.

Twicsy (twicsy.com)

Twicsy is a very user-friendly site, which boasts that it can search all Twitter photos, regardless of host. They have indexed almost 4,600,000,000 photos and estimate one million new photos added every day. The top search bar is the only search option and can handle any term including topics, names, and locations. Figure 9.02 shows a search for "ferguson protest" which identified 231 photos on Twitter. Clicking each image will direct you to another page on Twicsy that will display the full Twitter message, a larger version of the image, and additional images uploaded by the same user. To navigate to the original host of the image, in order to download the largest copy possible, click on the link within the text of the post that forwards to the photo-sharing site.

Figure 9.02: A Twicsy search result for Twitter images by keyword.

Twipho (twipho.net)

Twipho does not search all of the Twitter photo hosts, but it is a decent alternative to Twicsy. Additionally, it allows for a view of a live stream of recent Twitter images being posted. After many failed attempts, I gave up on generating a screen capture that was appropriate for a general audience. Logging into a Twitter account is required for this service.

Topsy (topsy.com)

Topsy was discussed earlier as a great way to search for deleted Twitter messages. This can also be valuable for photo and video searching. Each search on Topsy will default to a limited time frame. This will likely only display Tweets from the past seven to thirty days. If you are searching for photos, first conduct you query based on keyword or user name. The results will default to Twitter messages, but you can select the "Photos" option in the left menu to filter content. You can then choose the "All Time" option on the left menu to display all known photos that match your query. Figure 9.03 displays this option identifying multiple pages of photos relating to "OSINT".

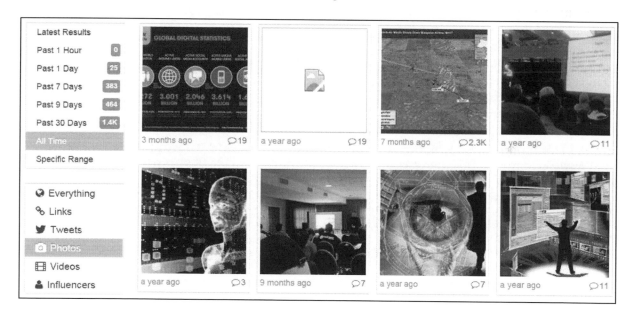

Figure 9.03: A Topsy photo search.

Instagram (instagram.com)

Instagram is a photo-sharing program that is now owned by Facebook. With well over 300 million active users, the amount of people that upload content daily from mobile devices is above 75 million. This application works with Twitter to distribute the photos. This service is quickly becoming very popular with most photo sharing Twitter users and should not be ignored. Searching for Instagram content through Twitter's website will not provide all of the content. Since this service is used in the form of an application on a mobile device, navigating to the main Instagram website is useless for searching. We must rely on third party services.

Iconosquare (iconosquare.com)

This is currently my first stop for Instagram research. If you know the user name of your target, it can be searched on any page within the site. For a direct approach, you can type the name directly after the website address. In the following example, the listed address would take you directly to the Instagram account of "ambermac":

http:// iconosquare.com/ambermac

Once you are on the user page, you will see detailed information about the account such as the real name of the user (if provided), a brief bio, any links to attached social networks, and all public photos available on Instagram. Figure 9.04 displays a typical result. Clicking on each photo will display the full size image and any comments associated with the photo. If you do not know the account user name, you can search within this site for possible accounts. In the example above, I searched "amber" and analyzed the results to identify my target. This site does not offer reliable keyword searching. For that, we will use Webstagram.

Webstagram (search.stagram.com)

Going to stagram.com will immediately direct you to web.stagram.com. Many people refer to this site as "Webstagram". To take advantage of the search capabilities of this service, you should replace "web" with "search" as shown in the title above. The search field on this page will allow you to search any keyword search term. This may be a person's name, an event, a location, or any keyword of interest. The results that appear will contain the searched term within the comment content or the user name. Clicking the image will enlarge the photo and reveal the user name of the account, any comments, and any tags associated with the image.

Worldcam (worldc.am)

This Instagram search site offers a new twist on locating photos. On this site, you can specify a specific location, such as a bar where a violent incident occurred, and you will be presented with photos captured at that location. Loading the website will take a moment as it attempts to identify your approximate location. You will see two search fields. Complete the second field first by typing the city and state until your desired location is listed. You should allow the website to specify the format of the location and not try to correct it by adding a state. Begin typing the target location in the first field until you see it listed. Select this entry and allow the photos to load. Figure 9.05 displays the information provided to search a wine bar in Chicago. Figure 9.06 display some of the dozens of photos that were captured inside the building. This could be used to investigate a specific incident, gather intelligence about the interior of the business, or identify employees visible in the background of the images. Each entry will identify the date, user name of the account holder, and brief description of the photo.

Figure 9.04: An Iconosquare search result.

Figure 9.05: A Worldcam search.

Figure 9.06: Three photos identified on Worldcam by the location captured.

Gram Feed (gramfeed.com)

The previous third party services allow you to search Instagram without providing any login credentials. This is very convenient, but you may be receiving limited results. Services that require an Instagram user name and password can often deliver expanded content that is not seen on the "anonymous" websites. Gram Feed requires you authorize its service through your Instagram account in order to view search results. I encourage this method when you possess an anonymous account that does not contain any personal information.

After credential verification, you will be allowed to search photos by keyword, profiles by user name, and posts by location. Aside from searching the Instagram API directly, this is the most comprehensive service I have found. Quick searches and interactive maps make this option stand out from the rest. One unique feature is the ability to filter any results by keyword or date.

Instagram API

My favorite way of searching for data on Instagram is through their Application Programming Interface (API). This method is detailed in Chapter Fourteen, but I believe a demonstration here is appropriate. Navigate to the following website in order to access these utilities.

http://inteltechniques.com/osint/instagram.html

This is a page I created that simplifies the API process and makes it fairly user friendly. Figure 9.07 displays the current state of the tool.

The first option allows you to enter an Instagram user name. This can be found on a person's profile page, individual post, or through the methods discussed previously. The result will include the following information on the last line.

```
"full_name":"Maria Bazzell","id":"6095673"}]}
```

The number at the end is the user number for the person that you searched. Placing that number in the second option on the custom tool will present the standard API view of that account. If you are using the custom browser extensions explained in Chapter Fifteen, this view should be very readable. If not, your result may look like random text.

Inside this page will be links to photos, friends, and general information about your target. Most importantly, if the target uses a mobile device and has the geo-location setting on, you will see GPS information about each post from the user. The following text is a small portion of the result for this user.

```
"profile_picture":"http:\\images.ak.instagram.com\profiles\profile_609567
3_75sq_1334043058.jpg",
"full_name":"MariaBazzell",
"id":"6095673"}
"location":{"latitude":26.340095093,"longitude":127.783305254},
"created_time":"1381461909",
"text":"Love the new h air!",
"from":{"username":"mverduzco20",
```

Placing those GPS coordinates into Google or Bing Maps will identify the location that the user posted this message and photo from. The API view will display all recent posts in chronological order with the newest at top.

The third and fourth options display a list of people the user is following on Instagram, and the people that are following the user. The final option will allow you to enter a GPS latitude and longitude of a location, along with the distance you want to search around that spot. A search of the GPS coordinates of Busch Stadium in St. Louis, Missouri produced many results. The following was a partial response identifying a link to a photo and the exact coordinates of the posting.

```
type: "image",
location: {latitude: 38.630882947,longitude: -90.191408481},
link: "http://instagram.com/p/geBKNESEUO/",
likes: {count:7
```

The linked image is of a man standing under the Arch in St. Louis, within one kilometer of the stadium. This option can be used by investigators researching a crime scene, security outfits monitoring a protest, or schools keeping a close watch on student activity. Also, remember that EchoSec, which was explained in Chapter Three, is an excellent tool to display Instagram posts from a specific location.

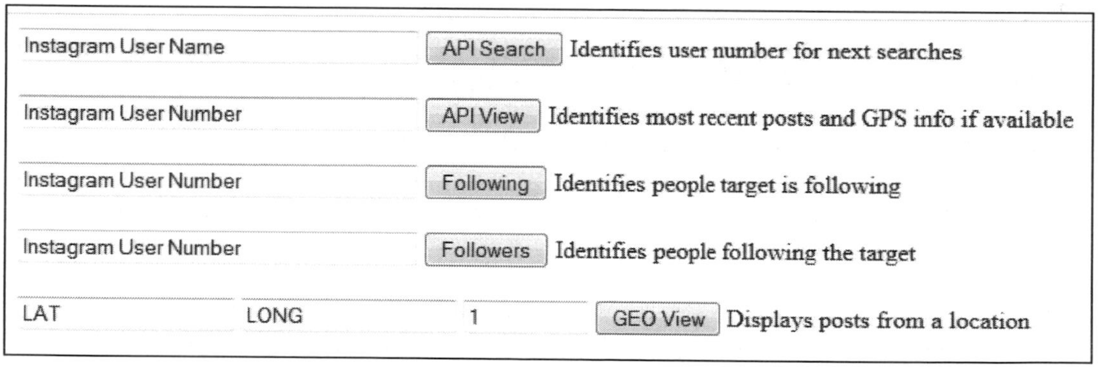

Figure 9.07: The custom Instagram tools on IntelTechniques.com

Banned Hashtags (http://thedatapack.com/tools/blocked-hashtag-search)

There is a long list of "Hashtags", or keywords, which cannot be searched within Instagram's mobile apps or third party web services. Most of these are vulgar, curse words, or otherwise inappropriate for print. Instagram dictates what words are offensive and blocks them. Surprisingly, "Photography" is on this list and is currently banned from being used as a hashtag. There is one online utility that will allow us to bypass this restriction.

In Figure 9.08, I conducted a search for the term "weed" on web.stagram.com. The results stated that "weed" was not found anywhere within Instagram. This seems very unlikely, so I conducted an identical search on the banned hashtag website listed above (Figure 9.09). This result identified dozens of photos posted within the past seven days that also identify each user name. If the terms that you are searching for on Instagram are responding with no results, you may be searching a banned term. A current list of banned words is located at thedatapack.com/banned-hashtags-instagram.

Figure 9.08: A search on Instagram for the term "weed".

Figure 9.09: An Instagram search on thedatapack.com for the term "weed".

Photo-Sharing Sites

In order to find a photo related to a target, the image must be stored on a website. The most common type of storage for online digital photos is on a photo-sharing site. These sites allow a user to upload photographs to an account or profile. These images can then be searched by anyone with an internet connection. Almost all of these hosts are free for the user and the files will remain on the site until a user removes them. There are dozens of these services, many allowing several gigabytes worth of storage.

Flickr (flickr.com)

Flickr, now owned by Yahoo, is one of the most popular photo-sharing sites on the internet. The majorities of these images are uploaded by amateur photographers and contain little intelligence to an investigator. There are many images in this "haystack" that will prove beneficial to the online researcher. The main website allows for a general search by topic, location, user name, real name, or keyword. This search term should be as specific as possible to avoid numerous results. An online user name will often take you to that user's Flickr photo album.

After you have found either an individual photo, user's photo album, or group of photos by interest, you can begin to analyze the profile data of your target. This may include a user name, camera information, and interests. Clicking through the various photos may produce user comments, responses by other users, and location data about the photo. Dissecting and documenting this data can assist with future searches. The actual image of these photos may give all of the intelligence desired, but the data does not stop there. Figure 9.10 displays a search on Flickr for photographs related to the Occupy Wall Street protesters. The search returned over 157,000 results.

Figure 9.10: A Flickr search by keyword.

If you encounter a heavy user of Flickr, you may see hundreds or thousands of photos spread across several albums. You may want to only see the most recent images uploaded regardless of which photo album they are in. To do this, you need to use Yahoo Pipes.

Yahoo Pipes (pipes.yahoo.com/pipes/pipe.info?_id=wm6OvlT62xGSOhDJ1fC6Jw)

This particular Yahoo Pipe will take any Flickr user ID and display only the most recent photos uploaded to that user account. To find the user ID number, click on a Flickr user's profile and look in the address. You will see a number separated by the "@" character. An example of this, as searched in Figure 9.11, is "62771906@N03". Some profiles will have a user name instead of a user number. To translate this, you can use IDGettr (idgettr.com). There are several Yahoo Pipes that automated search tasks. Find out more at pipes.yahoo.com.

Figure 9.11: A Yahoo Pipes search result on Flickr images.

My Pics Map (mypicsmap.com)

Flickr is one of the few remaining web services that do not remove the metadata stored within images. The data, which will be explained in detail in a moment, can often identify the location that a photo was captured. While Flickr offers their own interactive map to display the locations of user's photos, it seldom works properly. My Pics Map is a good alternative for this type of query. The home page will allow you to enter either a Flickr user number or photoset ID number. I usually only use this to see the locations of a specific Flickr user's photos. Figure 9.12 displays the photos of user 62771906@N03 that were captured in California, Oregon, and Colorado. You can zoom into each area to see exact detail of each photo and location. This can be a great resource to quickly determine the areas where a target has visited.

Flickr should never be the only photo-sharing site that is searched. Other sites, such as Photobucket (photobucket.com) and Fotki (search.fotki.com), may contain more personal photos than Flickr. Almost all of them have a search feature on the main page. This should be used for anything relating to your target including real name, screen name, or workplace. Picasa, a well-known photo sharing site from Google, now includes all user photos in their Google+ social networking service (see Chapter Three).

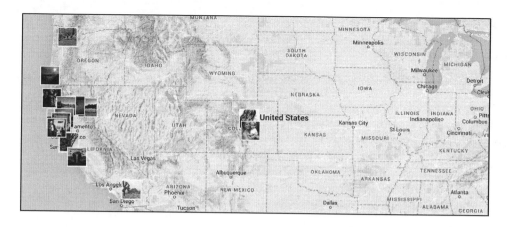

Figure 9.12: A search result of a Flickr user on My Pics Maps.

Flickr Map (flickr.com/map)

Flickr attempts to geo locate all of the photos that it can. It attempts to identify the location that the photo was taken. It will usually obtain this information from the Exif data, which will be discussed in a moment. It can also tag theses photos based on user provided information. Flick provides a mapping feature that will attempt to populate a map based on your search parameters. I have had rare success with this technique. For the mapping of Flickr photos, I prefer EchoSec. This amazing free service was explained in Chapter Three.

Picasa Web Albums (picasaweb.google.com)

Picasa was originally a privately owned company that provided a free downloadable application for photo management. After being purchased by Google, this application was improved and is widely used today. Recently, Google transferred Picasa user's photos to that user's Google+ account. Searching for these public photos has become difficult through the official Google+ channels. Fortunately, Google has not shut down the Web Albums section of the site. Here you can search for any photos uploaded to the public Picasa web albums. Similar to the other photo sharing sites, Picasa offers a search field ready for any input. The search results are similar to a Google Images search, with many advanced options. The filters include limiting to photos with or without faces, selection of aspect ratios and size, displaying photos or videos, and even a choice for camera manufacturer.

Exif Data

Every digital photograph captured with a digital camera possesses metadata known as Exif data. This is a layer of code that provides information about the photo and camera. All digital cameras write this data to each image, but the amount and type of data can vary. This data, which is embedded into each photo "behind the scenes", is not visible by viewing the captured image. You need an Exif reader, which can be found on websites and within applications. Keep in mind that some websites remove or "scrub" this data before being stored on their servers. Facebook, for example, removes the data while Twitter and Flickr often do not. Locating a digital photo online will not always present this data. If you locate an image that appears full size and uncompressed, you will likely still have the data intact. If the image has been compressed to a smaller file size, this data is often lost. Any images removed directly from a digital camera card will always have the data. This is one of the reasons you will always want to identify the largest version of an image when searching online. A software application to identify this data will be discussed later. The easiest way to see the information is through an online viewer.

Jeffrey's Exif Viewer (regex.info//exif.cgi)

I consider Jeffrey's Exif Viewer the online standard for displaying Exif data. The site will allow analysis of any image found online or stored on a drive connected to your computer. The home page, as seen in Figure 9.13, provides two search options. The first allows you to copy and paste an address of an image online for analysis. Clicking "browse" on the second option will open a file explorer window that will allow you to select a file on your computer for analysis. The file types supported are also identified on this page.

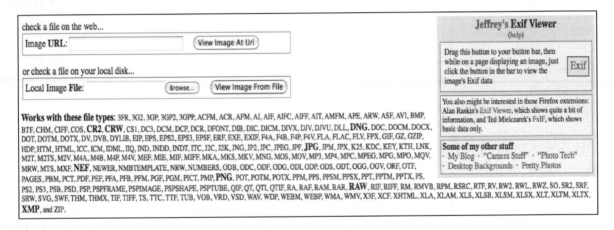

Figure 9.13: Jeffrey's Exif Viewer home page.

The first section of the results will usually provide the make and model of the camera used to capture the image. Many cameras will also identify the lens used, exposure settings, flash usage, date and time of capture and file size. In Figure 9.14, you can see that the camera used was a Canon EOS Digital Rebel with an 18 - 55mm lens at full 55mm setting. Auto exposure was selected, the flash was turned off, and the photo was taken at 2:30 pm on May 7, 2011. Not all of this will be vital for the researcher, but every bit of intelligence counts.

Scrolling down the analysis page will then identify many camera settings that probably provide little information to the researcher. These include aperture information, exposure time, sharpness, saturation and other image details. Mixed in with this data is the serial number field. This is most common in newer SLR cameras and will not be present in less expensive cameras. Figure 9.15 displays a serial number result. This camera will identify the make, model, and serial number of the camera inside every photo that it captures.

Camera:	Canon EOS Digital Rebel Also known as: Canon EOS Digital Rebel (US); Canon EOS 300D (Europe); Canon Kiss Digital (Japan)
Lens:	18 - 55 mm Shot at 55 mm
Exposure:	Auto exposure, $^1/200$ sec, f/9, ISO 100
Flash:	Auto, Did not fire
Focus:	AI Focus AF, Auto AF point selection, with a depth of field of from 1.19 m to 1 m.
Date:	**May 7, 2011** 2:30:01PM (timezone not specified) (9 months, 4 days, 17 hours, 9 minutes, 11 seconds ago, assuming image timezone of US Pacific)
File:	**2,048 × 3,072 JPEG (6.3 megapixels)** 2,380,938 bytes (2.3 megabytes) Image compression: 87%
Color Encoding:	**WARNING: Color space tagged as sRGB, without an embedded color profile. Windows and Mac web browsers will treat the colors randomly.** Images for the web are most widly viewable when in the sRGB color space and with an embedded color profile. See my Introduction to Digital-Image Color Spaces for more information.

Figure 9.14: The top portion of a Jeffrey's Exif viewer result.

Color Space	Unknown (-1)
Serial Number	520201773
Lens Info	70-200mm f/?

Figure 9.15: An Exif viewer result with a serial number.

A serial number of a camera associated with an image can be valuable data. This can help an analyst associate other photos found with a target's camera. If an "anonymous" image was found online that included a serial number in the Exif data, and another image was found of a target of the investigation, these two photos can be analyzed. If the serial number as well as make and model of camera match, there is a good likelihood that the same camera took both images. It is important to know that this data can be manipulated though. Using software such as Exif Tool (see Chapter Fifteen), a user can modify this data. While this is not a popular tactic to use, it is still possible. The difficult part of this is finding photos only knowing the serial number. Two new services will help with that.

Stolen Camera Finder (stolencamerafinder.co.uk)

This site was designed to help camera theft victims with locating their camera if it is being used by the thief online. For that use, you would find a photo taken with the stolen camera, and drop it into the site for analysis. This analysis identifies a serial number if possible. If one is located, the service then presents links to photo-sharing websites, such as Flickr, that contain photos with the same serial number. This is very creative, and we can use the same service for our own research.

On the home page, click the "no photo?" link in the lower center portion. This will now allow for a manual input of a serial number. Figure 9.16 displays a search result for the serial number entered. Clicking the "page" link will present you with options for payment. In 2013, this site became a premium service and full use is no longer free. However, we can still extract relevant data. Clicking the image thumbnail will open a new window with a compressed version of the image that was located. Conducting a reverse image search, which will be explained in just a moment, will often identify the original copies of this photo that appear online. This will often identify the photographer's screen name which can lead to more information. It is important to verify the make and model number as well, since different camera manufacturers may use overlapping serial numbers.

date	serial	model	urls	image preview
2012-01-23	2231205904 ✓	canon - canon eos 5d ?	page, image	
2011-12-11	2231205904 ✓	canon - canon eos 5d ?	page, image	
2011-12-03	2231205904 ✓	canon - canon eos 5d ?	page, image	

Figure 9.16: A result page on Stolen Camera Finder.

Camera Trace (cameratrace.com/trace)

An additional site, which is still free, that provides this service is called Camera Trace. Type in the serial number of a camera and the site will attempt to locate any online photographs taken with the camera. This service claims to have indexed all of Flickr and 500px with plans to soon add Smugmug, Picasa, and Photobucket. A sample search using a serial number of "123" revealed results for Panoramio, even though the site is not listed as being included in the results. The website urges users to sign up for a premium service that will make contact if any more images appear in the database. The fee for this is $10 per camera. The website at cameratrace.com/law-enforcement states that the service is free for law enforcement.

GPS

Many new SLR cameras, and almost all cellular telephone cameras, now include GPS. If the GPS is on, and the user did not disable geo-tagging of the photos in the camera settings, you will get location data within the Exif data of the photo. Figure 9.17 (left) displays the analysis of an image taken with a camera with GPS. The data is similar to the previous analysis, but includes a new "Location" field. This field will translate the captured GPS coordinates from the photo and identify the location of the photo. Further down this results page, the site will display an image from Google Maps identifying the exact point of the GPS associated with the photo. Figure 9.17 (right) displays this satellite view including a direction identifier. Since most cellular telephones possess an accelerometer, the device documents the direction the camera was facing. Most Android and iPhone devices have this capability. Your results will vary depending on the user's configuration of their GPS on the device.

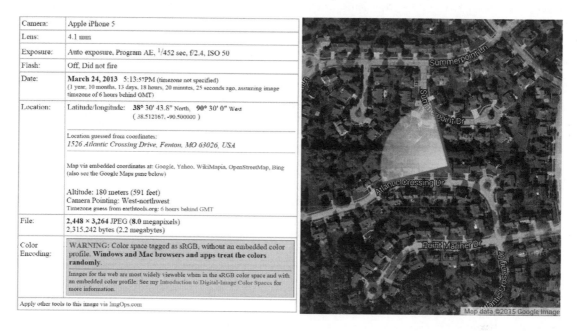

Figure 9.17: A Jeffrey's Exif Viewer result identifying location with map view.

Cropped Images

Another piece of information that we can look for from the Exif data is the presence of a thumbnail image within the photograph. Digital cameras generate a small version of the photo captured and store it within the Exif data. This icon size image adds very little size to the overall file. When a user crops the image, this original smaller version may or may not get overwritten. Programs such as Photoshop or Microsoft Photo Editor will overwrite the data and keep both images identical. Other programs, as well as some online cropping tools, do not overwrite this data. The result is the presence of the original and un-cropped image within the Exif data of the cropped photo. An example of this is seen in Figure 9.18. A cropped photo found online is examined through Jeffrey's Exif viewer. The cropped full size large photo is seen on the left. The embedded smaller original photo was not overwritten when cropped. We can now see what the image looked like before it was cropped.

This technique has been used by police to identify child pornography manufactures. These pedophiles will crop themselves out of illegal images to avoid identification. When photos of the children are found by police, an original un-cropped image may be enough to identify and prosecute a molester. This is not limited to law enforcement. Some tech savvy fans of television personality Catherine Schwartz examined a cropped photo on her blog in 2003. Inside the Exif data was the un-cropped version which exposed her breasts and quickly made the rounds through the internet.

Real world application: In a civil litigation, a subject claimed an injury that prohibited him from work, walking, and a normal life. The suit claimed damages from pain and suffering and sought a monetary judgment for future lack of ability to work. A brief scan of the subject's online photo album revealed fishing trips, softball games, and family adventure vacations. With Exif information data intact, exact dates, times, locations, and cameras were identified and preserved. The subject withdrew his lawsuit.

Figure 9.18: A Jeffrey's Exif Viewer summary result displaying an original un-cropped photo.

Exif Search (exif-search.com)

The idea of searching within the metadata stored within images has intrigued online researchers for years. Many people are surprised that Google has not tackled this obstacle. Exif Search is a service that allows limited search within this metadata, but it is far from perfect. The main page will allow you a single search field with a start and end date option. At the time of this writing, the date chooser was not functioning and the search field did not specify filters for location, keyword, or camera information. Fortunately, this service allows direct URL based search and we can manipulate addresses to conduct very specific searches. The following should help you structure your own addresses in order to obtain the appropriate information from this service.

To search by location, you can natively type in a city name through Exif Search. However, this is very broad and may present many unwanted results. Instead, you can specify an exact GPS coordinate and receive any results within five kilometers from that location. The exact address to enter into a web browser is demonstrated in the following URL. In this example, the latitude is 44.121923 and the longitude is -123.215868. You can modify these specifics for your own needs.

http://www.exif-search.com/index.php?la=44.121923&lo=-123.215868

If you type a make and model of camera into Exif Search, you will only conduct a keyword search for these terms. Instead, consider a direct URL that specifies that you want to search within the device information of the metadata. The following address would produce results for photos captured with a Canon 5D camera. Note that the "%20" in the address represents a single space.

http://www.exif-search.com/index.php?q=Canon%205d&device=1

Date range searches can also be conducted within the URL. The following example would search for images captured between January 1, 2014 and January 31, 2014.

http://www.exif-search.com/index.php?SD=2014-01-01&ED=2014-01-31

You can combine any search options into one single URL. The following address would search for any photos taken at the GPS coordinate of 44.121923, -123.215868 by an Apple iPhone between January 1, 2014 and January 31, 2014. Figure 9.19 displays the single result that matched these criteria.

http://www.exif-search.com/index.php?la=44.121923&lo=-123.215868&SD=2014-01-01&ED=2014-01-31&q=apple%20iphone&device=1

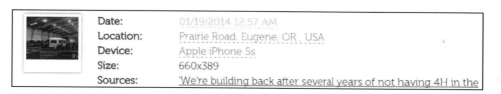

Figure 9.19: A search result on Exif Search.

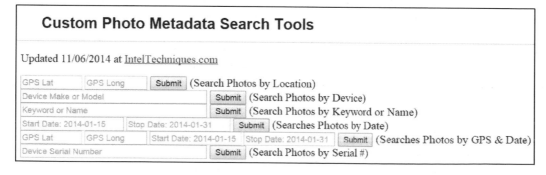

Figure 9.20: A custom search tool on IntelTechniques that allows search of Exif Data.

If these direct URL search queries are overwhelming, you can use a custom online tool that I created for this purpose. Navigate to inteltechniques.com/OSINT/photos.html and you will be presented with these search options that will present results within the same web page. Figure 9.20 displays this tool identifying the options available.

Reverse Image Searches

Advancements in computer processing power and image analysis software have made reverse image searching possible on several sites. While a standard search online involves entering text into a search engine for related results, a reverse image search provides an image to a search engine for analysis. The results will vary depending on the site used. Some will identify identical images that appear on other websites. This can be used to identify other websites used by a target. If you have a photo of a target on a social network, a reverse analysis of that photo may provide other websites that the target used the same image on. These may be results that were not identified through a standard search engine. Occasionally, a target may create a website as an alias, but use an actual photo of himself. Unless you knew the alias name, you would never find the site. Searching for the site by the image may be the only way to locate the profile of the alias. Some reverse image sites go further and try to identify other photos of the target that are similar enough to be matched. Some will even try to determine the sex and age of the subject in the photo based on the analysis of the image. This type of analysis was once limited to expensive private solutions. Now, these services are free to the public.

Google Images (images.google.com)

One of the more powerful reverse image search services is through Google. Rolled out in 2011, this service often goes undetected. On any Google Images page, there is a search field. Inside this field on the far right is a light blue camera icon that appears slightly transparent (Figure 9.21). Clicking on this icon will open a new search window that will allow for either an address of an online image, or an upload of an image file on your computer (Figure 9.22).

In order to take advantage of the online search, you must have the exact link to the actual photo online. Locating an image within a website is not enough. You will want to see the image in a web browser by itself, and then copy the address of the image. In Figure 9.23, I have found a website with a photo of my target. If I want to view the image from the actual location, I must right-click on the image and select "view image" with my Firefox browser. Chrome users will see "open image in new tab" and Internet Explorer users will see "properties" which will identify the URL of the image. Figure 9.24 displays the view of the image and the address bar identifies the exact location of the image online. This link is what you want in order to conduct a reverse image analysis. If you paste this link in the Google Images reverse online search (Figure 9.25), the result will be other similar images on other sites. In Figure 9.26, the result identifies exact duplicate images on other websites. Visiting these sites provides more information on the target.

Figure 9.21: Google Images search with camera icon.

Figure 9.22: Google Images reverse image search.

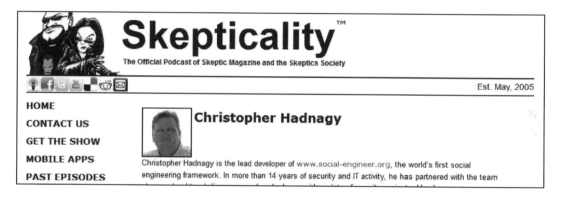

Figure 9.23: An image within a website.

Figure 9.24: An image viewed in a browser with URL to the location of the image.

Figure 9.25: A Google Image reverse search with the URL of an image.

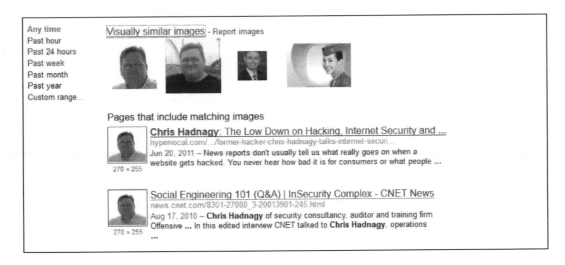

Figure 9.26: A Google Images reverse image results with duplicate photos.

Another way to use this service is to search for a target within the Google Images search page. The images in the results will present additional options when clicked. A larger version of the image will load inside a black box. The three options to the right of the image will allow you to visit the page where the image is stored, view the image in full size, or "Search by image". Figure 9.27 displays a result with these options. Clicking the "Search by image" link will present a new search results page with other images similar to the target image. In Figure 9.28, this identified additional identical photographs of the target. These connect to different websites which may contain more intelligence about the subject.

Figure 9.27: A Google Images result page from name search.

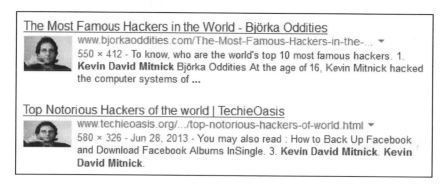

Figure 9.28: A Google Images result page from the "Search by image" option.

Tin Eye (tineye.com)

Tin Eye is another site that will perform a reverse image analysis. These results tend to focus on exact duplicate images. The results here are usually different than those found with Google. Since each service often finds images the other does not, both should be searched when using this technique. In Figure 9.29, an image of a subject as found on a website is analyzed. The results include three identical photos found on three different websites.

Bing Image Match

In 2014, Bing launched its own reverse image search option titled "Image Match". This feature can be launched from within any page on Bing Images by clicking the Image Match icon to the right of the search field. This service does not seem to be as robust as Google's. In my experience, I often receive either no result or misleading results. However, an a few occasions, I have received matched images that Google did not locate.

Figure 9.29: A Tin Eye search results page.

Nerdy Data (search.nerdydata.com/images)

This service was mentioned earlier in Chapter Two as a way to query source code of websites. The "Image Locator" option in the left menu will act as a reverse image search engine. This service is also not as strong as Google's option, but it should be used to enhance your results. Copy and paste any address of an image and Nerdy Data will seek other copies of it on the internet.

Yandex (images.yandex.com)

Russian search site Yandex has an image search option that can conduct a reverse image search. Similar to the other methods, enter the full address of the online image of interest and search for duplicate images on additional websites. Yandex does not allow you to upload an image from your computer.

Baidu (stu.baidu.com)

Similar to Yandex, the Chinese search engine Baidu offers a reverse image search. Baidu currently offers no English version of their website and only presents Chinese text. Navigating to the website offers a search box that accepts the address of an online image. The results will identify similar images on websites indexed by Baidu. Figure 9.30 displays search results for an image of hacker Kevin Mitnick. The address of the image is visible in the search box.

Karma Decay (karmadecay.com)

This service has a very specific specialty which can be beneficial to an internet researcher. It is a reverse image search engine that only provides positive results that appear on the website Reddit. It was originally launched as a way for users to identify when someone re-posted a photo that had previously been posted on the website. The user could then "down-vote" the submission and have it removed from the front page. We can use this in investigations to locate every copy of an individual photo on Reddit. You can either provide a link to an image or upload an image from your computer.

Pictriev (pictriev.com)

Pictriev is a service that will analyze a photo including a human face and try to locate additional images of the person. The results are best when of a public figure with a large internet presence, but it will work on lesser-known subjects as well. An additional feature is a prediction of the sex of the target as well as age. In Figure 9.31, the same image that was used in the last example displays Pictriev's prediction. It predicts that the subject in the photograph is male and approximately 44 years of age.

Figure 9.30: A Baidu reverse image search result.

Figure 9.31: A Pictriev search result showing predicted sex and age of a subject.

Real world application: These reverse image search sites can have many uses to the investigator. In 2011, I searched a photo of damage to a popular historic cemetery that was vandalized. The results included a similar photo of the suspect showing off the damage on a blog. An arrest and community service soon followed. While working with a private investigator, I was asked to locate any hotels that were using the client's hotel images on websites. A reverse image search identified dozens of companies using licensed photos without authorization. This likely lead to civil litigation. In 2013, a federal agent asked me to assist with a human trafficking case. They had a woman in custody that spoke little English. She was arrested during a prostitution sting and was suspected of being a victim of trafficking. A reverse image search from one online prostitution ad located all of her other ads which identified the regional areas that she had recently been working, a cellular telephone number connected to her pimp, and approximate dates of all activity.

Image Manipulation (fotoforensics.com)

It is common to find images on the internet that have been manipulated using software such as Photoshop. Often, it is difficult, if not impossible, to tell if these photos have been manipulated by visually analyzing them. This site uses a technique to determine not only if the photo has been manipulated, but which portions of the photo have changed. One site offers the following explanation of how the technology works.

"Error level analysis (ELA) works by intentionally resaving the image at a known error rate, such as 95%, and then computing the difference between the images. If there is virtually no change, then the cell has reached its local minima for error at that quality level. However, if there is a large amount of change, then the pixels are not at their local minima and are effectively original."

This site allows you to upload a digital image. After successful upload, it will display the image in normal view. Below this image will be a darkened duplicate image. Any highlighted areas of the image indicate a possible manipulation. While this site should never be used to definitively state that an image is untouched or manipulated, investigators may want to conduct an analysis for intelligence purposes only. Figure 9.32 displays original and manipulated images while Figure 9.33 displays the analysis of the images from Foto Forensics.

This site will provide an analysis of an image from the internet or a file uploaded from a computer. It is important to note that any images uploaded become part of the website's collection and a direct URL is issued. While it would be difficult for someone to locate the URL of the images, it could still pose a security risk for sensitive photographs.

Izitru (izitru.com)

The previous service will identify the areas of a photo that have been manipulated. If the edited content is not obvious, you may want a service that will provide additional analysis. Izitru may provide the details that you need in an investigation. I conducted a test with an original photo from a cellular telephone camera. Figure 9.34 (above) displays the result from the unmodified image. Figure 9.34 (below) displays the result after I modified a very small portion of the image. Identifying images that have been re-saved instead of copied could be valuable in civil litigation.

Figure 9.32: An original photograph (left) compared to a manipulated photograph (right).

Figure 9.33: The original photograph (left) and manipulated image (right) on Foto Forensics.

High Trust

This image passed all of our forensic tests, so the evidence strongly suggests it is an unmodified original file from a camera.

Potential file modification

Our forensic tests suggest this file has been re-saved since initial capture. Because this file is not a camera original, it is possible that it was modified.

Figure 9.34: A result from Izitru of an unmodified image (above) and manipulated image (below).

Chapter Ten

Videos

Online videos are almost as common as online photographs. The cameras in data phones can act as video cameras. In some situations, uploading a video to the internet is easier than a photograph. Video sharing sites such as YouTube have made video publication effortless. For investigations, a video can contain a huge amount of intelligence. When any abnormal event happens, people flock to their phones and start recording. These videos may capture criminal acts, embarrassing behavior, or evidence to be used in a civil lawsuit. Obtaining these videos is even easier than creating them.

YouTube (YouTube.com)

The most popular of several video-sharing sites is YouTube. The official YouTube site declares that 48 hours of video are uploaded every minute, resulting in nearly 8 years of content uploaded every day. It further states that over 3 billion videos are viewed each day. These impressive statistics confirm the need to include videos as part of a complete OSINT analysis. YouTube is easy to search from the main search field on every page. This field can accept any search term and will identify video content or user name. Users that upload videos to YouTube have their own "channel". Their videos are uploaded to this channel, and locating a user's channel will identify the videos uploaded by that user. Many people use YouTube as a social network, leaving comments about videos and participating in discussions about various topics. If you locate a video of interest, it is important to also retrieve this text information. Each comment below a video will include the user name that created the comment, which will link to that user's profile.

In Figure 10.01, a search for "school bus fight" returned over 192,000 video links on YouTube. Adding a search term such as the city or school name may help, but it may also prohibit several wanted videos from appearing. In this same screen capture, the "filter" option has been expanded. This button is above the first video result. This provides additional filter options including the ability to sort by relevance, upload date, view count, and ranking. To the right of these options is the ability to filter by videos that were uploaded today, uploaded this week, and uploaded this month. In Figure 10.02, the "uploaded this week" option was chosen. This resulted in only 437 videos which could easily be examined for any intelligence. Figure 10.03 displays the video page of a result from the search. The lower left portion of this page includes a link to the user's profile that submitted this video. This profile page includes all of the videos uploaded by that user and additional profile information.

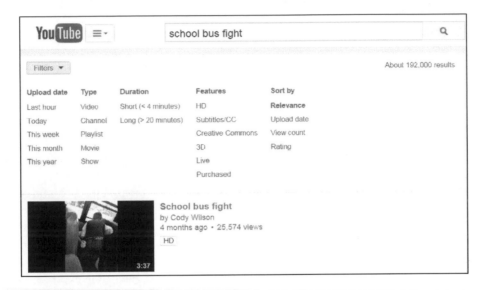

Figure 10.01: A YouTube search results page with the filter expanded.

Figure 10.02: A YouTube search results page sorted by videos uploaded this week.

Several YouTube "hacks" have surfaced over the years. Many of these stopped working as YouTube made changes to the environment. Of those still functioning, I find the following techniques helpful to my investigations.

Figure 10.03: A YouTube video page displaying the video, title, and uploader.

Print a Video (labnol.org/internet/print-youtube-video/28217)

Amit Agarwal at labnol.org developed a way to extract the YouTube story board that is visible as you move the slider bar throughout a video. These small screen shots are still images of frames captured during the video upload process. A piece of JavaScript executed while playing a video will open a new tab with the results. The website above should be visited to save the code. You can drag and drop the button into your Firefox or Chrome bookmarks toolbar as instructed on the page. Figure 10.04 is a partial display of a result using this method. It displays 10 frames out of the 101 that were presented during the query.

Figure 10.04: A story board capture from YouTube.

Bypass Age and Login Restriction

Several YouTube videos have been tagged as violent, sexual, or otherwise inappropriate for young viewers. Others demand that you log into a Google account in order to view the content for unclear reasons. Either way, this is an unnecessary roadblock to your investigation. As an OSINT investigator, I prefer to not be logged into any personal or covert account while I am researching. Any time you are searching through a Google product while logged into an account, Google is documenting your every move. This can be unsettling. The following techniques should remove this restriction.

Navigate to the following website and notice the inability to view the video. Figure 10.05 displays the result when accessing this link without a Google account.

https://www.youtube.com/watch?v=SZqNKAd_gTw

In this example, the YouTube Video ID is "SZqNKAd_gTw". In order to view this video through YouTube without a third party service, and without supplying the credentials for your personal Google account, you can generate the following URL. Replace "SZqNKAd_gTw" with the ID of your target video. The result will be the restricted video in full screen view. Some users report that this technique will also bypass videos that have a viewing country restriction.

https://www.youtube.com/v/SZqNKAd_gTw

If this technique should ever stop working, you can also use a non-Google service to achieve the same result. Navigate to the following website to access this same video number (SZqNKAd_gTw).

http://www.nsfwyoutube.com/watch?v= SZqNKAd_gTw

Notice that all of the addresses are very similar. This final link will take you to NSFWYouTube, a third party website, which will also remove the proof of age requirement. Please be warned that the video in this example contains very disturbing video, hence the blockage by YouTube.

Bypass Commercials with Full Screen

It seems lately that every YouTube video I play possess a 30 second commercial at the beginning. This is very frustrating when analyzing a large number of videos. A quick URL trick will bypass this annoyance. Navigate to the following address and notice the long commercial at the beginning.

http://www.youtube.com/watch?v=IEIWdEDFlQY

Alter this address slightly in order to force the video to play in full screen in your browser. This will also bypass any commercials. The URL should appear like the following.

https://youtube.googleapis.com/v/IEIWdEDFlQY

Notice that the video ID has not changed. Only the structure of the address is different.

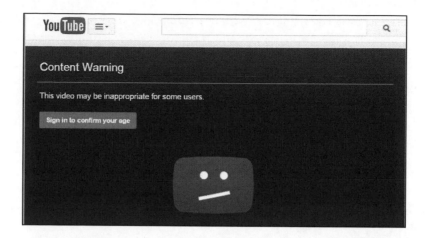

Figure 10.05: A YouTube content warning requiring user credentials to proceed.

Display Frames of Hidden Videos

When a user marks an uploaded video as private, you will not be able to see the content. However, even private videos possess at least four image frames that are publicly visible if a proper query is submitted. Navigate to the following address to load a private video.

http://www.youtube.com/watch?v=OmZyrynlk2w

Figure 10.06 on the left displays the result of this request. Using that same video ID, navigate to the following address to view the first still frame. Figure 10.06 displays the result of this second query on the right.

http://i.ytimg.com/vi/OmZyrynlk2w/0.jpg

The address that displayed the hidden image is not your only option. At least four images can be extracted from this specific video with the following addresses.

http://i.ytimg.com/vi/OmZyrynlk2w/0.jpg
http://i.ytimg.com/vi/OmZyrynlk2w/1.jpg
http://i.ytimg.com/vi/OmZyrynlk2w/2.jpg
http://i.ytimg.com/vi/OmZyrynlk2w/3.jpg

Metadata and Reverse Image Search (www.amnestyusa.org/citizenevidence)

Most of the details of a YouTube video can be seen on the native page where the video is stored. Occasionally, some of this data may not be visible due to privacy settings or profile personalization. In order to confirm that you are retrieving all possible information, you should research the data visible from YouTube's servers. The easiest way to do this is through the YouTube DataViewer from Amnesty International.

Select any YouTube video and copy the entire address of the page. Paste the video address into this service. The result will include the video title, description, upload date, upload time, four still images, and an option to conduct a reverse image search. Figure 10.07 displays a result. Clicking the "reverse image search" option next to a still frame opens a reverse image search on Google for the selected image. Figure 10.08 displays the result for the second image in Figure 10.07. It identified five websites that also host the target video.

Figure 10.06: A hidden YouTube video (left) that has had a still frame extracted (right).

Immediate Download Options

My preferred method for extracting YouTube videos will be explained in Chapter Fifteen. However, if you have no software or browser plugins available to you, there is another easy option. While you are watching any YouTube video, you can add the letters "PWN" to the beginning of the address in order to download the video to your computer. To test this, navigate to the following website.

http://www.youtube.com/watch?v=IEIWdEDFlQY

Now, add "PWN to the beginning, as indicated in the following address.

http://www.pwnyoutube.com/watch?v=IEIWdEDFlQY

You will be presented a new page with many options including the ability to download the video, download only the audio, convert the video to a different format, and bypass the age restriction as discussed earlier.

Figure 10.07: A search result from YouTube DataViewer.

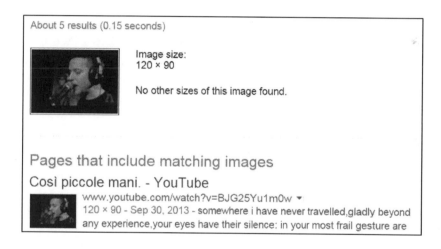

Figure 10.08: A reverse image search from a YouTube video.

Custom YouTube Search Tool (inteltechniques.com/osint/youtube.html)

If you feel overwhelmed at this point, I understand. I found myself getting confused about which address was the most appropriate for each technique. I created a web page that will walk you through the process. Navigate to the above address to access an all-in-one option. This page will allow you to enter only the user ID of each video of interest. Embedded JavaScript will formulate and execute each address for you. This should simplify the processes that were explained previously. Figure 10.09 displays the current state of this tool.

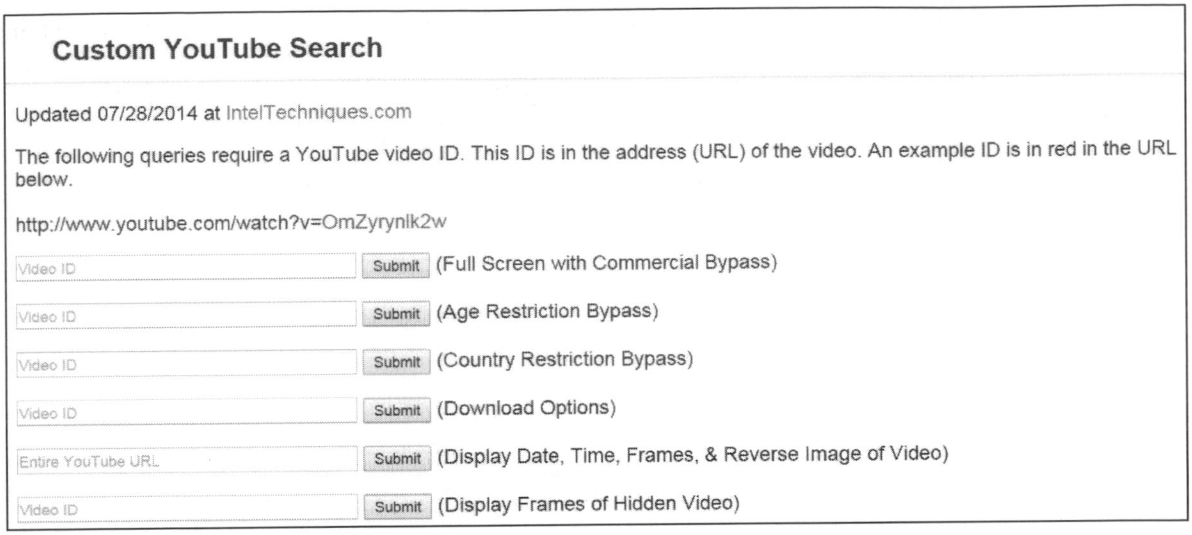

Figure 10.09: The custom YouTube search tool at inteltechniques.com.

YouTube is not the only video sharing service on the internet. Wikipedia identifies dozens of these sites, but searching each of them can become tedious. Fortunately, search engines like Google and Bing offer a search across all of the sites.

Google Videos (videos.google.com)

A search on Google Videos for "school bus fight" returned over 3 million results. These include the results identified in the previous YouTube search plus any videos from other sites that meet the search criteria. This will often lead to duplicate videos that have been posted by news websites and social networks. Google can filter these results by duration time, date and time captured, and video source. The top menu of any Google video results page will display these options. In Figure 10.10, a Google search for the term "female street fight", including filters for videos with a short duration that were posted this week from any source, returned over 1,000 results. These results could either be further filtered with search terms or quickly viewed by still frame to determine relativity to the investigation.

Bing Videos (videos.bing.com)

One feature that makes Bing a favorite site for searching videos is the instant video playback option. When viewing a video search results page, simply hovering the cursor over the video still shot will start the video playback from the beginning of the video. This eliminates the need to navigate to each video page for playback to determine the value of the video. Bing also offers filtering by length and source. The "select view" toolbar at the top of each search result page will allow you to sort the results by either the best match or the most recent. Whether using Google or Bing to locate videos, I recommend turning off the safe search feature. This feature is designed to prohibit some videos with adult content from displaying. With investigations, it is often these types of videos that are wanted. Figure 10.11 displays a search for "SIUE party" which returned 34 videos, most of them with footage of parties at a local university.

Figure 10.10: a Google videos result page using filters.

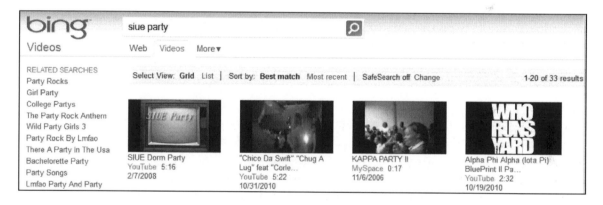

Figure 10.11: A Bing videos search result page.

Real world application: While investigating an aggravated battery that occurred in a housing project, a local police department searched on Google Videos for the terms "fight" and the city of occurrence. The first result was a YouTube video of the fight taken by an onlooker within five feet of the event. This footage, captured with a cellular phone, also displayed all of the witnesses to the fight. None of the subjects wanted to cooperate, but they were not necessary thanks to the video.

Facebook Videos

Facebook hosts the videos that users embed into their Facebook profiles. If you have already located a target's Facebook page, scrolling through the wall posts will likely present any videos that have been uploaded to the account. If you do not have a specific target and want to search these videos by keywords, this is possible through search engines. Google Videos will include Facebook videos in its video searches. Including the term Facebook in the search will place an emphasis on videos located on Facebook pages. This will not present every Facebook video fitting the criteria of the search. Using the site operator as discussed in Chapter One, you can specify a search to include only videos found on Facebook profiles. All Facebook profiles are hosted on the main Facebook domain under a subcategory of video. For example, the address of a video on Facebook would look like this:

http://www.facebook.com/video/video.php?v=1537495389593

The numbers at the end are associated with one unique video. A custom search on Google for a specific video may look like this:

site:facebook.com/video "school bus fight"

This search would attempt to locate any videos stored on the Facebook video servers that included the terms "school bus fight". Most of the videos located should link to the Facebook video page and play without being logged into a Facebook account.

World Star Hip Hop (worldstarhiphop.com/videos)

Lately, this video sharing website has captured a lot of attention from both the media and law enforcement. The site is infamous for possessing videos of violent fights, sexual activity, and hip-hop music. A search with the term "fight" produced over 100 amateur videos, mostly taken with a cellular telephone, depicting recent and brutal street fights with bloody endings. The site averages several million unique visitors every day. Without a doubt, some of those visitors are law enforcement looking to solve cases.

Internet Archive (archive.org/details/opensource_movies)

The premise of this site is to permanently store open source movies, which can include commercial and amateur releases. The search option at the beginning of every page allows for a specific section of the site to be searched. Selecting "community video" will provide the best results for amateur video. A large number of anti-government and anti-American videos are present and ready for immediate download. Unlike YouTube, this site does not make it easy to identify the user that uploaded the videos. Further, it does not link to other videos uploaded by the same user. To do this, you will need to look for some very specific text data.

Figure 10.12 displays a video located on the site after a search was conducted. Below the small video frame on the left are the options to play the video with different file types. Below these is a link titled "HTTP". Clicking the link provides a folder view of the actual files associated with the video (Figure 10.13). The last link on this list forwards to the metadata associated with the video. This data includes the title, description, creator, email address used to upload, and the date of upload (Figure 10.14). The file above the link forwards to the metadata that identifies every other video uploaded by this user.

Figure 10.12: A video file on the Internet Archive.

Index of /2/items/TheCiaCrackCocaineDrugTradeExpos/

../		
TheCiaCrackCocaineDrugTradeExpos.thumbs/	28-May-2009 19:29	-
TheCiaCrackCocaineDrugTradeExpos.gif	28-May-2009 19:29	154697
TheCiaCrackCocaineDrugTradeExpos.mp4	28-May-2009 19:27	24074121
TheCiaCrackCocaineDrugTradeExpos.ogv	28-May-2009 19:42	34556649
TheCiaCrackCocaineDrugTradeExpos_512kb.mp4	28-May-2009 19:36	34024334
TheCiaCrackCocaineDrugTradeExpos_files.xml	31-Dec-2010 19:13	7712
TheCiaCrackCocaineDrugTradeExpos_meta.xml	28-May-2009 19:42	732

Figure 10.13: A folder view of all files associated with a video on the Internet Archive.

```
<mediatype>movies</mediatype>
<collection>opensource_movies</collection>
<title>The CIA Crack Cocaine Drug Trade ExposÂ©</title>
- <description>
    Stated very simply, to fund the Nicaragua Contra army, the Central Intelligence Agency imported and helped distribute Cocaine produced
    in Nicaragua into America. This massive infusion of cocaine cr...
</description>
<subject>cia;cocaine;drug;trade;ExposÂ©;contra</subject>
<creator>theshowpodcast.com</creator>
<identifier>TheCiaCrackCocaineDrugTradeExpos</identifier>
<uploader>archive@theshowpodcast.com</uploader>
<addeddate>2009-05-28 19:27:53</addeddate>
<publicdate>2009-05-28 19:42:53</publicdate>
```

Figure 10.14: A text view of the metadata associated with a file on the Internet Archive.

TV News Archive (archive.org/details/tv)

At the time of this writing, the TV News Archive, another part or archive.org, had collected 672,000 television news broadcast videos from 2009-2015. Further, it extracts the closed captioning text from each video and provides a search option for this data. This allows you to search for any words verbally stated during these broadcasts in order to quickly locate videos of interest. Figure 10.15 displays the result for my search of the term "Bazzell". This resulted in 28 videos that mentioned someone with my last name within the broadcast. Selecting any result will play the video and all text from the closed captioning. The menu on the left will allow filtering by show title, station, date, language, and topic. I look forward to future years as this database builds.

Figure 10.15: A video result with closed captioning from the TV News Archive.

YouTube Closed Captions (serpsite.com/youtube-subtitles-download-tool)

YouTube attempts to provide captioning subtitles for as many videos as possible. This automated process transcribes any spoken dialogue within the audio of the video file and documents the words to text. To see this text while watching a video, click on the closed captioning icon (cc) in the lower left area of the video box. When the icon changes to a red color, the subtitles will display. These subtitles are contained within a small text file associated with the video. It also includes time stamps that identify the frame in which each piece of text is spoken. YouTube does not provide a way to obtain this text file, but Serpsite does. Copy an entire URL of any YouTube video with closed captioning. Paste this link into this website and execute the process. This will display the text from the captioning inside the video. These automated captions are not usually completely accurate. Slang and mumbled speech may not transcribe properly. Any time that you collect and submit a YouTube video as part of a report, I recommend obtaining this caption file as well. Even though the actual text may not be accurate, it can help during official proceedings with identifying a specific portion of a video.

Vine (vine.com)

Vine is a video sharing service that limits all videos to six seconds in length. It is very popular and many people use it in conjunction with Twitter and Instagram. Vine offers no search option for videos or users. For that, we must use Google or Bing. Use the "Site" operator on either service to search for information of interest. The most common search will be for a real name or user name. The following example would query any Vine videos posted by "Mike Skinner".

site:vine.co "mike skinner"

Notice that the domain to search is "co" and not "com". The result identified 52 videos by that user. Each link will play the short video and repeat it in a loop until you exit the window. You can also search within the text message included with each video. The following search would locate any videos on Vine that have both of the words "fight" and "Nashville" in the content.

site:vine.co "fight" "nashville"

Live Video Streams

If you are investigating any live event that is currently occurring, live streaming video sites can be a treasure of useful intelligence. These services offer the ability for a person to turn a cell phone camera into an immediate video streaming device capable of broadcasting to millions. The common setup is for a user to download a host service's application to a smart phone. Launching the application will turn on the video camera of the phone and the video stream is transmitted to the host via the cellular data connection or Wi-Fi. The host then immediately broadcasts this live stream on their website for many simultaneous viewers to see. An average delay time of five seconds is common. There are now several companies that provide this free service. The following are listed in my order of preference for investigative needs. Each site has a search option to enter the keywords that describe the live event you want to watch.

UStream (ustream.tv)
LiveStream (livestream.com)
Veetle (veetle.com)
LiveU (liveu.tv)

Bambuser (bambuser.com)
YouNow (younow.com)
VaughnLive (vaughnlive.tv)

Real World Application: During several large events, I have used UStream to capture the majority of my intelligence. In one investigation, I was assigned the task of monitoring social networks during a large protest that had quickly become violent to both officers and civilians. While Twitter and Facebook occasionally offered interesting information, UStream provided immediate vital details that made a huge impact on the overall response of law enforcement, fire, and EMS. The live video streams helped me identify new trouble starting up, victims of violence that needed medical attention, and fires set by arsonists that required an immediate response.

Chapter Eleven

Telephone Numbers & Addresses

There are hundreds of websites that claim the ability to search for information on telephone numbers and addresses. These vary from amazingly accurate results to sites that only include advertisements. If you have a target telephone number, you should be able to identify the person that uses the number and an address if the number is a landline. This can then lead to more intelligence and additional searches. The majority of cellular numbers can now be identified if they are registered in someone's name. If you have an address, you will want to identify the people associated with the address and any telephone numbers the subjects use. This section will highlight the sites that can assist you with these tasks.

Telephone Numbers

Google and Bing were once a great place to find basic information about a target phone number. These sites can still provide valuable information, but the amount of spam that will display in the results is overwhelming. Many of the links presented will link to sites that will charge a fee for any information associated. This information is usually the same content that could have been located with an appropriate free search. I do not recommend giving into these traps. Instead of basic search engines, you should focus your searches on designated telephone search engines.

Caller ID Databases

In 2013, I began experimenting with reverse caller ID data. These are the same databases that identify a telephone number on your landline caller ID display. Often, this will include the name associated with the number. Until recently, this was something that only appeared on landline numbers, but that has changed. Now many cellular telephone numbers have name information associated with them. This name information is usually extracted from the cellular telephone service provider. I was immediately shocked at the accuracy of these results while searching cellular telephone numbers that were otherwise untraceable. On many of my investigations, this technique has eliminated the need to obtain court subpoenas to discover subscriber information. On the day of this writing, a coworker identified a burglary suspect using this technique. He located a recently stolen item on Craigslist that included a cellular telephone number in the description. The reverse caller ID of this number returned to a local resident that lived near the victim. This result lead to a search warrant and collection of stolen electronics, worth thousands of dollars, which were almost sold on Craigslist.

The reason we can access this data is because it is necessary for telephone systems that do not already possess caller ID options. New systems that operate over the internet, referred to as VOIP systems, do not receive caller ID data natively. This is something that we have taken for granted while it was provided by our telephone companies. Today, many businesses must purchase access to this data from resellers. This presents us with an opportunity.

I scoured the internet for every business that provides bulk caller ID data to private companies. I contacted all of them and discovered that most will offer you a free trial to test their services. I have now tested all of them and identified those that are easy to access and give the best results. All of these services provide data through an application programming interface (API). Complete access will be explained in Chapter Fourteen. First, we will focus only on ways to search an individual number through a specific web address.

Privacy Star (http://www.privacystar.com/reverse-lookup)

This is not always the most accurate caller ID database site available, but it is the only website based option that we can use without creating an account. This address will connect you to a web page to test their caller ID services that are sold through their smart phone app. You can only attempt five lookups in a 24 hour period. However, deleting your temporary internet files or switching to another browser will often reset this limitation. This is a good start to identifying the owners of landline and cell phones, but it should never be the only search.

US Interlink (usinterlink.com/free)

Similar to Privacy Star, this service will allow a single telephone number lookup within its caller ID database. It will also attempt to identify the current and previous cellular service carrier. The majority of my searches revealed redundant information from other services. This can be valuable in order to increase your confidence in the results.

Open CNAM (opencnam.com)

Open CNAM provides two levels of caller ID service. The basic level is free and will work on most landline numbers. Some cellular numbers will display the owner, but most will give you an error encouraging you to use the premium service. Entering the following address into any web browser should give you a result on the telephone number provided in the address.

http://api.opencnam.com/v2/phone/+16184633505

The result is delivered via the API interface, which is text-only. It will appear exactly like the following.

ALTON CITY OF

This result is exactly what would appear on your caller ID screen if this number were to call you. The premium version will be discussed in a moment.

Caller ID Service (calleridservice.com)

Caller ID Service has provided good accuracy with cellular telephone searches. You must register for the service to gain access to a free trial, and the process is very easy. Navigate to the following exact site and complete the required information.

secure.calleridservice.com/index.cgi?mod=join

Upon completion, you will receive an email with an API license key that is valid for approximately 20 free successful searches. You will not be charged for empty results. You must validate this address by clicking the link included in the message. This is their way of verifying that you provided an accurate and real email address. The following information was sent to my account.

Username: jwilson555
Password: mb555555
Auth KEY: 0b253c059b9f26e588ab101f4c2332b496e5bf95
Balance : 0.12

You are now ready to submit requests for caller ID information. To do this, you must formulate an API request that includes your user name, authentication key, and target telephone number to search. This is easier than it sounds. All we need is a number to search. Figure 11.01 displays a LinkedIn result that includes the person's telephone number within the profile. This user, named Craig Williams, provided this information and identified it as a cellular number. The format for the web address, including our specific information, is the following URL.

cnam.calleridservice.com/query?u=jwilson555&k=c2332b496e5bf95&n=6187271233

This queries the domain (calleridservice.com), our user name (jwilson555), our authentication key (c2332b496e5bf95), and our target number (6187271233). The result from this address can be seen in Figure 11.02. The service confirmed that this cellular number belongs to Craig Williams.

Figure 11.01: A LinkedIn profile with a cellular telephone number.

Figure 11.02: A Caller ID Service result.

I recommend saving the address of your first query as a bookmark or favorite. However, you should leave off the target telephone number at the end of the address. This will prevent the service from charging you for a credit every time you load this template. You can then add the new target number of interest at the end of the bookmark and conduct your searches easily. Caller ID Services grants you $0.12 in free searches, which will allow you up to 25 querires. Obtaining an additional free trial will only require a different email address.

Service Objects (serviceobjects.com/developers/lookups/geophone-plus)

In 2014, Service Objects removed their free online telephone lookup demo titled GeoPhone Plus 2. However, they will still allow you to generate a free API license which will allow you 500 free searches. Navigate to this website and complete the "Free API Trial Key" offer. You will receive an email similar to the following.

This is your DOTS GeoPhone Plus 2 API Trial License Key: WS77-OAZ3-xXxX
This license key is used to authenticate your real-time transactions using our API. It includes 500 free transactions that can be used within a 30-day period.

You can now use this key within a custom URL to search the registered owners of landline and cellular telephone numbers. The exact format is the following. Note that you would change "8475551212" to the target telephone number and "WS77-OAZ3-xXxX" to your trial license key.

http://trial.serviceobjects.com/gppl2/api.svc/GetPhoneInfo?PhoneNumber=8475551212&TestType=full&LicenseKey=WS77-OAZ3-xXxX

The response will be in XML data format. However, it will be easy to read. Below is an example.

```
<Provider><Name>NEW CINGULAR WIRELESS PCS, LLC - IL</Name>
<City>NORTHBROOK</City>
<State>ILLINOIS</State>
<LineType>WIRELESS</LineType>
<Name>JOHN ADORJAN</Name>
<Address>12142 S. 22nd<Address/>
<City>Chicago<City/>
<State>IL <State/>
<DateFirstSeen>2014-06-20</DateFirstSeen>
```

This entry identifies the target number as a wireless service provided by Cingular since June of 2014. The registered owner of the number is John Adorjan residing at 12142 S. 22nd in Chicago. Before reverse caller ID lookups, this information would have required a subpoena.

In one recent example, a cellular telephone number searched on Service Objects revealed the name "Jennifer S" in the result. During an interview with this subject, she disclosed that "Jennifer S" is how she identifies her account on the telephone bill that she shares with other family members. She was unaware that this data was sent to the receiving number. On many searches, the full name will be present. This should explain why you may be noticing a caller's name on your caller ID display when he or she is calling from a cellular number.

Bulk Solutions (bulkcnam.com)

Bulk CNAM works very similar to Caller ID Services. You must register for a free account, and you will be granted limited free searches. You must provide a valid email address during the registration and will be required to validate that address after you receive an email with your license key. The custom address (URL) that we need to create only requires your license key and the target number. A user name is not necessary. The format of my free trial key is as follows.

cnam.bulkcnam.com/?id=b03c6513f688f89ee3f&did=6187271233

This queries the domain (bulkcnam.com), my free trial license (b03c6513f688f89ee3f), and my target telephone number (6187271233). Figure 11.03 displays another confirmation that our target number belongs to Craig Williams.

Figure 11.03: A Bulk Solutions caller ID search result.

A premium subscription to Bulk Solution costs $0.009 per successful query.

CID Name (cidname.com)

This service is my personal favorite of all of the caller ID providers. You must contact them for a free trial, but it will only involve a brief telephone conversation. I recommend asking for a free trial in order to test their results on your Asterisk VOIP system. This is a very common setup and the person you are talking to will understand. I also told the representative that I was currently using Bulk Solutions, which was technically true, and that I wanted to see if CID Name could provide better results, which was also true. The eager sales person should quickly send you a trial key good for 25 free searches. The format for our address to query with this service is as follows.

https://dip.cidname.com/6187271233/d3a6e863c&output=raw&reply=none

This queries the domain (cidname.com), our target number (6187271233), and our license key (d3a6e863c). Figure 11.04 displays the result for our number. This service did not identify the name. However, when a name is not available, it will provide the general area of the telephone registration if available. This is a great example of why one service is never enough. I recommend that you use all of these services every time.

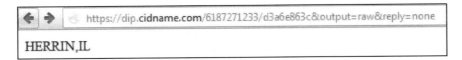

Figure 11.04: A CID Name caller ID search result.

Open CNAM Plus (opencnam.com)

Open CNAM was the first API option that was discussed in this chapter. This limited free version will usually not return results on cellular numbers. A search of our target number from earlier produces the following error.

CNAM for phone "+16187271233" is currently unavailable for Hobbyist Tier users.

A result for this number requires a premium account, which is currently priced at $0.004 per successful query. The entire process can be completed through their website. After a payment of at least $1.00, you will be issued an account number and license key as described in the previous tutorials. The following address contains the structure of a proper query.

http://api.opencnam.com/v2/phone/+16187271233?account_sid=f100cef5&auth_token=AU5c43d8

This queries the domain (opencnam.com), the target number (16187271233), our account ID (f100cef5), and our license number (AU5c43d8). Note that Open CNAM requires a "1" before the ten digit number. Figure 11.05 displays the result from a search on our target number. It has also confirmed that the number is likely registered to Craig Williams.

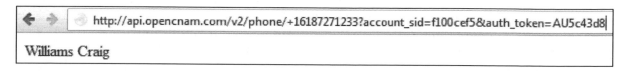

http://api.opencnam.com/v2/phone/+16187271233?account_sid=f100cef5&auth_token=AU5c43d8

Williams Craig

Figure 11.05: A Caller ID search result from Open CNAM Plus.

Everyone API (everyoneapi.com)

This service is owned by the same company as Open CNAM (Telephone Research LLC). The difference with this option is that it will display the cellular company that previously owned the number before it was ported. It will also search the number in a social network database. My research indicates that it is simply pulling Facebook data in the same way that was discussed in Chapter Three. This premium service is a bit more expensive than the previous options, but a complete telephone number search can be obtained for less than ten cents. The format of the URL for the request is as follows. You would replace "8475551212" with your target number, "xxx" with your account SID, and "yyy" with your license key. Below this URL is a typical response received.

https://api.everyoneapi.com/v1/phone/+18475551212?data=name,carrier&account_sid=xxxx&auth_token=yyyy&pretty=true

```
"carrier": {"name": "Verizon Wireless"},
"carrier_o": {"name": "Cricket Wireless"},
"name": "Brian Parker"
"number": "+16189720091",
```

This result indicates that the target number was registered through Cricket Wireless before the current registration through Verizon Wireless. This number is currently associated with a social network profile of "Brian Parker".

Caller ID database results are my current favorite way to extract cellular and landline information from telephone numbers. They have been much more reliable than standard website search engines that often display inaccurate and dated information. Almost every day, I am contacted by an investigator that is stuck on a telephone number involved in an investigation. Lately, these are usually Craigslist style theft cases or subjects inappropriately contacting children over mobile devices. If the telephone number is registered to someone, we have a 90% success rate in identifying the person through these methods. If the telephone is a "burner" style device that is not registered to anyone, these methods will not produce any valid results.

There are other caller ID options available on the internet. I encourage you to investigate any companies that have surfaced since this research. Some services may no longer offer a free trial period to test the database. I have purchased premium memberships through CID Name and Open CNAM. A $10 purchase will allow you over 1,000 queries at each provider.

In Chapter Fourteen, I will explain how you can create a simple web page that will query all of these services at once when you provide a single telephone number. The results will all display immediately for you. I use my own custom page every day. If this is overkill for your needs, there are plenty of web based search engines that are easy to use.

Pipl (pipl.com)

One of the easiest search engines for telephone numbers is Pipl. This is the same search page that was discussed for name searches earlier in the book. The same search field will handle a telephone number. This number should not be entered in the standard separated format such as 555-445-8543. Instead, enter the number without dashes or spaces similar to 5554458543. This can increase the accuracy and number of results. The results page will first identify any profiles created with the target number. These profiles can be visited for more content related to the number. The information received from this profile often includes full name, address, date of birth, and relatives. Figure 11.06 displays the first result received after searching a telephone number. The "Suggested searches" area contains the profiles created by Pipl. Figure 11.07 shows one of these profiles that identify the year of birth, complete address, and several relatives. Scrolling further down this page (not in screen capture) would display links to more results that would verify this information.

This is not the limit of the information you can get from Pipl about a telephone number. There is nothing else to search on the official profile, but there is data stored that you may want. Pipl maintains a street listing of all of the households on a specific street that is cross-referenced by telephone number. Unfortunately, there is no simple way to access this on the Pipl site. To get this information, you can use Google. Conduct the following style of search on the Google main page, replacing the listed number with the target number.

site:pipl.com 5554458543

This should provide a single result that will link to the Pipl page that identifies all residences on the same street as the house with the target telephone number (Figure 11.08). This lists the telephone number and address of each household. The telephone numbers are links that will open a profile on that number.

Real world application: As a detective, I have been tasked on several occasions to assist with background checks on Police Officer applicants. Occasionally, the current address of the applicant is out of state and visiting the neighbors is not optimal. Entering the telephone number of the applicant's residence in this fashion will display all of the neighbors' telephone numbers and addresses. Visiting the associated profiles will identify enough information to make contact via telephone and conduct an interview.

Figure 11.06: A Pipl search result by telephone number.

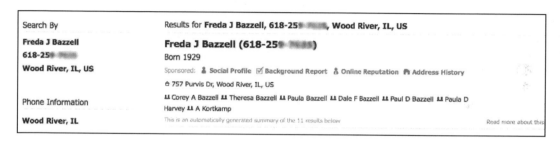

Figure 11.07: A Pipl profile by telephone number.

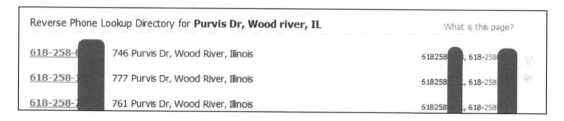

Figure 11.08: A Pipl neighborhood search result by telephone number.

That's Them (thatsthem.com)

This service has been mentioned as a strong search engine for real names, email addresses, and user names. It also possesses a telephone search that will cross reference all of the other categories. Clicking the "Reverse Telephone" link at the top and entering your target telephone number will execute all possible queries. Figure 11.09 displays a result from a landline number. This data includes the owners name, address, email address, cellular telephone number, recent IP address, and vehicle information. It should be noted that this information is associated with a deceased relative. However, it was 100% accurate.

Paul Bazzell

$ Buy A Background Check For Paul

Primary Contact info:

618-259-7625 Landline

$ Purchase Criminal Check for Paul   Ad

$ Purchase Background Check on Paul   Ad

✔ Valid Email Address
pbazzell@gmail.com

757 Purvis Dr 57
Wood River Illinois 62095

IP Address: 192.138.102.113

Alternate Contact info:

618-553-5620

Automobiles Associated with Paul Bazzell

2002 Ford Focus
VIN: 1fafp34372w126826

Figure 11.09: A telephone search result from That's Them.

411 (411.com)

411 offers several reverse search options. For telephone numbers, focus on the "Reverse phone" tab. This will present a single search field. The phone number should be entered into this field without any dashes or spaces similar to 5554458543. The results will include profiles created by 411 for review. Clicking on any of these profiles will present the full profile information. It is common for each household resident to possess a separate profile. All should be checked.

White Pages (dexknows.whitepages.com)

This site will often provide the same results as 411. Occasionally, a non-landline number result may appear here when it would not appear on 411.

Cell Revealer (cellrevealer.com)

There are several websites that claim to reverse search a cellular telephone number. Most of these use databases with outdated or inaccurate information. Cell Revealer does not use these databases. It accesses the caller ID information attached to the cellular telephone number as discussed earlier as well as provider information. Figure 11.10 displays the Cell Revealer search result for our target number from earlier. It did not identify the name, but it did confirm the location. Additionally, it identified the date and time of the registration of that number as well as the provider, Cingular Wireless.

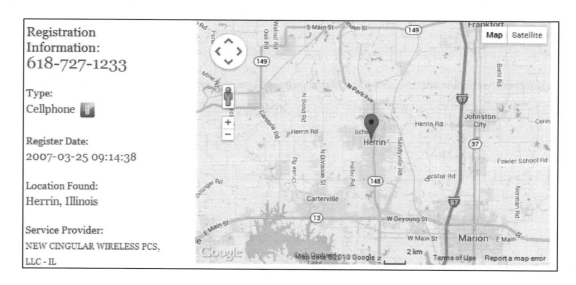

Registration
Information:
618-727-1233

Type:
Cellphone

Register Date:
2007-03-25 09:14:38

Location Found:
Herrin, Illinois

Service Provider:
NEW CINGULAR WIRELESS PCS,
LLC - IL

Figure 11.10: The Cell Revealer search page.

Reverse Genie (reversegenie.com/reverse_phone)

Reverse Genie offers several reverse search options. The strongest are the phone and email search. If a cellular number is located in the Reverse Genie database, it will attempt to locate an address associated with the owner of the number. It will then provide a map identifying the area of the target and the telephone service provider. An alternative to this service is Number Guru (numberguru.com).

Infobel (infobel.com)

Infobel can conduct telephone and address searches on international subjects from almost every country. Several of the links will forward you to external third party services that will appear within an Infobel window. Any links identified as "Infobel" will search an internal database of numbers. The results will identify telephone numbers and addresses for the target searched.

Who Calls Me (whocallsme.com)

Who Calls Me is a user submitted site to report annoying telephone calls from telemarketers and automated systems. If a call is received, the user can enter the number listed on the caller ID to view other people's experiences in identifying the caller. This site also encourages the searcher to leave a comment about the number that was searched. The database is surprisingly large and accurate. Figure 11.11 displays a recent comment that details an experience with a caller. Law Enforcement can use this information to investigate complaints from citizens about telephone harassment. The private sector can use this information to gauge customer complaints about their telemarketing employees.

I just received a call just now. I spoke with a lady first...she was saying that i did a check fraud to pay day loan and so forth and that i will be serve if i don't resolve this...then she transfer me to an attorney name John Davis. I asked him where he from he stated new york....and he was just really scaring me about all these charges $2,000.000 when the lady i spoke with said $1,000.00. Anyway, then he kept saying that it will only cost me $315.00 if i can resolve this today. He also mentioned something about that they will get it from my refund cause they are also connected with IRS...then when i said i don't even work...he was so surprise that no it states that you work and so on...anyway how i ended this was ok can i have the number so i can call back and i said so he is from the attorney office right? then he got really upset and said what don't i understand cause we are going in circles here...ATTORNEYS are professional especially when they talk and this guy he a total jerk and ghetto!!!! anyways they need to catch these people!!!! REPORT PEOPLE if you get this call!
thank you

Caller: ATTORNEY JOHN DAVIS FROM NY
Call Type: Debt Collector

Figure 11.11: A WhoCallsMe search result from a telephone number.

Alternatives to this site are 800 Notes (800notes.com) and Number Guru (numberguru.com). The experience is very similar with equally accurate data. A search through both should quickly identify suspicious numbers found on a caller ID log, cellular phone history, or telephone detailed billing.

Craigslist (craigslist.org)

Craigslist has already been discussed in earlier chapters, but the phone search options should be further detailed. Many people use Craigslist to sell items or services. The posts that announce the item or service available will often include a telephone number. These numbers will belong to a landline or cellular provider. This can be a great way to identify unknown telephone numbers.

Some posts on Craigslist will not allow a telephone number to be displayed on a post. It is a violation of the rules on certain types of posts. Some people choose not to list a number because on automated "scrapers" that will grab the number and add it to databases to receive spam via text messages. Either way, the solution that most users apply to bypass this hindrance is to spell out the phone number. Instead of typing "314-555-1212", the user may enter "three one four five five five one two one two". Some will get creative and post "314 five five five 1212". This is enough to confuse both Craigslist's servers as well as the spammers. This can make searching difficult for an analyst. The hard way to do this is to conduct several searches similar to the following.

site:craigslist.org "314-555-1212"
site:craigslist.org "314" "555" "1212"
site:craigslist.org "three one four" "five five five" "one two one two"
site:craigslist.org "314" "five five five" "1212

This list can get quite long if you try to search every possible search format. One search that will cover most of these searches in a single search attempt would look like the following.

site:craigslist.org "314"|"three one four" "555"|"five five five" "1212"|"one two one two"

The "|" symbol in this search is the same as telling Google "or". In essence, we are telling Google to search "314" or "three one four", then "555" or "five five five", and then "1212" or "one two one two". With this search, you would receive a result if any combination of the following was used.

314-555-1212   314.555.1212   3145551212   314 555 one two one two   three one four 555-1212

This search will not catch every possible way to post a phone number. For example, if the user had typed "314 555 twelve twelve", the above technique would not work. The researcher must consider the alternative ways that a target will post a number on a website. It may help to imagine how you would post the target number creatively on a site, and then search for that method. Additionally, searching for only a portion of the number may provide results. You may want to try searching only the last four digits of the number. This may produce many unwanted results, but your target may be within the "haystack". This technique is not unique to Craigslist only. The same searches would get you results on other sites, such as Backpage, by changing the domain name as follows.

site:backpage.com "314"|"three one four" "555"|"five five five" "1212"|"one two one two"

If the manual approach to this seems overwhelming, I created an online tool that will attempt to replicate this process. It will allow you to enter any telephone number and will search the numerical and written combinations on both Google and Bing. It can be found at the following website.

inteltechniques.com/OSINT/telephone.html

Figure 11.12 displays an actual search result from a telephone number. The search was performed when only a target cellular number was available. This search provided the target's first name and full email address. The email address can now be searched to discover an abundance of information on the target.

```
2011 Chevrolet Impala LS
4 Door Sedan, Automatic
Current Mileage: 23,744
Color: Tan
Interior: Tan cloth
CD player
Asking $14,075

Great condition. Non-smoker. Always parked in a garage.
Please call 618-656-4308 or email jmgusewelle@hotmail.com
```

Figure 11.12: A Craigslist post found through Google from a telephone number.

Facebook (facebook.com)

In Chapter Three, a method of searching cellular telephone numbers on Facebook was explained. This technique is currently one of the most successful methods of identifying the owner of a cellular number. If there is any chance that your target is on Facebook, the number should be searched with that technique.

Spy Dialer (spydialer.com)

This service takes a new approach on identifying the user of a cellular telephone. Most cellular users have an outgoing voicemail message that identifies them by name. Others create a custom message with their own voice. Any of this can help determine the user of the number. Spy Dialer attempts to connect to the service provider of the cellular number, extract the outgoing voicemail message, and present it to you in mp3 format for listening and downloading. All of this is normally completed without ringing the target's telephone. You should note that on some occasions, the target telephone number rang during testing. It did not identify the caller, but the unusual single ring may raise suspicion with a paranoid target. In my experience, this happens about 10 percent of the time. If the target dials the Nevada based number of the missed call, he or she will be notified that a Spy Dialer call was placed. My successes with this method outweigh the risk. I have had several investigations that involved "anonymous" cash cellular telephones that announced the owner's name on the outgoing message. When a successful result is displayed, you can click the link below the player to download the audio file to your computer.

Sly Dial (slydial.com)

This service conducts an inquiry into a cellular telephone the same way as Spy Dialer's attempt. It contacts the cellular provider of the telephone number and sends you straight to the outgoing voicemail message of the target. However, there are two big differences.

Sly Dial does not work through a website. Instead, you must call a general Sly Dial telephone number and follow the automated prompts. You must listen to a brief advertisement before your call is placed. Finally, the service will play you the target's outgoing voicemail message through this audible telephone call. Since a website is not involved, there is no option to download an audio file of the call. We can obtain an audio copy of this message by placing the call through Google Voice and recording the session by pressing the "4" button on the dial pad.

Sly Dial does not usually ring the suspect's telephone. It will likely not show "missed call" or any other indicator that a call occurred. In my testing, less that 5 percent of the attempts actually cause the target telephone to ring only one time. Calling the missed call back reveals nothing about the identity of the number. Ultimately, there is a very small chance that the target will know that someone attempted a call. In the rare occurrence that the telephone rings, the target will never know the identity of the person making the calls.

To use the Sly Dial service, call the following telephone number from any telephone service including landlines, cellular lines, or VOIP.

267-759-3425 (267-SLYDIAL)

Follow the directions during the call. If this number does not work, visit slydial.com for updated directions.

Escort Ads (escortads.xxx)

If you have any suspicion that the target of your investigation is involved in prostitution, drugs, or any related activity, Escort Ads should be checked against the telephone number of your subject. This website aggregates all of the prostitution classifieds and review sites into one search. It extracts the telephone numbers from all online classified pages and allows you to search by the target telephone number. Figure 11.13 displays a search result from a number listed in a Backpage post. It identifies 37 online photos, 20 escort ads, several reviews by "Johns", ages used by the target, the last known location, and locations visited based on postings in online classifieds. Any time I have a target telephone number that is likely involved in criminal activity, I conduct a brief search on this site.

Figure 11.13: A partial search result from escortads.xxx.

Grocery Reward Cards / Loyalty Cards

Most grocery chains have adopted a reward/loyalty card system that mandates the participant enroll in their program. The consumer completes an application and receives a plastic card to use during checkout for discounts. Many of these stores only offer a sale price if you are a member in the program. Most consumers provide a cellular telephone number to the program and use that number during checkout. This eliminates the need of possessing a physical card in order to receive the discount. Instead, they type their cell number into the card swiping machine to associate the purchase with their membership. These programs contain a huge database of telephone numbers and the registered users. There is no online database to access this data. However, you can obtain this data if you are creative.

Assume that your target telephone number is 847-867-5309. If you have tried every technique mentioned at this point to identify the owner and failed, you may consider a query with a local grocery chain. The easiest method is to enter the store, purchase a pack of gum, and enter the target telephone number as the reward/loyalty program number. You will likely receive a receipt with the target's name on the bottom. Figure 11.14 (left) displays apportion of the actual receipt that I received when using this number. If you prefer to avoid entering a store, drive to the company's gas station outside of the store. Figure 11.14 (right) displays the notification I received when entering this same number at the pump. Note that this number is fictional. However, it has been registered at practically every grocery store in the United States. Try to use it the next time you make a purchase.

Figure 11.14: A receipt (left) and gas pump (right) identifying the owner of a cell telephone number.

Addresses

The target of your investigation may be an address. You may want to know who lives at a residence or receives mail sent to a specific address. You may want to know what businesses were located at a location prior to the current tenant. There are dozens of websites that possess databases of address information. I have outlined a few that I have had success with in the past.

White Pages (whitepages.com)

This is the official White Pages website that will conduct a reverse address search. Click on the "Address & Neighbors" tab and enter the address. Entering the zip code instead of the city and state will eliminate spelling errors or formatting inconsistencies. The results will include known residents and neighbors. Often, these neighbors listed will include current and previous residents. This data is pulled from public information and is rarely complete.

Voter Registration (blackbookonline.info/USA-Voter-Records.aspx)

Many people will have their address and telephone number unlisted in public telephone books. This prevents their information from appearing on some websites. If any of these people are registered voters, their address may still be public. In order to locate this data, you will need to connect to the county clerk of the county of residence. The link here will display a list of all fifty states. Clicking the state of the target will present all of the counties with known online databases of voter registration content. Figure 11.15 shows a small portion of a public database from Madison County, Illinois. This will display the full name of the voter and full address. This can be sorted by name or address depending on what information you have about the target.

```
Township-Edwardsville    Precinct-1
                                                HOME
TP-PR-TAX-W CN LG REP SWIC      NAME            MAILING ADDRESS

14-01-102-1 13 56 112    HERIN, CANDICE DAWN    1001 N 2ND ST EDWARDSVILLE 62025
14-01-102-1 13 56 112    PATTISON, KAREN L       1001 N 2ND ST EDWARDSVILLE 62025
14-01-102-1 13 56 112    PATTISON, STEPHEN R     1001 N 2ND ST EDWARDSVILLE 62025
14-01-102-1 13 56 112    FEAR, LOREN G           1003 N 2ND ST APT 3 EDWARDSVILLE 62025
14-01-102-1 13 56 112    CORT, LILLEY ROSE       1103 N 2ND ST EDWARDSVILLE 62025
14-01-102-1 13 56 112    ROACH, JASMINE L        1103 N 2ND ST EDWARDSVILLE 62025
14-01-102-1 13 56 112    WATERSON, PAMELA J      1103 N 2ND ST EDWARDSVILLE 62025
14-01-102-1 13 56 112    WILLIAMS, SANDRA D      1207 N 2ND ST EDWARDSVILLE 62025
14-01-102-1 13 56 112    ROCKWELL, CELESTE M     1301 N 2ND ST EDWARDSVILLE 62025
14-01-102-1 13 56 112    ROCKWELL, MICHAEL D     1301 N 2ND ST EDWARDSVILLE 62025
14-01-102-1 13 56 112    ARMSTRONG, JANE C       1302 N 2ND ST EDWARDSVILLE 62025
```

Figure 11.15: A voter registration page identifying addresses.

Melissa Data (melissadata.com/lookups/zipnumber.asp)

Melissa Data has many tools to filter through public data. This particular tool will accept a zip code and house number. The result will be every possible address that would fit this criteria including the full street name, 6 + 4 zip code, and links to an aerial map of the address (Figure 11.16). This can be helpful if you only know the address number but not the street name. This is also a way of verifying if the target address you are searching really exists.

Zillow (zillow.com)

This is a popular real estate information site. Entering an address will identify data such as purchase price history, sale status, satellite view map, estimated value, and surrounding real estate information. If the house is for sale or was recently for sale, and the home was listed on a real estate site, you will probably see the sale information here. If this includes interior photographs, which most do, you can view the interior of the house. This can help identify the layout of the building.

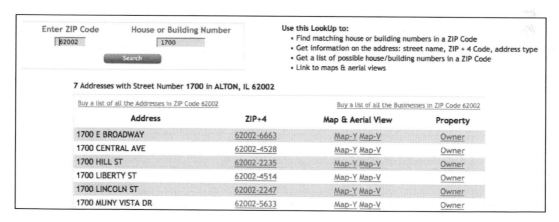

Figure 11.16: A Melissa Data result identifying addresses.

Google (google.com)

If all else fails, or you believe you are missing something, check Google. Searching the address should identify any leftover information about your target address. When searching, place the street address in quotes excluding the city. An example search may appear like this:

"1234 Main" "Bethalto" IL

This will mandate that any results include the exact address and the exact city name, but they do not necessarily need to be right next to each other on the page. If you place the entire address including the city inside a single set of quotes, you would miss any hits that did not have this data connected on the same line.

Spokeo (spokeo.com)

Spokeo was explained earlier as a tool to search a target's real name. A reverse address search will also provide interesting information. Choosing the "Address" option and supplying a full address will identify the last names of any occupants. This is obtained from sources such as utility bills and shipments. The first names of the subjects will be masked and only the first initial is visible. Paying a monthly fee will eliminate this masking, but is usually unnecessary. Instead, a custom search on Google will usually identify the target names. The following example should help explain.

Searching your target address on Google often presents too many results to be effective. Figure 11.17 displays the results of an address search. None of these identify any occupants. The same search on Spokeo identifies the target's first initial as "P" and last name as "Bazzell". A Google search of "bazzell" "757 Purvis" immediately identifies the full name of the target. This technique eliminated results that were not helpful and focused on relevant content. Figure 11.18 displays the first two results on Google that identify full names, a telephone number, a wedding announcement, and relatives. Additional results identified previous addresses, associates, and more family members.

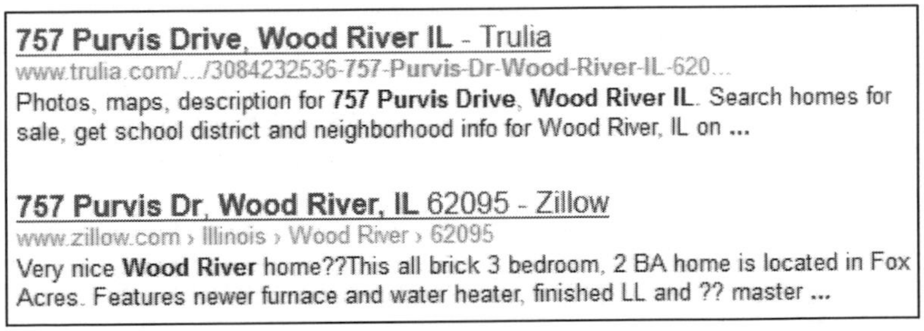

757 Purvis Drive, Wood River IL - Trulia
www.trulia.com/.../3084232536-757-Purvis-Dr-Wood-River-IL-620...
Photos, maps, description for **757 Purvis Drive, Wood River IL**. Search homes for sale, get school district and neighborhood info for Wood River, IL on ...

757 Purvis Dr, Wood River, IL 62095 - Zillow
www.zillow.com › Illinois › Wood River › 62095
Very nice **Wood River** home??This all brick 3 bedroom, 2 BA home is located in Fox Acres. Features newer furnace and water heater, finished LL and ?? master ...

Figure 11.17: A Google search result of an address.

Metro East-Central Residence Pages - Page 23 : DexPages - Metro ...
pageserver2.dexpages.com/guide/IL/Metro_East-Central/.../23.asp
Tel:(618)462-4985. **BAZZELL**, Paul & Freda Contact Details: Main address: **757 PURVIS DR WD RVR 62095**- - - - - Metro East-Central, IL ,. Tel:(618)259-7625 ...

Page 22, Alton Telegraph, Sunday, May 29, 1988 - Newspaper ...
newspaperarchive.com/alton-telegraph/1988-05-29/page-22/
May 29, 1988 – ... **Bazzell** Bob Harvey The engagement of Paula Baz zell to Bob Harvey is announced by her Paul and Freda **Bazzell** of **757 Purvis** Wood Her ...

Figure 11.18: A Google search result of an address with last name included.

Real world application: In hostage situations, SWAT teams want to have all of the information possible about a target building before entry. The satellite and street views are helpful, but the interior view could be more vital. Using Google and Bing, a search of the building should identify any current or previous real estate sale information. If this was within the past decade, these pages usually include digital photographs of the interior of the building. While these may be outdated, they can still provide beneficial information about the layout of the building. Such knowledge would be appreciated by a SWAT team about to make entry.

Online Maps (Chapter Four)

Online maps were explained in Chapter Four, but these services deserve another mention. Entering an address into any of the online map sites will present a satellite view, street view, or 45 degree angled view of the address. This data can be valuable to the identification of assets such as vehicles and boats.

Additional Resources

Many of the telephone number and address search sites present the same information. Occasionally, you may find one site that offers additional information from the rest. If you want to exhaust these options, the following should be visited.

wp.superpages.com
people.yahoo.com
searchbug.com
phonenumber.com
10digits.us

freephonetracer.com
fonefinder.net
mobilephoneno.com
skipease.com/reverse

Chapter Twelve

IP Addresses & Websites

An IP address or a website may become a target of an investigation. IP addresses are often obtained from an email message or connection over the internet. When legal process is served to online content providers, a list of IP addresses used to log into the account is usually presented as part of the return of information. Serving legal orders to identify and obtain IP addresses is outside the scope of this book. However, several techniques for collecting a target's IP address using OSINT are explained in this chapter. A personal website is commonly located during an analysis of a target's online presence. There may be a large amount of information about the website to be gained that is not available within the actual online content. This chapter explains analysis possibilities when an IP address or website is encountered.

MaxMind (maxmind.com)

MaxMind offers up to 25 free IP address searches daily. The results are the most comprehensive I have seen for a free website. While GPS coordinates of an IP address are available, this most often returns to the provider of the internet service. This usually does not identify the exact location of where the IP address is being used. The country, region and city information should be accurate. If an organization name is presented in the results, this indicates that the address returns to the identified company. The exception here is when an internet service provider is identified. This only indicates that the IP address belongs to the specified provider. Figure 12.01 displays a MaxMind result that translates an IP address into information including business name, general location, and internet service provider. This can be used to determine if the IP address that a target is using belongs to a business providing free wireless internet. This can be important intelligence.

Alternate websites include IP Fingerprints (ipfingerprints.com) and IP2Location (ip2location.com).

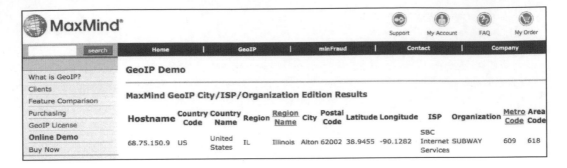

Figure 12.01: A MaxMind IP address search result.

Bing IP (bing.com)

Once you have identified an IP address of your target, you can search for websites hosted on that IP address. A specific search on Bing will present any other websites on that server. If your target is stored with a large host such as GoDaddy, there will not be much intelligence provided. It will only list websites that share a server, but are not necessarily associated with each other. If the user is hosting the website on an individual web server, this search will display all other websites that the user hosts. This search only works on Bing and must have "ip:" before the IP address. An example of a proper search on Bing would look like the following.

ip:67.199.100.78

The results of this search identify every local website hosted by a specific local website design company (Figure 12.02).

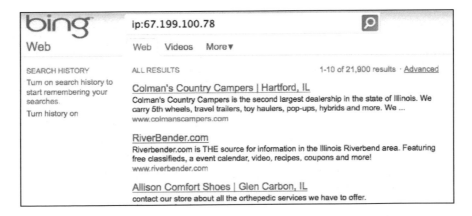

Figure 12.02: Associated websites as identified by Bing.

Email Trace (ip-adress.com/trace_email)

If you would like to analyze an email header in order to identify the IP address and sender information, you have two options. You can look through a few sites and teach yourself how to read this confusing data, or you can use an automated service. Email Trace provides a large text box that an entire email header can be copied into for analysis. The response includes the IP address and location of the sender, interactive map identifying the originating location, internet service provider, and links to additional information from an IP search. Anyone wanting more information from an email threat should start here. An alternate site that performs the same function is MX Toolbox (mxtoolbox.com/EmailHeaders.aspx).

Websites

Websites, also known as domains, are the main site at a specific address. For example, the website www.computercrimeinfo.com/blog is on the domain of computercreiminfo.com. The "www" or anything after the ".com" is not part of the domain. These addresses should be searched for additional information.

Spy On Web (spyonweb.com)

Spy On Web is one of many sites that will search a domain name and identify the web server IP address and location. It also conducts a "whois" query which will give you registration information of a website. This will include the name of the person that registered the website, the administrative contact person, and technical contact person. The summary will also include the physical address, email address, and telephone number of these contacts if provided. Figure 12.03 displays the general information about the website including the IP address of the shared server.

The advanced feature of this service is the ability to reverse search website analytics. Analytics are commonly installed on websites in order to track usage information. This data often identifies the city and state a visitor is from, details about the web browser the user is using, and keywords that were searched to find the site. Only the owner of the website can view this analytic data. Spy On Web determines the specific number assigned to the analytics of a website. If the owner of this website uses analytics to monitor other websites, the analytic number will probably be the same. Spy On Web will now conduct a reverse search of this analytic number to find other websites with the same number. In other words, it will search a website and find other websites that the same owner may maintain. Additionally, it will try to identify user specific advertisements stored on one site that are visible on others. It will reverse search this to identify even more websites that are associated with each other. A couple of examples should simplify the process.

A Spy On Web search for the website "inteltechniques.com" produces a "Google Analytics" result. It identifies seven additional domains that are using the same Google Analytics account for online monitoring. This identifies an association between these websites (Figure 12.04). It is likely that these results will identify other websites maintained by the same subject that created the target website.

Domain name:	inteltechniques.com (whois)
IP Address:	97.74.215.62 (whois)
Analytics Id:	UA-8231004
Alexa Rank:	**774,843** (details)
Page Rank:	1/10
Last Seen:	15.10.2014

Figure 12.03: A Spy On Web result identifying a Google Analytics ID.

Figure 12.04: A Spy On Web result identifying associated domains.

SameID (sameid.net)

While Spy On Web is my preferred overall whois analysis tool, there are additional options that should be checked for reverse analytics. SameID performs the same type of query and attempts to locate any other domains that share the same analytics or advertisement user numbers as your target. This will provide new websites related to your target. During a search of computercrimeinfo.com, it identified all 10 domains that I manage. This was the only website that accomplished this. Further, it identified a new domain that I had established after only two weeks of activation. This service also recognizes Amazon affiliate numbers, which means that if your target website has an advertisement for Amazon on it, SameID will locate any other websites with the same affiliate ID number.

SameID is a premium service and only allows five domain searches per day. You may have extended success by searching Google when your free queries have been exhausted. If you were researching inteltechniques.com, the following search on Google would likely display results that are not redacted.

site:sameid.net "inteltechniques.com"

Domain Analyzer (analyzer.cc)

This service provides an abundant amount of information about a domain that is not visible within the target website. Figure 12.05 is a small portion of the results that identifies the Google Analytics ID number and various technologies used within inteltechniques.com. Overall, the following information was revealed about this domain.

Siteadvisor security rank
Visitors per day
Value of domain
Pageviews per day
Google Analyitcs ID number
Server operating system
Web framework

Facebook shares
Twitter posts
Overall internet ranking
All internal page links
All external page links
Robots.txt data
Page title & description

Historic screenshots
Server location
Server IP address
Domain creation date
Domain expiration date
Domain changed date
DNS services

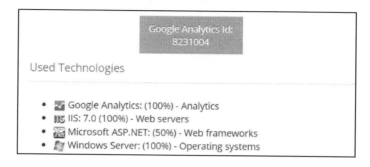

Figure 12.05: A Domain Analyzer search result.

PubDB (pub-db.com)

Another free domain analysis service is PubDB. It is not as robust as others mentioned. However, it occasionally identifies information that was not available with other services. One of its strengths is the ability to identify a Google Adsense affiliate number within a website and cross reference that data to other related domains. Figure 12.06 displays an example of this. The target website of notla.com reveals an Adsense ID of "pub-3941709854725695" (left). Clicking this hyperlink reveals three additional domains that also possess this Adsense number (right). This indicates that the same person may have created all four websites.

Domain Crawler (domaincrawler.com)

The results on this service will likely be redundant to the previously mentioned websites. However, the data here could be used to validate the information that you have already collected. Domain Crawler will attempt to identify any analytics or advertisement codes and will allow you to cross-reference these to other websites. A search for computercrimeinfo.com only identified three related websites. The results were accurate. Another similar site is **Reverse Internet** (reverseinternet.com).

Figure 12.06: A PubDB result identifying domains with the same Google Adsense ID number.

Net Comber (netcomber.com)

This option for reverse analytics is my least favorite. The engine that powers this service is very thorough and locates amazing results. However, it is a premium website and demands payment to disclose results that are not redacted. One or two results will be displayed while the majority will be masked. This provider could still be used to validate your findings from the other services.

Real world application: While investigating an "anonymous" website that displayed photo evidence of a reported felony, I discovered that the registration information was inaccurate. A search of the website on these services identified a Google analytics number and an additional website that possessed the same number. That additional website was the personal blog of the suspect. An arrest was made the same day.

Nerdy Data (search.nerdydata.com)

Nerdy Data was mentioned in Chapter Two as a search engine that indexes the source code of websites. If you have located a Google Analytics or Adsense ID number of a website using the previous methods, you should consider searching this number through Nerdy Data. A search of my Google Analytics number of UA-8231004 revealed five domains that possess the same data. This number, visible only within the source code of the website, can be seen in Figure 12.07.

Computer Crime Presentations and Training by Michael Bazzell

computercrimeinfo.com | view source ☑

```
[r].q||[]).push(arguments)},i[r].l=1*new Date();a=s.createElement(o),  m=s.getElementsB
yTagName(o)[0];a.async=1;a.src=g;m.parentNode.insertBefore(a,m)  })(window,document,'sc
ript','//www.google-analytics.com/analytics.js','ga');  ga('create', 'UA-8231004-3', 'a
uto');  ga('require', 'displayfeatures');  ga('send', 'pageview');</script></body></htm
l>
```

Figure 12.07: A Nerdy Data result identifying websites associated with a Google Analytics number.

Nerdy Data also has a backlinks search that identifies websites that possess a link to your target. The results here should be similar to those found with the Small SEO Tools backlink checker. However, multiple tools should always be used when available. A search of labnol.org produced 667 websites that had referenced the target. Figure 12.08 displays the results with an option to download, view as a list, or view as screenshots. Figure 12.09 displays the screenshot view option. This allows you to quickly locate results of interest.

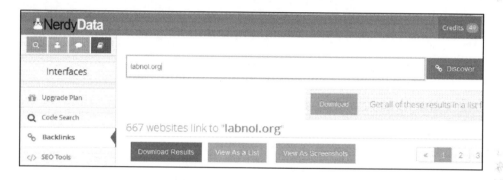

Figure 12.08: A Nerdy Data Backlinks search result.

Figure 12.09: A Nerdy Data Backlinks search result with the screenshot option enabled.

Who Is Hosting This (whoishostingthis.com)

For a quick look at where a website is hosted, try WhoIsHostingThis. Results are minimal and to the point. A search of my own site revealed GoDaddy as my host and the IP address of the server my site is on (Figure 12.10). This will be important in our next search. This is not a complete search for all available information, but this will identify only these key pieces of information without confusion.

Real world application: Law enforcement often serves subpoenas to get information from website hosts. This site offers a simple start to find the company hosting the content. Once an investigator knows where a website is hosted, then a court order can be sent and information collected.

Figure 12.10: A Who Is Hosting This summary.

WhoIsMind (whoismind.com)

"Whois" websites are plentiful and rarely unique. I prefer Domain Dossier (centralops.net), but many others will provide the same information. They all query user registration data for domain names and provide any hosting details available. WhoIsMind offers additional search options not present on other websites. The standard search page allows for a query of a domain name, IP address, or email address. The domain and IP address searches present identical information as other services. However, an email address search presents any domain names associated with the address. This unique option allows you to locate websites that were registered by your target. Further, it appears to store historical information. A search of an old email address, mbazzell@charter.net, identified a previous registration of my website yourcomputernerds.com. This service, combined with the email assumptions search described earlier, can lead to the discovery of websites associated with your target's user name.

Whoisology (whoisology.com)

This service appeared in 2014 and becomes more powerful every month. It is much more than a whois lookup tool. Technically, it is a *reverse* whois lookup. However, that description is not powerful enough to convey the search options available within this website. The home page of Whoisology presents a single search field requesting a domain or email address. Entering either of these will display associated websites and the publicly available whois data. This is where the features begin.

The first basic feature that you see is the display of standard whois data that will identify the registered administrative contact, registrant contact, technical contact, and billing contact. These will often be the same individual for most personal websites. The advanced feature within this content is the ability to immediately search for additional domains associated within any field of this data. As an example, a search for the domain of computercrimeinfo.com reveals the following data.

Name	Michael Bazzell (6)
Email	mike@computercrimeinfo.com (1)
Street	1700 E Broadway (7)
City	Alton (6,428) (+323)
Region	Illinois (1,244,506) (+51,793)
Zip / Post	62002 (2,535) (+110)
Phone	16184628253 (4) (+1)

The name, address, and other data can be found on any whois search website. However, the numbers in parentheses identify the number of additional domains that match those criteria. In this example, there are a total of six domains registered to Michael Bazzell, and seven domains registered to the address of 1700 E Broadway. Clicking on any of these pieces of data will launch a new page with all of the matching domain information. As an example, clicking on Michael Bazzell will display the six domain names associated with my name. Clicking 1700 E Broadway will display the seven domain names associated with that address. One of these is a new domain that is not directly associated with me. However, since it was registered with the same address, there is now a connection.

This type of cross reference search has not been found through other services. Another powerful feature of Whoisology is the historic archives. This service constantly scans for updates to domain registrations. When new content is located, it documents the change and allows you to search the previous data. As an example, a search of computercrimeinfo.com reveals the current administrative contact telephone number to be 6184628253. However, a look at the historic records reveals that on October 16, 2012, the same contact number was 6184633505. This can be a great way to identify associated telephone numbers that have since been removed from the records.

Similar to WhoIsMind, Whoisology will provide details from the search of an email address. In my experience, Whoisology will provide a more detailed and accurate response. A search of the email address brad@notla.com revealed the following five domains associated with that account.

notla.com
albanyscavengerhunt.com
snowplowshow.com
phonelosers.com
phonelosers.org

If you ever encounter an investigation surrounding a domain or any business that possesses a website, I highly encourage you to conduct research through Whoisology. They also offer access through their API at a cost. The individual queries through their website are free.

Domain History (domainhistory.net)

Domain History is similar to Whoisology. However, it does not offer many option for cross reference search of data fields. It does offer a historical view of the whois registration data as well as related domains based on email address. A search of the domain notla.com revealed the standard whois data, an associated email address of brad@notla.com, and two additional domains associated with that email address. There were over a dozen historical records of this domain's registration details. Most of them were very recent and identified redundant information. However, one historical record was from six months prior and identified a previous domain registrar.

Change Detection (changedetection.com)

Once you locate a website of interest, it can be time consuming to continually visit the site looking for any changes. With large sites, it is easy to miss the changes due to an enormous amount of content to analyze. This is when sites like Change Detection come in handy. Enter the address of the target page of interest as well as an email address where you can be reached. This service will monitor the page and send you an email if anything changes. Figure 12.11 displays the format of the change indications that will be sent via email. Anything highlighted is either new or modified content. Anything that has been stricken through indicates deleted text. Visual Ping offers an additional feature. You can select any portion of a web page and monitor only that section for any changes. This could be used to monitor only the changes to a person's profile photo or latest blog post. Parents are encouraged to set up and use these services to monitor their child's websites. It does not work well on some social networks such as Facebook, but can handle a public Twitter page fine.

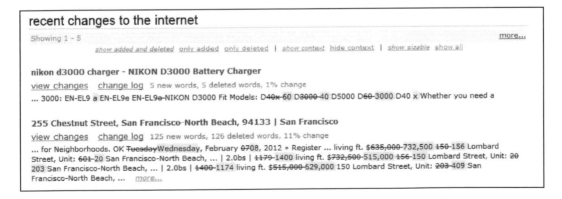

Figure 12.11: Changes to websites as detected by Change Detection.

Visual Ping (visualping.io)

If you found the service provided by Change Detection helpful, but you are seeking more robust options, you should consider Visual Ping. This modern Swiss website allows you to select a target domain for monitoring. Visual Ping will generate a current snapshot of the site and you can choose the level of monitoring. I recommend hourly monitoring and notification of any "tiny change". It will now check the domain hourly and email you if anything changes. If you are watching a website that contains advertisements or any dynamic data that changes often, you can select to avoid that portion of the page. Figure 12.12 displays the monitoring option for inteltechniques.com. In this example, I positioned the selection box around the content of the Latest Videos section of this page. I also chose the hourly inspection and Tiny Change option. If anything changes within this selected area, I will receive an email announcing the difference.

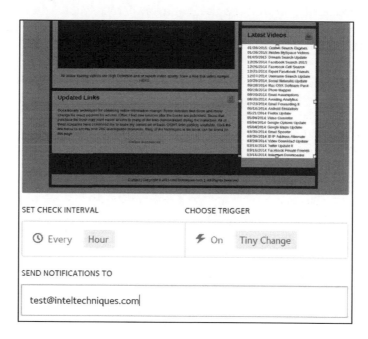

Figure 12.12: A portion of a web page monitored by Visual Ping for changes.

Built With (builtwith.com)

A quick analysis of a target website may identify the technologies used to build and maintain it. Many pages that are built in an environment such as WordPress or Tumblr often contain obvious evidence of these technologies. If you notice the YouTube logo within an embedded video, you will know that the creator of the site likely has an account within the video service. However, the presence of various services is not always obvious. Built With takes the guesswork out of this important discovery. Entering my domain of inteltechniques.com into the Built With search immediately identifies my web server operating system, email provider, web framework, website analytics, video services, mailing list provider, blog environment, and website code functions. While much of this is geek speak that may not add value to your investigation, some of it will assist in additional search options through other networks. Another option for this type of search is **Stats Crop** (statscrop.com).

WordPress Sites

WordPress has made creating a personal website extremely easy. Many people that decide to create a personal blog choose WordPress as the format. When you encounter a personal website that was created with WordPress, there are additional search options. The best way to identify if a site was designed with WordPress is to scroll to the bottom of the page and look for any design reference to WordPress. It will usually appear similar to "Copyright WordPress© 2008–2013". Users are encouraged to apply security updates to their WordPress site, but many people ignore these requests. Typing some specific text after the website name on a user's unpatched WordPress site can display additional information. An actual example should explain the method.

The website "dailypicksandflicks.com" is a WordPress site that has not been updated since version 3.5. Visiting the site presents the public view including any intentional content on the home page. Adding the text "/wp-content/uploads/" without quotes behind the website address presents an "Index" view of the uploaded content to the site (Figure 12.13). You can now access any content uploaded to the website by the owner. This may include photos not present on the basic site. Additionally, it will usually allow access to the full size photos uploaded to the account even if the user decided to compress them for space consideration. These original images could still have the Exif content in them that can produce new intelligence. This will not work with all WordPress sites. Figure 12.14 displays the results for any data uploaded to the blog in August of 2013.

Figure 12.13: A WordPress blog.

Figure 12.14: A WordPress blog's uploaded content.

Pentest-Tools (pentest-tools.com/reconnaissance/find-subdomains-of-domain)

This unique tool performs several tasks that will attempt to locate hidden pages on a domain. First it performs a DNS zone transfer which will often fail. It will then use a list of numerous common subdomain names and attempt to identify any that are present. If any are located, it will note the IP address assigned to that subdomain and will scan all 254 IP addresses in that range. In other words, it will attempt to identify new areas of a website that may not be visible from within the home page. The following example may help to clarify.

The website at hope.net is very basic and provides links to various Hackers On Planet Earth (HOPE) conference websites. It then appears to have no further content to be analyzed. Searching for hope.net on Pentest-Tools provides additional intelligence. It identifies the following subdomains present on the web server:

radio.hope.net
w.hope.net
archive.hope.net
www.hope.net

x.hope.net
wwww.hope.net
ww.hope.net
api.hope.net

Typing in these addresses into an address bar in a browser generates new pages that contain valuable data. This method has helped me locate "hidden" pages which contain several forum messages from users of the site. Previous editions of this book have discussed additional providers for this type of service. Pentest-Tools is the only provider that continues to function. The rest have disappeared.

Shared Count (sharedcount.com)

This website provides one simple yet unique service. It searches your target domain and identifies its popularity on social networks such as Facebook and Twitter. A search of labnol.org produced the following results.

Facebook Likes: 348
Facebook Shares: 538
Facebook Comments: 148
Facebook Total: 1034
Twitter Tweets: 0

Google+1s: 4202
Pinterest Pinned: 1
LinkedIn Shares: 172
Delicious Bookmarks: 44
StumbleUpon Stumbles: 0

This information would lead me to focus on Google+ and Facebook first. It tells me that several people are talking about the website on these services. I also know now that 44 people have bookmarked the site on Delicious, and I could go track down those people. I have used this tool to successfully identify pedophiles that are interested in a child pornography website and students at a high school that were commenting on a blog that encouraged harassment of a specific student.

Small SEO Tools: Backlinks (smallseotools.com/backlink-checker)

After you have determined the popularity of a website on social networks, you may want to identify any websites that have a link to your target domain. This will often identify associates and people with similar interests of the subject of your investigation. There are several online services that offer a check of any "backlinks" to a specific website. Lately, I have had the best success with the backlink checker at Small SEO Tools. A search of my own website, inteltechniques.com, produces 264 websites that have a link to mine. These results include pages within my own websites that have a link to inteltechniques.com, so this number can be somewhat misleading. Several of the results disclosed websites owned by friends and colleagues that would be of interest if I were your target.

Small SEO Tools: Plagiarism Checker (smallseotools.com/plagiarism-checker)

If you have identified a web page of interest, you should make sure that the content is original. On more than one occasion, I have been contacted by an investigator that had been notified of a violent threat on a person's blog. I was asked to track down the subject before something bad happened. A quick search of the content identified it as lyrics to a song. One of many options for this type of query is the plagiarism checker at Small SEO Tools.

You can use this tool by copying any questionable text from a website and paste it into this free tool. It will analyze the text and display other websites that possess the same words. This service uses Google to identify anything of interest. The benefit of using this tool instead of Google directly is that it will structure several queries based on the supplied content and return variations of the found text. Figure 12.15 displays results from text that was identified on nine different websites. Clicking the links seen here will open the Google search result page that found the text. This example confirms that none of the supplied text had original content. Another option for this type of search is **Copy Scape** (copyscape.com).

Figure 12.15: A Plagiarism Checker search result.

Reddit Domains (reddit.com)

Reddit was discussed in Chapter Seven as a very popular online community. The primary purpose of the service is to share links to online websites, photos, videos, and comments of interest. If your target website has ever been posted on Reddit, you can retrieve a listing of the incidents. This is done through a specific address typed directly into your browser. If your target website was phonelosers.org, you would navigate to the following website.

reddit.com/domain/phonelosers.org/

This example produced 16 Reddit posts mentioning this domain. These could be analyzed to document the discussions and user names related to these posts.

Robots.txt

Practically every professional website has a robots.txt file at the "root" of the website. This file is not visible from any of the web pages at the site. It is present in order to provide instructions to search engines that crawl the website looking for keywords. These instructions identify files and folders within the website that should not be indexed by the search engine. Most engines comply with this request, and do not index the areas listed.

Locating this file is relatively easy. The easiest way to view the file is to open it through a web browser. Type the website of interest, and include "robots.txt" after the forward slash (/). The file for Reddit can be found at the following address.

http://www.reddit.com/robots.txt

If this technique produces no results, you can conduct a Google or Bing query to identify any files. The following search on either search engine would identify robots.txt files from the website Twit.tv.

site:twit.tv "robots.txt"

Figure 12.16 displays the Google search result. You can see that an instructional file is located at "inside.twit.tv", which may have prevented you from finding it manually. Figure 12.17 displays a portion of this robots.txt file. The first line indicates that this website was created by Squarespace, and is likely stored on their servers. The last line identifies a login page that could be accessed by typing in the direct address (inside.twit.tv/display/login). This information would not have been located through a search engine.

The following text is a portion of an actual robots.txt file located on a web server of a college.

```
Disallow:  /eListen/
Disallow:  /employeelisting/
Disallow:  /uploadedfiles/
```

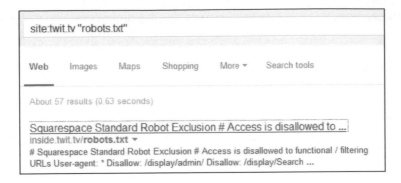

Figure 12.16: A Google search result for a robots.txt file from a website.

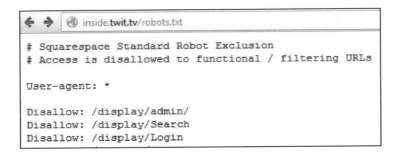

Figure 12.17: A portion of a robots.txt file on a website.

These instructions are telling the search engines to avoid scanning the folders eListen, employeelisting, and uploadfiles. It is likely that there is sensitive information in these directories that should not be available on Google or Bing. We can now type these directories after the domain name of our target to identify interesting information. If this was the robots.txt file on my website, you would type the following addresses into your browser.

Inteltechniques.com/eListen
Inteltechniques.com/employeelisting
Inteltechniques.com/uploadedfiles

This particular file is not from my website, so these examples will not provide any information. Another portion of this text file is the following.

```
Disallow: /AssetManagement.config
Disallow: /AssetManagementbkup20070925.Config
```

These instructions request that the listed web pages are not indexed by any visiting search engines. While these pages will be excluded from Google, Bing, and others, we can type them in directly to see the data. If these were found within my robots.txt file, you would type each of the following into a web browser.

Inteltechniques.com/AssetManagement.comfig
Inteltechniques.com/AssetManagementbkup20070925.Config

Most robots.txt files will not identify a secret area of a website that will display passwords, raunchy photos, or incriminating evidence. Instead, they usually provide insight into which areas of the site are considered sensitive by the owner. If you have a target website and have exhausted every other search method, you should also visit this file. It may direct you toward a new set of queries to find data otherwise ignored by search engines.

Wigle (wigle.net)

Wigle is a crowd sourced database of wireless access points. Users in all areas of the country conduct scans of wireless devices in their area, identify details of each device, and submit this data to Wigle in order to map the found devices on the site. This allows anyone to browse an area for wireless access points or search an address to locate specific devices. Additionally, you can search for either a specific router name or MAC address and locate any matching devices. The results will include links that will display the results on an interactive map. Most of the world has been covered. In order to take advantage of the search features, you will need to register for a free account. Generic or misleading information can be used that does not identify you.

There are many investigation uses for this service. You can identify the wireless access points in the immediate area of a target's home. Figure 12.18 displays a map of a neighborhood with the associated routers. In this view, you can identify the router names including possibly sensitive information.

An investigator could also search by the target's name. This may identify routers that have the target's name within the SSID. Figure 12.19 displays a search result for "Bazzell". It identifies seven access points that probably belong to relatives with my last name. These results identify the router name, MAC address, dates, encryption method, channel, and location of the device. This can easily lead an investigator to the home of a target.

Many internet users will use the same name for their wireless router as they use for their online screen name. Assume that your target's user name was "Hacker21224". A search on Wigle for "Hacker21224" as a router name will produce only one result. This will identify the router's MAC address, encryption type, and GPS coordinates. A search on Google Maps of the supplied GPS coordinates will immediately identify the home address, a satellite view of the neighborhood, and a street view of the house of the target. All of this intelligence can be obtained from a simple user name. These results would not appear on any standard search engines.

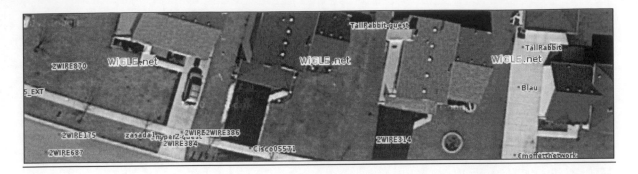

Figure 12.18: A Wigle search result by location identifying router names.

map it	netid	ssid	comment	name	type	freenet	paynet	firsttime	lasttime	flags	wep	trilat	trilong	dhcp	lastupdt	channel
Get Map	00:1F:33:38:D2:1E	bazzell			infra	?	?	2012-08-31 04:04:33	2012-09-05 04:12:06		2	36.10634995	-97.05599976	?	20120905041207	4
Get Map	00:18:E7:D2:58:F2	bazzell-ap			infra	?	?	2012-02-05 10:31:02	2012-02-05 00:14:09		2	26.31480408	127.81907654	?	20120205001523	6
Get Map	00:1E:52:78:8D:88	Bazzell AC		Bazzell AC		?	?	0000-00-00 00:00:00	2011-08-26 14:51:50	0000	?	47.42412567	8.57739544	?	20110826145152	9

Figure 12.19: A Wigle search result by name identifying sensitive information.

SHODAN (shodanhq.com)

SHODAN is a search engine that lets you find specific computers (routers, servers, etc.) using a variety of filters. General search engines, such as Google and Bing, are great for finding websites. However, they do not search for computers or devices. SHODAN indexes 'banners', which are metadata a device sends back to a client. This can be information about the server software, what options the service supports, or a welcome message. Devices that are commonly identified through SHODAN include servers, routers, online storage devices, surveillance cameras, webcams, and VOIP systems. Network security professionals use this site to identify vulnerabilities on their systems. Criminals use it to illegally access networks and alter devices. We will use it to locate specific systems near a target location. In order to take advantage of SHODAN's full search capabilities, you must create a free account. Only a name and email address is required. The following example will identify how to locate live public surveillance cameras based on location.

The target for this search is Mount Pleasant, Utah. The following search on SHODAN produced 9,684 results.

country:US city:"Mount Pleasant"

There are two flaws with this search. First, you may receive results from other cities named Mount Pleasant. Second, you will likely receive too many results to analyze effectively. The following search will focus only on the specific GPS location of interest (Lat=39.55, Long=-111.45).

geo:39.55,-111.45

There were 238 results for this search. This is much more manageable and all of the results will be devices in the target area. Adding more specific search criteria will filter the results further. The following search identified only one device.
geo:39.55,-111.45 netcam

Figure 12.20 displays this search result. The next to last line identifies this device as a "Netcam". The result also identifies the internet service provider as "Central Utah Telephone" indicating the user has a DSL connection. To connect to the device, you would click on the IP address identified as 63.78.117.229. Clicking through each of these results may be time consuming. You can add a search term to filter your results.

Replicating this search for a GPS location in a large city will produce many results. Clicking the IP address will take you to the page that will connect to each device. You must be careful here. Some devices will require a user name and password for access. You could try "admin" / "admin" or "guest" / "guest", but you may be breaking the law. This could be considered computer intrusion. However, many of the webcam and netcam results will not prompt you for a password and connect you to the device automatically.

There is likely no law violation when connecting to a device that does not prompt you for credentials. Figure 12.21 displays the live camera feed from the result in the previous example. This is just one of several searches you can do to discover devices by name, location, IP address, etc. The following list identifies the appropriate search operators for each type of query. **Shodan Maps** (maps.shodan.io) allows you to conduct any of these searches based on location alone.

City: Name of the city (ex. city:"San Diego")
Country: 2-letter country code (ex. country:US)
GPS: Latitude and longitude (ex. geo:50.23,20.06)
OS: Operating system (ex. os:Linux)
IP Address: Range (ex. net:18.7.7.0/24)
Keyword: (ex. webcam)

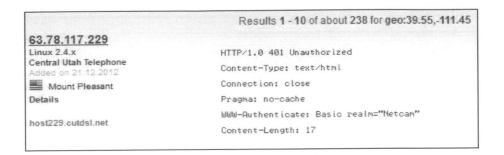

Figure 12.20: A SHODAN search result from a GPS location.

Figure 12.21: A live camera feed located through SHODAN.

Obtaining a Target's IP Address

You may want to know the IP address of the person you are researching as provided by their internet service provider. This address could be used to verify an approximate location of the person, to provide law enforcement details that would be needed for a court order, or to determine if multiple email addresses belong to the same subject. All of those scenarios will be explained here while I explain the various services that can be used.

What's Their IP (whatstheirip.com)

For many years, this was my favorite option for identifying the IP address of a target. There are many options now, and all of them will be explained here. This specific technique involves some trickery and the need to contact the target from a covert account. For this demonstration, assume that your target has a Facebook page that he checks regularly. You can send him a private message that includes "bait" in the form of an online link. Before you send the message, you must create the link.

Navigate to whatstheirip.com and provide your email address. The target will not see this address, but I recommend an anonymous account. This will generate two website links that are unique to you. I always prefer the first option, as it looks less suspicious. Two links issued to me are as follows.

http://www.bvog.com/?post=IDAftMfYZQx9Sj7rp
http://www.hondachat.com/showthread.php?t=IDAftMfYZQx9Sj7rp

If a person visits the first link, they receive a notification that the website is no longer available. It is basically a blank page with an error at the top. The second link connects to what appears to be an online forum about cars, but the post requested is unavailable. Both of these links are designed to make the target believe that whatever was on these pages previously is no longer available.

Your goal is to get your target to click on one of these links. When he or she does, this service will capture their IP Address and forward it to you. There are two main ways to effectively complete this task.

Email: The easiest solution would be to email them a link. However, do not just send the link and hope for the best. I recently had a Craigslist investigation where a suspect was selling a stolen iPad through the website. I sent an email from a covert account that was verbatim as the following example.

Hi. I saw your ad on craigslist. I want to buy that iPad for my dad. I have cash and I live about 20 minutes away. I just need to know if it is the model 1 or 2. This link has a picture of what the back should look like. If it does, let me know and I can bring you cash today.

http://www.bvog.com/?post=IDAftMfYZQx9Sj7rp

When the target clicked on the attached link, he saw exactly what you see in Figure 12.22. Within one second of him clicking the link, I received the email visible in Figure 12.23. I immediately knew an approximate location and the IP address of the suspect. A subpoena to the internet service provider verified an actual address.

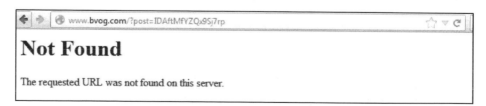

Figure 12.22: The "Not Found" page generated by "whatstheirip.com".

Figure 12.23: A response from "whatstheirip.com" identifying a target's IP address.

IP Logger (iplogger.org)

An alternative to whatstheirip.com is IP Logger. This service applies the same concept as whatstheirip.com but works differently. Instead of sending you an email when a target clicks a link, you must view a log file within the IP Logger website. Additionally, this service supports transparent and custom images that will track your target for extra covert privacy. A detailed set of instructions should explain the processes with several options.

The main website gives you an option to "Generate an invisible IPLOGGER". This button will forward you to another page with a custom transparent image created specifically for you. This image is very small and invisible to human eyes. You can place this image on any personal website, forum, or blog. When a target visits the page, this image captures the IP address and other details of that user. All of this happens without the target knowing. When I clicked this, I was presented with Figure 12.24.

Notice that it issued me the image address of "iplogger.org/1Wzp3.jpg". I then created a post on a web forum about wireless hacking. This generic post is displayed in Figure 12.25. Notice that the image is not visible. When making the post, I chose the "media" option, and inserted the link above.

Now that this is in place, any time that anyone views this specific page, their information will be extracted and recorded. I can click on the button labeled "View Log" in Figure 12.24 to see the results. Figure 12.26 displays this log moments after the post. I can identify the IP addresses from people in New York, Michigan, and Illinois that recently viewed this page.

In this scenario, I will now know the IP addresses of people reading my post and other posts on the same page. This could also be used on comment boards, blogs, or any type of web forum that allows images to be included in your post.

The next option that we have with this service is to provide a target web page that we want to monitor. Previously, I discussed sending a link to a suspect as bait about someone posting his information online. When the target clicked the link, an error from a blank website was returned. In this scenario, we are going to give the target a link that will actually forward to Twitter in order to eliminate any suspicion about a broken link.

On the main IP Logger page, there is an option to "Generate short IP Logger URL". I supplied the following web address to forward to the target. IP Logger responded with the result visible in Figure 12.27.

https://twitter.com/osint

This verifies that if anyone opens the web page "iplogger.org/2iXV", he or she will be forwarded to "twitter.com/osint". When this happens, IP Logger will capture the IP address of the target and allow us to see the information. Since "iplogger.org/2iXV" looks somewhat suspicious, we will change this to a shortened link at "goo.gl", Google's link shortening service. Figure 12.28 displays the result.

Figure 12.24: An IP Logger response with a custom invisible image for tracking.

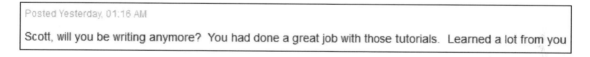

Figure 12.25: An online post including the invisible image from IP Logger.

N	Date, Time	ip	Country	Region	City
1	11.11.2013 02:43:39	69.207.19.16	United States	New York	Buffalo
2	11.11.2013 02:39:31	24.11.222.147	United States	Michigan	Warren
3	11.11.2013 02:38:35	97.92.227.166	United States	Illinois	Glen Carbon

Figure 12.26: The results from IP Logger identifying IP addresses of targets.

Figure 12.27: An IP Logger response with a shortened URL that forwards to a Twitter page.

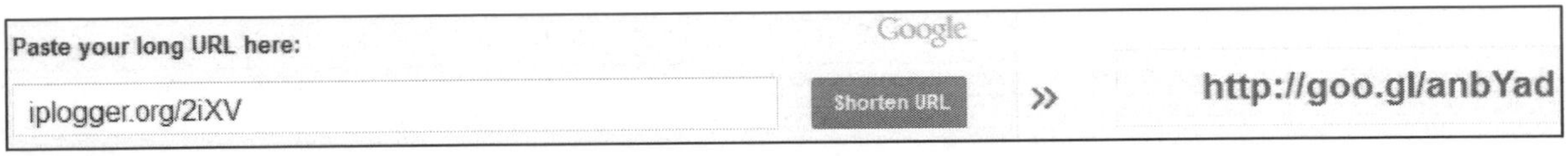

Figure 12.28: A Google response from a shortened URL request.

A quick summary should clear up any confusion. The IP Logger service created us a special link that will forward to a Twitter page. This link captures the target's IP information. Because the link was suspicious looking, we used the Google shortening service to create a new and innocent looking link (goo.gl/anbYad). Anyone that clicks this Google link now will be forwarded to the Twitter page and we will have their IP address.

We can now send this Google link to the target through an email, blog post, or social network as described earlier. Receiving the Twitter page, or any page that would be of interest to your target, should eliminate any concern about this being a trap. We can visit the log visible in Figure 12.26 using the listed IP Logger ID number to see the results.

The last option we have is to use our own image to hide the tracking code. On the following website, I have an invisible man photo.

http://computercrimeinfo.com/bio.html

This image is used on advertisements and brochures related to my public speaking events because I do not like to have photos of me on the internet. The actual image is located at the following location.

http://computercrimeinfo.com/img/invisible.jpg

On the main IP Logger page, I supplied this image address on the "Generate picture code" option. I was given the response visible in Figure 12.29. IP Logger created a new image online that will forward to the real image. I placed this image, "iplogger.org/3UzK.jpg, on the following website.

http://computercrimeinfo.com/bio2.html

If you navigate to this site, you will notice that it appears identical to the first website that possesses my bio. The difference is that this new address possesses a tracking code within the photo that forwards you to the invisible man image. Basically, just opening this page and viewing that image records your IP address. To test this, insert the IP Logger ID number of 2805751652657 on the IP Logger main page and view the results. You will see not only your IP address, but every other viewer's IP address as well. I have had recent success with this technique in the following scenario.

I was communicating with an unknown subject about illegal matters on a web forum about hacking and stolen credit card numbers. I wanted to find out his IP address in order to discover his true identity with a court order. Using the Twitter search techniques mentioned earlier, I located an old photo of a person's debit card that appeared on twitter.com/needadebitcard. I chose this option because he had recently made a post about cancelling the card. I told the hacker that I had an image of a freshly stolen debit card that I was willing to share. He requested proof, so I created an IP Logger link based on that online image, and embedded that link into the web forum that we were communicating in. Within a few moments, I visited the log for this image and discovered his IP address in Newark, New Jersey.

Figure 12.29: An IP Logger response with a link to a forwarded image.

Blasze (blasze.tk)

A newer option for IP identification is Blasze. At the time of this writing, it was more popular than the previous two methods. It works very similar to Whats Their IP. The difference is that you can forward the target to a desired link that may not raise any suspicion. As an example, assume that you want to send your target an email message that will identify his IP address. You want him to click on a link, but you do not want him to receive an error similar to what is presented by whatstheirip.com. Instead, you want him to actually navigate to a safe website in order to eliminate any concern that he was compromised.

The Blasze website will ask you to enter a real website that you want your target to see. In this example, I will use the Reddit Netsec page located at reddit.com/r/netsec. When I supplied this link to Balsze, it generated a unique internet address (URL) of blasze.tk/DQ7ORY. This is the page that you want your target to open. It will forward him to the Reddit website, but it will first capture his information. Blasze will also generate a web page that will allow you to monitor the captured details. You should bookmark or save this link. In this example, the address for monitoring the forwarding link was http://blasze.tk/track/JYHFLR.

If your target clicks on the blasze.tk/DQ7ORY link, Blasze will track the information from his internet connection. However, this suspicious URL may make your target skeptical. Before the link is sent, I recommend using a URL shortening service that will make the link appear more trustworthy. I prefer to use Google for this. Navigate to the website goo.gl and enter the Blasze link provided to you (blasze.tk/DQ7ORY in this example). Google will generate a new link that will appear similar to http://goo.gl/dIviMz. Now, you can send a link that is less suspicious looking.

In this example, you would send your target the link of goo.gl/dIviMz. When clicking this link, it automatically forwards to the Blasze service and connects to blasze.tk/DQ7ORY. When this link is executed, it automatically forwards to the original "safe" site of reddit.com/r/netsec. Overall, the target clicks on a shortened Google link and sees the Reddit page. If this were my investigation, I would have sent a message similar to the following.

Hi David. Sorry, you don't know me, but I thought you should know that the project that you have been working on has leaked and is currently being discussed on Reddit here: goo.gl/dIviMz.

Obviously, you would want to use an anonymous email account. If your target opens the link, and sees the Reddit page, it will likely create confusion, but will look less suspicious than opening a link that generates an error message. You can then navigate to the Blasze link monitoring page, http://blasze.tk/track/JYHFLR in this example, and see the results. Figure 12.30 displays my test results. The target clicked on the link at 22:30 hours on February 2, 2015. He was using a Chrome web Browser (version 40.0), had an IP address of 68.225.11.142, and uses Cox as an internet service provider (ISP). MaxMind reports the residential IP address to be in Irvine, California.

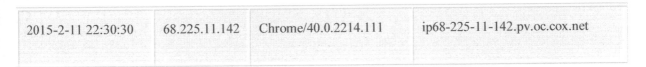

| 2015-2-11 22:30:30 | 68.225.11.142 | Chrome/40.0.2214.111 | ip68-225-11-142.pv.oc.cox.net |

Figure 12.30: A link monitoring report from Blasze identifying the IP address of a target.

You may choose to send these links from a spoofed email account. If I were to email you from *mikethehacker@gmail.com* and request that you open a link, you would likely delete the message. However, what if the email came from someone that you worked with? It is easy to control the display of a sender's email address and name. There are many software applications that will allow this manipulation. However, the easiest way is through an online service.

Emkei (emkei.cz)

The service will allow you to immediately send an anonymous email message from within the website. You can completely control the sender's name, email address, subject, and message. The recipient will receive an email as normal. However, the "From" section will contain any spoofed information that you desire. Combining this utility with the tracking services mentioned previously can increase the success of the methods. Always test this technique by sending a message to yourself first.

Anonymous Email (anonymousemail.me)

I recently noticed that anonymous messages from Emkei were being marked as spam by Gmail. Because of this, I began using the free service from Anonymous Email to send messages that appear to be coming from someone else. I have found that Gmail is not currently identifying these as spam. My tests all landed directly in the inbox of the recipient.

Social Network

If you do not know your target's email address, you can send this same link to them through their social networks, such as Facebook. In September of 2013, I was investigating an incident that involved an anonymous Facebook profile that was harassing several people with violent threats. A search warrant to Facebook would get what I needed. However, that can take several weeks. Instead, I sent a private message to the Facebook profile with the following text.

I don't know who you are, but I thought you should know that another Facebook user has posted your home address over on another site. You may want to take it down or at least be aware: http://www.bvog.com/?post=IDAftMfYZQx9Sj7rp

Obviously, this private information was not present. However, it was enticing enough to make the target click the link. That was all I needed in order to identify the IP address and approximate location of the target. If your person of interest is very tech savvy, he or she will know about this trick. If that might jeopardize your investigation, avoid this technique.

BananaTag (bananatag.com)

This premium service offers a free version that is limited to five emails per day. It requires you to use a Gmail account and install a plugin through your web browser. In my tests, antivirus companies did not alert on the process. An occasional test on your end should be conducted if you continuously use this service. After you create your account and install the plugin as directed on the website, you will have a new feature within your Gmail account. Next to the standard "Send" button visible when you compose a new email, you will see a button titled "Track & Send". Clicking this button will inject a small piece of code into your message. When the message is read, you will receive an email announcing the event. You will need to login to your BananaTag account to see the details. Figure 12.31 displays details of the following email that I sent to my supervisor to determine his location (sorry boss).

LT, disregard that last message, I figured it out. MB

The response identified his IP Address, the operating system of his computer, the type of computer, the web browser, and the approximate location. This information tells me that he is likely at home and not replying from a mobile device.

A message could be sent to multiple email addresses of your investigation. Changing each message may convince a single person using multiple accounts to click each link. This can verify that the multiple accounts actually belong to the same target.

My complaint with BananaTag is the amount of steps involved to access the service. When conducting techniques like this, I prefer to use methods that do not require registration and the installation of software. If this is something you will do on a regular basis, it is worth the configuration time. If you only need to identify one or two IP addresses, I recommend "Whats Their IP" and a bit of creativity.

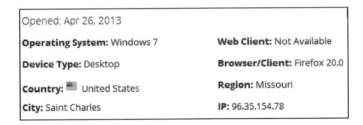

Figure 12.31: A BananaTag response.

Get Notify (getnotify.com)

Similar to BananaTag, Get Notify tracks the opening of email messages and presents the connection information of the target. However, this service is completely free and does not require Gmail as your email provider. You will need to create an account through the Get Notify website and you will be limited to five email messages per day.

After you have registered the email address that you will be using, you can send emails from that account as usual. However, you will need to add ".getnotify.com" after each email recipient. Instead of sending an email address to the valid account of Michael@inteltechniques.com, you would send the message to Michael@inteltechniques.com.getnotify.com. This will force the email message to go through Get Notify's servers and route the message to the valid address. When your target reads the email message, Get Notify will track the user's IP address, geographical location, and notify you whether your message was viewed for a length of time or deleted right away. Figure 12.32 displays a result from Get Notify.

Get Notify works by adding a small invisible tracking image in your outgoing emails. When your email recipient opens your message, this image gets downloaded from a Get Notify server. Get Notify will know exactly when your sent email was opened and it notifies you through an email that your sent message is read by the recipient. You can also view log files within your online account. The tracking image inserted by Get Notify is invisible to the recipient. Optionally you can specify your own images to be used as tracking images by going to the preferences section after signing in to GetNotify.com. Your recipient will not see ".getnotify.com" at the end of his or her email address. If you want to send a single email to multiple recipients, you should add ".getnotify.com" at the end of every email address.

Email Tracking Details	
Opened at	13-Apr-2014 at 5:42:25 PM (GMT-06:00)
Location	Mountain View, United States (80% likelihood)
Recipient IP	66.249.85.65
Language	
Web Browser	Firefox 3.0.7
Operating System	Windows XP
User Agent String	Mozilla/5.0 (Windows; U; Windows NT 5.1; de; rv:1.9.0.7) Gecko/2009021910 Firefox/3.0.7 (via ggpht.com GoogleImageProxy)
Read Duration	Please see the live tracking details of this email for email read duration.

Figure 12.32: A Get Notify result identifying a target's IP address, location, and operating system.

There are countless scenarios that may make these techniques beneficial to your online research. While I used it for law enforcement, especially in tracking down stolen goods on Craigslist, civilians can use it for many different things. Private investigators have used it on dating websites while hunting cheating spouses. Singles have used it to verify that the potential mate that they have been chatting with for weeks is really local and not in another state or country. The possibilities are endless.

Chapter Thirteen

Government Records

Open source government information has never been easier to obtain. A combination of a more transparent government, cheaper digital storage costs, and widespread broadband internet access has placed more information online than ever before. There is no standard method of searching this data. One county may handle the queries much differently than another county. The following resources and techniques should get you started.

County & Court Records

A Google search of your county clerk should identify whether an online database is available. As an example, St. Clair County, Illinois (circuitclerk.co.st-clair.il.us/icjSearch.htm), has their court records online. Searching only a last name will present profiles with full name, date of birth, physical identifiers, case history, fines, pending appearances and more. Navigating the website will expose charged crimes even if they were dismissed. This can be extremely useful in civil litigation.

There are several websites that help connect you to publicly available county government records. These sites allow you to drill-down to your local records. The main page will prompt for the state desired. The result will be a list of links that access each county's court information. Some rural areas are not online, but an occasional search should be done to see if they have been added. Of these services, I have found the following to be useful.

Black Book (www.blackbookonline.info/USA-Counties.aspx)
Public Records Online (publicrecords.onlinesearches.com)

SSN Validator (ssnvalidator.com)

A simple way to verify if a number is valid is at SSN Validator. This does not provide the personal information attached to the number, only verification that the number is valid. A typical response will include the state that issued the number, the year issued, and verification that the number was assigned (Figure 13.01).

Date of this report:	February 16, 2012
State of Issuance:	Illinois
Approx. Date of Issuance:	1975
Issuance Status:	According to Social Security Administration data, this SSN has been issued.
SSA Death Masterfile:	No record as of 10-01-2011
STATUS:	THIS SSN HAS BEEN VALIDATED!

Figure 13.01: A summary from SSN Validator.

Birthday Database (birthdatabase.com)

This site should identify the full name, date of birth, and city and state of birth of your target (Figure 13.02). The only available search fields are first name, last name, and approximate age. The age field is not required, but may help eliminate multiple results.

MICHAEL	S BAZZELL	1961-	Zephyrhills	FL	Find Public Record
MICHAEL	D BAZZELL	1961-	Louisville	KY	Find Public Record
MICHAEL	A BAZZELL	1953-	Granite City	IL	Find Public Record
MICHAEL	J BAZZELL	1948-	Jacksonville	FL	Find Public Record
MICHAEL	BAZZELL	1948-	Buffalo	NY	Find Public Record

Figure 13.02: A Birth Database result.

Social Security Death Index (genealogybank.com/gbnk/ssdi)

This public index of death records is stored on a genealogy site. The only required information is the first and last name. The results will identify birth year, death year, state of last residence, and state of SSN issue.

Legacy (legacy.com)

There are many websites that search for death related information such as social security indexes and ancestry records. A leader in this area is Legacy. This site indexes online obituaries and memorials from approximately 80 percent of all online newspapers. The search on this site is straightforward and results can identify family members and locations.

Asset Locator (blackbookonline.info/assetsearch.aspx)

Black Book Online's Asset Locator is the most comprehensive list of sources for the search of real estate, judgments, bankruptcies, tax liens, and unclaimed funds. This page will allow you to select the type of asset you are researching and the state of the target. This will then create a new page with all of the options for that state. It will provide direct links to the sites for a search of the target. This often includes online databases of public employee salaries, vehicle registrations, property tax records, and dozens of other categories.

DMV Records

Track Somebody (tracksomebody.com/?cat=3) offers a list of contact information for each state. Written requests may obtain the information you are looking for. Notations of the states that demand a request in person are included. This page does not provide any online search function, but the information is useful.

Campaign Contributions (data.influenceexplorer.com)

Any contributions to political campaigns are public record. Searching this is now easy thanks to three separate websites. The most comprehensive is Influence Explorer. It provides an overview of campaign finance, lobbying, earmark, contractor misconduct and federal spending data. The main page allows for a search of individual and business names. The site provides over twenty years of past data.

Money Line (politicalmoneyline.com)

This site will search with information as minimal as a last name. Including the full name and year will provide many details about the target. This includes occupation, the recipient of the contribution, the amount, the type of contribution, and a link to the official filing that contains the information. After an initial search is conducted, you will receive additional search tabs that will allow you to search by zip code, occupation, and year. Figure 13.03 displays a typical result when searched by zip code.

No.	Name	Occupation/Employer	City	State	Zip	Recipient	Type	Date	Amount
1.	ALYEA, DANIEL	SELF-EMPLOYED PHYSICIAN	ALTON	IL	62002	Romney For President Inc	CONTRIB	9/25/2012	$ 1,000
2.	ANGELIDES, MICHAEL J.	SELF-EMPLOYED ATTORNEY	ALTON	IL	62002	Obama For America	MEMO (FILER'S % OF CONTRIBUTION GIVEN TO JOINT FUNDRAISER)	10/15/2012	$ 2,500
3.	AUSTIN, CYRUS	IUPAT DISTRICT COUNCIL 58 BUSINESS REPRESENTATIVE	ALTON	IL	62002	International Union Of Painters And Allied Trades Political Action	CONTRIB	1/7/2011	$ 250

Figure 13.03: A campaign contribution report from Money Line.

Melissa Data (melissadata.com/lookups/fec.asp)

Melissa Data is an alternative to Money Line. The site allows you to search a zip code and identify all political donations for a specified year. The results should be identical to Money Line, but may occasionally contain unique data.

Criminal Information

If a target has a criminal past, there is probably evidence of this on the internet. County court searches will identify most of this information, but this requires a separate search on each county's website. There are a handful of services that attempt to locate nationwide information by name.

Family Watch Dog (familywatchdog.us)

This is one of the leading sites in identifying public criminal information about sex offenders. The main page includes a "Find Offender" area on the left side. You can search here by address or name. The name search only requires a last name to display results. This will identify registered sex offenders that match the criteria specified. This will include a photograph of the target and details of the offense.

Felon Spy (felonspy.com)

This site can appear difficult to navigate at first. Most of the search fields for information forward to a sponsored result that will demand a fee for the information. The only free way to search this data is to click on the "Begin Search" button overlapping the map in the middle of the page. The only fields that should be searched on this page are in the top row and include address, city, and state. Entering any address in a target neighborhood will display markers on a map of convicted felons in that area (Figure 13.04).

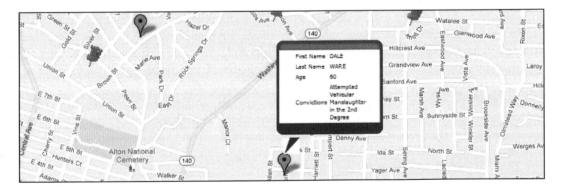

Figure 13.04: A Felon Spy neighborhood report.

Crime Reports (crimereports.com)

Crime Reports delivers a very comprehensive map of criminal incidents, traffic accidents, registered sex offenders, police reports, and emergency incidents. The only option for search is an address. Alternatively, you can move the map to a desired location. After you have selected an area on the map of interest, you can select the types of notifications to populate the map. These include violent crimes, property crimes, traffic issues, and emergency incidents. As long as you are only viewing a specific neighborhood and not an entire metropolitan area, you should be fine selecting all of the reports. This will mark all of the incidents on a map (Figure 13.05). These markers can be selected for further information about the incident.

The marker will expand to display any details available about the incident. This often includes the date, time, address, crime, report number, and investigative agency. This type of detail can assist with an accurate filing of a Freedom Of Information Act (FOIA) request. Additionally, neighboring police departments can access data from another jurisdiction without a common report management system.

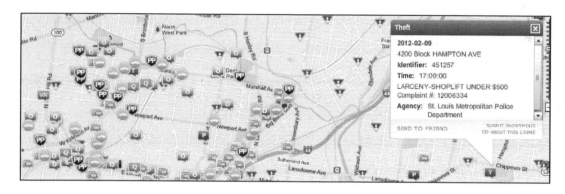

Figure 13.05: A Crime Reports detailed summary.

Inmate Searches

Both federal and state prisons offer prisoner details online. The amount of detail will vary by state, but most will include photographs of the target and details of the crime. In most states, this information is maintained in public view after the target is released if the subject is still on probation or parole. Federal prisoners can be located at www.bop.gov/inmateloc. A first and last name is required for search.

Each state maintains its own database of prisoner information. A great collection of links to each state's content is on The Inmate Locator at theinmatelocator.com. Selecting the state of interest will forward you to the appropriate website.

High Programmer (highprogrammer.com/cgi-bin/uniqueid)

Most states use some type of algorithm to create a driver's license number for a person. Often, this number is generated from the person's name, sex, and date of birth. After you have determined your target's middle initial and date of birth from the previous websites mentioned, you can use this data to identify the target's driver's license number. High Programmer will automate this process for the following states:

Florida	New Hampshire
Illinois	New York
Maryland	Washington
Michigan	Wisconsin
Minnesota	

Military Duty Status (dmdc.osd.mil/appj/scra)

The website requires only a last name and date of birth in order to access a current active duty status report. This PDF document will open which identifies current status, leave of duty date, and future call-up date. The required information is easily obtainable through the previously discussed methods. Figure 13.06 displays a typical report with redacted information.

Selective Service Verification (sss.gov/regver/wfverification.aspx)

This website requires a last name, social security number, and date of birth of the target. The result will identify the person's full name, selective service number, and date of registration (Figure 13.07).

On Active Duty On Active Duty Status Date			
Active Duty Start Date	Active Duty End Date	Status	Service Component
███	NA	███	NA
This response reflects the individuals' active duty status based on the Active Duty Status Date			

Left Active Duty Within 367 Days of Active Duty Status Date			
Active Duty Start Date	Active Duty End Date	Status	Service Component
███	███	No	NA
This response reflects where the individual left active duty status within 367 days preceding the Active Duty Status Date			

The Member or His/Her Unit Was Notified of a Future Call-Up to Active Duty on Active Duty Status Date			
Order Notification Start Date	Order Notification End Date	Status	Service Component
NA	NA	No	NA
This response reflects whether the individual or his/her unit has received early notification to report for active duty			

Figure 13.06: A redacted Military Duty Status report.

Figure 13.07: A redacted Selective Service report.

Further Research

There are several websites that provide links to the numerous online government records. Some of the better collections can be located at the following websites.

Public Records Databases:
vinelink.com
brbpub.com/free-public-records
blackbookonline.info
publicrecords.searchsystems.net

Marine Records:
www.boatinfoworld.com
www.marinetraffic.com

Aircraft Records:
www.blackbookonline.info/Aviation-public-Records.aspx

VIN Records:
thatsthem.com/vin-search
www.checkthatvin.com
www.nicb.org/theft_and_fraud_awareness/vincheck

Vehicle Registration Records:
www.reversegenie.com/plate.php

Chapter Fourteen

Application Programming Interfaces (API)

This chapter will be the most technical of the book. It stands alone and is not required reading to understand the rest of the chapters. While none of these search methods are required to find OSINT information about a target, they will speed up the process and find new data. These techniques will automate the search process across several resources. The results will be text only pages, without ads or graphics, which eliminate confusing or unwanted content. If you are willing to invest a little time learning the process, the reward will be worth it.

An application programming interface (API) is an interface for software components to communicate with each other. API's are used all over the internet. For example, when you use websites mentioned earlier such as AllMyTweets or WebStagram, you are taking advantage of an API. These sites display Twitter and Instagram information about a target. They obtain this information from the Twitter and Instagram API's. Twitter, just like many social sites, allows the public access to the API of its content. This allows developers to create new uses for the data and attracts more users.

Think of an API as a link to the large servers that hold all of the content of a website like Twitter. Going to twitter.com is one way to access the information stored by Twitter. Another option is to bypass the website and communicate with the API that has a direct link to all of the data on the servers. This API access will be more efficient for certain types of data.

Websites that take advantage of a single service's API are great, but they are just the tip of the iceberg. New services collect data from multiple APIs and combine the results. These APIs allow access to any user's entire social network information. If you supply a user name or email address, these services will fetch all online accounts associated with that subject. This can provide an immediate list of profiles that are associated with a target. This can save many hours of researching the information on traditional websites.

Some of the API's detailed here will only provide information that you could otherwise obtain on the official website. The benefit of this API access is that only the content related to your target is presented. You will not receive sponsored links, ads, or misleading text and graphics. If you have multiple targets to research, using the API instead of the web interface will be much faster. You can even automate the search and execute hundreds of queries all at once. Ideally, you can create your own web form of all of these techniques to use when needed. This chapter will explain the entire process. Figure 14.01 is the form that I created that allows me to use API's with very little effort.

Before attempting any API searches, I recommend installing both the Firefox web browser and the JSONView add-on. Both of these are explained in Chapter Fifteen. This combination of software will present all of the results within a standard web page. This page can then be printed, saved, or captured as a screen shot, the same way that you would document a website. Using Internet Explorer to open most API web pages in this section will produce undesired results.

Most of these services are designed to handle large volumes of requests. If you have a long list of names, email addresses, or telephone numbers, API's can produce results much faster than traditional website searches. To take advantage of this automated feature, you will need to understand how scripts and batch files work. This is outside the scope of this book. If your agency has a need for bulk queries, it is worth approaching a programmer to create a customized solution. Otherwise, a few explanations should help understand the manual search techniques.

Pipl (dev.pipl.com)

I explained earlier how Pipl can be a huge resource for information about a real name, email address, telephone number, or user name. The website is easy to navigate, but the API provides only the relevant data and it is easier to digest. A Pipl API key is required to conduct any searches and can be obtained for free at their site. The XXXXXXXXXX in all of these results should be replaced with your API key. The same API key will work for all four of the techniques detailed here. As of this writing, replacing "XXXXXXXXXX" in the following examples with "sample_key" will bypass the need for a valid key. However, you will be limited to 25 searches per day from your IP address.

Real name search:

https://api.pipl.com/search/v4/?first_name=freda&last_name=bazzell&city=wood%20river&state=il&exact_name=false&no_sponsored=true&key=XXXXXXXXXX

Email address search:

https://api.pipl.com/search/v4/?email=jennifer.brandel@gmail.com&no_sponsored=true&key=XXXXXXXXXX

pipl.com	Email Address		Submit Query (Social network info-ENHANCED)	
pipl.com	User Name		Submit Query (Social network account info)	
pipl.com	Phone #		Submit Query (Reverse Telephone)	
pipl.com	First Name	Last Name	City	State Submit Query
rainmaker	Email Address		Submit Query (Social network account info-TEXT)	
FullContact	Email Address		Submit Query (Social network account info-HTML)	
FullContact	Telephone Number (10 Digits Only)		Submit Query (Social network account info)	
FullContact	Twitter Handle		Submit Query (Social network account info)	
FullContact	Facebook Username		Submit Query (Social network account info)	
FullContact	Email Address		Submit Query (Verify Anonymous Email Account)	
RapLeaf	Email Address		Submit Query (Provides gender, age and location)	
Yellow Pages	Telephone #		Submit Query	
Yellow Pages	First Name	Last Name	City	State Submit Query
Yellow Pages	Number Street		City	State Submit Query
SMITH JOHN 555-555-5555	Phone Number		Submit Query (Basic Caller ID Database)	
facebook	User Number		Submit Query (Facebook profile updated time)	
facebook	User Name		Submit Query (Facebook account info)	
Instagram	Instagram User Name		API Search (ID User Number)	
Instagram	Instagram User Number		API View	
Instagram	Instagram User Number		Followers	
Instagram	Instagram User Number		Following	
Instagram	LAT	LONG	1	GEO View
flickr	Email Address		Submit Query (Locate Flickr Page)	
Toofr!	First Name	Last Name	Domain	Submit Query
BriteVerify	Email Address		Submit Query (Verify Email Address)	

Figure 14.01: A custom API search page hosted at inteltechniques.com.

User name search:

https://api.pipl.com/search/v4/?username=osintgeek&no_sponsored=true&key= XXXXXXXXXX

Telephone number search:

https://api.pipl.com/search/v4/?phone=##########&no_sponsored=true&key= XXXXXXXXXX

These structured requests should start to look familiar now. In the previous examples, the data is detailed as follows.

https://api.pipl.com/search/v4?: This tells Pipl to use the latest version (v4).

first_name=freda&last_name=bazzell: This identifies the first and last name of the target.

city=wood%20river&state=il: This identifies the city and state of the target.

email=jennifer.brandel@gmail.com: This identifies the email address of the target.

username=osintgeek: This identifies a user name of the target.

phone=##########: This represents a target telephone number and should be the actual number.

&no_sponsored=true: This tells Pipl to exclude any advertisements.

&key= XXXXXXXXXX: This represents your actual API key.

The most useful of these API requests is an email address search. When it is conducted, the associations of the target's email address with any social networks or online communities will be displayed. Any accounts created with the email address supplied would be included. Figure 14.02 displays one of the links listed in a summary of a target email address. This link identifies the personal website of the subject. Clicking the link will forward you to the subject's site.

```
- source: {
    @is_sponsored: false,
    url: http://jennyanything.com/contact.html,
    domain: "jennyanything.com"
  },
- names: [
  - {
      first: "Jennifer",
      last: "Brandel",
```

Figure 14.02: A Pipl API result.

You could now bookmark the URL that you created to get the information. Each time you wanted to check another email address, you could visit the bookmark and edit the email address to match that of your target. I prefer to create a form that simplifies this process.

To do so, you need to create a web page. The page does not need to be uploaded anywhere on the internet, and you can execute the page from your computer's hard drive. If you have web development software, it will make it easy. If not, a text editor will work just fine. If you are a Windows user, open Notepad and type the following in a new text document.

```html
<html><head></head><body>
<script type="text/javascript">
function dopipl1(firstpp, lastpp, citypp, statepp) {
window.open('https://api.pipl.com/search/v4/?first_name=' + firstpp + '&last_name=' + lastpp + '&city=' +
citypp + '&state=' + statepp + '&exact_name=false&no_sponsored=true&key=XXXXXXXXXX', 'pp1window');
}</script>
<form onsubmit="dopipl1(this.firstpp.value, this.lastpp.value, this.citypp.value, this.statepp.value); return
false;">
<input type="text" name="firstpp" size="18" value="First Name" />
<input type="text" name="lastpp" size="18" value="Last Name" />
<input type="text" name="citypp" size="12" value="City" />
<input type="text" name="statepp" size="5" value="State" />
<input type="submit" /></form>
<script type="text/javascript">
function dopipl2(email) {
window.open('https://api.pipl.com/search/v4/?email=' + email +
'&no_sponsored=true&key= XXXXXXXXXX, 'pipl2window');
}</script>
<form onsubmit="dopipl2(this.pp2.value); return false;">
<input type="text" name="pp2" size="40" value="Email Address" />
<input type="submit" /></form>
<script type="text/javascript">
function dopipl3(ppuser) {
window.open('https://api.pipl.com/search/v4/?username=' + ppuser +
'&no_sponsored=true&key= XXXXXXXXXX, 'pipl3window');
}</script>
<form onsubmit="dopipl3(this.pp3.value); return false;">
<input type="text" name="pp3" size="40" value="Screen Name" />
<input type="submit" /></form>
<script type="text/javascript">
function dopipl4(ppphone) {
window.open('https://api.pipl.com/search/v4/?phone=' + ppphone +
'&no_sponsored=true&key= XXXXXXXXXX, 'pipl4window');
}</script>

<form onsubmit="dopipl4(this.pp4.value); return false;">
<input type="text" name="pp4" size="30" value="Phone #" />
<input type="submit" /></form>
</body></html>
```

Save this file as pipl.html. When you open the file, it should appear in a web browser and look like Figure 14.03. A digital version of this file is at inteltechniques.com/api/4.txt, which can be copied and pasted from the site.

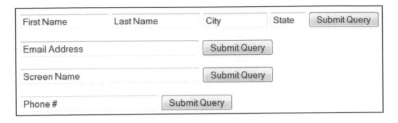

Figure 14.03: An entry form for the Pipl API.

Fliptop (fliptop.com)

Fliptop acquired Qwerly in 2011. Qwerly was an amazing resource in locating social network information associated with a target's email account. Qwerly took an extra step beyond providing stored information about an email address. If a profile on the target was not complete, it would go out and fetch any accounts associated with the email address. Performing the search a second time, after a few minutes had passed, would present the data that was obtained. This same service is now available through Fliptop. An API key is required from the site listed above, but it is no longer free. However, I have found that by contacting them directly, a limited trial key can be issued to prospective new clients. The URL is not as complex as others and should look like this:

http://api.fliptop.com/beta/person?email=lorangb@gmail.com&api_key=XXXXXXXXXX

The only parts you need to change are the email address portion and the API key at the end. The result will appear similar to the following.

```
"age": "",
"company": "FullContact Inc.",
"email": "lorangb@gmail.com",
"first_name": "Bart",
"gender": "",
"image_url": "http://www.linkedin.com/mpr/mpr/shrink_80_80/p/2/000/086/2c8/2444fae.jpg",
"klout_influence": 47,
"last_appended_date": "Thu Feb 09 04:16:46 GMT+00:00 2012",
"last_name": "Lorang",
"location": "Denver",
"memberships": {
        "twitter": "http://twitter.com/lorangb",
        "linkedin": "http://linkedin.com/pub/bart-lorang/3/19/a22"
"name": "Bart Lorang",
"title": "Co-Founder & CEO",
```

Results will often identify social networks using an alias and personal blogs. The links all forward directly to the source of the information. If you do not receive any results, attempt the search again in a few minutes. Fliptop will try to find any information about the target and deliver when asked the next time. In 2012, Fliptop added the ability to conduct API searches on Facebook names and Twitter handles. This can often identify the Facebook profile of a Twitter user and vice versa. All of this data correlates with Fliptop's email address database, so the Facebook or Twitter information could lead to a large amount of associated content. For Facebook, the URL should appear as follows:

http://api.fliptop.com/beta/person?facebook=http://facebook.com/bart.lorang&api_key= XXXXXXXXXX

In this example, the Facebook user URL is http://facebook.com/bart.lorang. This is the address that would display the target's Facebook page. The result will appear similar to the following.

```
image_url": "https://fbcdn-profile-a.akamaihd.net/251881980_n.jpg",
name": "Mike Murphy",
first_name": "mike",
last_name": "murphy",
gender": "Male",
memberships": {
    "facebook": "http://facebook.com/mike cary",
    "myspace": "http://www.myspace.com/476745282"
```

The Twitter search is very similar, and the URL should appear similar to the following:

http://api.fliptop.com/beta/person?twitter=http://twitter.com/mikemorton89&api_key= XXXXXXXXXX

In this example, the Twitter URL is http://twitter.com/mikemorton89. This is the address that would display the target's Twitter page. The result will appear similar to the following:

```
image_url": "https://fbcdn-profile-a.akamaihd.net/h93_873564440_n.jpg",
name": "Michael Morton",
gender": "Male",
location": "St Louis, Missouri, United States",
memberships": {
    "klout": "http://beta.klout.com/mikemorton89",
    "facebook": "http://www.facebook.com/mikemorton89",
    "twitter": "http://twitter.com/mikemorton89"
```

Creating an entry form for these searches is similar to the previous examples. The following is the exact text that would create a page for repeated searching.

```
<html><head></head><body>
<script language="JavaScript" type="text/javascript">
functiondofliptop(email) {
window.open('http://api.fliptop.com/beta/person?email=' + email +
```

```
'&api_key=XXXXXXX', 'fliptopwindow');
}</script>
<form onsubmit="dofliptop(this.ftemail.value); return false;">
<input type="text" name="ftemail" size="40" value="Email Address" />
<input type="submit" /></form>
<script type="text/javascript">
function dofliptop2(twitter) {
window.open('http://api.fliptop.com/beta/person?twitter=http://twitter.com/' + twitter +
'&api_key=XXXXXXX', 'fliptopwindow');
}</script>
<form onsubmit="dofliptop2(this.fttwitter.value); return false;"><input type="text" name="fttwitter" size="40"
value="Twitter Handle" />
<input type="submit" /></form>
<script language="JavaScript" type="text/javascript">
function dofliptop3(fb) {window.open('http://api.fliptop.com/beta/person?facebook=http://facebook.com/' + fb +
'&api_key=XXXXXXX', 'fliptopwindow');
}</script>
<form onsubmit="dofliptop3(this.ftfb.value); return false;">
<input type="text" name="ftfb" size="40" value="Facebook Username" />
<input type="submit" /></form>
</body></html>
```

Save this file as fliptop.html. When you open the file, it should appear in a web browser and look like Figure 14.04. A digital version of this file is at inteltechniques.com/api/5.txt, which can be copied and pasted from the site.

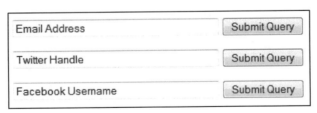

Figure 14.04: A created Fliptop search form.

Full Contact (developer.fullcontact.com)

Another search similar to Fliptop is Full Contact. It provides a reverse search of any social networks or personal sites associated with the target email address. One of the advantages of this service over Fliptop is that Full Contact will attempt to find new information while you wait. A second search is occasionally required. Full Contact will scour the hundreds of social APIs for any relevant data. You can also specify in what format you want the results. This provides an additional option of a HTML view which provides icons and photographs. The following is the basic URL with a text view.

https://api.fullcontact.com/v2/person.json?email=lorangb@gmail.com&apiKey=XXXXXXXXXX

This URL is detailed as follows.

https://api.fullcontact.com/v2/person: This refers to the site and version.

.json: This is the format output. Another option is HTML.

email=lorangb@gmail.com: This specifies the email address to search.

apiKey=XXXXXXXXXX: This represents the API key which you will provide.

The result of this search includes dozens of associated social networks, photographs, profiles, and organizations with direct links. Next is a small excerpt.

```
    "familyName": "Lorang",
        "givenName": "Bart",
        "fullName": "Bart Lorang",
        "chats": [
                        "client": "gtalk",
                        "handle": "lorangb@gmail.com"
                        "client": "skype",
                        "handle": "bart.lorang"
        "websites": [
                        "url": "http://rainmaker.cc/"
    "photos": [
                    "typeName": "Twitter",
                    "type": "twitter",
                    "typeId": "twitter",
                    "url": "http://a0.twimg.com/profile_images/1364842224/Bart_Profile_1_normal.jpg"
            },
                    "typeName": "Tungle Me",
                    "type": "tungleme",
                    "typeId": "tungleme",
                    "url": "https://tungle.me/public/bartlorang/Image"
                    "typeName": "Myspace",
                    "type": "Myspace",
                    "typeId": "Myspace",
                    "url": "http://a2.ec-
                    images.Myspacecdn.com/profile01/114/97c130815ed44e47a19080f970706dbe/s.jpg"
    ],
    "demographics": {
            "age": "32",
            "locationGeneral": "Denver, Colorado, United States",
            "gender": "Male",
            "ageRange": "25-34"
        },
    "socialProfiles": [
            {
                    "id": 5998422,
                    "typeName": "Twitter",
                    "following": 489,
                    "followers": 662,
```

"username": "lorangb",
"bio": "CEO & Co-Founder of @FullContactApp and @FullContactAPI - Tech
Entrepreneur and Angel Investor.",
"type": "twitter",
"typeId": "twitter",
"url": "http://www.twitter.com/lorangb",
"typeName": "Facebook",
"type": "facebook",
"typeId": "facebook",
"url": "http://facebook.com/bart.lorang",
"id": "651620441",
"username": "bartlorang"

These links can lead to intelligence that may have taken hours to locate by traditional search methods. The HTML view option may be preferred when a large amount of data is available. The view displays a compressed result, which includes icon links to the target's social network profiles. The URL would be changed to the following address, with the result displayed in Figure 14.05.

https://api.fullcontact.com/v2/person.html?email=lorangb@gmail.com&apiKey=XXXXXXXXX

Figure 14.05: A Full Contact result in HTML view.

In 2012, Full Contact added new search features to their API. You can now search by Facebook name, Twitter handle, and telephone number. Also, you can search an email address to identify the likelihood that it is an anonymous account. The Facebook search URL would appear like the following.

https://api.fullcontact.com/v2/person.html?facebookUsername=bart.lorang&apiKey=XXXXXXXX

In contrast to Fliptop, Full Contact only requires the Facebook user name and not the entire address. In this example, "bart.lorang" is the user name, and the entire Facebook profile address would be http://facebook.com/bart.lorang. This can be very useful when you do not know the email address of the target but have located a Facebook page. This would now help you identify all of the social networks of the target which should lead to the email address. The Twitter URL would appear as follows.

https://api.fullcontact.com/v2/person.html?twitter=bartlorang&apiKey=XXXXXXXX

In this example, "bartlorang" is the Twitter handle.

The telephone search API of Full Contact is in a beta stage, and is very unreliable. I believe that this piece could prove to be very valuable in the future. The search URL should appear like the following.

https://api.fullcontact.com/v2/person.html?phone=+16182597625&apiKey=XXXXXXXX

The telephone number in this search is 618-259-7625. Neither hyphens nor spaces should be used when constructing the URL, and a "1" should preceded the ten digit number.

The final offering from Full Contact provides a unique service that I have not encountered before. When you provide an email address, Full Contact offers information that may identify it as an anonymous account. If your target's email address is John@hushmail.com, most analysts would identify that domain as one that is associated with private email services. However, john@sharklasers.com may not seem so obvious. Both accounts belong to a service that provides disposable email accounts. Full Contact will attempt to identify these for you. The URL of the request should appear as follows.

https://api.fullcontact.com/v2/email/disposable.html?email=john@sharklasers.com&apiKey=XXXX

In this example, the email address is john@sharklasers.com. The result will appear as follows.

```
<message>
Email username is not sub addressed. Email's domain is likely associated with disposable email addresses.
</message>
```

Creating a web form for all of these searches is done the same way as all of the rest. The following is the exact text that would create the page. Remember to change the XXXXXXXXXX to your exact API key provided by Full Contact.

```
<html><head></head><body>
<script type="text/javascript">
function dofullcontact(femail) {
window.open('https://api.fullcontact.com/v2/person.html?email=' + femail +
'&apiKey=XXXXXXXX', 'contactwindow');}</script>
<form onsubmit="dofullcontact(this.femail.value); return false;">
<input type="text" name="femail" size="40" value="Email Address" />
<input type="submit" /></form>
```

```
<script type="text/javascript">
function dofullcontact2(phone) {
window.open('https://api.fullcontact.com/v2/person.html?phone=+1' + phone +
'&apiKey=XXXXXXXX', 'contactwindow2');}</script>
<form onsubmit="dofullcontact2(this.fcp.value); return false;">
<input type="text" name="fcp" size="40" value="Telephone Number (10 Digits Only)" />
<input type="submit" /></form>
<script type="text/javascript">
function dofullcontact3(twitter) {
window.open('https://api.fullcontact.com/v2/person.html?twitter=' + twitter +
'&apiKey=XXXXXXXX, 'contactwindow3');}</script>
<form onsubmit="dofullcontact(this.fct.value); return false;">
<input type="text" name="fct" size="40" value="Twitter Handle" />
<input type="submit" /></form>
<script type="text/javascript">
function dofullcontact4(fb) {
window.open('https://api.fullcontact.com/v2/person.html?facebookUsername=' + fb +
'&apiKey=XXXXXXXXX, 'contactwindow4');}</script>
<form onsubmit="dofullcontact(this.fb.value); return false;">
<input type="text" name="fb" size="40" value="Facebook Name" />
<input type="submit" /></form>
<script type="text/javascript">
function dofullcontact5(anon) {
window.open('https://api.fullcontact.com/v2/email/disposable.html?email=' + anon +
'&apiKey=XXXXXXXX, 'contactwindow'5);}</script>
<form onsubmit="dofullcontact(this.anon.value); return false;">
<input type="text" name="anon" size="40" value="Email Address" />
<input type="submit" /></form>
</body></html>
```

Save this file as fullcontact.html. When you open the file, it should appear in a web browser and look like Figure 14.06. A digital version of this file is at inteltechniques.com/api/6.txt, which can be copied and pasted from the site.

Figure 14.06: A Full Contact custom search page.

Facebook (developers.facebook.com)

The Facebook Graph API is a very robust engine that could fill several chapters with information. Our scope will limit the instruction to three techniques that can be used for OSINT needs. The first task is to view the basic profile information of a target. While logged into Facebook, you could navigate to the following profile to see the target's information.

facebook.com/bart.lorang

You can add the word "graph" to the beginning of this URL in order to retrieve basic account details. This will be only a few pieces of information, but it can be executed without providing login credentials. Therefore, a programmer could create a program that scraped basic Facebook information without dealing with user accounts and credentials. The proper address would appear as below.

graph.facebook.com/bart.lorang

The results will be the following text data.

```
"id": "651620441",
"name": "Bart Lorang",
"first_name": "Bart",
"last_name": "Lorang",
"link": "http://www.facebook.com/bart.lorang",
"username": "bart.lorang",
"gender": "male",
"locale": "en_US"
```

This provides us the target's Facebook user number, full name, gender, and country. The next two options will require a token from Facebook. This is similar to a license key and is unique for each person. Before we can proceed, we must obtain this token. The following instructions will help you create an app, get a token, and extend your token's expiration time.

Navigate to developers.facebook.com/apps and register to create new apps. Click the "Create New App" button, assign any name to your app, and click "continue". Note the "AppID and "App Secret as visible in Figure 14.07.

Figure 14.07: Facebook API app details.

Navigate to developers.facebook.com/tools/explorer and click the "Graph API Explorer" menu and select your new app. Mine is called "Test". Click the "Get Access Token" to generate a unique number for your app. A new window will open titled "Select Permissions". Select each checkbox in this view and click the "Get Access Token" button. Figure 14.08 displays this option. Figure 14.09 displays the access token provided by Facebook.

This token is ready to use. However, it will expire in two hours. This limitation can be extended to 60 days with a specific request. In order to complete this request, we will need the App ID, App Secret, and Access Token that has been provided to us from Facebook. Our "Test" app has the following information.

App ID: 530334577056519
App Secret: 62997cca2a9701325e183779d4b03917
Access Token: CAAHiViQT2wcBAJjaI0aP7Q5vrtY2znOI3I9MwKZBElZCBDwPFUQmKUJajbaQbZCLeq4tl
pRXtVLigZCZCXB3bv23XEYVyIqcIBXux9b5qLhO2W28hdRL0SyAOQJGyZA3oOB9IIgofFzYyimqWjCGUzjDh
QD3BSZCzs3myxwFyRTYKxoijkZAMDhXrrthZAiZCwDcSM6tsvjeKiUAZDZD

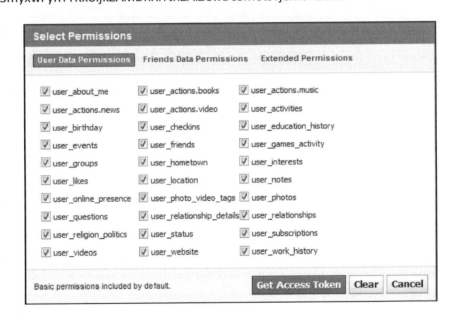

Figure 14.08: Permission options within a Facebook app.

Figure 14.09: A Facebook access token.

Create a web address (URL) in your web browser with the following structure.

https://graph.facebook.com/oauth/access_token?client_id=APPID&client_secret=APPSECRET &grant_type=fb_exchange_token&fb_exchange_token=ACCESSTOKEN

You will replace APPDID, APPSECRET, and ACCESSTOKEN in the above address with the actual data. Our test example would be the following address.

https://graph.facebook.com/oauth/access_token?client_id=530334577056519&client_secret=62997 cca2a9701325e183779d4b03917&grant_type=fb_exchange_token&fb_exchange_token= CAAHiViQT2wcBAJjal0aP7Q5vrtY2znOI3I9MwKZBElZCBDwPFUQmKUJajbaQbZCLeq4tlpRXtVLigZCZCX B3bv23XEYVylqclBXux9b5qLhO2W28hdRL0SyAOQJGyZA3oOB9IlgofFzYyimqWjCGUzjDhQD3BSZCzs3 myxwFyRTYKxoijkZAMDhXrrthZAiZCwDcSM6tsvjeKiUAZDZD

If you were successful, you will receive an immediate response with a new access token. Figure 14.10 displays the result for this example.

Figure 14.10: An extended token response from Facebook.

The result identifies the access token number and the expiration in seconds. This will translate to 60 days. When this token expires, repeat the process to generate a new number. We can now use this token to request extended information without being logged into Facebook. We can use the following address to display specific details about the target user name or number.

https://graph.facebook.com/USERNAME?fields=first_name,last_name,middle_name,gender,birthda y,age_range,address,education,,about,bio,cover,currency,devices,hometown,id,languages,locale,loc ation,political,relationship_status,religion,security_settings,significant_other,timezone,username,w ebsite,work,albums,checkins,events,family,likes,photos,tagged,accounts,interests,groups,locations,s tatuses,permissions,picture,subscribedto,subscribers,videos,posts&type=user&access_token=TOKEN

This address requests the basic information listed such as time zone, bio, and check-ins. The privacy settings of the target will determine what information you will receive. This address is probably overkill and requests a lot of information that is rarely displayed. However, it is better to ask for too much than not enough. An actual address based on our new token and the target name of bart.lorang would be the following.

https://graph.facebook.com/bart.lorang?fields=first_name,last_name,middle_name,gender,birthda
y,age_range,address,education,email,about,bio,cover,currency,devices,hometown,id,languages,loca
le,location,political,relationship_status,religion,security_settings,significant_other,timezone,userna
me,website,work,albums,checkins,events,family,likes,photos,tagged,accounts,interests,groups,locat
ions,statuses,permissions,picture,subscribedto,subscribers,videos,posts&type=user&access_token=C
AAHiViQT2wcBAApkxCcDyCIJpLLED77fgVjt1MfnNs5KwAfmMWusp3iRF92si7uoZALLf6ZBE5kmyzqPIc
uQe174OtcZCN6uOM8A7m7UZAXCcUlK3CwDOnRZACcRQCKZBBYZBGDQzFb5noCfzoGQmWLJqSteVI
du1fUA41TOajseVLWhZCeCPLVWAIpEhXbCcP4ZD

The result is as follows.

    "first_name": "Bart",
    "id": "651620441",
    "gender": "male",
    "last_name": "Lorang",
    "locale": "en_US",
    "username": "bart.lorang",
    "posts": {
        "data": [
            "id": "651620441_10153318481590442",
            "from": {
                "name": "Bart Lorang",
                "id": "651620441"
            "story": "Bart Lorang likes a link.",
            "story_tags": {
                "0": [
                    "id": "651620441",
                    "name": "Bart Lorang",
                    "offset": 0,
                    "length": 11,
                    "type": "user"
            "privacy": {
                "value": ""
            "type": "status",
            "created_time": "2013-10-11T03:53:22+0000",
            "updated_time": "2013-10-11T03:53:22+0000"
    "paging": {
        "previous":
"https://graph.facebook.com/651620441/posts?access_token=CAAHiViQT2wcBAApkxCcDyCIJpLLED77fgVjt1
MfnNs5KwAfmMWusp3iRF92si7uoZALLf6ZBE5kmyzqPIcuQe174OtcZCN6uOM8A7m7UZAXCcUlK3CwDOn
RZACcRQCKZBBYZBGDQzFb5noCfzoGQmWLJqSteVIdu1fUA41TOajseVLWhZCeCPLVWAIpEhXbCcP4ZD
&limit=25&since=1381463602&__previous=1",
        "next":
"https://graph.facebook.com/651620441/posts?access_token=CAAHiViQT2wcBAApkxCcDyCIJpLLED77fgVjt1
MfnNs5KwAfmMWusp3iRF92si7uoZALLf6ZBE5kmyzqPIcuQe174OtcZCN6uOM8A7m7UZAXCcUlK3CwDOn
RZACcRQCKZBBYZBGDQzFb5noCfzoGQmWLJqSteVIdu1fUA41TOajseVLWhZCeCPLVWAIpEhXbCcP4ZD
&limit=25&until=1381463601"
    "picture": {
        "data": {

"url":"https://fbcdn-profile-a.akamaihd.net/hprofile-ak-ash3/195544_651620441_1809836487_q.jpg",
"is_silhouette": false

This identifies recent activity of the target on Facebook. This information could all be located within the target's Facebook profile. The benefits with this query are that you do not need to be logged into an account and a programmer could use this data to automate the collection process.

The last technique that will be explained is a simple query to identify the date and time that a target updated his or her Facebook profile information. This often includes basic data such as the name displayed or the profile image. The structure of the address is as follows.

https://graph.facebook.com/USERNAME?fields=updated_time&type=user&access_token=TOKEN

The address for our token with a target of bart.lorang would be the following.

https://graph.facebook.com/bart.lorang?fields=updated_time&type=user&access_token= CAAHiViQT2wcBAApkxCcDyCIJpLLED77fgVjt1MfnNs5KwAfmMWusp3iRF92si7uoZALLf6ZBE5kmyzqPI cuQe174OtcZCN6uOM8A7m7UZAXCcUlK3CwDOnRZACcRQCKZBBYZBGDQzFb5noCfzoGQmWLJqSteVl du1fUA41TOajseVLWhZCeCPLVWAlpEhXbCcP4ZD

The result is the following.

"updated_time": "2013-11-01T03:20:45+0000",
"id": "651620441"

This discloses that the target last updated something on his profile on 11/1/2013 at 03:20 GMT. As with the other methods, this action does not require you to be logged into a Facebook account.

We can now create a single web page that will allow us to easily conduct searches for all of this information. The following is the exact text that would create the page. Remember to change my token to your exact token key provided by Facebook.

```
<head></head><body>
<script type="text/javascript">function dofbuser(username)
{window.open('http://graph.facebook.com/' + username, 'frame1');}
</script><form onSubmit="dofbuser(this.username.value); return false;">
<input type="text" name="username" size="40" value="Facebook User Name" />
<input type="submit" />(Displays User Number)<br />
<iframe allowScriptAccess='always' name='frame1' id='frame1' width='450px' height='200' frameborder=1>
</iframe></form>

<script type="text/javascript">
function dofbupdate(username2) {window.open('https://graph.facebook.com/' + username2 + '?
fields=updated_time&type=user&access_token=CAAHiViQT2wcBAApkxCcDyCIJpLLED77fgVjt1MfnNs5KwAf
mMWusp3iRF92si7uoZALLf6ZBE5kmyzqPIcuQe174OtcZCN6uOM8A7m7UZAXCcUlK3CwDOnRZACcRQCK
```

ZBBYZBGDQzFb5noCfzoGQmWLJqSteVldu1fUA41TOajseVLWhZCeCPLVWAIpEhXbCcP4ZD', 'frame2');}
</script><form onSubmit="dofbupdate(this.username2.value); return false;"><input type="text"
name="username2" size="40" value="Facebook User Name" /><input type="submit" />(Displays Last
Updated Date/Time)
<iframe allowScriptAccess='always' name='frame2' id='frame2' width='350px'
height='110' frameborder=1> </iframe></form>

<script type="text/javascript">function dofbinfo(fbinfo) {window.open
('https://graph.facebook.com/' + fbinfo +
?fields=first_name,last_name,middle_name,gender,birthday,age_range,address,education,email,about,bio,cov
er,currency,devices,hometown,id,languages,locale,location,political,relationship_status,religion,security_settin
gs,significant_other,timezone,username,website,work,albums,checkins,events,family,likes,photos,tagged,acco
unts,interests,groups,locations,statuses,permissions,picture,subscribedto,subscribers,videos,posts&type=user
&access_token=CAAHiViQT2wcBAApkxCcDyCIJpLLED77fgVjt1MfnNs5KwAfmMWusp3iRF92si7uoZALLf6ZB
E5kmyzqPlcuQe174OtcZCN6uOM8A7m7UZAXCcUlK3CwDOnRZACcRQCKZBBYZBGDQzFb5noCfzoGQm
WLJqSteVldu1fUA41TOajseVLWhZCeCPLVWAIpEhXbCcP4ZD', 'frame3');}</script><form
onSubmit="dofbinfo(this.fbinfo.value); return false;"><input type="text" name="fbinfo" size="40"
value="Facebook User Name" /><input type="submit" />(Displays Basic Account Info)
<iframe
allowScriptAccess='always' name='frame3' id='frame3' width='950px' height='1000' frameborder=0>
</iframe></form></body></html>

Save this file as facebook.html. When you open the file, it should appear in a web browser and look like
Figure 14.11. A digital version of this file is at inteltechniques.com/api/7.txt, which can be copied and
pasted from the site.

Instagram (instagram.com/developer)

The search features of the Instagram API were explained and demonstrated in Chapter Nine. In order
to avoid redundancy, I will only explain the process to obtain a token and create a custom Instagram
search web page in this chapter.

Navigate to instagram.com/developer and log into your Instagram account. Create a new account if
necessary. Click on the "Manage Clients" button and then the "Register a New Client" button. Provide
a name for your new client, any description, any website address, and repeat that address on the
"OAuth" line. You can use the same website that I used in this example, which is visible in Figure 14.12.
The response will include a Client ID and Client Secret. We will use this information to create our
token.

Similar to Facebook, we must request a token from Instagram. Fortunately, these tokens do not expire,
so we will only need to do this once. Create a URL based on the following structure.

https://instagram.com/oauth/authorize/?client_id=CLIENTID&redirect_uri=WEBSITE&response_type=t
oken#

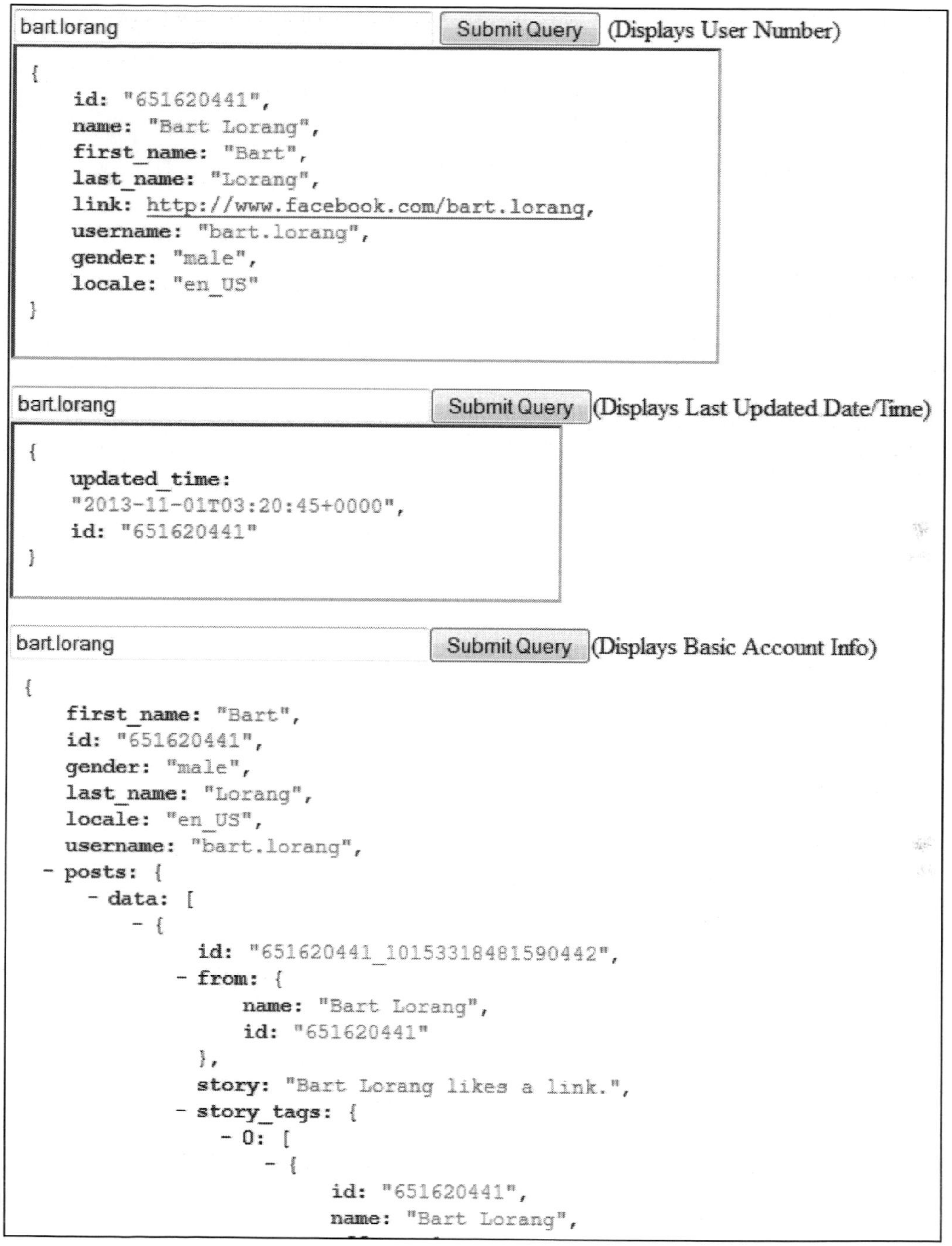

bart.lorang   [Submit Query] (Displays User Number)

{
    id: "651620441",
    name: "Bart Lorang",
    first_name: "Bart",
    last_name: "Lorang",
    link: http://www.facebook.com/bart.lorang,
    username: "bart.lorang",
    gender: "male",
    locale: "en_US"
}

bart.lorang   [Submit Query] (Displays Last Updated Date/Time)

{
    updated_time:
    "2013-11-01T03:20:45+0000",
    id: "651620441"
}

bart.lorang   [Submit Query] (Displays Basic Account Info)

{
    first_name: "Bart",
    id: "651620441",
    gender: "male",
    last_name: "Lorang",
    locale: "en_US",
    username: "bart.lorang",
  - posts: {
    - data: [
        - {
            id: "651620441_10153318481590442",
          - from: {
                name: "Bart Lorang",
                id: "651620441"
            },
            story: "Bart Lorang likes a link.",
          - story_tags: {
            - 0: [
                - {
                    id: "651620441",
                    name: "Bart Lorang",

Figure 14.11: A custom Facebook API page with embedded search results.

CLIENT ID	c027a4ea360b46b49954704bb2803d95
CLIENT SECRET	6f9216944521454fbf3c7a72b7dce1bc
WEBSITE URL	http://inteltechniques.com
REDIRECT URI	http://inteltechniques.com

Figure 14.12: An Instagram API details page.

Our address based on the information in Figure 14.12 would be the following.

https://instagram.com/oauth/authorize/?client_id=c027a4ea360b46b49954704bb2803d95&redirect_uri=http://inteltechniques.com&response_type=token#

The response will include a confirmation box from Instagram that you must authorize. You will then be forwarded to the address that you provided (inteltechniques.com). The address bar of this page will include your new token from Instagram. The address on my page was the following.

http://inteltechniques.com/#access_token=241310026.c027a4e.66b6a1616d6d491c93e0af9f6261652

This token can be used to create our custom web page that we can use to conduct the searches described in Chapter Nine. The following is the exact text that would create the page. Remember to change my token to your exact token key provided by Instagram. Note that the last GPS option requires the Client ID as provided by Instagram.

```
<head></head><body>
<script type="text/javascript">
function dotw1(tw1) {window.open('https://api.instagram.com/v1/users/search?q=' + tw1
+'&count=999&access_token=241310026.c027a4e.66b6a1616d6d491c93e0af9f6261652',
'twitterwindow');}</script><form onsubmit="dotw1(this.tw1.value); return false;"><input type="text" name="tw1"
size="40" value="Instagram User Name" /><input type="submit" value="API Search" />Identifies user number
for next searches<br /><br /></form>

<script type="text/javascript">function dotw2(tw2) {window.open('https://api.instagram.com/v1/users/' + tw2 +
'/media/recent?access_token=241310026.c027a4e.66b6a1616d6d491c93e0af9f6261652', 'twitterwindow');}
</script><form onsubmit="dotw2(this.tw2.value); return false;"><input type="text" name="tw2" size="40"
value="Instagram User Number" /><input type="submit" value="API View" />Identifies most recent posts and
GPS info if available<br /><br />

<script type="text/javascript">function doig4(ig4) {window.open('https://api.instagram.com/v1/users/' + ig4 +
'/follows?access_token=241310026.c027a4e.66b6a1616d6d491c93e0af9f6261652', 'twitterwindow');}
</script></form><form onsubmit="doig4(this.ig4.value); return false;"><input type="text" name="ig4" size="40"
value="Instagram User Number" /><input type="submit" value="Following" />Identifies people target is
following<br /><br /></form>

<script type="text/javascript">function doig5(ig5) {window.open('https://api.instagram.com/v1/users/' + ig5 +
'/followed-by?access_token=241310026.c027a4e.66b6a1616d6d491c93e0af9f6261652', 'twitterwindow');}
```

```
</script></form><form onsubmit="doig5(this.ig5.value); return false;"><input type="text" name="ig5" size="40"
value="Instagram User Number" /><input type="submit" value="Followers" />Identifies people following the
target<br /><br /></form>

<script type="text/javascript">function dotw3(lat, long, distance)
{window.open('https://api.instagram.com/v1/media/search?lat=' + lat + '&lng=' + long + '&distance=' + distance
+'?client_id=c027a4ea360b46b49954704bb2803d95&access_token=241310026.c027a4e.66b6a1616d6d491c
93e0af9f6261652', 'twitterwindow');}</script><form onsubmit="dotw3(this.lat.value, this.long.value,
this.distance.value); return false;"><input type="text" name="lat" size="20" value="LAT" /><input type="text"
name="long" size="20" value="LONG" /><input type="text" name="distance" size="10" value="1" /><input
type="submit" value="GEO View" />Displays posts from a location<br /><br /></form></body></html>
```

Save this file as instagram.html. When you open the file, it should appear in a web browser and look like the example in Chapter Nine. A digital version of this file is at inteltechniques.com/api/8.txt, which can be copied and pasted from the site.

Reverse Caller ID Engines

Chapter Eleven explained the various reverse API methods that can identify landline and cellular telephone numbers. The API process was documented for searching each individual company for caller ID information. This section will explain how to create a web page search tool that will execute a search across all companies for a single telephone number.

The following is the exact text that would create the page. Remember to change "XXX" on each line to your exact token key provided by each caller ID service.

```
<head></head><body>
<script type="text/javascript">function docidall(cidall) {
window.open('http://api.opencnam.com/v2/phone/+1' + cidall, 'frame1');
window.open('http://api.opencnam.com/v2/phone/+1' + cidall + '?account_sid=XXX&auth_token=XXX',
'frame2');
window.open('http://cnam.bulkcnam.com/?id=XXX&did=' + cidall, 'frame3');
window.open('http://cnam.calleridservice.com/query?u=USERNAME&k=XXX&n=' + cidall, 'frame4');
window.open('http://trial.serviceobjects.com/gppl/geophoneplus.asmx/GetPhoneInfo_V2?PhoneNumber=' +
cidall + '&TestType=full&LicenseKey=XXX, 'frame5');
window.open('https://dip.cidname.com/' + cidall + '/XXX&output=raw&reply=none', 'frame6');}

</script><form onsubmit="docidall(this.cidall.value); return false;"><input type="text" name="cidall" size="40"
value="Phone Number" /><input type="submit" />(BASIC Caller ID Database) <br /><br /></form>
<iframe allowScriptAccess='always' name='frame1' id='frame1' width='650px' height='40' frameborder=0>
</iframe>  <br />
<iframe allowScriptAccess='always' name='frame2' id='frame2' width='650px' height='40' frameborder=0>
</iframe><br />
<iframe allowScriptAccess='always' name='frame3' id='frame3' width='650px' height='40' frameborder=0>
</iframe><br />
<iframe allowScriptAccess='always' name='frame4' id='frame4' width='650px' height='40' frameborder=0>
</iframe><br />
<iframe allowScriptAccess='always' name='frame6' id='frame6' width='650px' height='40' frameborder=0>
```

```
</iframe>
<iframe allowScriptAccess='always' name='frame5' id='frame5' width='650px' height='540' frameborder=0>
</iframe>
</form></body></html>
```

Save this file as phone.html. When you open the file, it should appear in a web browser and look like Figure 14.13. A digital version of this file is at inteltechniques.com/api/cid.txt, which can be copied and pasted from the site.

Figure 14.13: A custom web page to search several reverse caller ID services.

You should now have nine HTML files that can each be executed to conduct multiple searches. You can also place all of these on one page similar to Figure 14.01. In addition to the nine HTML files available online, I have created an all-in-one page for you at inteltechniques.com/api/all.txt. You will need to change the API keys to match yours and then save the file with the extension "html". At the time of this writing, I am experimenting with several new APIs. The final summary of each is not ready for publication, but I want to identify the services and current status of each.

Service Objects (serviceobjects.com/products/email/email-insight)

Service Objects offers several API search options based on sources of data. Chapter Eleven explained how to use their reverse caller ID service through their website on a free trial basis. This company also offers an email lookup utility that will occasionally identify the location, age range, gender, income, education, and residence information of the user of the account. This is similar to TowerData. However, Service Objects displays more information during the free evaluation. Obtaining a free trial allows you up to 500 searches within a 30 day timeframe. Provide an email address, any name, and any telephone number to immediately be issued an active API key. Create a URL based on the following structure.

http://trial.serviceobjects.com/ei/emailinsight.asmx/GetContactInfoByEmail?Email=EMAILADDRESS&LicenseKey=XXXX-XXXX-XXXXX

I navigated to the following URL based on my API key and sample email address which produced the result seen directly below it.

http://trial.serviceobjects.com/ei/emailinsight.asmx/GetContactInfoByEmail?Email=m.wilson72@hot mail.com&LicenseKey=WS67-QRI1-OZH4

```
<EmailInsightResult>
<City>Santa Barbara</City>
<County>Santa Barbara</County>
<State>CA</State>
<Country>United States</Country>
<PostalCode>93105</PostalCode>
<AddressType>Residence</AddressType>
<Latitude>34.446925</Latitude>
<Longitude>-119.742822</Longitude>
<Age>45-54</Age>
<Gender>Male</Gender>
<HouseholdIncome>100K-125K</HouseholdIncome>
<Education>Unknown</Education>
<Homeowner>True</Homeowner>
<HomeMarketValue>350K-500K</HomeMarketValue>
</EmailInsightResult>
```

I now know that the data available for this email address indicates that the user is a male aged 45-54, he lives in Santa Barbara, California, and is a home owner with a residence valued at $350,000-$500,000.

Creating a web page to search this data is very easy. Save the following code as serviceobjects.html. When you open the file, it should appear in a web browser and look similar to the other custom tools created in this chapter. A digital version of this file is at inteltechniques.com/api/so.txt, which can be copied and pasted from the site.

```
<html><head></head><body>
<script type="text/javascript">function doservice(email) {window.open
(' http://trial.serviceobjects.com/ei/emailinsight.asmx/GetContactInfoByEmail?Email' + email
+'&LicenseKey=XXXX-XXXX-XXXX', servicewindow');}
</script>
<form onsubmit="doservice(this.service.value); return false;">
<input type="text" name="service" size="40" value="Email Address" />
<input type="submit" /></form>
</body></html>
```

TowerData (dashboard.towerdata.com/users/sign_up)

TowerData is a company that builds products to analyze large amounts of information. They help businesses sort through large customer email databases and obtain information about the customers.

They offer free access to the basic API that communicates with their data. This service will give us the location, sex, and age range of the user of a specific email address. It uses several sources of data including social networks and marketing data. For a small fee, you can obtain more information than these three categories, but this tutorial will only focus on the free data.

TowerData's API, as well as most APIs, will require a unique API key. This is a license issued to you and no one else. Visiting the website above will allow you to create an account and request your key. Once you have the key, you need to construct a very specific URL, or internet address, to conduct the search. An example of this address would look like this:

https://api.towerdata.com/v5/td?email=test@test.com&api_key=xxxx&format=html

This search is detailed as follows.

https://api.towerdata.com: This is the main domain of the service.

v5/td?: This identifies to TowerData that we are using the latest version (v5) of the API.

email=test@test.com: This specifies the email address that we want to search.

api_key=xxxx: This represents your API key issued by TowerData.

format=html: This tells TowerData to present the results in a standard HTML view on a web browser.

If you were to request this data using your API key and a valid email address, the result would be the following.

```
"location": "Chicago, Illinois, United States",
"age": "25-34",
"gender": "Female"
```

You could now bookmark the URL that you created to get the information. Each time you wanted to check another email address, you could visit the bookmark and edit the email address to match that of your target. I prefer to create a form similar to those discussed previously. Open Notepad and type the following in a new text document.

```
<html><head></head><body>
<script type="text/javascript">function dotower(email) {window.open
('https://api.towerdata.com/v5/td?email=' + email +'&api_key=xxxx&format=html', 'towerwindow');}
</script>
<form onsubmit="dotower(this.raf2.value); return false;">
<input type="text" name="raf2" size="40" value="Email Address" />
<input type="submit" /></form></body></html>
```

Save this file as towerdata.html. When you open the file, it should appear in a web browser and look like Figure 14.14. A digital version of this file is at inteltechniques.com/api/1.txt, which can be copied and pasted from the site.

Figure 14.14: A TowerData query form.

You can now type in any email address, click Submit Query, and a new tab will open with the results from TowerData. You could make a separate page for each of the services discussed in this chapter. Instead, consider creating a page similar to Figure 14.01. The graphics and descriptions are not necessary. If you want to create something more visually pleasing, information on web design is plentiful on the internet.

Mashape (mashape.com)

Mashape is a collection of several APIs from several companies. They also offer their own API that can be used to access the data from other businesses. This collection includes both paid and free services, and most will allow you to test the product within this website. I am currently using this website for testing of individual email addresses through Email Sherlock, Email Validator, and Social Media Email Search. Results can vary, but there is much potential with this type of combined services. I recommend creating a free account and experimenting with the various APIs.

Chapter Fifteen

Software Applications

Up to this point, every technique that has been discussed will work on any computer regardless of operating system (OS). This includes Windows, Mac, and Linux. As long as the system has an internet connection and a web browser, you can perform all the methods for searching. This chapter focuses on software applications that can assist with your OSINT searching. All of these programs will only work on a computer with a Windows operating system. This will include the majority of readers. If you have a Mac or Linux OS, you can use virtualization software to run Windows within it. The internet will deliver all of the information you need on that topic.

Many of the programs detailed here can be executed as a "portable application". This means that the program can be downloaded and started without installation. All of the files needed are within the application and ready to go. This can be convenient when an application is needed on another computer. You can download the programs to a portable flash drive and execute them directly from the drive. Storing these applications on a portable drive will keep you prepared to conduct queries from any location. I recommend visiting **Portable Apps** (portableapps.com), **Pen Drive Apps** (pendriveapps.com), and **Portable Freeware** (portablefreeware.com).

All of the software mentioned in this chapter is free for personal use. Before using, read any text files included to ensure that you are not violating any of the terms of service. I have yet to come across any concerns. Most of these programs are updated regularly. These updates are very important. They often correct software bugs and add new features. Some, but not all, of these applications will notify you when an update is available. Visit the application website occasionally to see any updates.

All programs mentioned in this book are legal to use. They are tools that should be used responsibly. Some of them may be considered hacker tools, often used for malicious or devious purposes by an individual. It is my intent that the programs will be used only to obtain information legally. It is the responsibility of the reader to do so.

Firefox (mozilla.org)

The most vital application in this chapter is the Firefox web browser. All of the searching methods that you have learned must be conducted within a web browser. Most people settle for Internet Explorer, which is included with Windows. I do not recommend using that browser for OSINT analysis. The Firefox browser has a feature called "add-ons" or "extensions". These are small applications that work within the browser that perform a specific function. They will make searching and documentation much easier. There is not an official Firefox portable application on the website, but you can always find the latest portable release at portableapps.com/apps/internet/firefox_portable. I also use, and encourage others to use, the Chrome web browser. However, many of the extensions that I need are only compatible with Firefox.

The browser will not look much different from the browser you were previously using. When installing and executing, choose not to import any settings from other browsers. This will keep your browser clean from unwanted data. The extensions detailed here will include a website for each extension. You can either visit the website and download the extension or search for it from within Firefox. The latter is usually the easiest way. While Firefox is open, click on "Tools" and then "Add-ons" in the menu bar. This will present a new page with a search field in the upper right corner. Enter the name of the extension and install from there.

Extensions

There are thousands of extensions available for Firefox. Some are helpful, some are worthless, and some are just fun. This chapter will discuss sixteen of them:

> Copy All Links: Quickly copy all hyperlinks from a website
> Disconnect: Block trackers from collecting your information
> Docs Online Viewer: Quickly launch online documents within browser
> DownloadHelper: Download media from a page with click of a button
> DownThemAll: Automatically download ALL media found on a page
> Empty Cache Button: Immediately delete invasive cookies and internet cache
> Exif Viewer: Identify Metadata embedded inside a photograph
> Facepaste: Automatically download Facebook photo albums
> FireShot: Generate screenshots of partial and entire web pages
> FoxySpider: Crawl a website for photos, audio, video, etc.
> Geolocater: Force your browser to spoof your location
> GTranslate: Right-click language translation
> Hola: Temporarily change your location to allow restricted content
> JSONView: View API JSON results in browser
> List.it: Create, sort, and print notes from an investigation
> MementoFox: View previous versions of a website
> Minimap Add-on: Display location notifications in an embedded map

Nimbus: Alternative screen capture for large web pages
NoScript: Block any script from launching within a website
Resurrect Pages: Enable historical search on deleted websites
Search Image Everywhere: Conduct automatic reverse image searches
User Agent Switcher: Emulate various browsers and devices
Vibe: Collect information about email addresses within web pages

Copy All Links (addons.mozilla.org/en-us/firefox/addon/copy-all-links/)

This simple add-on will identify any hyperlinks within the source code of an individual web page. It will store the links within your operating system's clipboard, which will allow you to paste them into any application of your choice. While only a small utility, it can quickly turn a large project into a completed task. After installing, I recommend navigating to the "options" menu within the add-on and selecting "Copy only clickable links". This will eliminate many unwanted results. Using the utility is fairly straight forward. While on any website, right-click anywhere in the page and highlight the "Copy All Links" option in the menu. This will present you with options to either copy the links in the current tab or within all open tabs of your browser. You can then choose to copy all file sharing links, direct file links, or all links. I always recommend the last option. The links will be stored in your clipboard and you can paste them into Notepad, Excel, or any other productivity application. There are unlimited uses for Copy All Links, and below are a few of my favorite.

Facebook: When I am on my target's list of Facebook friends, I will use Copy All Links to quickly record each hyperlink to an individual's profile. I will then paste these into Excel for later analysis.

Twitter: When I am viewing a Twitter profile, I will use this utility to capture all links to external websites and photos.

Instagram: When using the Instagram API view of a target's followers, I use this tool to capture direct links to each of their profiles.

Performing screenshots in these examples would never identify the direct links to the visible content. A combination of screen captures and link collection should provide a much more comprehensive report.

Disconnect (addons.mozilla.org/en-us/firefox/addon/disconnect/)

In previous editions of this book, I have recommended Ghostery for protection from tracking websites. I have now switched to Disconnect. I believe that it is more effective and there is less risk of your personal data being released. Disconnect is a browser extension that stops major third parties from tracking the webpages you go to. Disconnect can make your web experience more private, less cluttered, faster, and safer. Every time you visit a site, Disconnect automatically detects when your browser tries to make a connection to anything other than the site you are visiting. They call these other attempted connections "network requests". Disconnect then categorizes these network requests into different groups (Google, Facebook, Twitter, Advertising, Analytics, Social and Content). By default, Disconnect blocks all of the network requests in each category except Content. Content is unblocked by default because it often includes network requests that, if blocked, would "break" the site you are visiting. Blocked categories have green icons and unblocked categories have gray icons. You can block or unblock categories by clicking the icon associated with that category. You can also get more granular by clicking on the ">" on the right side of each category, which will open up a list of all the trackers in that category. Blocked trackers are checked and unblocked trackers are unchecked. You can block and unblock categories by checking and unchecking them. Finally, you can unblock all network requests on a given site by clicking "whitelist".

Docs Online Viewer (http://www.deekshith.in)

You will likely encounter several types of documents during your searches. Some of these will require specific software such as Adobe Reader, Microsoft Word, or Open Office in order to view the files. This extension will allow you to view all of these documents within the web browser. It takes advantage of Google Docs to display each document inside of a new tab. You will see a new icon displayed next to each document within search results. Figure 15.01 displays a search result with the "eyeball" icon to the right. Clicking this image will open each document within the browser instead of launching Microsoft Word.

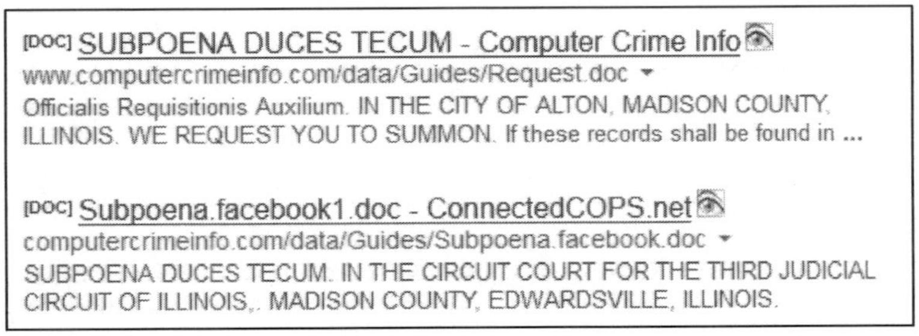

Figure 15.01: A search result with the Docs Online Viewer extension.

Download Helper (downloadhelper.net)

This extension will assist with downloading media that is located during your search. It works well with videos such as those found on YouTube. When this extension is enabled, an icon will appear within your browser that looks like three circles. Any time you open a website that includes media content, such as a video, these circles will start to spin. This is an indication that the media on the page can be extracted. Click on the down arrow to the right of this icon to present the download options. Do not click on the icon directly, as this will only present random websites with video content. Figure 15.02 displays the menu options.

This view presents the different sizes of the video that can be downloaded. If the video is going to be used in court, I recommend downloading all sizes available. If you only want a personal archive, the largest size should be downloaded. You will now have a pure digital extraction of the target video. This is better than a screen capture or recording of the video because there is no loss of data or analog conversion. The files can then be archived on CD or DVD.

If downloading a large amount of videos, this extension will make the work easy. When you are on any YouTube page, highlight any area of videos by holding down the left mouse button and dragging to select the area. Right-click anywhere within this area and choose "Download videos from YouTube Link(s)". This will start a batch download process and save all of the videos to the default storage location on the computer. These videos will be in the MP4 format.

Real world application: While assisting with a large investigation, I was provided a long list of links to YouTube videos of interest to a specific incident. Instead of visiting each link and downloading the files manually, I created a blank HTML formatted web page with all of the links. After opening the page within Firefox, and highlighting all of the links, a right-click provided the ability to download all of them at once. This could now run for a few hours while hundreds of videos were archived and titled according to the video title.

Figure 15.02: A Download Helper menu.

Down Them All (downthemall.net)

This extension can also make downloading a large amount of media files easy. If you locate a page of several audio or video files, it can be time consuming to save them all. Additionally, you run the risk of accidentally skipping a file. Down Them All provides a solution. As an example, the Defcon website (defcon.org) contains media archives of each Defcon hacking conference available for download. Viewing the Defcon 19 links presents hundreds of files to obtain. You could save each of them individually, but that is not efficient. While on the target page, click on "Tools", "Down Them All Tools" and then "Down Them All". This will present a new window with every link available on the website page.

You can highlight the files that you want to save or right-click and choose "select all" to save everything. The lower section of this window allows you to choose where you want to save the data and any filters you want to include. In Figure 15.03, I chose to only download the videos and documents from the page and to save them to my Temp directory. Clicking "Start" will begin the automated download. These files can get quite large and may take a while to complete. Archiving to DVD is optimal.

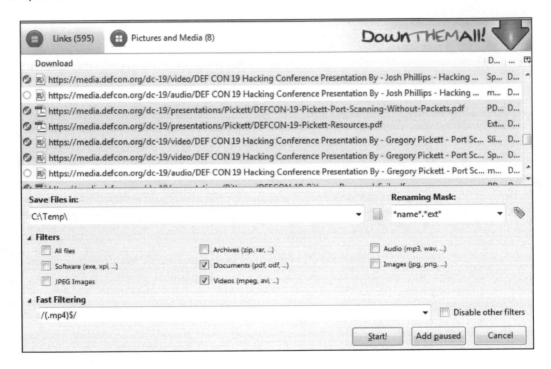

Figure 15.03: A Down Them All window.

Empty Cache Button (addons.mozilla.org/en-us/firefox/addon/empty-cache-button)

This add-on creates a small icon in your browser that appears similar to an eraser. You can click this at any time to immediately remove internet cache from within that browser. This includes memory cache, disk cache, offline cache, and favicon cache. A similar feature is available when you close your browser. However, this simple feature allows you to empty your cache without closing your current session.

Exif Viewer (araskin.webs.com/exif/exif.html)

This extension provides right-click access to the Exif data embedded into images. Chapter Nine explains what Exif data is and how it can be useful. With this extension enabled, you can right-click on any full size image located on a web page. The menu option is "View Image Exif Data" and a new window will open when selected. This window will identify any available metadata about the image. Figure 15.04 displays partial results that identify the make and model of the camera used to capture the image.

- Camera Make = Canon
- Camera Model = Canon PowerShot A590 IS
- Picture Orientation = normal (1)
- X-Resolution = 180/1 ===> 180
- Y-Resolution = 180/1 ===> 180
- X/Y-Resolution Unit = inch (2)
- Last Modified Date/Time = 2009:07:02 10:35:16
- Y/Cb/Cr Positioning (Subsampling) = centered / center of pixel array (1)

Figure 15.04: A result from Exif Viewer.

FacePaste (addons.mozilla.org/en-US/firefox/addon/facepaste)

Encountering a Facebook profile with thousands of photos can be overwhelming and a thorough analyst will archive all photos associated with a target. This task could take weeks if completed manually. FacePaste provides right-click access to a new menu option labeled "Download Facebook Album(s)". You only need to right-click on any photo album on the main photos page of a profile. Selecting this option will present a new window that will prompt you to select the albums to download and the location where to save them. Figure 15.05 (left) displays a window ready for execution. All of the target's photos will be downloaded to a folder titled "Temp" at the root of my C drive. They will be numbered in order and any duplicate folder names will be merged into one. Figure 15.05 (right) displays a finished response identifying the successful results.

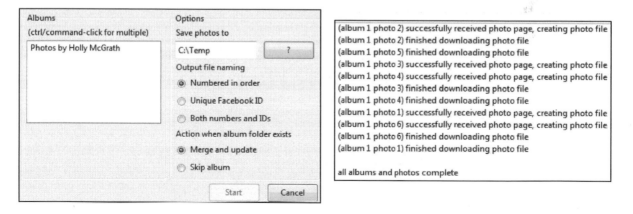

Figure 15.05: The FacePaste input and activity windows.

FireShot (getfireshot.com)

Documenting and archiving your progress with an OSINT investigation is as important as the intelligence discovered. The general rule is that if you do not have proof of your findings, then they never existed. FireShot provides you with an easy solution to capturing all of your results. When enabled, this extension is in the form of a button in the upper right portion of your browser. It appears as a red square containing the letter "S". Clicking the down arrow directly to the right of the icon presents a menu with many options. The best option is to select "Capture entire page" and then "Save as PDF". This will then create a PDF document of the entire page exactly as it appears in your browser and save it to anywhere you choose. The file can later be archived to a removable disc. The title of the document will match the title of the web page and it will be date and time stamped to identify when it was captured.

This method is preferred over a standard screen capture for several reasons. A typical screen capture only captures the visible area and not the entire page. You must then open a program to "paste" the data into and then save the file. The FireShot extension automates this and saves it in a format that is difficult to edit. This can be beneficial during testimony.

By accessing the "Preferences" area of the menu, you can assign default action so that you can simply click the button to complete the process each time. I recommend the following tweaks within the FireShot preferences.

General: Default: Capture Entire Page and Save as PDF
Editor: General: Confirmations: Display message=no/Open Folder=No
Editor: Capturing: File Name: %t - %u - %y - %m - %d - %H - %M - %S
Editor: Display: Watermark: Template:
      Captured: %H:%M:%S, %d-%m-%y.
      Original Image size: %w x %h pixels.
      Target Website: %u

FoxySpider (addons.mozilla.org/en-US/firefox/addon/foxyspider)

FoxySpider can be used to create a thumbnail gallery containing links to rich media files of any file types you are interested in. It can also crawl deep to any level on a website and display the applicable files it found in the same gallery. It is useful for different media content pages such as music, video, images, and documents. You can narrow and expand the search to support exactly what you want. Once the thumbnail gallery is created you can view or download every file that was fetched. After FoxySpider is installed, a button will appear to the left of the Firefox address bar. Click it to start a crawl process, which will start from the currently viewed webpage. Clicking again during a crawl, while focusing on the created gallery, stops the crawl process.

GeoLocator (addons.mozilla.org/en-us/firefox/addon/geolocater)

Most modern browsers possess the ability to share your current location with the website that you are connecting to. This is beneficial when you want to quickly navigate to your current geographical area within a location enhanced website. Mapping websites such as Google and Bing take advantage of this technology in order to immediately display your current location on an online map. As an OSINT researcher, I never allow my browser to share my current location with a web service. However, I may choose to share a false location in order to fool the data collection system. Geolocater allows us to submit this false information.

After installing the add-on, you will have a new option in the Firefox Tools menu titled "Geolocater". Highlighting this menu will present the "Manage" option which will open a new configuration window. The configuration options within Geolocater are not obvious and it took a while for me to understand the best method of spoofing my location. The following instructions should help you quickly setup your add-on.

Click on the red map marker in the upper right corner next to two grey markers. This will create a new location. The middle map marker should now also be red. Click on this to toggle the map mode. This should present new fields to enter location information. Enter a name for your Location and the desired location address. Under the country field, choose the "-" option. Change the accuracy option to the minimum (50 feet). Figure 15.06 displays a completed entry identifying my desired location as Disneyland. When finished, click the last map marker which should now appear red with a green checkmark. This will save the setting and you can choose to immediately begin using this location. Navigating to Bing Maps and allowing it to locate you should identify if your spoofed location was effective.

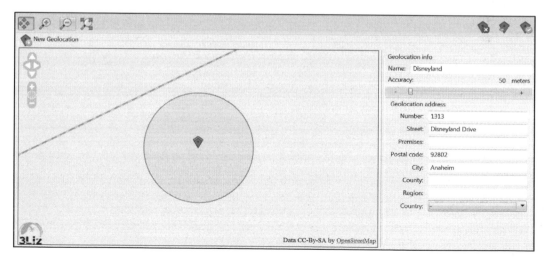

Figure 15.06: A Geolocater configuration page.

GTranslate (addons.mozilla.org)

If you find yourself using Google's free language translation service to translate foreign text into English, this extension will be a welcome addition to your Firefox browser. When installed, any text you highlight and right-click will present a new menu option. This will automatically translate the text into English without leaving the target website. This will work on any site including social networks. Figure 15.07 displays a Twitter post translated to English through the extension.

Figure 15.07: The GTranslate Extension.

Hola (hola.org)

I urge you to use caution with this add-on. When initiated and left to run continuously, it may cause your internet connection to have issues. When applied appropriately and disabled after use, you should have no problems. Hola allows you to obtain protected content when your current location is prohibited from accessing it. A demonstration should explain the process.

If you navigate www.bbc.co.uk/iplayer/live/bbcone, you will likely be greeted with an announcement that you cannot view this live video stream. This is because the BBC only allows viewing from within the U.K. Figure 15.08 (left) displays this warning. With the Hola program enabled, it will automatically launch a proxy service that will change your assumed location. In this case, it automatically selected the U.K. and reloaded the page. Figure 15.08 (right) displays the new announcement that will allow you to play the video stream. Within the Hola add-on, you can choose to appear to be connecting from any country. Figure 15.09 displays the results when I connected to Google and selected Afghanistan as my country. It forwarded me to google.com.af, an Arabic version of Google.

Figure 15.08: A notification from the BBC before executing Hola (left) and after execution (right).

Figure 15.09: A Google search window while using a Hola connection from Afghanistan.

JSONView (jsonview.com)

This extension will probably go unnoticed, which is a good thing. JSONView allows JSON files to be opened and viewed within a web page instead of saving them and viewing the files in a text editor. This only applies to the API discussions in Chapter Fourteen. Many of these APIs deliver the results in a view that is not intended for web browsers, even Firefox. With the extension installed, the API results should appear within the browser. Without this extension, some of the API searches will not function.

List.it (welist.it)

This is a very recent extension that I now rely on daily. When enabled, you possess a sidebar on the left side of the browser ready for notes and links from your investigation. You can create as many fields as you like, move them around, and delete them as necessary. Figure 15.10 displays an example of results obtained during an investigation. This includes manually entered text as well as links copied and pasted. You can also right-click on any link and send it directly to your list. When finished, the print button in the upper portion will generate a properly formatted report to print for your records. The white area to the right is what would be printed.

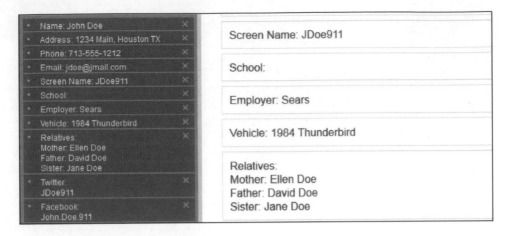

Figure 15.10: A partial List.it menu bar and report template.

MementoFox (mementoweb.org)

Chapter One discussed The Wayback Machine, a free service that archives previous versions of websites. Searching a website manually involves visiting the Wayback website and entering each website of interest individually. This extension embeds this option within our browser. Any time you are viewing a target website, use the slider visible in the toolbar to seek a previous archive. Figure 15.11 displays the website "phonelosers.org" as archived on 05/25/2003. You could move the slider further to the left to go back to an earlier date. You can also enter a date manually, and the extension will locate the archive closest to that date.

I believe the biggest strength of this extension is that it provides a constant reminder to use this type of service. With the slider bar present on every page you visit, there is no excuse to not check for previous archives. Clicking the grey clock on the upper left at any time will return you to the live website.

MiniMap (minimap.spatialviews.com)

This extension comes with three mapping components. The main and most powerful is a map sidebar. In this sidebar you can drag and drop addresses or locations you find on web pages and they will be automatically located. However, the easiest way to use it is to copy any location information and right-click it. Figure 15.12 displays a Twitter API page that identified GPS information. Highlighting the GPS coordinates and right-clicking presented a Minimap option. Selecting that opened the identified location on a map in the sidebar.

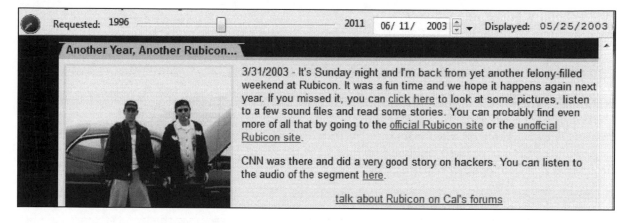

Figure 15.11: An archived website accessed through the MementoFox extension.

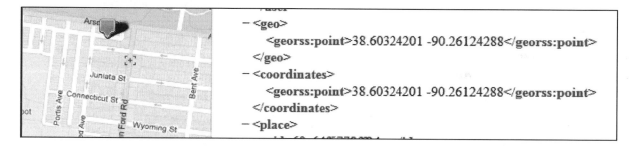

Figure 15.12: A MiniMap sidebar generated from GPS coordinates.

Nimbus (addons.mozilla.org/en-US/firefox/addon/nimbus-screenshot)

While FireShot is my preferred screen capture utility within Firefox, there are some instances where it does not perform well. If you have a target's Facebook page that has a lot of activity present, this may create a screen capture too large for FireShot. When this happens, I use Nimbus as a backup. Nimbus allows you to specify whether you want to capture only the visible portion of the page, the entire page, or a custom selection from the page. The drop-down menu presents these choices and the result is saved as a PNG file.

NoScript (noscript.net)

Disconnect, the add-on mentioned earlier, blocks a large number of trackers imbedded into websites. NoScript, an add-on only available on Firefox, possesses the ability to block all scripts within any web page. This software may be overkill for the casual web investigator. Those that are privacy conscious will greatly benefit from its powerful features. Installing the software can be completed at the website above. The default configuration of this software will block practically any script programmed to execute when you load a web page. This will include advertisements, tracking cookies, applications, and anything else that is not native to the display of the web page. This protection can often block core content required to properly view the website. The following instructions will explain how to properly configure NoScript.

Clicking the new "S" icon in the menu area of your browser will present the NoScript menu for the website currently loaded. There are options within this menu if you want to enable scripts. If NoScript is blocking something on a website and is preventing it from displaying the content you want, use the following guide to correct the issue. I recommend taking action in the following order which starts with minor changes and ends with disabling NoScript completely from the website.

✓ Attempt to identify the blocked script that is desired. If you can identify the specific script, select "Temporarily allow" next to the script name. This will allow the script to load one time. However, the next time you load that website, the script will be blocked again.

✓ If you decide that any allowed script should not run in the future, you do not need to take any action. If you want to block the script right away, you can click the "Forbid" option next to the script name.

✓ If you decide that the temporarily unblocked script should always be allowed, select the "Allow" option below the "Temporarily" option next to that script. It will now always allow that specific script on any website. This may be beneficial to always allow a desired login or social network.

✓ The "Temporarily allow all this page" option near the bottom of the menu will reload the current website and allow any scripts as if NoScript were not installed. This can be beneficial when you cannot access the desired website appropriately and do not know which script is the culprit.

✓ The "Allow all this page" option will always allow all scripts to run on the current website. This can be beneficial when you commonly visit a trusted website, such as your bank or other financial service. Enabling this setting will advise NoScript to never block scripts on that page.

✓ If you are currently only using trusted websites and are frustrated with NoScript blocking desired content, you can choose "Allow Scripts Globally". This completely disables NoScript and you are not protected. You can reverse this action by selecting "Forbid Scripts Globally".

If you choose to use NoScript, you do not need to use the Disconnect or Ghostery extensions mentioned previously. I believe that NoScript is a superior service and provides more protection. In exchange for this security, you sacrifice convenience in your daily internet browsing. I hope that you find this inconvenience worth the reward of a safer online experience. The following describes my NoScript settings.

✓ I have a default NoScript installation and configuration within Firefox. I block all scripts while browsing and searching the internet.

✓ If I encounter a website that I cannot view properly, and it is a reputable website, I will select the "Temporarily allow all this page option" for a single use allowance.

✓ The first time I connect to trusted websites such as my bank, financial services, email, or educational site, I choose the "Allow all this page" to permanently allow the scripts.

✓ When I am conducting important business, such as financial transactions or creating accounts on business websites, I select "Allow Scripts Globally". As soon as I am finished, I choose "Forbid Scripts Globally". My individual settings are still maintained.

Resurrect Pages (github.com/arantius/resurrect-pages)

This extension also provides archived views of websites. Resurrect replaces the standard "Page not found" error when you try to load an invalid website. Instead, you will see several new buttons that will attempt to load a cached or archived copy of the website. These serve as a reminder to look for deleted information. Figure 15.13 displays the new result when you visit a website that no longer exists.

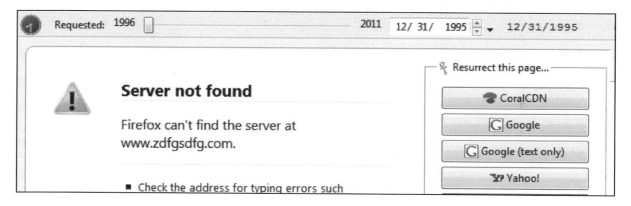

Figure 15.13: A 404 error with Resurrect Pages enabled.

Search Image Everywhere (snark.co.il)

Chapter Nine explained reverse image search engines and how they can identify more target photographs. Popular options include Google Images and Tin Eye. This extension automates the reverse search when an image is right-clicked. When clicked, an option of "Search Image Everywhere" is present. When selected, five new tabs open in your browser. Each tab connects to a reverse photo service and analyzes the target photo for duplicate copies on the internet. This can be very convenient if you have several images to search. It can eliminate the need to open each image to locate the URL to copy. This extension performs this task behind the scenes.

User Agent Switcher (chrispederick.com/work/user-agent-switcher)

Occasionally, you may visit a website that does not want to cooperate with Firefox. Browsers notify websites of their identity and websites can alter or refuse content to certain browsers. One example is that some older websites require Microsoft's Internet Explorer to view the content. Even though Firefox is capable of displaying the information, a website can refuse the data to the browser. Another example is mobile websites that display different content if viewing from an iPhone instead of a computer. This can now all be controlled with User Agent Switcher. When enabled, you will have new options in the "Tools" menu. The sub-menu "User Agent Switcher" will give you options to change your reported browser to three versions of Internet Explorer or an iPhone. Selecting the iPhone will ask websites to deliver data for mobile view, which can reveal new services. In order to test this, you can navigate to geolocha.com and view the page through a web browser. It should notify you that the site requires an iPhone. If you change the agent to the iPhone setting and reload the page, you will enter a chat room for iPhone users. This technique can lead to new content discovery.

Vibe (addons.mozilla.org/en-US/firefox/addon/vibe-for-firefox)

Vibe is an easy to use people research tool. You can use it to find the person associated with an email address. After installing the add-on, hover or click on any email address that you see within a website. This could be on a social network profile or within a news article. From an email address, Vibe will attempt to find the associated name, designation, work history, social media handle, and topics of interest. Vibe requires membership credentials and provides access for free.

Chrome Extensions

All of the previously mentioned add-ons are available for the Firefox browser. Some of them are also available on the Chrome browser. While Firefox is my choice for investigations, there are a couple of extensions that are only available for Chrome.

Falcon (falcon.io)

Falcon monitors the social networks that you visit and supplies additional details about the targets that you are researching. The plugin can be accessed by clicking the "F" icon in the upper right corner of the browser. It will only load if the page that you are on is supported. Examples of supported pages include Twitter, Google+, Facebook, YouTube, and ten others. Figure 15.14 displays a Twitter profile with the Falcon bar visible in the right column. Hovering on the link in his profile for his wife, "summertomato", identified her full name, location, Facebook account, AboutMe account, Google+ page, YouTube page, Foursquare details, and personal blog. You can keep this column visible at all times. Any time that you click a social network link or hover over a person's user name, any available details will display within the app. This is similar to some services and APIs that have been discussed. The advantage with this utility is that it is completely automated.

Figure 15.14: A Falcon response to a user name on a Twitter page.

This plugin also possesses a search option. At the top of every Falcon results column, there is a search field. You can enter an email address, Twitter handle, Facebook user name, or any other moniker. You must be on a website such as Twitter in order to launch this option. In my Chrome browser, I have Twitter as my home page and Falcon enabled. This way, as soon as I start Chrome, I am ready to conduct a search.

Prophet (recruitingtools.com)

Prophet is very similar to Falcon and will often return redundant results. Occasionally, I receive data that was not available from Falcon. The install and execution of Prophet is also similar to Falcon. With Prophet, you should click on the black arrow button in the upper right of your browser in order to launch the menu which will display any found results. Figure 15.15 displays the results from the same previous profile which provides links to her Facebook, Google+, Klout, Twitter, Instagram, and personal website pages.

Figure 15.15: A Prophet result within the Chrome browser.

TOR Browser (torproject.org)

TOR is an acronym for The Onion Router. Basically, it allows you to mask your IP address and appear to be browsing the internet from a false location. Normally, when you connect to the internet and browse to a website, that website can identify the IP address that was assigned to you from your internet service provider. This can often identify the city and state that you are in and possibly the business organization where you are currently located. In some instances, it can identify the building you are in if you are using public wireless internet access. The owner of the website can then analyze this information which may jeopardize your investigation. This is one of the many reasons that I recommend the Disconnect add-on for Firefox which was explained earlier. Disconnect will block most of the analytic code within websites that monitors your information, but it will not stop everything. Occasionally, you may want to change your IP address to make you appear to be someone else in a different country. This is where TOR excels.

The TOR bundle available for free download is completely portable and requires no installation. After download, unzip the file and extract all of the data. You are now ready to start the program by double clicking the "Start TOR Browser" icon. The first task that TOR will complete is to create a connection to a TOR server. This connects you to a server, usually in another country, and routes all of your internet traffic through that server. After the connection is successful, it will load a custom version of the Firefox browser. Now, every website that you visit through this browser will assume that you are connecting through this new IP address instead of your own. This provides a layer of privacy to stay hidden from a suspect. This may be overkill for most investigations. If you are only searching and monitoring common services such as Facebook, Twitter, or YouTube, this service is not needed. If you are visiting personal websites and blogs of a tech savvy hacker, you should consider TOR. When using TOR, you will notice a drastic decrease in the speed of your internet. This is normal and unavoidable.

Figure 15.16 displays my IP address without using the TOR browser as reported by whatismyipaddress.com. It identifies the city and state I was in at the time, the internet service provider, the organization providing me the wireless internet access, and a map with the location marked. Any website that I visited would announce this information to the website owner. Figure 15.17 displays this same information when visited with the TOR browser running. It identifies my location as Kota Bogor Tengah, Indonesia. It also recognizes the TOR network which announces that this IP address is not accurate. This would prevent a target from identifying me through my traffic to his or her website. To stop the service, close the browser. This will disconnect the TOR network and stop all services.

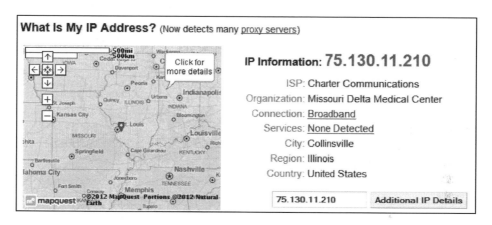

Figure 15.16: An IP address identification through whatismyipaddress.com.

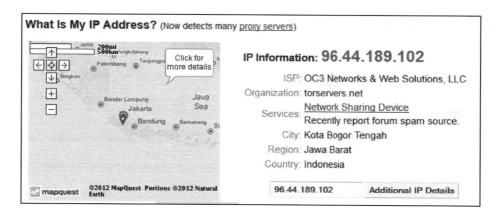

Figure 15.17: A masked IP address identification through whatismyipaddress.com.

Tweet Deck (tweetdeck.com)

This application replicates some of the Twitter search methods discussed in Chapter Three. The benefit of the application is that it will store any user settings and reload these settings on launch of the program. You must create a free account in order to use the program. This is actually a good thing. With this account, you can log into any copy of the program on any computer and access your saved settings. The account does not need to contain any private information, just a user name and password. After logging into the program, you will have to attach a Twitter account. This will be your user name and password for your personal Twitter account. I hope that by now you have created a fictitious account. You are now ready to set up your screen.

Each of the columns in the program can be modified. I suggest deleting the current columns since they are configured for a person that wants to send messages, not watch them. To delete these, highlight a column and click the gear icon in the upper right corner of the column. This will give you the option to "Remove column". Once you have a clean slate, you can customize the screen.

To add a specific user's Twitter stream, click on the "Add Column" button and then "Timeline". Search for the user name. When located, highlight the name and click "Add Column". You can now view a live stream of posts to and from that target. To add a column of search results, click "Add Column, then "Search". Enter your search term and select "Add Column". To display any mentions of a topic, click "Add Column", then "Mentions" and search for the term of interest. Choose "Add Column" when complete. You will now have three columns of information populating the software. Figure 15.18 displays columns searching for the term "flash mob", mentions of "OccupyWallSt", and posts to and from user "sriney8".

This tool is recommended for analysts that are responsible for monitoring live Twitter data. Archiving is not possible, but screen captures or a video capture would work.

Figure 15.18: A Tweet Deck display screen.

4K Stogram (4kdownload.com/products/product-stogram)

4K Stogram, which I refer to as Instagram Downloader, is a standalone software application available for PC, Mac and Linux. The program allows you to download and backup all Instagram photos and videos from a user at once. The default download option is a setup file that will install to your computer. However, a portable option is also available within the "Download" tab. Launching the program presents only one single entry field which is ready for any Instagram user name. Clicking "Follow" will begin the extraction of all public photos and videos from the specified account.

The files will be saved to your default documents directory in a subdirectory titled 4kstogram. The options within this program are not obvious. The following instructions should help you make the most of the program.

✓ Allow the collection process to complete before navigating to the content folder. A grey counter in the upper right should identify the number of photos and videos that have been collected.

✓ Hover over the user name directly above the collected photos. This will activate two icons immediately to the right. The first will stop the collection process and the second will open the folder where the files are being collected.

✓ Click on the red "X" directly to the far right of the user name. This will remove the current search from the program view. This will not remove any files. You must remove all content manually through the operating system when desired.

✓ If you are seeking files from private accounts, and you possess an account that is "friends" with the target, you can enter your credentials within 4K Stogram to access the restricted account.

Creepy (ilektrojohn.github.com/creepy)

Creepy is an application created to display a user's location on a map. This is determined by the GPS data stored within a Twitter or Instagram post, or the Exif data inside a photograph on Flickr. This can identify places visited by a target with the date and time that they were present. The program will allow for searching of any combination of Twitter user names, Instagram user names, or Flickr user IDs.

In December of 2013, a new version of Creepy was released that corrected old bugs and introduced new features. This also complicated the configuration process, but the software walks you through the steps. Before attempting a search, click on "Edit" in the menu and then "Plugins Configuration". In order to use Flickr, you will need an API key from them. This process is explained at flickr.com/services/api. The Instagram and Twitter plugins will ask you to log into each account and will guide you through the API setup process. Look for the button titled "Run Configuration Wizard".

Create a new project and enter the user name of your target. Select the networks that you want to search and click "Search" to find the accounts. Any accounts identified will be displayed below. Click "Add to Targets" to select the accounts desired. Continue this process until you have added any accounts of your target. Accept the default options and click "Next" and "Finish" to start the query. Figure 15.19 displays a Twitter account ready for analysis.

The application will identify posts that contain GPS information from the selected accounts. It will then map out each post on an embedded Google map. The column on the right will display all of the geo-located posts in chronological order (Figure 15.20). You can double-click any of them to see additional information. The map will change so that the center marker is the location of the chosen message. The lower right window will display the message and a link to the original source.

The result of a Creepy response of Instagram or Flickr locations will look similar to the Twitter result. The lower window will display the title of the photograph and a link to the original file. The map will center the marker on the location of the photo according to the GPS or Exif data (Figure 15.21).

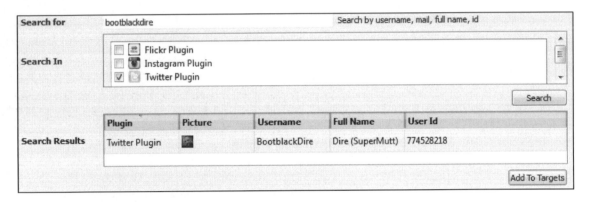

Figure 15.19: A Creepy user search screen.

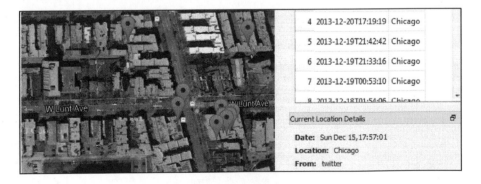

Figure 15.20: A Creepy Twitter result.

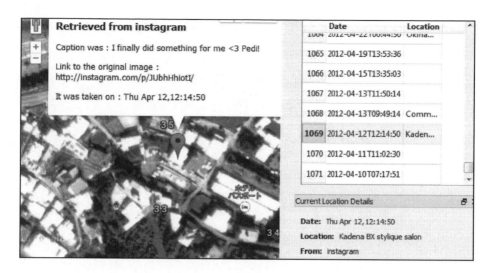

Figure 15.21: A Creepy Instagram result.

The latest version will allow you to enter multiple targets from numerous accounts. Each project will automatically be saved within the application and available to you with the next launch. You can right-click any project to delete it. The program allows you to export a project to a standard CSV file or a Google Maps KML file. The KML option allows you to open the analysis within Google Maps. After being dormant and useless for most of 2013, this application is now very valuable to my OSINT investigations.

4K Video Downloader (4kdownload.com/products/product-videodownloader)

4K Video Downloader allows download of video, audio, and subtitles from YouTube in the highest quality available. It will download the files as fast as your computer and connection will allow. Downloading is simple and straightforward. Navigate to your target's YouTube page and select the video tab to see all of the uploaded content. Copy the entire address (URL) of this page and launch 4K Video Downloader. Click the first icon titled "Paste Url". This will begin the process of identifying uploaded videos, parsing the links, and presenting the download options. Figure 15.22 (left) displays the blank entry form received when launching the program. Figure 15.22 (right) displays the download screen. In this example, I have selected to download all 24 videos in MP4 format. The highest quality versions will be obtained and any subtitle information will be downloaded as text files. The entire content will be saved to my desktop. This free version will limit you to a download of 25 videos or less per page.

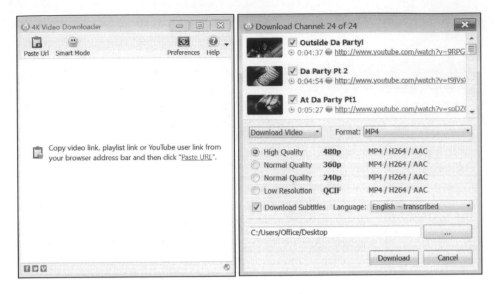

Figure 15.22: The 4K Video Downloader entry screen (left) and download options (right).

Video Manipulation Utilities (ffmpeg.org)

When I was in law enforcement, one of my assignments was to obtain any video evidence from various crime scenes. This might be video footage of an armed robbery from a convenience store camera system or personal video captured through a cellular telephone camera by a witness. Either way, I often encountered many problems. Some surveillance systems required rare video codecs in order to view the media. Some personal videos were very short and difficult to see because of quick movement. I developed scripts to take advantage of open source tools that helped with the various struggles that I had involving digital video.

The following techniques will require the executable files ffmpeg.exe and ffplay.exe. Downloading the correct version of FFmpeg can be difficult. Navigating to the following website will present dozens of options for various operating systems. In order to make this easier, you can type in the exact address below and download the latest version for Windows.

http://inteltechniques.com/data/ffmpeg.zip

Video Codec Player

When you identify an online or offline video that offers value to your investigation, you should save and archive the file. This video, if gathered from a digital surveillance system, may require a video codec that you do not possess. If you cannot view the video, it has no value. I recommend using ffplay.exe as your best chance of viewing videos that require unknown codecs. You can play a video file by executing instructions via a command line. However, I prefer to create a batch file that will simplify the process every time.

Extract the two files (ffplay.exe and ffmpeg.exe) from the compressed file mentioned previously. Save them inside a folder titled "video" on your desktop. In this same folder, create a new text file and title it player.bat. Be sure to change the file extension from txt to bat. Windows will now recognize this text file as a set of instructions. Type the following text into this new file.

```
set /p VIDEO=Video file name (with extension) on Desktop:
ffplay.exe "%userprofile%\desktop\%VIDEO%"
```

Double-click this new batch file and you should be prompted to enter the name of an unplayable video file. Note that you must supply the entire file name, including the file extension, and the video file must be placed directly on the desktop. You should now be able to play the previously unplayable file. Note that some video files will still not play. However, this method should eliminate many of the problems.

Video Converter

If you are able to now play the previously unplayable video file, you should consider converting it to a more universal format. During my investigations, I was often asked to forward any video evidence to a prosecutor. If I had a hard time playing the video, it was certain that the prosecutor would have difficulty. Therefore, I always submitted both the original evidence video and a converted copy that should play on any computer. We can use the ffmpeg.exe file to convert any playable video to a standard MP4 format. Create another text file within your video folder and title it converter.bat. Type the following text into the document and save it.

```
set /p VIDEO=Video file name (with extension) on Desktop:
ffmpeg.exe -i "%userprofile%\desktop\%VIDEO%" -vcodec mpeg4 "%userprofile%\desktop\%VIDEO%.mp4"
```

Double-click this new batch file and you should be prompted to enter the name of an unplayable video file. Note that you must supply the entire file name, including the file extension, and the video file must be placed directly on the desktop. This should create a new video file on your desktop that will have the same title as the previous file but with the extension MP4. This file should play on any modern computer system.

Video Frame Extraction

You may also want to extract the still frames from the video for deeper analysis. Law enforcement may want to extract the stills of online videos for distribution to the media with the hope of identifying a suspect. There are many expensive programs designed to offer a solution for this, but this free program works just as well. The ffmpeg.exe file downloaded earlier will extract still images from practically any video. Create another text file within your video folder and title it extract.bat. Type the following text into the document and save it.

set /p VIDEO=Enter full name of video file on desktop:
md "%userprofile%\desktop\frames"
ffmpeg.exe -y -i "%userprofile%\desktop\%VIDEO%" -an -r 4 "%userprofile%\desktop\frames\img%%3d.jpg"

It is very important that these files do not have a "txt" extension. If you double click this file and it opens within Notepad, the file extension is "txt" and not "bat". Change the file extension and you should see a black box open similar to Figure 15.23. In this example, I have a video titled youtube01.flv on the desktop of my computer. After entering this file name of the video, press enter on your keyboard and you should see the program begin processing the video. When complete, you should see a new folder on your desktop titled "frames" which will contain numerous still images in chronological order. These are the frames from your video which can now be printed, distributed, or enhanced. Figure 15.24 displays one of the several still image files extracted from my target video.

Figure 15.23: The command prompt of FFmpeg requesting file name.

Figure 15.24: A still frame extracted by FFmpeg.

Video Metadata (mediaarea.net/en/MediaInfo/Download/Windows)

Most smartphone devices store data within every video captured. This includes the software version and model of the phone, the date and time of the video, and the GPS location of the device during the capture. It also documents the direction that the phone was facing during the capture as determined by the internal accelerometer. There are several ways of extracting this type of information. I have found MediaInfo to be the easiest solution.

Navigating to this download website will present you with many options. Most users download the universal installer which will quickly install the required software. Unfortunately, it will also display advertisements and attempt to trick you into installing unnecessary software that is difficult to remove. My preference is to download the 32 bit "CLI" option. This is a command line version which will require a bit more work to make it run. However, you do not receive any unwanted bundled software.

Download the compressed file and unzip it to a folder called metadata. Create a new text file within this same folder and title it metadata.bat. Be sure that this file no longer possesses a txt file extension. Type the following text into this new batch file.

```
set /p VIDEO=Enter full name of video file on desktop:
mediainfo.exe "%userprofile%\desktop\%VIDEO%" > "%userprofile%\desktop\%VIDEO%".txt
```

Double-click the metadata.bat file and you should be prompted to enter the name of a video file residing on your desktop. Place any video file of interest on your desktop and enter that file name. This will create a new text file on your desktop that will have the same name as your target video. The content of this new "report" will contain all of the available information about that video from the metadata. The following partial information was retrieved from a test video that I extracted from a co-worker's cellular telephone.

Complete name:	C:\Users\Office\desktop\2.mov
Format :	MPEG-4
Format profile:	QuickTime
File size :	1.00 MiB
Duration:	10s 712ms
Overall bit rate:	787 Kbps
Recorded date :	2013-08-26T07:46:36-0500
©xyz :	+38.8890-090.1599+161.000/
Model :	iPhone 4S
Writing application:	6.1.3

This information identifies the location that target video was captured, the make and model of the device, and even the operating system within the iPhone. While many people realize that their phones record GPS within the photos that they take, they do not always know that this applies to videos as well.

Stream Transport (streamtransport.com)

Some video sites make it difficult to download the videos. Occasionally, the Download Helper extension and the 4K Video Downloader program cannot archive the file playing in the web browser.

Stream Transport can usually solve this issue. Stream Transport must be installed on the computer and cannot currently work as a portable application. When executed, the program launches similar to a web browser. Type or paste in the address of the video file that you want to download. When you begin playing the file, you should see a stream of data directly below the video playback window. To the right of this is a "Download" button. Clicking this will begin the download process in a new window. When complete, you will have an identical digital replica of the video file that can be archived to DVD. Figure 15.25 displays a video file on Vimeo being downloaded in a second window. This program will also work on some live streams of video using the same method.

Figure 15.25: The Stream Transport video download application.

CamStudio (camstudio.org)

If all else fails and you cannot retrieve a pure copy of a video, you can always create a video screen capture while the video plays. This is not the recommended plan, but is better than not archiving the footage. Cam Studio is completely free and simple to use. It can also work as a portable application from a flash drive. Upon launch, the program is ready to start recording. Before hitting the record button, I suggest visiting the "Video Options" menu under "Options". If you are going to use this recording as official documentation of an investigation, you should increase the quality to 100%. This will create a large file, but the quality is worth the size. Now, you must choose what "Region" you want to record. Your options are "Full Screen" or "Fixed Region". If you are working on a single monitor, "Full Screen" should work fine. If you have multiple monitors and do not want everything on them captured, you should select a region. This should be the only mandatory configuration changes. You are now ready to record.

Clicking the red record button will start the recording and place the menu icon in the taskbar. When you are finished recording your screen, right-click on the menu in the taskbar and choose "Stop". This will prompt you to title your video and choose a storage location. This video is now ready for archiving.

This screen recording technique could also be used to capture an entire OSINT search and analysis. You could start the video before any searching is conducted and let it record while you navigate through websites. This could then be used for reference later to review the steps taken to locate any vital data. Some investigators like to archive this for court to confirm that the data obtained was indeed located legally and through open source methods. If you do choose to record your research, I encourage you to disable the "Record Audio" feature, which will prevent your microphone from recording your voice.

FastStone Capture (faststone.org)

If still captures are needed of anything on your screen, you have several options to generate them. You could capture a screen shot with the print screen button and paste it into a program that will allow you to save it. However, this is a hassle and time consuming. You could print the page you are viewing, but this gets difficult on some sites, such as Facebook. You could save the entire web page to your hard drive and recreate it as needed, but this is overkill. I recommend an automated screen capture. FastStone Capture will do this for free. Some configuration is necessary, but since the application is portable, you can take your changes with you.

Launching the program will present a small icon in the lower right area of your taskbar. It will look similar to a red and green triangle. Right-click on this and choose "settings". This will present several settings that you can customize for your needs. You can choose which combination of keys will create a new capture and where the captures will be saved. You can also choose what type of file is created. I use the PDF option. PDF files are more difficult to modify than image files, and this can be helpful in courtroom testimony. By default, the files created will be titled according to the current date and time of the computer. This will assist in documenting your actions in a summary report. One last option you should select is the auto-save option. This will eliminate the need to confirm the saving of each image as it is created. To access this setting, right-click on the icon in the taskbar and choose "Output" and then "To File (Auto-Save)". Now, every time that you create a screen capture, it will automatically save the PDF file to your computer without prompting. By default, it will create a capture of the entire application that you are working in. In most situations, this will be your web browser. This will include both the content and the URL of the page you are viewing.

You can use this tool to document and archive all of your findings. I often let this program run and take a screen capture every time I find anything relative to my target. I then save all of the files to a CD or DVD and submit the disc with the report.

Photo Trail Mapper (github.com/excocitato/PhotoTrailMapper)

This free program was created by the same team that distributed the Facebook and Twitter visualizers that are now defunct. Photo Trail Mapper will allow you to analyze a folder of photographs and visually plot the locations of each capture onto a map. Figure 15.26 displays nine photos captured in various locations. The lines connecting them identify the path taken based on the photo capture dates. You can zoom into each photo to identify the exact location of the capture. Additionally, you can use the export option to create a spreadsheet of partial metadata from all photos. Figure 15.27 displays this exported result from these sample images.

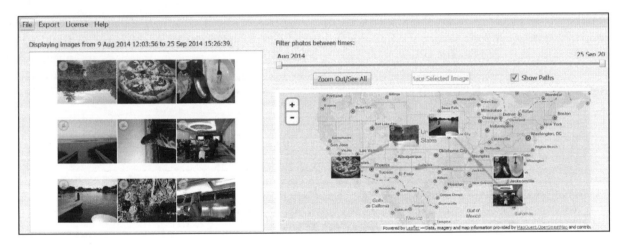

Figure 15.26: A photo location analysis through Photo Trail Mapper

Camera Make	Date	Latitude	Longitude	Position Data Source
SAMSUNG SCH-I545	8/9/2014 12:03	39.35263822	-104.7643585	GPS from EXIF data in photo
SAMSUNG SCH-I545	9/16/2014 18:16	33.78931044	-117.9193802	GPS from EXIF data in photo
SAMSUNG SCH-I545	9/17/2014 17:57	33.50652311	-86.79887386	GPS from EXIF data in photo
SAMSUNG SCH-I545	9/21/2014 18:39	33.77067947	-78.78749844	GPS from EXIF data in photo
SAMSUNG SCH-I545	9/22/2014 8:26	33.74721525	-78.80355831	GPS from EXIF data in photo
SAMSUNG SCH-I545	9/23/2014 9:11	28.25308036	-81.62351222	GPS from EXIF data in photo
SAMSUNG SCH-I545	9/25/2014 11:08	41.25836944	-95.92529292	GPS from EXIF data in photo
SAMSUNG SCH-I545	9/25/2014 12:07	41.25821303	-95.92536161	GPS from EXIF data in photo
SAMSUNG SCH-I545	9/25/2014 15:26	41.32160944	-95.89912414	GPS from EXIF data in photo

Figure 15.27: An exported spreadsheet of metadata created by Photo Trail Mapper.

Exif Tool (sno.phy.queensu.ca/~phil/exiftool)

The details about how Exif data is stored within images was discussed in Chapter Nine. This data can be very valuable to an investigation. The resources mentioned earlier require internet access and the image to be uploaded to a website. For most situations, this is not a problem. Some investigations may involve classified material that is prohibited from being uploaded to any public network. Under these circumstances, Exif Tool becomes useful. The program is portable and allows you to browse to an image. It will then display all stored Exif information about the image. This will include camera details and GPS coordinates if available. Since this application does not use the internet for information, you will not receive a map of the location. You will only get the numerical coordinates.

JPEG Snoop (impulseadventure.com/photo)

If Exif Tool does not provide enough data, or displays a view of the data that you do not like, take a look at JPEG Snoop. This portable application provides a very detailed report of all of the Exif information that is stored. The report can be saved to a log file or printed. The best feature of this software is the batch process ability. You can select an entire folder of images and conduct an analysis of all of them at once. A report can be generated of the results, which can be archived to disk. JPEG Snoop will not display a map and does not require internet access (Figure 15.28).

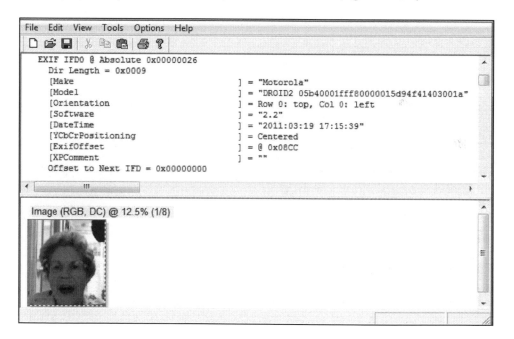

Figure 15.28: An image analysis in JPEG Snoop.

SmartDeblur (github.com/Y-Vladimir/SmartDeblur)

You may eventually locate a digital image of interest to your investigation that is blurry, distorted, or otherwise flawed. This happens to me often in the form of surveillance photos and video screenshots. There are commercial applications available that will assist with this situation, but they can be expensive. Another solution, Photoshop, is not only expensive, but difficult to use. My current free solution for this is SmartDeblur. Figure 15.29 displays a blurry photo loaded within the SmartDeblur application.

Adjusting the defect type, radius, smoothness, and correction strength will often clear up an image. Figure 15.30 displays the same image after slight manipulation with the tool. The new settings are visible in this demonstration. Further adjustments will likely make the remaining text legible. I recommend a lot of practice with this program before it is needed for an image of importance.

Real World Application: I recently used this application to identify the license plate of a suspect vehicle as captured from a home surveillance system. The original image was too blurry to be helpful. The manipulated image provided all of the digits of the vehicle's registration. This technique is also used by several people on Reddit's "PicRequest" as explained in Chapter Seven.

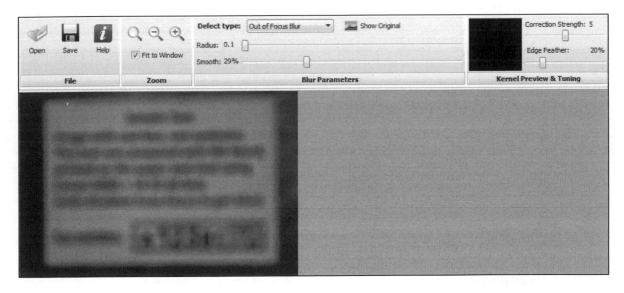

Figure 15.29: A blurry image opened in SmartDeblur.

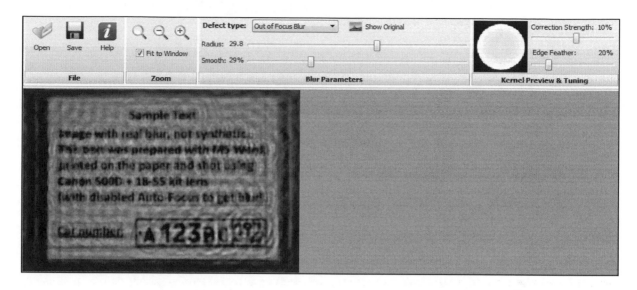

Figure 15.30: An enhanced image edited with SmartDeblur.

Google Earth (earth.google.com)

Google maps is an online website that was discussed in Chapter Four. Google Earth is a standalone application that takes the Google Map data to another level. With this application, we have access to many mapping tools. These tools can import data from spreadsheets and help you visualize the content. In order to maintain the scope of open source intelligence, I will focus on only a few specific tools.

Within the application, the first step is to display your location of interest. This can be accomplished by typing the address or GPS coordinates in the upper left search field. When you see your target location and have set the zoom to an appropriate level, you are ready to start adding layers. By default, you will only see the satellite imagery of the location. The menu on the left possesses options for adding new content to this view. The last box in this menu is titled "Layers". Inside of this menu are several data sets that can be enabled and disabled by the checkbox next to each. The following details will explain the layers of interest.

Photos - Digital images uploaded through social networking sites Panaramio.com and 360cities.net
Roads - Text layer of road names
3D Building - Alternative 3D view of some locations
Gallery - User submitted content including YouTube videos

I recommend disabling all layers and then enabling one at a time to analyze the data that is added to your map view. Figure 15.31 displays a view of Chicago including the Photos, Roads, and Gallery layers.

Figure 15.31: A Google Earth view with layers enabled.

Another Google Earth tool available that is often overlooked is the Historical Imagery option. This can be activated by selecting the "clock" icon in the upper menu bar of the application. This will open a slider menu directly below the icon. This slider can be moved and the result will be various satellite images of the target location taken at different times. Figure 15.32 displays the same target area with the Historical Imagery option enabled. The view has been changed to the satellite image obtained on 05/30/2008. Usually, the quality of the images will decline as you navigate farther back in time. This can be useful in identifying changes in the target location such as building modifications, additional vehicles, and land changes. Drug enforcement agents often use this tool to monitor suspected drug growth at a target location.

Figure 15.32: A Google Earth view from historic imagery.

FOCA (informatica64.com/foca.aspx)

FOCA has many uses. Some are legit, and some are a little sneaky. Everything that the program can do is legal, but I will only focus on the areas that should pass any ethics debate. FOCA's biggest strength is the ability to extract metadata from documents. You can drag and drop a document into the program, and it will analyze the file's hidden data and present a summary. Though there are many programs that can do this. FOCA stands out by automating the search process by searching, downloading, and analyzing all documents on a web server with very little input. The entire process follows.

When you launch FOCA, you will see the main program with few action choices. Click on "Project" and then "New project". Create a project name and provide the target website if you have one. Choose a location to store any documents located and include any notes necessary. Click the "Create" button to create your project. You will be prompted to name your project file, which will be the target domain name by default. Choose the same location as you chose to save the documents. You are now ready to begin analysis.

If you have any locally saved documents to analyze, you can now "drag and drop" them into the program. When the file is visible in the program, right-click on it and choose "extract all metadata". The left column will now have the analyzed content ready. Clicking on the file name under the "Documents" section will display the full metadata of the document. This will often include dates and times associated with modifications of the file, user names of people that modified it, printers that have printed the file, revision history, email addresses of the owner, and software version information. Figure 15.33 displays a partial result of a file summary that displays the company, computer user name, and email address of the target. This information is probably stored inside every document created on that computer.

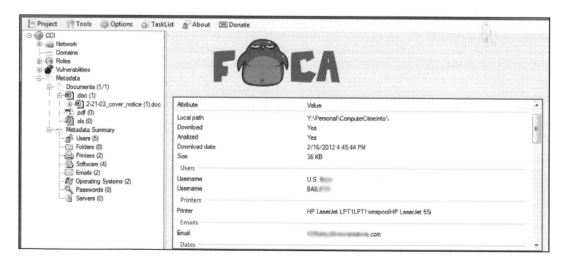

Figure 15.33: A partial FOCA analysis.

If you do not have any individual documents to analyze, you can begin to look for them now. On the same main menu, you should see various check boxes in the upper right corner. Uncheck the box next to "Exalead". You can try a search with this enabled, but it tends to cause problems due to Exalead's API rules. Now click the "search all" button. The program will use Google and Bing to search for any documents on the target website that were indexed by the search engines. In my example, it located 107 documents on the very informative website irongeek.com. When it is finished searching, right click on any of the files located and click "Download All". This will save a copy of all documents found to the location on your computer that you chose earlier. This can take some time depending on the amount and size of the documents. Even though we have not analyzed any of the documents yet, simply having a copy of all of them could prove beneficial for further intelligence.

After the files have finished downloading, right-click on any of them and select "Extract All Metadata". This will extract each document's raw metadata. When complete, right-click any file and select "Analyze Metadata". This will analyze all of the extracted content and categorize the results by various topics. The left column will now display several new subfolders under "Documents". This analysis may take some time if there are a large number of documents.

The first section will identify the documents by file type. Figure 15.34 identifies 107 documents on the website irongeek.com. This includes 51 PDFs, 52 Powerpoints, and 1 Open Office document. The "Users" summary identifies five user names associated with the account, including the website owner, Adrian Crenshaw.

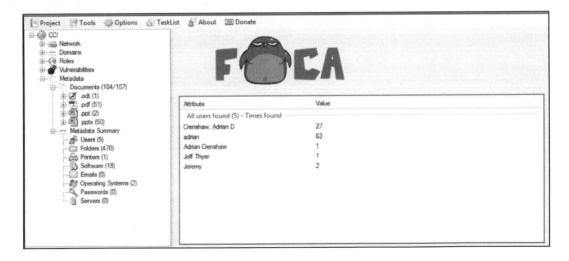

Figure 15.34: A partial FOCA analysis.

There are several scenarios where this program can prove valuable. People that run illegal websites often use fraudulent information during the registration process. If a website has been identified as a target, this registration (whois) information becomes useless. If the target stores any documents on the website that are indexed by Google or Bing, you can extract the metadata from these files. Often, these subjects use a real name for the login name for their computers or as part of the registration of software. When this data is captured within the documents, you now have a lead on the identity of the target. As with most open source intelligence, this data is user created and you cannot always assume that the information is correct. However, it can provide great intelligence for additional searches. Another great reason to use this tool is to make sure that you did not miss any documents during the analysis of a website. Most sites have several pages in folders and subfolders. This is one way to locate all documents that are publicly available.

HTTrack (httrack.com)

There are several ways to make an exact copy of a website. I choose HTTrack because it is portable software and works quickly. The software will walk you through the process of saving a website. You may want to do this when you locate a target website and are concerned that the site could be taken down. Any time that you find any content that will be used in court, you should archive the entire site. This application automates the process. The result is a locally stored copy that you can navigate as if it were live. This is beneficial in court when internet access is not appropriate.

When the application loads, clicking the "next" button will bring you to the project screen. Give your project a title, preferably the website name, and choose a location to save all of the data. Click next and then "add URL". Enter the exact website that you want to archive. Do not enter in any login or password. Click "next" and then "finished" and you are done. The application will begin extracting all public information from the site. This can take a while, depending on the size of the site. When complete, you will have an exact copy which you can navigate and search offline. Archiving to CD or DVD creates a replica that can be held for future analysis.

SEO Spider (screamingfrog.co.uk)

This program was designed to assist in Search Engine Optimization (SEO). This is the process of tweaking a website so that it will appear higher in search engine results. We can use it to identify all public pages, images, links, CSS files, and other data within our target's website.

After installing and executing the free software, I conducted a search of "phonelosers.org". The entire process completed in approximately four minutes. Figure 15.36 displays a small portion of the results. Overall, this program identified 2,436 unique pages, 4,604 images, and 6,123 external links that were located within the target website. This tool will often identify much more data than a person can locate manually. On several occasions, this application has provided evidence that would have been otherwise missed.

You can right-click on any result and open the data within a web browser. It will connect to the selected content within the target's live website. A complete user guide can be found at http://www.screamingfrog.co.uk/seo-spider/user-guide.

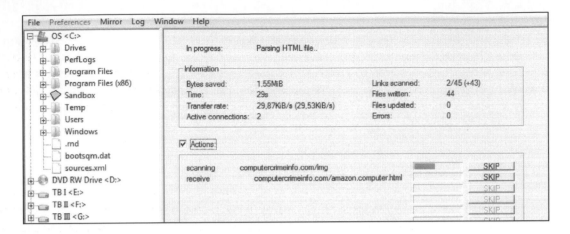

Figure 15.35: HTTrack website archiving.

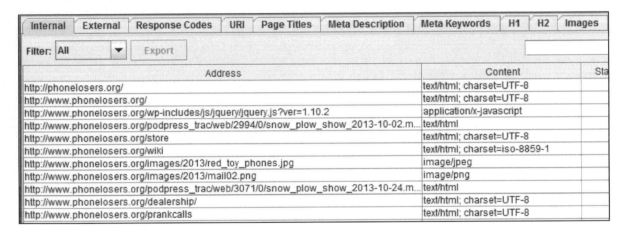

Figure 15.36: A partial search result from SEO Spider.

Domain Hosting View (nirsoft.net)

This application will take any website domain and retrieve all public information about the registration and host. This will commonly include the names and contact information of people associated with the account. It will identify the physical host, which will be needed in the case of serving legal process. This is the same information as the "whois" searches conducted in Chapter Twelve but with a cleaner interface. You can only search one domain at a time with this tool. If you have several domains to search, you should use the WhoisThisDomain tool from the same website. Upon execution, it will present a window that will accept multiple IP addresses or domain names. The "View" menu offers a single combined report of all queries.

IP Net Info (nirsoft.net)

If you have an IP address instead of a domain, IP Net Info will perform the same series of searches for you. The first screen will allow you to enter multiple IP addresses and search them all. This is convenient when an investigator has received login IP addresses from an online provider such as Yahoo or Facebook. Both Domain Hosting View and IP Net Info will export the results as a text file for archiving.

Maltego (paterva.com)

No book about OSINT would be complete without a mention of Maltego. This application automates much of the OSINT search and collection process. An entire book could (and should) be devoted to the operation of this application. Attempting to document its many uses here would not do the program justice. A user manual can be found at ctas.paterva.com/view/Userguide.

Chapter Sixteen

Android Emulation

For several years, online researches have been navigating through various social networking websites for information about individuals. Whether it was older sites such as Friendster and MySpace, or newer networks such as Twitter and Facebook, we have always flocked to our web browsers to begin extracting data. Times have changed. Today, an entire generation of social network users rarely touch a traditional computer. They operate completely from a cellular telephone or tablet. Many of the networks that individuals engage through will only operate on a mobile device. Services such as SnapChat, Tinder, and Kik do not allow a user to access content from a traditional web browser. As this shift occurs, investigators must transition with it.

This chapter will focus on the huge amount of information available through mobile platforms that is not accessible through a web browser. I will explain three methods of emulating a portable device within a traditional computer. Before we dive into the nuts and bolts of making things work, we should discuss why emulation is the way to go. In my investigations, documentation is my primary reason for launching a simulated mobile device within my computer operating system. If I conducted my investigation on an actual smart phone, documenting my findings can be difficult. Mobile screen captures only cover a small amount of visible content. Extracting any captured images can be a hassle. Referencing my findings within a final report can become very tedious. When using Android emulation within my traditional computer, I can easily create numerous screen captures, record a video of my entire investigation, and paste my results directly into the report.

Privacy and security are also important reasons to consider emulation versus directly investigating from a portable device. I have seen many law enforcement investigators conduct a search or use an app directly from their personal or work phones. This opens that device to scrutiny and discovery. An attorney could rightfully request a copy of the investigator's phone in order to conduct an independent forensic analysis. That would make most people nervous. Additionally, if I encounter malicious software or a virus from my portable device, it could affect all future investigations using that hardware. Emulation will remedy both of these situations.

The idea of Android emulation is to recreate the mobile operating experience within an application on your computer. This application will execute in the same manner that your web browser, word processor, or email client would open. It will have the exact same appearance as if you were staring at a telephone or tablet. Any actions that you take within this emulated device will not affect anything else on your computer. Think of it as an encapsulated box, and nothing comes in or gets out. A great feature of emulation is that you can create unlimited virtual devices. You could have one for every investigation in order to prevent any contamination.

Some readers will question why I chose to explain Android emulation instead of iPhone. The most obvious reason is the number of options. I will explain two software solutions and an online option for recreating the Android environment on your computer. The iPhone simulator will only function on Apple computers and has very limited features. The Android techniques will work on any major operating system. Additionally, we can create Android virtual machines that possess all original functionality. The iPhone simulator will not connect to most applications and features.

There are more options for Android emulation than what I present in this chapter. My goal is to focus on the most user-friendly and feature rich solutions that are available without cost. My overall emulator of choice is Genymotion.

Genymotion (genymotion.com)

This application-based solution is extremely easy to use. It works with Windows, Mac, and Linux operating systems. I will provide details for the Windows installation, but the principles apply across all platforms. The operation of virtual devices after installation is identical on all operating systems. First, you will need to install the application.

Navigate to the download area of the website and click on the "Get Genymotion" link. You will be required to create an account for the free service. This can be completed using anonymous information and any real email address that you have access to. This setup file will contain both the Genymotion application and a virtual machine application called Virtual Box. Accepting all default installation options will install all of the required files. When the setup process has completed, you will have a new icon on your desktop titled Genymotion.

Execute this application and note that a Google Nexus 10 virtual machine is pre-installed and ready for launch. Instead of accepting this default option, consider creating your own machine in order to learn the process for future investigations. I recommend deleting this machine by clicking the trash icon to the right of the title. Perform the following instructions in order to create your custom Android devices.

✓ Create a new device by clicking the "Add' Icon in the menu. Select the "Custom Phone – 4.4.4 – API 19 – 768x1280" option. This will create a new emulator of the latest public Android release (4.4.4) in a default vertical telephone view (768x1280). It will not have any branding from a specific manufacturer.

✓ Launch the new device by clicking the "Start" icon. The machine will load in a new window which should appear similar to the screen of an Android telephone. Click "OK" to any feature notifications. Figure 16.01 (left) displays the default view of the home screen.

✓ Navigate within the Android emulator by single clicking on icons and using the "Back" icon in the lower left that appears similar to a left facing arrow.

✓ Consider the following customizations to improve the look and feel of the device. Figure 16.01 (right) displays the view of the home screen after these configurations have been made.

> Drag the camera icon up and drop it in the "Remove" option.
> Click the "Applications" icon (six dots within circle), and choose "Settings".
> Choose "Display", then "Sleep", and select "30 Minutes".
> Choose "Security", then "Screen Lock", and choose "None".
> Press and hold the clock to drag up and remove.

You now have a functioning replica of a standard Android device. However, you are missing several features. The biggest void is the absence of key applications such as Google Play and Gmail. Without core Google services, you cannot download apps to your device as part of your investigation tools. This has been the biggest hurdle with emulation. However, there is finally a fix. Perform the following instructions to add the ability to download any app within the Google Play repository.

✓ Navigate to https://goo.im/gapps/gapps-kk-20140606-signed.zip/ and click the white "Download Now" button directly below the file information. If this link should disappear, try androidhost.org/bDyyW.

✓ Drag and drop the downloaded compressed file into your open Android virtual machine. You should see a message that reads "File transfer in progress". You will receive a warning about the file being a "flashable archive". Click "OK" to accept the warning. Click "OK" when you are notified of the successful copying of the files.

✓ Click "OK" to accept any errors that are reported after the installation. Turn off the virtual device by closing the active window.

✓ Re-start the virtual machine. Multiple restarts may be required to eliminate all startup errors.

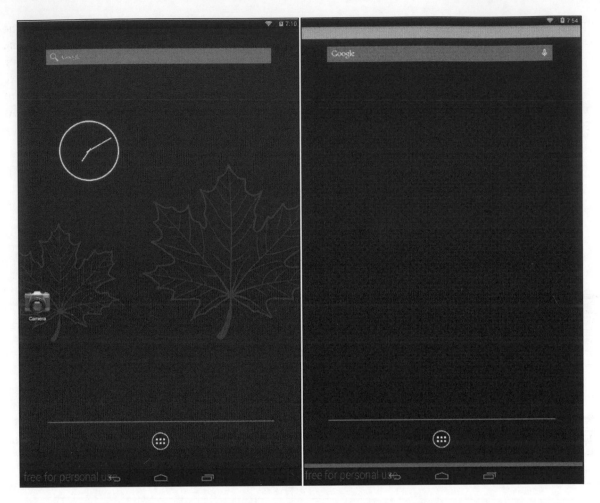

Figure 16.01: A Default Android home screen (left) and the custom version free of clutter (right).

Your device should now prompt you to connect to an existing or new Google account. Consider using an anonymous account that is not used for anything else. I do not recommend creating a new account from within this virtual machine because Google will likely demand a cellular telephone number for verification. I prefer to create the Google accounts from a traditional computer before connecting to the virtual Android device. After syncing with an active Google account on your new device, you should now be able to activate the Google Play store. You should also now see all core Google services in your applications menu. Figure 16.02 (left) displays the standard applications included with the emulator and Figure 16.02 (right) displays the new Google options.

The addition of Google Play will allow you to natively install Android applications as if you were holding a real telephone or tablet. Launch Google Play and you will be able to search, install, and execute any app to your new virtual device. After you install a new program, click on the applications menu (circle with six dots in it). Click and hold the new app and you will be able to drag it to your home screen. Figure 16.03 displays the screen of my default investigation emulator. The top row contains chat apps, the second row contains social network apps, the third contains location-based apps, the fourth contains Google services, and the last contains Android utilities. I will later explain how these programs can be used for intelligence collection. First, you should understand the features embedded into the Genymotion software.

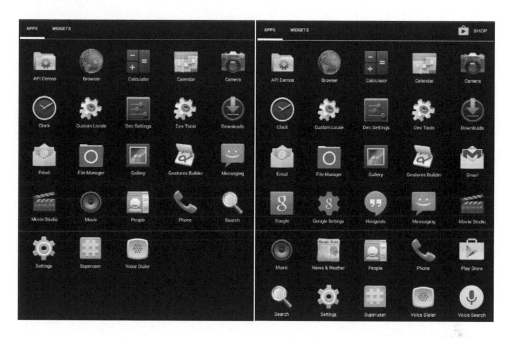

Figure 16.02: A default application list (left) and a version with Google services installed (right).

When you launch an Android virtual machine, you will see a column on the right side of the window and a row of icons horizontally on the bottom. The bottom icons are part of the emulated Android system. Clicking the first icon will navigate you backward one screen from your current location. If you are within an app, this would take you back one step each time that you press it. The second icon represents the "Home" option and will always return you to the home screen. The third button is the "Recent Apps" option and it will load a view of recently opened applications.

The icons on the right of the emulator are features of Genymotion and allow you to control aspects of the Android machine from outside of the emulator. Figure 16.03 displays this column of options. The guide on the following page should help explain each of these features.

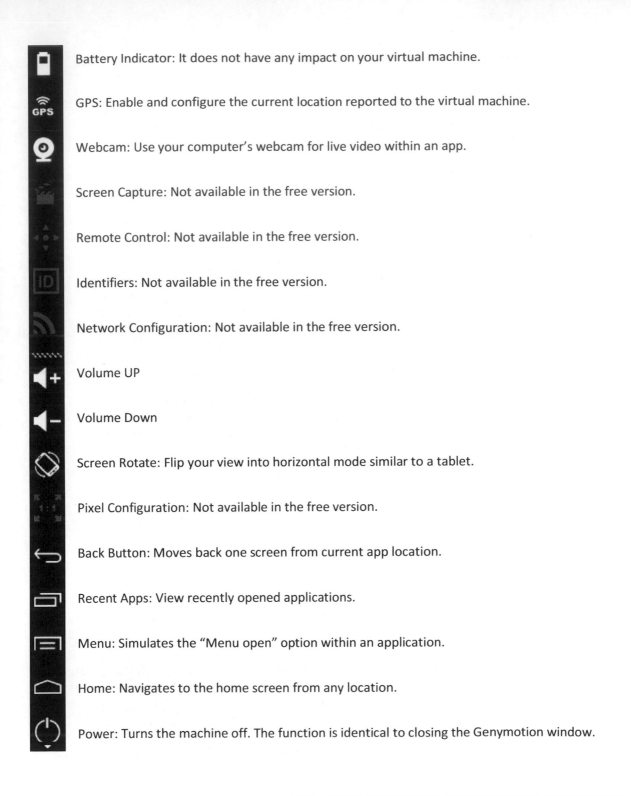

Battery Indicator: It does not have any impact on your virtual machine.

GPS: Enable and configure the current location reported to the virtual machine.

Webcam: Use your computer's webcam for live video within an app.

Screen Capture: Not available in the free version.

Remote Control: Not available in the free version.

Identifiers: Not available in the free version.

Network Configuration: Not available in the free version.

Volume UP

Volume Down

Screen Rotate: Flip your view into horizontal mode similar to a tablet.

Pixel Configuration: Not available in the free version.

Back Button: Moves back one screen from current app location.

Recent Apps: View recently opened applications.

Menu: Simulates the "Menu open" option within an application.

Home: Navigates to the home screen from any location.

Power: Turns the machine off. The function is identical to closing the Genymotion window.

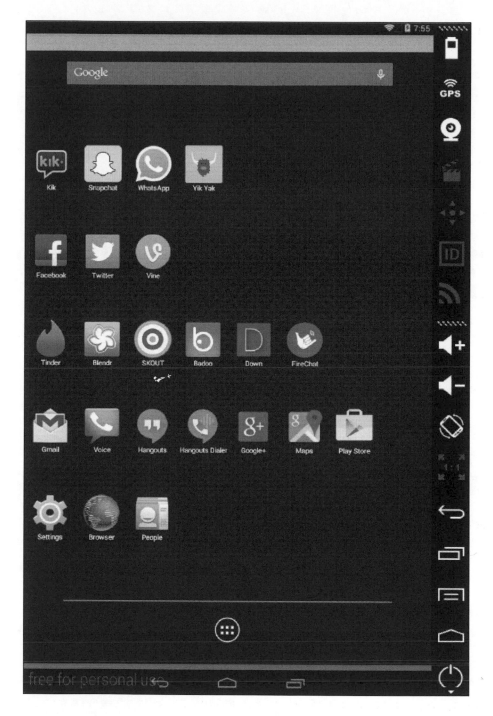

Figure 16.03: A custom Android emulator home screen with several apps installed into groups.

The GPS option within Genymotion is the most beneficial feature of their toolset. Clicking this icon will launch the GPS menu. Clicking the Off/On switch will execute the location spoofing service and a pre-configured GPS latitude and longitude will be provided. You can either supply the exact coordinates directly or click on the "Map" button to select a location via an interactive Google map. Figure 16.04 (left) displays the default GPS menu in the disabled state. Figure 16.04 (right) displays the menu with the exact coordinates of the Denver International Airport entered. I recommend changing the altitude, accuracy, and bearing settings to "0". Close this window and you will see a green check mark in the GPS button to confirm that your location settings are enabled.

Now that you have selected a location to broadcast through your device, you should test this configuration. My preferred way of doing this is to open Google Maps within the Android emulator and click the small blue target inside the white circle in the lower left. This will zoom Google Maps into the location that it believes you are located. You could also load the Bing Maps web page within a browser and ask it to center to your location. With both of these options, you may be prompted to "Allow" or "Deny" the device from obtaining your location details. You must choose "Allow" for this to function. After you have your desired location configured and you have confirmed accuracy, you can start to put this feature to work. The following tutorials will explain how location-aware applications could be used in investigations. You can download each of these apps from the Google Play store within your Android virtual machine.

Facebook: The Facebook app on Android will appear similar to a compressed view of a standard profile page. The benefit of the mobile app is the ability to check into places. When you click the "Check In'" tab in the upper right corner, Facebook will present businesses near your current spoofed location. With my configuration, Facebook presented the terminals and airlines at the Denver airport. If you choose a location, and create a post on your timeline, Facebook will verify that you were there. I have used this when I need to portray that I am somewhere I am not. This method can help you establish credibility within your fake profile. You could easily create the illusion that you were working at a business all day or out clubbing all night.

Real World Application: I once helped a domestic violence victim confuse her ex-husband with this technique. He stalked her every move online. After wasting his time going to random places trying to find her, and always finding the location to be closed, he began doubting the information that he uncovered about her whereabouts.

Twitter: The first time that you use Twitter within your Android environment, you will be asked if you want to share your location. While I usually discourage this type of activity, sharing your spoofed location can have many benefits. Similar to Facebook, you can make yourself appear to be somewhere that you are not. You may want to confuse your target. If you know that he or she will be monitoring your social networks using the techniques in Chapter Three, this method should throw them off.

Yik Yak: This anonymous social media app is very popular with protesters and organized gatherings. It uses your location data and allows you to communicate with strangers within a ten mile radius. With my configuration, I can watch people chat from the Denver Airport. I once used this app while investigating a group of looters that were ruining an otherwise peaceful protest. Because many of the undesirables participating in the looting do not know each other, they rely on apps like these to communicate. I was able to intercept live communication about the next business that they would target. When using, be sure to always expand the replies to individual posts.

Tinder: This dating app relies on your location in order to recommend people in your area that want to "hook up". It will use your Facebook account in use on your device for the login credentials. The preferences menu will allow you to specify the gender, age range, and distance of the targeted individuals. Most people use this to identity members of the opposite sex within a mile of their current location. The users can then chat within the app. I have used this to identify whether a target was at home or other location.

Real World Application: During one investigation, I discovered that my target was a Tinder user. I set my GPS in my Android emulator to his residence. I could then search for men his age and identify if he was at home. If I did not get his profile as a result, I could change my GPS to his work address or favorite bar. When I received his profile in the results, I knew that he was at the spoofed location. I could do all of this from anywhere in the world.

Blendr/Badoo: These apps use the same database of user profiles. It is similar to Tinder but does not require a Facebook account. This could be an additional option for locating a target that uses dating apps. The same method applied to Tinder would work on this network as well.

Skout: This app uses your Facebook account to populate data in your profile. The "Meet People" area will present individuals currently in the area of your supplied GPS coordinates. In addition to identifying the location of targeted individuals, this app could be used to identify people that are currently at a crime scene or gathering. I once used this technique to simply document people that were present near a state capitol during a credible bomb threat. When these people denied their presence during interviews, I had data that disagreed with their statements. Those that were lying quickly recanted their false statements and saved investigators a large amount of time.

Down: Formally called "Bang with Friends", this is another dating app based on your friends within your Facebook profile. If you have a covert profile that includes your targets as friends, launching this app will identify those friends that are also on Down.

Real World Application: I once used this during a cheating spouse investigation. I connected with a covert female Facebook profile that was friends with the suspected cheating spouse. Launching the Down app confirmed that he had an account. Swiping "Down" on his profile alerted him that I wanted to "get down" with him. This quickly resulted in a very incriminating chat that was later used in litigation.

FireChat: FireChat is a mobile app which uses wireless mesh networking to enable smartphones to connect via Bluetooth, Wi-Fi, or Apple's Multipeer Connectivity Framework without an internet connection. Though it wasn't designed with the purpose in mind, throughout 2014 it was used as a communication tool in civil protests. Launching the app within your emulator will identify live messaging and numerous chat rooms. These rooms can often contain valuable intelligence about live events from people directly involved. A social network login is not required and people can use any pseudonym desired. I have used this only to obtain details of events. I have never had success in identifying individuals within the service.

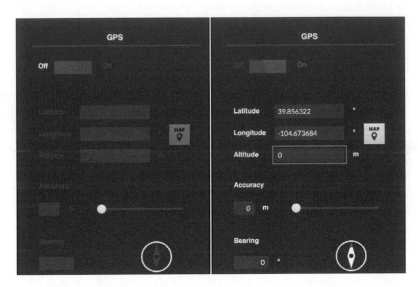

Figure 16.04: A disabled Genymotion GPS menu (left) and spoofed GPS (right).

There are many other similar apps. Now that you have an idea of how to integrate mobile applications into your investigations, you can apply the same techniques to the next future wave of popular apps. Many social network apps have no association with location. This content can still have value to an investigation. Some apps, such as SnapChat and Kik, only function within a portable device. You cannot load a web browser on a traditional computer and participate with these networks. However, you can access them from within your Android virtual machine. The following tutorials may help you find new uses for these popular apps.

SnapChat: This popular photo messaging application allows a user to capture photos, record videos, add text and drawings, and send them to a controlled list of recipients. These sent photographs and videos are known as "Snaps". Users set a time limit for how long recipients can view their Snaps, after which they will be hidden from the recipient's device and deleted from Snapchat's servers. Many teenagers use this app for "sexting" by sending and receiving nude photos. You must use a portable device in order to participate in SnapChat's network. Your Android emulator will allow you to interact with users as if you were using a mobile device. However, I prefer to use the SnapChat app as an intelligence gathering tool. The following tutorial will allow you search cellular telephone numbers to identify the associated SnapChat user names.

✓ Launch your Android virtual machine and open the "People" app to see your contacts. This will likely be empty. Create a new contact by clicking the "Add User" option in the upper right portion of the window. Figure 16.05 (left) displays this icon. Enter the target cellular telephone number in the "Name" and "Phone" fields. Click "Done" when finished.

✓ Launch the SnapChat app and either create a new account or log into an existing account. Creating your new account through your emulator is acceptable. Click the "menu" option (three horizontal lines) in the lower right portion of the screen. This will present the "My Friends" menu.

✓ Click the "Add Friend" icon in the upper right corner. Click the "Address Book" icon directly right of the "Add User" icon. This will extract the telephone numbers that are in your address book and reverse search them through SnapChat. Any numbers that are associated with a user will be present here. You will see the number and user name. Figure 16.05 (right) displays a result.

Real World Application: I have used this technique several times in the past three years. While it does not identify an individual's real name, it does provide a user name. Most of the time, researching this user name on other networks such as Twitter provides real identifiers for the target. I was once able to identify a subject that was sending death threats to various students at a local high school.

Kik Messenger: Kik is an instant messaging application for mobile devices. It is modeled after BlackBerry's Messenger and uses a smartphone's data plan or Wi-Fi to transmit and receive messages. It also allows users to share photos, sketches, mobile webpages, and other content. You must create a free account within the app and you can then search any user name or Kik number. Many users do not share personal details, but you can still use the app during your investigation for covert communication with a target.

Real World Application: Child exploitation is prominent on Kik Messenger. Pedophiles have been quoted in news sources stating "I could go on it now and probably within 20 minutes have videos, pictures, everything else in between off the app. That's where all the child porn is coming off of." and "I can get anybody I want. I can achieve my sexual glorification through this app". In 2014, a parent confiscated her 15 year old daughter's cellular telephone after it was discovered that the minor was sending nude photos of herself to an older man at his request. I was able to use my Android emulator to log in as the child, continue conversations with the pedophile, and develop evidence to be used during prosecution. Documentation was easy with screen captures and screen recording.

WhatsApp: WhatsApp Messenger is an instant messaging app for smartphones that operates under a subscription business model. The proprietary, cross-platform app enables users of select feature phones to use the Internet to communicate. In addition to text messaging, WhatsApp can be used to send images, videos, and audio media messages. Locations can also be shared through the use of integrated mapping features. It is the most globally popular messaging app with more than 600 million active users. You will need to create an account and provide a telephone number for verification. This number can be a cellular, landline, or VOIP number. I have had success using free Google Voice numbers. After you have an account, you can communicate directly with any target using the service. I have found that several of my targets refuse to converse over traditional text messaging, but freely text over WhatsApp. If you conduct any online covert operations, you should have this set up ahead of time.

Figure 16.05: An Android contact profile (left) and a SnapChat friend discovery (right).

I hope that you now have a desire to create numerous Android emulators and configure each for your investigation needs. Figure 16.06 displays my current collection. The first is my standard Android 4.4.4 emulator that has no customization. It is a clean machine that contains only default settings. The second machine contains only voice related apps such as Google Voice, Google Hangouts, and numerous voice over IP (VOIP) programs that allow free telephone calls. I use these for an extra layer of anonymity when placing covert phone calls. The third option is only for investigations. I have all of the apps that have been mentioned here and each is configured to a covert Facebook account. The fourth machine is only for testing new apps that I may introduce into my investigations. It is important to understand the application before launching it in a covert environment. The last machine contains only location-based apps. I can use them to either announce a fake location or investigate a distant location.

The paid version of Genymotion will allow you to clone any machine. This is very beneficial when you have a custom emulator that contains a lot of configuration. You can instantly make a copy of that machine and use a new version for each investigation. However, the free edition of this software has disabled this feature. Instead, you will need to manually create each machine that you want to use.

The benefit of this is that you will keep your skills sharp. It should only take you ten minutes to create a new machine and incorporate the Google core services.

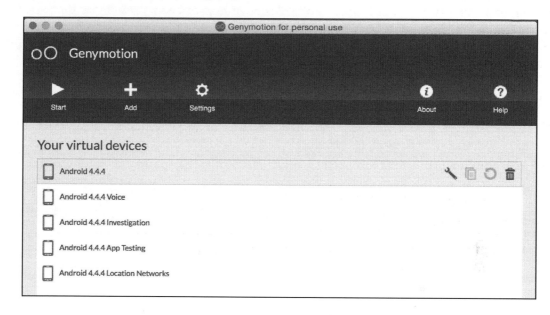

Figure 16.06: A Genymotion menu with a selection of virtual Android devices.

Google Android Emulator (developer.android.com)

There are other options for Android emulation besides Genymotion. If you have reservations about creating an account through that service, you could execute Android virtual machines through Google's native emulator. I have found this to be more difficult than Genymotion, but it is important to have options in case a service ever disappears. The tutorial for this method will not be as detailed as the previous. I will provide enough information to get a machine running. Installing Google Play is very difficult and requires various configuration techniques depending on the exact operating system running. I only recommend this option for advanced users.

✓ Download the installer from http://developer.android.com/sdk/index.html. Install it to any location that you desire.

✓ Execute "SDK Manager.exe". It will launch an "Android SDK and AVD Manager". By default "Installed packages" will be highlighted. On the pop up select "Choose Packages to Install". There will be some default packages selected already. Click "Install".

- ✓ Select "Virtual Devices" to create a new virtual machine. Click on "New" and enter a descriptive name. Choose the highest number such as "Android 4.4 – API Level 17". Click on "Create AVD".

- ✓ Select the Virtual device that you created and click on Start. Clicking "Start" will launch another pop-up. Click "Launch" to proceed.

This should execute an Android virtual machine similar to Genymotion. It will not have the sidebar features that Genymotion has. The procedure for installing Google Play varies by operating system version. Visit developer.android.com/google/play-services/setup.html for the current instructions.

Manymo (manymo.com)

The final Android emulation service discussed in this chapter is Manymo. You do not need an account to launch an emulator, but you will be restricted on the length of time that your machine will stay open. You can launch Android emulators from within a web browser. All of the processing and data storage is occurring on Manymo's servers. You will notice a bit of a delay while interacting with a machine. However, there are no resource requirements from your computer. If you have an older computer that cannot keep up with the previous methods, this may be a better option. After you create your account, use the following tutorial to launch your first emulator.

- ✓ Click on "Launch Emulators" in the upper right portion of the website.

- ✓ Choose the size of Android device that you desire. I recommend either the first or second option. The first will appear horizontal similar to a tablet and the second will appear vertical similar to a smart phone. Click "Launch".

You will now have a functioning emulator within your web browser. However, you will only see stock apps and will not have access to Google Play. I have been unable to find a way to allow Google Play to load within a Manymo emulator. However, you can load individual apps within the service. Before you can upload an app, you will need to download the app's APK file. Consider a file with an APK extension similar to an application with an EXE extension. Google uses APK for every app. The following instructions should obtain any app file from the Google Play account and allow you to execute it within your Manymo emulator.

- ✓ Navigate to play.google.com and search for the desired app. A search for SnapChat revealed the app to be at play.google.com/store/apps/details?id=com.snapchat.android.

- ✓ Navigate to http://apps.evozi.com/apk-downloader/ and enter the URL of your desired app. Click "Generate Download Link". After the file has been fetched, click "Click here to download". The APK file for that app will download to your computer.

✓ Navigate to Manymo.com/emulators and select the "App" link next to "Launch with" in the upper right corner. Click "Upload an App" in the upper right, browse to your downloaded APK file, and select it. Click "Continue" to upload the app to the Manymo servers.

✓ Choose the desired size of the emulator and select "Launch". A new tab will open and the emulator will execute. Navigate to the applications menu and launch the uploaded app. Figure 16.07 displays my result of the SnapChat app loaded within an Android emulator within a web browser.

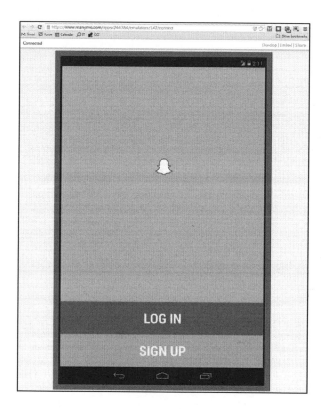

Figure 16.07: A Manymo emulator with an uploaded APK file of SnapChat.

I encourage you to attempt all three methods of accessing mobile applications from your computer. Genymotion is obviously the most robust. However, having an understanding of other options will prevent your investigations from stalling when one service is unavailable. I believe the future of OSINT collection will become more focused on mobile apps that have no website search option. In order to conduct thorough online investigations, mobile environment emulation is required.

Chapter Seventeen

Radio Frequency Monitoring

Monitoring radio frequencies is considered an open source technique. It does not require the internet and the information obtained can be quite valuable. In the past, this method of collecting information was conducted using expensive hardware such as emergency receivers and console radios. Today, a few bucks or a computer can provide all of the equipment necessary to take advantage of this free information.

Hardware

There are two paths you can take in reference to hardware requirements to monitor the airwaves. Dedicated devices, such as police scanners and desktop receivers, are easier to configure. A Software Defined Radio (SDR) is more complicated and requires a computer. However, the monitoring possibilities are greater. Overall, I recommend that a novice begin with a handheld police scanner.

Police Scanners

These affordable devices referred to as police scanners are actually capable of monitoring much more than emergency radio traffic. Practically any modern unit is capable of receiving the frequencies discussed in this chapter. More expensive units that allow for "trunked" frequencies are beneficial for monitoring government communications, but not necessary for the bulk of the radio spectrum. My personal scanner that was used for all of the methods discussed in this chapter was a Radio Shack PRO-2055. At the time of this writing, pre-owned devices were available for under $50 on Craigslist. One benefit of this type of scanner is that it can be programmed either manually or through computer software. Since the instructions for programming a scanner will vary by device, it will not be explained here. The instruction manual for the device should provide the proper instructions. Figure 17.01 displays the front of a desktop scanner.

Figure 17.01: A Radio Shack PRO-2055 police scanner.

Software Defined Radio (SDR)

Some radio receivers require a computer in order to operate. These advanced systems offer many features that are not available on typical hardware scanners. These systems contain the basic hardware required to receive the frequencies and then pass data to a computer. Special software on the computer controls the hardware and allows for advanced monitoring. This can include decoding alpha-numeric pagers, receiving digital satellite imagery from weather satellites, identifying beacons from airplanes and ships, and deciphering amateur radio signals or Morse code. Explanation of these types of devices exceeds the scope of this book. If you have an interest in this, I recommend researching the topic on the internet. Beginner devices such as the RTL2832U based USB receiver can be purchased for $30. Higher end devices can sell for several thousand dollars. I only recommend these for tech savvy individuals.

Antennas

There are several books dedicated to theories and suggestions on proper antenna creation, alignment, and placement. The techniques discussed here do not require that level of sophistication. The supplied antenna of a police scanner should work fine. Obviously, better antennas will allow you to receive signals from a farther distance. If you find the techniques explained here successful to your investigations, then I would consider further research into superior antennas.

Frequencies

Most commercial receivers will monitor radio frequencies between 25 MHz and 1300 MHz. There are usually gaps in this coverage which will not affect the techniques described here. The techniques explained in this chapter will monitor public frequencies available on all models. All frequencies listed in this chapter are displayed in megahertz (MHz).

Family Radio Service (FRS)

If you go to the local department store and purchase a pair of 2-way family radios, you will be transmitting on a public radio frequency that can be monitored with a scanner. The Family Radio

Service (FRS) is a radio system authorized for use without a license since 1996. Figure 17.02 displays an example of this type of device.

Figure 17.02: Typical Family Radio Service portable radios.

There are 14 FRS channels available which operate on 14 specific frequencies. The following table identifies these frequencies.

Channel 01 - 462.5625	Channel 06 - 462.6875	Channel 11 - 467.6375
Channel 02 - 462.5875	Channel 07 - 462.7125	Channel 12 - 467.6625
Channel 03 - 462.6125	Channel 08 - 467.5625	Channel 13 - 467.6875
Channel 04 - 462.6375	Channel 09 - 467.5875	Channel 14 - 467.7125
Channel 05 - 462.6625	Channel 10 - 467.6125	

The most common use for these radio frequencies is by families on vacation or at large events. They allow parents to keep in contact with their children. Criminals have found uses for them as well. Subjects often referred to as "spotters' use them to notify drug dealers when police are approaching a specific area. Additionally, illegal business operations such as gambling rooms and prostitution houses will use them to communicate cheaply and "anonymously". While this may afford the users some privacy protection against personal identification, the transmissions are completely public. Since the transmissions can travel several miles, the audio can be intercepted safely and without detection. Programming and monitoring these frequencies in known criminal areas may provide raw intelligence about your investigation. These are not the only frequencies to consider.

Multi-Use Radio Service (MURS)

The Multi-Use Radio Service (MURS) is an unlicensed two-way radio service that was established in 2000. The radios are capable of a range of ten miles when using decent antennas. The following table identifies the MURS frequencies.

151.820	151.880	151.940	154.570	154.600

General Mobile Radio Service (GMRS)

Additional public frequencies, known as General Mobile Radio Service (GMRS) frequencies require a license to legally transmit audio. Most people ignore this requirement and it is seldom enforced. The radios that transmit on these frequencies can use up to 50 watts, allowing the signal to travel farther. All MURS and GMRS frequencies should be programmed and monitored in the same way as FRS frequencies. The following table identifies the GMRS frequencies:

Channel 01 - 462.550	Channel 07 - 462.700	Channel 13 - 467.650
Channel 02 - 462.575	Channel 08 - 462.725	Channel 14 - 467.675
Channel 03 - 462.600	Channel 09 - 467.550	Channel 15 - 467.700
Channel 04 - 462.625	Channel 10 - 467.575	Channel 16 - 467.725
Channel 05 - 462.650	Channel 11 - 467.600	
Channel 06 - 462.675	Channel 12 - 467.625	

Monitoring FRS, GMRS, and MURS frequencies can be crucial to several types of investigations. The following are a few scenarios that can take advantage of this method.

✓ Police officers can monitor criminals that use two-way radios as part of criminal activity.

✓ Security staff can monitor families that may need emergency assistance.

✓ Agents can monitor groups that may be planning violence at protests.

✓ Investigators can monitor businesses under investigation.

Citizen Band (CB)

Many people associate Citizen Band (CB) radios with truck drivers. This is often appropriate, but truckers are not the only people that transmit on such frequencies. Since CB is low power, the receiver must be within a few miles of the transmitter. There are 40 channels available in this band. Communication on these channels may include traffic issues, witnesses to major accidents, reports of reckless drivers, and the occasional sermon. Many state patrol vehicles include a CB radio for receiving and transmitting. The following table identifies the frequencies and channels.

Channel 01 - 26.965	Channel 11 - 27.085	Channel 21 - 27.215
Channel 02 - 26.975	Channel 12 - 27.105	Channel 22 - 27.225
Channel 03 - 26.985	Channel 13 - 27.115	Channel 23 - 27.255
Channel 04 - 27.005	Channel 14 - 27.125	Channel 24 - 27.235
Channel 05 - 27.015	Channel 15 - 27.135	Channel 25 - 27.245
Channel 06 - 27.025	Channel 16 - 27.155	Channel 26 - 27.265
Channel 07 - 27.035	Channel 17 - 27.165	Channel 27 - 27.275
Channel 08 - 27.055	Channel 18 - 27.175	Channel 28 - 27.285
Channel 09 - 27.655	Channel 19 - 27.185	Channel 29 - 27.295
Channel 10 - 27.755	Channel 20 - 27.205	Channel 30 - 27.305

Channel 31 - 27.315	Channel 35 - 27.355	Channel 39 - 27.395
Channel 32 - 27.325	Channel 36 - 27.365	Channel 40 - 27.405
Channel 33 - 27.335	Channel 37 - 27.375	
Channel 34 - 27.345	Channel 38 - 27.385	

Real World Application: Two truck drivers in Arkansas were engaged in a heated argument with each other over their CB radios. The argument turned into a physical altercation that resulted in severe injuries. Responding police were monitoring a CB frequency while two other truckers were following the suspect. This communication helped police identify and arrest the suspect.

Marine Channels

Frequencies for marine use are not titled in the same fashion as other groups. Some channels are skipped and others are amended with the letter "A" at the end. There is a general understanding within marine circles of the type of radio traffic on each channel, but there is no enforcement of these designations. For example, many channels are reserved for commercial traffic only, but some disregard this rule. Many people disregard scanning this type of radio traffic because they do not live near waterways. Some criminal groups have purchased portable "walkie-talkie" style marine radios in non-water areas and communicate without fear of authentic marine vessels hearing their traffic. I recommend programming all of the frequencies into your scanner in the same bank as other civilian frequencies.

Real world application: While assisting a law enforcement agency during a large protest, I monitored marine frequencies for suspicious traffic. I immediately identified a small group of people communicating with portable marine radios. They were using them to coordinate meeting locations for arriving groups. While this intercepted traffic did not pose a threat, the intelligence was beneficial to the mission to keep everyone safe.

01A	156.050	17	156.850	63A	156.175	79A	156.975
05A	156.250	18A	156.900	65A	156.275	80A	157.025
06	156.300	19A	156.950	66A	156.325	81A	157.075
07A	156.350	20	161.600	67	156.375	82A	157.175
08	156.400	20A	157.000	68	156.425	84	161.825
09	156.450	21A	157.050	69	156.475	85	161.875
10	156.500	22A	157.100	70	156.525	86	161.925
11	156.550	23A	157.150	71	156.575	87	157.375
12	156.600	24	161.800	72	156.625	88A	157.425
13	156.650	25	161.850	73	156.675	AIS 1	161.975
14	156.700	26	161.900	74	156.725	AIS 2	162.025
15	156.750	27	161.950	77	156.875		
16	156.800	28	162.000	78A	156.925		

Room Monitors

There are several ranges of frequencies assigned by the FCC that are used by personal devices. These include a groups of frequencies designated for one-way monitoring devices often used as "baby monitors". These devices come in pairs. One unit is a transmitter that is placed in a room to be monitored, such as a nursery. The second unit is a receiver that can be up to 1000 feet away that will broadcast the audio from the other unit. Often, these include a switch on each unit to switch between two or three different channels. This is because all of these devices use the same frequencies. If you received interference from a neighbor's device, you could switch the channel. The channels assigned to these units fall in three ranges. The 49 MHz models are older and cheaper units that operate on a frequency similar to older cordless phones. The following frequencies are assigned to these units.

49.300   49.830   49.845   49.860   49.875   49.890

The 900 MHz models are more popular and are also used in wireless video cameras with audio. Houses that have consumer grade wireless surveillance cameras operate within this band. Often these devices transmit audio and video to a base station that is connected to a television in the house. I have seen many of these during search warrant executions. I believe any good tactical operations plan should include a sweep of this frequency range before execution of a search warrant. This can identify the presence of wireless systems used to provide early notice of law enforcement at the door. This can be a huge officer safety concern. There are too many frequencies available to these devices to list here. Instead, I recommend a scan of the following two ranges. Be warned that you may encounter cordless telephones within this range. If you do, block the frequency in order to avoid any law violations.

902.000 MHz - 908.000 MHz   923.000 MHz - 928.000 MHz

The 2.4 GHz models are often encrypted and change frequencies sporadically. Additionally, most basic scanners cannot monitor this range. Only expensive highly specialized devices can accurately monitor this traffic.

Real World Application: A police department in a Chicago suburb executed a search warrant on the home of a child predator. The suspect heard the entry from a basement room where he possessed the receiver of a wireless audio room monitor. This early warning allowed him time to destroy evidence and flee through a basement window. A standard frequency scanner could have notified the officers that a wireless system was present. This may have prompted a closer analysis for cameras and modifications could have been made to the operations plan.

Wireless Microphones

Wireless microphones or "cordless" microphones can be found transmitting throughout the radio frequency spectrum. They are most often in the 42 MHz, 70-74 MHz, 170-220 MHz, and 580-800 MHz ranges. Many modern professional wireless microphone systems are frequency agile and tunable to different frequencies. Wireless microphone power levels are normally very low in order to reduce the potential for interference. Clear reception requires close proximity or use of directional antennas. The following frequencies should receive audio from most of the existing wireless microphone systems. If you expect to receive a wireless transmission, and none of these frequencies are active, you should search by "nearby frequencies" (Page 402).

169.445	72.9000	174.8000	183.4000	194.4000	204.8000
169.505	73.1000	175.2500	184.2000	195.2000	205.6000
170.245	73.3000	175.6000	184.6000	195.4000	206.3500
170.305	73.6000	176.4000	184.8000	195.8000	206.4000
171.045	75.1000	178.2000	185.2000	196.2000	208.2000
171.105	75.5000	178.6000	186.8000	196.6000	208.6500
171.845	75.7000	179.2000	187.6000	197.4000	210.8000
171.905	75.9000	180.8000	188.4000	198.7500	211.6000
72.1000	82.5000	181.2500	190.2000	199.6000	212.4000
72.3000	82.8000	181.6000	192.8000	200.4000	
72.5000	83.8000	182.4000	193.2000	202.2000	
72.7000	86.8000	183.2000	193.6000	202.6500	

Real World Application: While attending a computer security conference, a non-scheduled presentation was offered to select attendees in reference to new exploits being used on corporate networks. Since I did not receive an invitation, I was not allowed entry. I connected my headphones to a portable scanner and began scanning the common ranges used by wireless microphones while sitting in the hallway outside of the closed door session. Within moments, I had discovered the frequency used by the speaker's wireless lapel microphone and was able to listen to the entire presentation. It is likely that I was able to hear the speaker clearer than most of the live audience since I had the isolated microphone feed.

Hotels and Convention Centers

Most hotels use some type of two-way radio systems as part of their daily operations. Many larger hotels in major cities use a group of channels and isolate traffic for maintenance, housekeeping, security, and valet. This traffic can identify valuable information during a targeted investigation. A security protection detail that is assigned to a high profile subject may want to monitor the frequencies of the hotel where the subject is staying. The traffic may identify employees discussing the subject and announce vulnerabilities including the assigned room number and specific requests by the subject. The vehicle information may be broadcasted on the valet channel and gossip may be heard on the operations channels. This information could be devastating if used maliciously. Additionally, traffic on the hotel security channel could identify a threat to a target before the security detail is involved. Law enforcement analysts should begin monitoring a specific hotel's frequencies the moment a serious event occurs at the location such as an explosion, hostage situation, bomb threat, homicide, armed robbery, etc. This live information can be vital to the investigation. Hotels do not use a standard set of frequencies or band on the radio spectrum. Discovering the frequencies to monitor is easy thanks to Radio Reference.

Radio Reference (radioreference.com)

This is the most complete collection of current frequencies assigned to government agencies and private businesses on the internet. It was discussed briefly in Chapter Seven and online monitoring of emergency communications was explained. You can also use this database to identify practically any active frequency. Basic search methods can be completed without a premium account. The search field in the upper right portion of every page can locate a set of frequencies based on a business name. Additionally, you can browse by location and identify all businesses in a specific area. This section will explain both methods.

A search of "Chicago Palmer House" on Radio Reference identifies all of the frequencies used by the Palmer House Hilton hotel in downtown Chicago. This hotel is often used by dignitaries and public officials. Figure 17.03 displays the results including the assigned call sign, frequency, and number of units allowed to access the frequency. Within these ten frequencies are the channels assigned to security, housekeeping, maintenance, and administration. The valet at this location now uses Nextel cellular service. These active channels can be monitored from several miles away using a basic scanning device.

You can also browse the Radio Reference database to locate frequencies of interest. Clicking the "Databases" link at the top of every page will present an interactive United States map. You can click any state and will be presented all of the counties in that state. Selecting a county will present the options of government and business frequencies for that area. Figure 17.04 displays the results for US Cellular field. It identifies thirteen frequencies assigned to Security, Parking, Maintenance, Operations, and others. This could be used to quickly begin monitoring these frequencies if a threat or catastrophe occurred at that location.

Entity	Callsign	Frequency	Units
THOR PALMER HOUSE HOTEL DBA/PALMER	WQEB345	451.28750	50
THOR PALMER HOUSE HOTEL DBA/PALMER	WQEB345	451.58750	50
THOR PALMER HOUSE HOTEL DBA/PALMER	WQEB345	456.28750	50
THOR PALMER HOUSE HOTEL DBA/PALMER	WQEB345	456.58750	50
THOR PALMER HOUSE HOTEL DBA/PALMER	WQEB345	461.68750	50
THOR PALMER HOUSE HOTEL DBA/PALMER	WQEB345	461.96250	50
THOR PALMER HOUSE HOTEL DBA/PALMER	WQEB345	462.21250	50
THOR PALMER HOUSE HOTEL DBA/PALMER	WQEB345	466.68750	50
THOR PALMER HOUSE HOTEL DBA/PALMER	WQEB345	466.96250	50
THOR PALMER HOUSE HOTEL DBA/PALMER	WQEB345	467.21250	50

Figure 17.03: A Radio Reference search result.

Frequency	License	Type	Tone	Alpha Tag	Description
461.45000	WQAU450	RM	67.0 PL	CWS Security	Security - Main (as of June 2010)
462.05000	WPXR683	RM	732 DPL	CWS Ops F-3	Guest Relations Operations [F-3]
461.20000	WPLI617	RM	67.0 PL	CWS Parking	Parking [F-6]
456.56250		M	051 DPL	CWS 456.5625	Food-Beverage service
463.72500	WPLL482	RM	466 DPL	CWS Maintnce	Maintenance
464.28750		M	67.0 PL	CWS Ticketng	Ticketing
464.51250		M	226 DPL	CWS Food	Food
464.55000		M	047 DPL	CWS Ops46455	Operations
464.67500	WQDD864	RM	223 DPL	CWS Concessn	Sportservice - Concessions
464.81250		M	466 DPL	CWS Food	Food
464.83750		M	051 DPL	CWS Janitor	Janitorial
464.95000	WPLL482	RM	67.0 PL	CWS Ops D	Operations (infrequently used)
464.75000		RM	67.0 PL	CWS Sec old	Security - Main (old)

Figure 17.04: A Radio Reference search result.

Retail Businesses

The next time you are shopping at a large store such as Wal-Mart or a clothing store such as Old Navy, pay attention to the employees. Most of them will either have portable radios in their pockets or wireless headsets. This is how they communicate to request more cashiers, announce a lunch break, verify a price, and direct employees to different areas. When you order food at the drive-through at a fast food restaurant, you are probably talking through a two-way radio device. When you are at a large concert, there are several people around you communicating through radio systems. This will include servers carrying drink orders, security, and even the backstage crew working with the musicians. This is all available to you through radio frequency monitoring. Practically anywhere your investigation takes you will present possibilities in intelligence collection through these methods. The frequencies of the businesses in your location should be available on Radio Reference.

Real World Application: Detectives in a St. Louis suburb were investigating a report that an employee at a local fast food restaurant was distributing cocaine while working. Covert Officers inside the business never noticed any unusual activity. After monitoring the drive-through frequency, they overheard several orders for a specific non-food item that was not on the menu. They later determined that this was the code word for one gram of cocaine. Several arrests were made.

News Media

During large investigations, various print and video news outlets will occasionally obtain information before the police do. This may be through witness reports or diligent efforts of a skilled reporter. Usually, it is due to the financial resources of the media company. These companies are quick to send a helicopter to the scene of a crime or a news van to a victim's house to capture video footage. While most ground reporters use cellular telephones to communicate with the news room, helicopters use radio frequencies. These powerful transmissions can be received several miles away. The frequencies for your area can be found on Radio Reference.

Real World Application: An Illinois police department was investigating a missing person that was last seen near a rock quarry. A news helicopter was flying overhead filming officers walking in the bottom of the quarry. The pilot observed what he thought may be the victim's body and began transmitting this through the radio system to the news desk. An alert officer monitoring the helicopter from a portable radio heard the report and determined the location of the body based on the pilot's description to his co-workers.

Emergency Communications

One last obvious group of interesting frequencies is that of emergency personnel such as police, fire, and EMS. Law enforcement officers should keep the frequencies of surrounding agencies stored in their scanners. This can provide valuable information such as pursuits, major incidents, and crimes related to their own jurisdiction. Those not in law enforcement can also use this technique for intelligence gathering. News reporters would want to monitor all local emergency channels for immediate notification of the next hot scoop.

Nearby Frequencies

If you cannot locate the specific target frequency to load into your scanner, you have one other option. Most modern devices include a feature that will quickly scan all of the major bands of frequencies for any that are in your immediate area. Uniden radios refer to this as the "Close Call" option while others label it as "Signal Stalker". Basically, it scans for the strongest frequencies and ignores weak signals. This may be the only way that you can identify the frequency that you are searching for. This will often identify local frequencies of interest that are not listed on Radio Reference or are unlicensed.

Wireless Video Cameras

Surveillance systems with a Digital Video Recorder (DVR) are very common in homes and businesses. An abundance of electronics from China has made these affordable for anyone. In the past, the solution was to install cameras that were wired directly into a DVR. This caused a web of hidden wires inside walls and ceilings. Today, most people choose a wireless system that broadcasts live video on the 900MHz, 1.2GHz, or 2.4GHz spectrum. The consumer models rarely encrypt the signal, and any generic video receiver can view the live stream. The FCC has assigned specific blocks of frequencies for the wireless channels used by these devices. Because of this, new handheld receivers have been created that can scan all of these frequencies and display any wireless video on a small screen. These range in price from $400 to $500. A Google search for "wireless video scanner" will present many options. A decent unit with a quality antenna will display any wireless video being transmitted within an entire residential block. These can also be used to detect unauthorized hidden video devices.

Always use discretion when scanning for wireless video signals. While completely legal to view, using the collected video to harass, intimidate, stalk, burglarize, or defraud someone is obviously illegal and unacceptable. Many people have been arrested for abusing this technology.

Chapter Eighteen

OSINT Workflow Processes

I have conducted numerous OSINT training programs over the past few years. Regardless of the audience, I receive one question at every event.

"Is there a standard process or workflow for OSINT?"

My short answer was always "no". I had always looked at each investigation as unique. The type of investigation dictated the avenues and routes that would lead me to valuable intelligence. There was no cheat-sheet that could be used for every scenario.

While I still believe that there is no template based solution for this type of work, I now admit that some standards can be developed. This chapter will display my attempt at creating valuable workflows that can quickly assist with direction and guidance. These documents are presented in five views based on the information being searched. Each example should be considered when you are researching the chosen topic. The categories are Email Address, User Name, Real Name, Telephone Number, and Domain Name.

Each example will try to show the standard path that I would take when provided the chosen type of data, such as an email address. The goal with my investigations is to get to the next topic. For example, if I am given an email address, my goal is to find any user names and real names. When I have a user name, my goal is to find any social networks and verify an email address. When I have a real name, the goal is to find email addresses, user names, and a telephone number. When I have a telephone number, my goal is to verify the name and identify a physical address and relatives. When I have a domain name, my goal is to locate a real name and address. The cycle continues after each new piece of information is discovered.

Each example will identify only the technique used. It will not display the actual address to navigate to. However, every method listed within these charts is explained throughout this book. These documents do not contain every avenue that may provide good information. They only display the basics. Think of them as the obvious steps to take when you receive a target to search. The results of your queries can lead you to more places than can display on a single page in this book. These are just the first priorities.

Below is an excerpt from the Email Address worksheet.

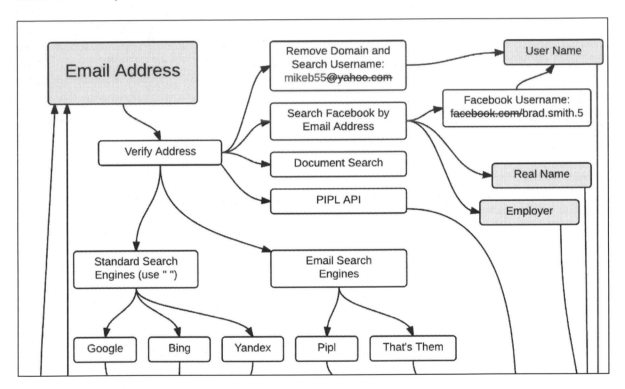

The written translation of this would be to take the email address and search it within both email validation tools online. Then conduct searches of the address within quotation marks on the main search engines. After that, conduct searches across both email search engines. Any results would be sent to the non-visible area of this example. You can see that these later are sent back up to start the search over with new content. The next step would be to remove the domain from the address and search only the user name as directed in the User Name worksheet. Conduct a search of the email address through the Facebook technique and pass on the user name to the User Names worksheet. Search the target's real name through the techniques on the Real Name worksheet. Finally, use the Full Contact and Pipl API services to identify any further information. You would then continue through the remainder of the chart.

If you find the following information beneficial, you are welcome to download digital copies on my website at the following address.

inteltechniques.com/data/workflow.zip

I ask that you leave the references to my website within them if you plan on distributing, publishing, or printing them.

I believe that all of these will always be a work in progress. As everything else in OSINT changes, these will too. I will try to keep them updated on the website. If you have suggestions, I am honored to receive and apply them. If you would like to create better formulas, I encourage you to get creative. I used the website LucidChart.com to create each of these. I also made all of these public within the Lucid Chart website so that you can take advantage of my starting point. The following links will connect you to a live environment that will allow you to replicate the work in seconds.

Email Address:
http://www.lucidchart.com/invitations/accept/5282ad5a-b0dc-4442-a4a5-4a440a00dd05

User Name:
http://www.lucidchart.com/invitations/accept/5282ad70-58dc-4546-8758-0a460a00c875

Real Name:
http://www.lucidchart.com/invitations/accept/5282ad8b-c4d0-4db3-98f2-25d00a00c875

Telephone Number:
http://www.lucidchart.com/invitations/accept/5282ad9a-64a4-4435-9073-3ce80a00c875

Domain Name:
http://www.lucidchart.com/invitations/accept/5282acc9-f324-43b2-af40-04c00a00c875

Location:
http://www.lucidchart.com/invitations/accept/9d446294-580e-49ba-a88f-2437cc392b6f

I begin with the email address worksheet because it is always my preferred piece of target information. This unique piece of data usually provides the most accurate results. The following chart will walk you through how I start with the address and work my way toward the target's user names, real name, employer, social networks, and personal websites.

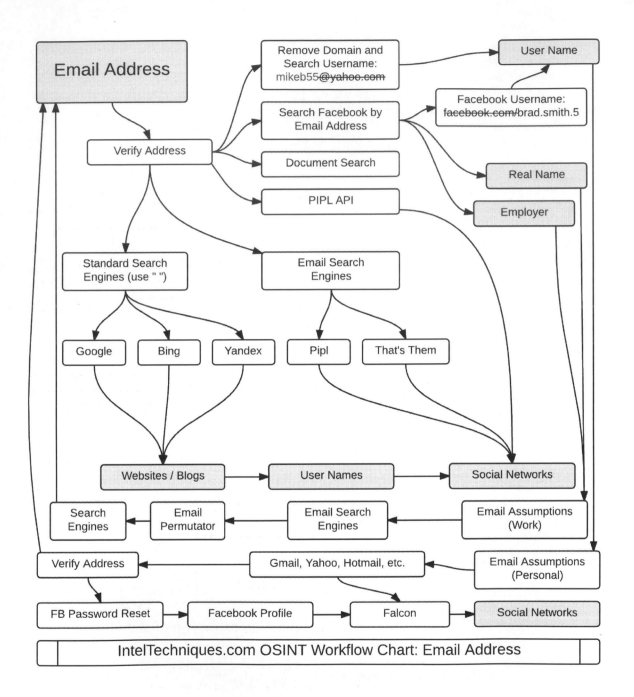

Email Address

Remove Domain and Search Username: mikeb55@yahoo.com

User Name

Verify Address

Search Facebook by Email Address

Facebook Username: facebook.com/brad.smith.5

Document Search

Real Name

PIPL API

Employer

Standard Search Engines (use " ")

Email Search Engines

Google   Bing   Yandex   Pipl   That's Them

Websites / Blogs   →   User Names   →   Social Networks

Search Engines   ←   Email Permutator   ←   Email Search Engines   ←   Email Assumptions (Work)

Verify Address   ←   Gmail, Yahoo, Hotmail, etc.   ←   Email Assumptions (Personal)

FB Password Reset   →   Facebook Profile   →   Falcon   →   Social Networks

IntelTechniques.com OSINT Workflow Chart: Email Address

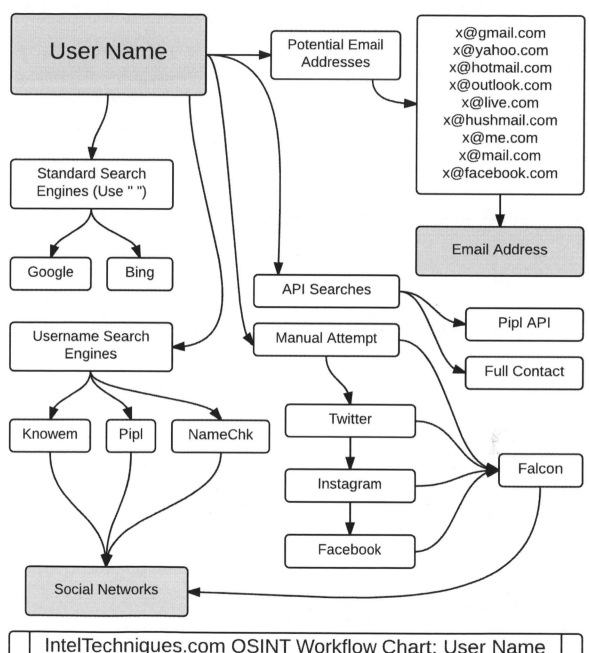

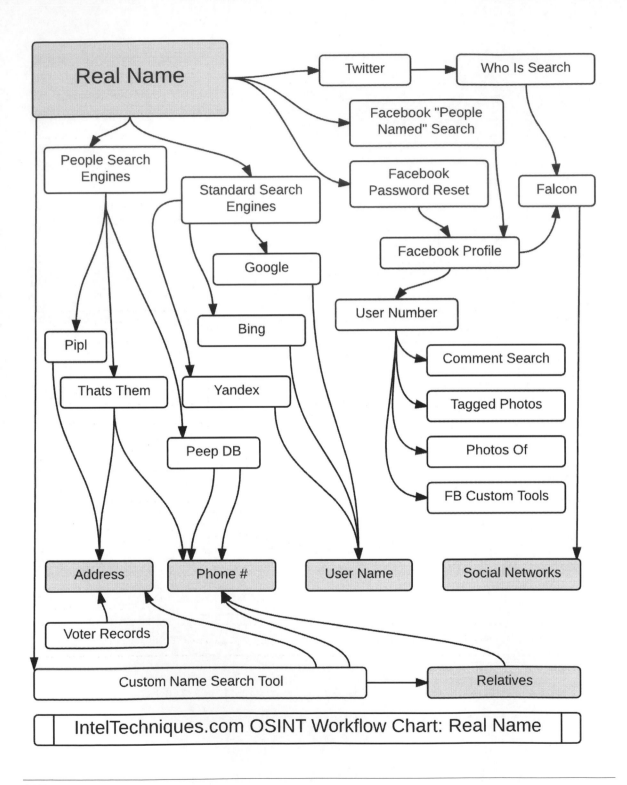

IntelTechniques.com OSINT Workflow Chart: Real Name

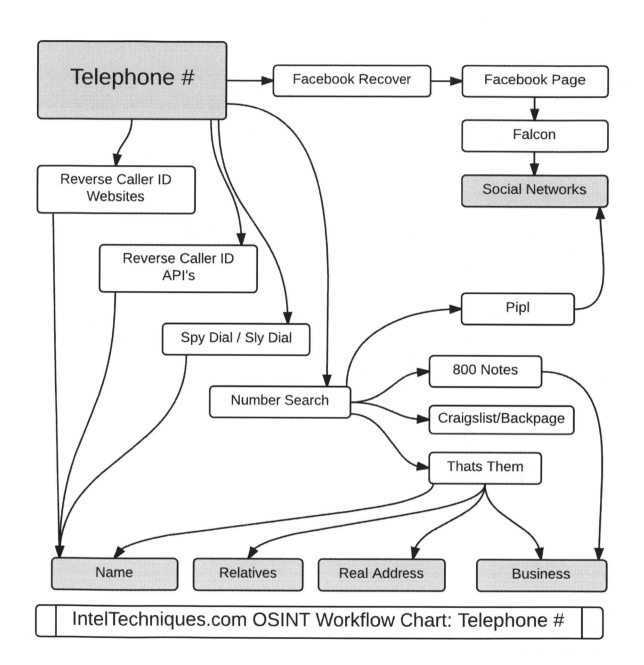

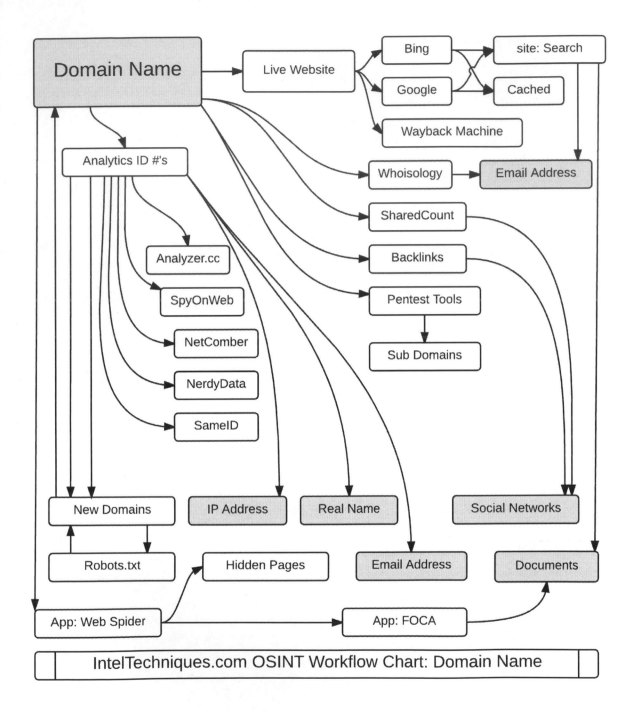

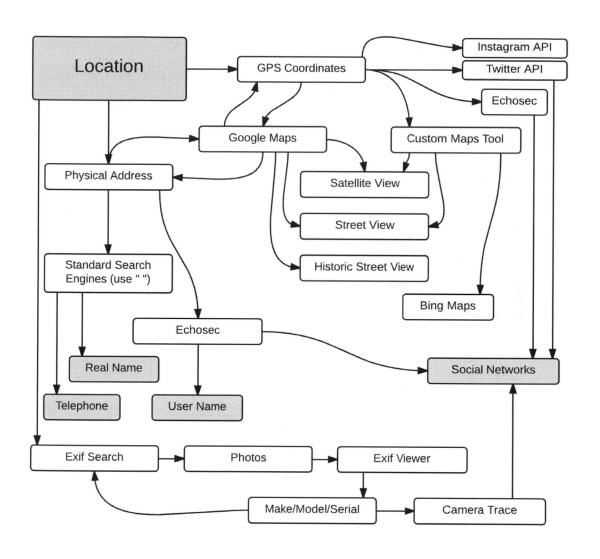

IntelTechniques.com OSINT Workflow Chart: Location

Conclusion

What now?

I hope the techniques presented have sparked your interest in finding new avenues of research and investigations. With patience and diligent effort, this book will be a helpful reference guide to assist in performing more accurate and efficient searches of open source intelligence.

Permanently documenting these techniques on paper ~~may~~ will provide outdated content. Technology changes quickly and methods must adapt to keep up. Ten years from now, this book may be an amusing piece about how we once managed our online data.

To keep up with the changes in various methods and OSINT data collection, subscribe to my blog at **IntelTechniques.com**. The chances are good that as you read this, new content has been posted about the very topic you are researching. The same website will allow you to access all of my current investigation links. Look for the "Online Resources" link. I also offer an online OSINT video training course that includes over 40 hours of HD videos, access to all of the API's explained here, a custom online search tool, and a software pack of every application ready to use.

Thank you for reading.

Index

Save 25%

Inteltechniques.com

Online OSINT Training Videos

Thank you for purchasing a copy of this book. Use the following website to receive 25% off your purchase of monthly or yearly access to over 140 online OSINT training videos.

inteltechniques.com/bookvideos.html

Printed in Great Britain
by Amazon.co.uk, Ltd.,
Marston Gate.